SOTHIS PRESS

Sothis Press aims to completely reimagine the public domain book with an emphasis on universal access to captivatingly designed print editions. We believe that technology will enable every single book ever published to be perpetually accessible in beautiful print form. Sothis is beauty in ubiquity.

www.sothis.press
1 Waterhouse Square, London, ECIN 2ST

A Summary of the Law of Bills of Exchange, Cash Bills, and Promissory Notes

John Bayley

SOTHIS PRESS

ISBN 978-1-0365-2321-3

A Summary of the Law of Bills of Exchange, Cash Bills, and Promissory Notes
is in the public domain.

This edition is published by
 The company
is registered in England and Wales.
The Company Number is 14900389.

SUMMARY

OF THE LAW OF

BILLS OF EXCHANGE,

CASH BILLS,

AND

PROMISSORY NOTES.

By SIR JOHN BAYLEY, Knt.
ONE OF THE JUSTICES OF HIS MAJESTY'S COURT OF KING'S BENCH.

THE FOURTH EDITION:
WITH CONSIDERABLE ADDITIONS.

LONDON:
PRINTED BY A. STRAHAN,
LAW-PRINTER TO THE KING'S MOST EXCELLENT MAJESTY;
FOR JOSEPH BUTTERWORTH AND SON, 43. FLEET-STREET;
J. & W. T. CLARKE, PORTUGAL-STREET; AND
J. COOKE, ORMOND-QUAY, DUBLIN.
1822.

PREFACE

TO

THE FOURTH EDITION.

THIS edition contains the cases since the last, and a new chapter upon the Forgery of Bills and Notes.

THE profession has sustained a great loss in Mr. Barnes. He was a man of great promise, and most respected where best known: had he been living, this edition would have come from him; but his death, and other circumstances, have induced the original author to prepare and superintend this edition.

BEDFORD-SQUARE, 1822.

TABLE

OF

CITED CASES.

TABLE OF CONTENTS.

CAP. IX.

CAP. X.

CAP. XI.

CAP. XII.

CAP. XIII.

CAP. XIV.

A

SUMMARY OF THE LAW OF

BILLS OF EXCHANGE

AND

PROMISSORY NOTES.

CAP. I.

A BILL of Exchange is a written order or request, and a Promissory Note a written promise, for the payment of money absolutely and at all events, the one owing its existence and privileges to the law and custom of merchants, the other to the 3d and 4th Anne, c. 9. (1)

(1) Before the statute of Queen Anne many attempts were made to put promissory notes on the footing of bills of

The person who makes a bill is called the Drawer, the person to whom it is addressed the

---

exchange, but without success, vide Pearson v. Garrett, 4 Mod. 242. Clerke v. Martin, Lord Raym. 757. Salk. 129. Burton v. Souter, Lord Raym. 774. and Williams v. Cutting, Lord Raym. 825. Salk. 24. 7 Mod. 154. 11 Mod. 24. and see 4 Term. Rep. 151, 152.

'By the 3d and 4th Anne, c. 9. § 1. Whereas it hath been 'held, that notes in writing, signed by the party who makes the 'same, whereby such party promises to pay unto any other 'person, or his order, any sum of money therein mentioned, 'are not assignable or indorsable over, within the custom of 'merchants, to any other person; and that such person to 'whom the sum of money mentioned in such note is payable, 'cannot maintain an action by the custom of merchants against 'the person who first made and signed the same; and that any 'person to whom such note should be assigned, indorsed, or 'made payable, could not within the said custom of merchants, 'maintain any action upon such note against the person who 'first drew and signed the same:' Therefore, to the intent to encourage trade and commerce, which will be much advanced, if such notes shall have the same effect as inland bills of exchange, and shall be negotiated in like manner: Be it enacted, that all notes in writing, that after the 1st day of May, in the year of our Lord 1705, shall be made and signed by any person or persons, body politic or corporate, or by the servant or agent of any corporation, banker, goldsmith, merchant or trader, who is usually, intrusted by him, her or them, to sign such promissory notes for him, her or them, whereby such person or persons, body politic and corporate, his, her or their servant or agent as aforesaid, doth or shall promise to pay to any other person or persons, body politic and corporate, his, her or their order, or unto bearer, any sum of money mentioned in such note, shall be taken and construed to be, by virtue thereof, due and payable to any such person or persons, body politic and corporate, to whom the same is made payable, and also every such note payable to any person or persons, body politic and corporate, his, her or their order, shall be assignable or indorsable over,

Drawee, and the person in whose favour it is made the Payee.

If the Drawee accepts the bill, he is called the Acceptor.

The person who makes a note is called the Maker, and the person to whom it is payable the Payee.

When a bill or note is indorsed, the person indorsing it, is called the Indorser, the person to whom it is indorsed the Indorsee.

A note while in the hands of the payee, has this resemblance to a bill, that it is for the payment of money absolutely and at all events, and when transferred it is exactly similar to a bill of exchange (2).

---

in the same manner as inland bills of exchange are or may be, according to the custom of merchants; and that the person and persons, body politic and corporate, to whom such sum of money is or shall be by such note made payable, shall and may maintain an action for the same, in such manner as he, she or they might do, upon any inland bill of exchange, made or drawn according to the custom of merchants, against the person or persons, body politic and corporate, who, or whose servant or agent as aforesaid, signed the same; and that any person or persons, body politic and corporate, to whom such note, that is payable to any person or persons, body politic and corporate, his, her or their order, is indorsed or assigned, or the money therein mentioned ordered to be paid by indorsement thereon, shall and may maintain his, her or their action for such sum of money, either against the person or persons, body politic and corporate, who, or whose servant or agent as aforesaid, signed such note, or against any of the persons who indorsed the same, in like manner as in cases of inland bills of exchange.

(2) In Heylin v. Adamson, Burr. 669. The question was, whether the indorsee of a bill was bound to make a demand

Sect. 2. — No particular (3) words are necessary to make a bill or note; any order or promise which from the time of making it cannot be complied with or performed without the payment of money, is a bill or note.

---

upon the drawer as the indorsee of a note must upon the maker, and per Lord Mansfield, "while a note continues in its original "shape of a promise from one man to another, it bears no "similitude to a bill; but when it is indorsed, the resemblance "begins; for then it is an order by the indorser upon the "maker to pay the indorsee, which is the very definition of a "bill: the indorser is the drawer, the maker of the note the "acceptor; and the indorsee, the person to whom it is made "payable; and all the authorities, and particularly Lord Hard-"wicke, in a case of Hamerton v. Mackarell, M. 10 Geo. II. "put promissory notes on the same footing with bills of ex-"change." And in Brown v. Harraden, 4 Term Rep. 148. where the court decided that three days grace should be allowed on promissory notes, Lord Kenyon observed, that the effect of the statute was, that notes were wholly to assume the shape of bills; and Buller J. added, that the cases cited in the argument showed clearly, that the Courts of Westminster had thought the analogy between bills and notes so strong, that the rules established with respect to the one, ought also to prevail as to the other; that the language of the preamble of the Act was express, that it was the object of the legislature to put notes exactly on the same footing with bills, and that the enacting part pursued that intention. The same doctrine is to be found in Carlos v. Fancourt, 5 Term Rep. 482. Edie v. East India Company, Burr. 1224.

(3) D. Lord Raym. 1397. Str. 629. 8 Mod. 364.

Chadwick v. Allen, Str. 706. A note was in these words: "I do acknowledge that Sir Andrew Chadwick has delivered "me all the bonds and notes, for which 400*l.* were paid him on "account of Col. Synge, and that Sir Andrew delivered me "Major Graham's receipt and bill on me for 10*l.* which 10*l.*

Thus an order or promise to (4) deliver, or that I. S. (5) shall receive money, or to be (6) accountable or (7) responsible for it to him or order, is a good bill or note.

But a mere (8) acknowledgment of a debt without any promise to pay, is not a bill or note.

" and 15*l.* 5*s.* balance due to Sir Andrew I am still indebted, " and do promise to pay," and upon demurrer to the declaration, the court held it a note within the statute.

(4) D. acc. Lord Raym. 1397.

(5) D. 8 Mod. 364.

(6) Morris v. Lea, Lord Raym. 1396. Str. 629. 8 Mod. 326. Plaintiff sued as indorsee upon a note by which the defendant promised to be accountable to A. or order for 100*l.* value received; and after verdict for the plaintiff it was insisted in arrest of judgment, that this was not a negotiable note: sed per cur., no precise words are necessary to be used in a bill or note: Deliver such a sum makes a good bill; by receiving the value the defendant becomes a debtor, and when he promises to be accountable for it to A. it is the same as a promise to pay to A. and it is the stronger, because it is to be accountable to A. or order, and it would be an odd construction to expound the word accountable, to give an account, when there may be several indorsees. Judgment for plaintiff.

(7) D. 8 Mod. 364.

(8) Fisher v. Leslie, 1 Esp. N. P. C. 426. An unstamped slip of paper with "I. O. U. eight guineas," written upon it, and signed by the defendant, was offered in evidence under the money counts, and objected to as being either a promissory note, or a receipt, and therefore requiring a stamp; but Lord Kenyon held that it was neither a promissory note nor a receipt, and received it in evidence. But see Guy v. Harris, sittings after Easter Term, 1800, cor. Lord Eldon, C. J. contra, Chitty 243. n.

A note was (9) in these words, "borrowed of I. S. 50*l.* which I promise *not* to pay:" and per Lord Macclesfield, the word *not* shall be rejected, for a man shall never say, I am a cheat and have defrauded.

An order to pay money will be a bill, though instead of the ordinary direction to the drawers, the word "*at*" is prefixed to their names. (10)

Especially if from fraud it is written in such a manner as to be intended to escape observation, and to make the instrument pass as a bill. (11)

The order may be addressed to the person making it, in other words, a man may draw upon him-

---

(9) Cited per Lord Mansfield in Russell v. Langstaffe. B. R. M. 21 Geo. III. and in Peach v. Kay, sittings after Tr. 1781. and per Lord Harwicke, 2 Atk. 32.

(10) Shuttleworth v. Stephens, 1 Campb. 407. In an action against defendant as drawer of a bill, the instrument was in this form: "Two months after date pay to the order of J. J. 78*l*. 11*s*. value received, T. S.—at Messrs. John Morson and Co." Lord Ellenborough held this was properly declared on as a bill of exchange, and plaintiff had a verdict.

(11) Allan v. Mawson, 4 Campb. 115. In an action against defendant as drawer of a bill, the instrument was as follows. "Two months after date pay L. H. or order 40*l*. value received, G. M. @/r Jno. Perring and Co's." The "*at*" was in very small letters in the hook of the S. Plaintiff presented it for acceptance, and on refusal brought this action within the two months: the question was, whether plaintiff was intitled to treat this as a bill of exchange, and Gibbs, C. J. thought he would have been on the authority of Shuttleworth v. Stephens, 1 Campb. 407. had the word "*at*" been distinctly written; but he left it to the jury whether it was not fraudulently written to escape detection, and to induce a belief that the instrument was a bill, the jury thought it was, and found for plaintiff.

self; but in legal operation it is rather a note than a bill. (12)

Sect. 3.—Bills and notes must be for the payment of money only; an order or promise to pay money *and do some other act* is not a bill or (13) note.

And they must be for the payment of money in specie: an order or (14) promise to pay money *in good East India Bonds*, or in cash, or Bank of England Notes, (15) is not a bill or note.

---

(12) Starke v. Cheeseman, Tr. 11 W. III. Carth. 509. Christopher Cheeseman being in Virginia, drew upon Christopher Cheeseman in Ratcliffe, which in truth was himself; and an action being brought against him upon the bill, he suffered judgment by default, without taking any objection on this ground, though he did upon others, and the plaintiff had judgment.

Dehers v. Harriot, Tr. 2 W. and M. 1 Show. 163. A. drew a bill payable by himself in Dublin; an action was afterwards brought thereon, and the plaintiff recovered.

Robinson v. Bland, Burr. 1077. The defendant being at Paris drew a bill for 672*l.* on himself in London; the consideration was partly money lost at play in Paris, and partly money lent at the time and place of play, and upon that ground a case was reserved for the opinion of the court; but no objection was made that the defendant drew the bill upon himself.

Joselyn v. Laserre, Fort. 282. A man may draw a bill upon himself. See also Mar. 3.

(13) Martin v. Chauntry, Str. 1271. on error from the court of Common Pleas, the court of King's Bench held that a note to deliver up horses and a wharf, and pay money at a particular day, was not a note within the statute, and reversed the judgment which had considered it as such.

(14) Anon. Buller's Ni. Pr. 272. a written promise to pay 300*l.* to B. or order, in three good East India Bonds, was held not to be a note within the statute.

(15) Ex parte Imeson, Hil. 1815. Case from Chancery,

And they must be for a specific amount. A bill or note for a given sum, and for whatever else may be due to the payee, is not, even between the original parties, a bill or note. (16)

Nor is it good for the sum it specifies. (16)

But an order of promise to pay so many "pound" instead of "pounds" is a bill or note. (17)

---

on the question, whether a country bank was debtor to the holder of certain of their notes, which he had taken from third persons, not from the bank; the notes were for payment some of five guineas, some of one guinea "in cash or Bank of "England notes;' and after argument the court held the bank not debtor to this holder, for these notes were not within the statute, because a delivery of bank notes, which might be of less value than cash, would satisfy them, and they were not absolutely and at all events for payment of money in specie.

Rex v. Wilcox, Easter, 1808. Indictment for forging and uttering a promissory note; the note was to "pay the bearer on "demand one guinea in cash or Bank of England notes;" it was issued by the Pontefract bank. A case was reserved for the consideration of the twelve judges, on the question, whether this was a note within the statute; and a majority of them held it was not; and upon a representation to the crown, the prisoner was pardoned.

(16) Smith v. Nightingale, 2 Stark. 375. Defendant gave Eastling this note, "I promise to pay James Eastling, my head "carter, 65*l.* with lawful interest for the same, three months "after date, *with all other sums that may be due to him.*" Eastling's administratrix sued thereon; Lord Ellenborough thought it no note, even for the 65*l.*, but an agreement, and it not having an agreement stamp, he nonsuited the plaintiff.

(17) Rex v. Post, Pasch. 1806. Prisoner altered a note for one pound into a note for ten, by substituting ten for one before the word "Pound" in the body of the note, and also in the corner. It was urged that a note for payment of ten *pound* was not a money note. On a case reserved, the judges were clear that it was, and that a capital conviction of the prisoner for forgery was right.

Negotiable bills or notes made in England for less than (18) twenty shillings are void; and all negotiable bills or notes made in England (excepting Bank of England notes, and notes payable to the bearer on demand), for twenty shillings and less than (19) five pounds, unless made conformably

(18) By 48 Geo. III. c. 88. sect. 2. it is enacted, "that "all promissory or other notes, bills of exchange, or "draughts, or undertakings in writing, being negotiable or "transferable for the payment of any sum or sums of money, "or any orders, notes, or undertakings in writing, being nego-"tiable or transferable for the delivery of any goods, specify-"ing their value in money, less than the sum of twenty shillings "in the whole, heretofore made or issued, or which shall here-"after be made or issued, shall, from and after the 1st day of "October, 1808, be, and the same are hereby declared to be, "absolutely void and of no effect; any law, statute, usage or "custom, to the contrary thereof in any wise notwithstanding."

(19) By 17 Geo. III. c. 30. § 1. made perpetual by 27 Geo. III. c. 16., it is enacted, that all promissory or other notes, bills of exchange or draughts, or undertakings in writing, being negotiable or transferable, for the payment of twenty shillings, or any sum of money above that sum and less than five pounds, or on which twenty shillings or above that sum, and less than five pounds, shall remain undischarged, and which shall be issued, within that part of Great Britain called England, at any time after the 1st day of January, 1778, shall specify the names and places of abode of the persons respectively to whom, or to whose order, the same shall be made payable, and shall bear date before or at the time of drawing or issuing thereof, and not on any day subsequent thereto, and shall be made payable within the space of twenty-one days next after the day of the date thereof; and shall not be transferable or negotiable after the time thereby limited for payment thereof; and that every indorsement to be made thereon shall be made before the expiration of that time, and bear date at, or not before the time of making thereof; and shall specify the name and place of abode of the person or persons to whom, or to whose order the money

with certain regulations, are also void; and the

---

contained in every such note, bill, draught, or undertaking, is to be paid; and that the signing of every such note, bill, draught, or undertaking, and also of every such indorsement, shall be attested by one subscribing witness at the least; and which said notes, bills of exchange, or draughts, or undertakings in writing, may be made or drawn in words to the purport or effect as set out in the schedule hereunto annexed, No. 1 and and 2. And that all promissory or other notes, bills of exchange, or draughts, or undertakings in writing being negotiable or transferable, for the payment of twenty shillings, or any sum of money above that sum and less than five pounds; or on which twenty shillings, or above that sum and less than five pounds, shall remain undischarged, and which shall be issued within that part of Great Britain called England, at any time after the said 1st day of January, 1778, in any other manner than as aforesaid; and also every indorsement on any such note, bill, draught, or undertaking, to be negotiated under this act other than as aforesaid, shall, and the same are hereby declared to be, absolutely void.

SCHEDULE,

No. 1.

(*Place*) (*Day*) (*Month*) (*Year*)

'Twenty-one days after date, I promise to pay to A. B. of '(*place*) or his order, the sum of for value received by

'Witness, E. F. C. D.'

And the Indorsement, toties quoties.

(*Day*) (*Month*) (*Year*)

'Pay the contents to G. H. of (*place*) or his order,

'Witness I. K. A. B.'

No. 2.

(*Place*) (*Day*) (*Month*) (*Year*)

'Twenty-one days after date, pay to A. B. of (*place*) or his 'order, the sum of value received, as advised by

'To E. F. of (*place*) C. D.'

'Witness G. H.'

person issuing or negotiating them (20) liable to a penalty not exceeding twenty pounds, nor less than five.

These regulations are, that they specify the name and place of abode of the person to whom or to whose order they are made payable; that they be attested by one subscribing witness; that they bear date at or before the time when they are issued; and be made payable within twenty-one days after the date.

But all notes payable to bearer, issued by the Governor and Company of the Bank of England, are (21) good and valid in law, notwithstanding their

---

And the Indorsement, toties quoties.

(*Day*) (*Month*) (*Year*)

'Pay the contents to I. H. of (*place*) or his order

'Witness L. M. A. B.'

(20) By 48 Geo. III. c. 88. § 3. where the bill or note is for less than twenty shillings; and by 17 Geo. III. c. 30. § 2. where such bills or notes as fall within that Act, are not made conformably with the regulations there prescribed.

(21) By 37 Geo. III. c. 28. it is enacted, "That all promissory notes, and other notes for payment of money, which since the second day of March, one thousand seven hundred and ninety-seven, have been, or which hereafter shall be issued by the Governor and Company of the Bank of England, payable to bearer, notwithstanding the same shall have been, or shall be, made and issued for the payment of any sum of money under the sum of five pounds, shall be good and valid in the law, to all intents and purposes, in like manner as if the same had been made and issued for the sum of five pounds, or up-

being for the payment of less than 5*l.* And the act of the 17th Geo. III., so far as it relates either to the making void of promissory notes, or draughts, or undertakings in writing *payable on demand to the bearer thereof,* for any sum of money less than 5*l.* in the whole, or to the restraining the publishing or uttering and negotiating of any such notes, draughts, or undertakings, was, during the late war, (22) suspended until six months after the ratification of a definitive treaty of peace; and the stamp-act now in force, 55 G. III. c. 184., which imposes stamps on such notes, implies that they are to be considered as valid.

Sect. 4. — A bill or note must purport that the money mentioned in it shall be payable absolutely and at all events; if it purports to make the payment depend on any uncertainty or contingency, the instrument is not, except in certain cases as to the stamp duties, a billor note; and if it is not a bill or note ab initio, no subsequent (23) event can make it so.

---

wards; and no person concerned, or who has acted in, or who shall or may be concerned or act in, the making, uttering, publishing, or negotiating such notes, shall be subject or liable to any penalty or forfeiture whatsoever in respect thereof.

(22) By 37 Geo. III. c. 32. and 45 Geo. III. c. 25.

(23) See Colehan v. Cooke, Willes 393. and Hill v. Halford, post 16. and Blankenhagen v. Blundell, post. 30,

Thus an order or promise to pay money provided (24) the terms mentioned in certain letters shall be complied with, provided (25) I. S. shall not be surrendered to prison within a limited time, provided (26) I. S. shall not pay the money by a particular

---

(24) Kingston v. Long, B. R. M. 25 Geo. III. The Plaintiff brought an action as Indorsee against the Defendant, as acceptor, upon an order importing to be payable, *provided the terms mentioned in certain letters written by the drawer were complied with*, and the court held clearly that the plaintiff could not recover, though the acceptance admitted a compliance with the terms, for the order was no bill, until after such compliance, and if it were not a bill when drawn, it could not afterwards become one.

(25) Smith v. Boheme, 3 Lord Raym. 67. cit. Lord Raym. 1362. 1396. Action by payee against the makers upon a note promising to pay plaintiff or order on demand 71*l.* 12*s.* 10*d.* or to surrender the body of Samuel Boheme in an action brought against him by plaintiff. Verdict for the plaintiff and judgment; and on error brought in the King's Bench, the court held that this was not a note within the statute, because the money was not absolutely payable, but depended upon the contingency whether the defendants should surrender Samuel Boheme to prison; and the judgment was reversed 9th of June, 1724.

(26) Appleby v. Biddulph. cit. 8 Mod. 363. 4 Vin. 240—pl. 16. An action was brought on this note, "I promise to pay to "T. M. 50*l.* if my brother doth not pay it within six weeks;" and after verdict for the plaintiff, the court arrested the judgment, because the maker was only to pay it on a contingency.

Ferris v. Bond. B. R. Trin. 2. Geo. 4. A note was in these words, "I John Connor, promise to pay John Ferris or his or- "der, 50*l.* with interest, at six months' notice, dated 24th of "June, 1808. (Signed,) I Connor.——Or else Henry Bond." In an action upon this against Bond, the question was reserved whether this was as to Bond, a note within the statute; and the court after argument held it was not, because Bond's engagement only was to pay if Connor did not; and a rule for a nonsuit was made absolute.

day, provided (27) I. S. shall leave me sufficient, or I shall otherwise be able to pay it, or when I. S. (28) shall marry, is no bill or note on account of the contingency to which the payment is subjected. An order or promise to pay out of my (29) growing subsistence, or (30) fifth payment when due,

---

(27) Roberts v. Peake, Burr. 323. The plaintiff as indorsee of a note sued one of the makers; the instrument was in these words: "We promise to pay A. B. 116*l.* 11*s.* value received on "the death of George Henshaw, provided he leaves either of "us sufficient to pay the said sum, or if we shall be otherwise "able to pay it;" and upon a case reserved, the court held it was not a negotiable note, because it was payable eventually and conditionally only, and not absolutely and at all events, and a nonsuit was entered. See Williamson v. Bennett, post.

(28) Beardsley v. Baldwin, Str. 1151. A note to pay money within so many days after the defendant should marry, was (on consideration) held not to be a negotiable note; and in Pearson v. Garrett. Comb. 227. and 4 Mod. 242. (which was before the statute,) an action having been brought upon a note by which the defendant promised to pay the plaintiff sixty guineas if he (the plaintiff) should be married within two months, the court inclined against the note, because it was to pay money on a mere contingency, and judgment was given on demurrer for the defendant.

(29) Jocelin v. Laserre, Fort. 281. 10 Mod. 294. 316. Evans drew upon Jocelin, and required him to pay Laserre 7*l.* a month out of Evans's growing subsistence. Laserre sued Jocelin, and had judgment, but upon a writ of error that judgment was reversed, because this draught was not a good bill of exchange, in as much as it would not have been payable, had Evans died, or had his subsistence been taken away.

(30) Haydock v. Linch, Lord Raym. 1563. Rogers drew upon Linch and requested him to pay Haydock 14*l.* 3*s.* out of the fifth payment when it should become due, and it should be allowed by Rogers. Linch accepted the draught, and Haydock sued him, but the court on demurrer to the declaration held this was no bill of exchange, and gave judgment for the defendant.

or out of (31) money when received, is no bill or note on account of the uncertainty whether the subsistence or payment will become due, or the money be received.

So an order to pay a sum out of (32) rents or (33) other money in the hands of the person to whom it is addressed is no bill, because he may not have rent or other money in his hands sufficient to discharge it.

---

(31) Dawkes v. Lord Deloraine, Blackst. 782. 3 Wils. 207. A draught was in these words: "8th of January, 1768, Seven weeks after date, pay Mrs. Dawkes, 32*l*. 17*s*. out of W. Steward's money as soon as you shall receive it, for your humble servant, Deloraine. To Timothy Brecknock, Esq." Brecknock accepted the bill, but it not being paid, Mrs. Dawkes brought an action upon it, against Lord Deloraine, who pleaded that Brecknock had not received W. Steward's money, and upon demurrer to his plea, insisted that this was not a bill of exchange. The court after argument, held the objection good; because it was payable out of a particular fund, and on an event which was future and contingent, viz. the receipt of W. Steward's money, whereas a bill ought to be subject to no event or contingency, except the failure of the general personal credit of the persons drawing or negotiating it. In Wilson, 262. is a report from hearsay of a determination that a promise to pay a sum of money, on the receipt of the Payee's wages due from a ship in government service, was a good note; but that may perhaps be questioned, because the maker might never receive the wages.

(32) Lord Raym. 1362. Str. 592. Fort. 282.

(33) Jenny v. Herle, Lord Raym. 1361. 8 Mod. 265. Str. 591. Herle sued Jenny upon a bill drawn by him upon Pratt, and payable to Herle to this effect: "Sir, you are to pay Mr. Herle "1945*l*. out of the money in your hands belonging to the pro-"prietors of the Devonshire mines, being part of the consideration "money for the purchase of the manor of West Buckland."

So a promise to pay (34) *on the sale or produce immediately when sold, of the White Hart inn, St. Albans, and the goods, &c.* is no note: although it be averred in the declaration upon such promise that the White Hart and goods were sold before the action was commenced.

So an instrument in the form of a note, but with a memorandum written upon it, stating that it is taken for (35) securing the payment of all such ba-

---

Herle had judgment in the Common Pleas, but upon a writ of error, the court of King's Bench held this was no bill of exchange, because it was only payable out of a particular fund supposed to be in Pratt's hands, and the judgment was accordingly reversed.

(34) Hill v. Halford and another in Error. 2 B. and P. 413. The defendants in Error sued Hill as maker of a note, thereby promising to pay them 190*l.* " on the sale or produce, immediately when sold, of the White Hart, St. Albans, Herts, and the goods, &c. value received." The declaration averred a sale of the inn and goods before the commencement of the action. After judgment in K. B. by default, writ of inquiry executed, and general damages recovered, Hill brought a writ of error in the Exchequer Chamber, and the court held that this promise could not be declared on as a note, and therefore reversed the judgment.

(35) Leeds & al. v. Lancashire. 2. Camp. N. P. C. 205. The defendant, Marriott, and Ball gave a joint and several promissory note to the plaintiffs for 200*l.* No time for payment was mentioned in the note. On the back was written, " The within " note is taken for security of all such balances as Jas. Mar- " riott may happen to owe to Thos. Leeds and Co. not extend- " ing farther than the within named sum of 200*l.* but this note " to be in force for six months, and no money liable to be called " for sooner in any case." This memorandum was written before the note was signed by the defendant or Ball. It appeared in an action upon this note, that in the course of mercanti le

lances as shall be due from one of the makers to the payee, to the extent of the sum mentioned therein, or that if any dispute shall arise respecting the subject which is the consideration for it, it shall be void, is no note. (36)

So an instrument acknowledging the receipt of draughts for the payment of money, and promising to pay the money specified in the draughts, is (37) not a promissory note. For the payment of the money depends upon the draughts being honoured.

---

dealings, Marriott had become indebted to the plaintiffs, and that on their refusing to deal with him any longer without some guarantee, the above instrument, which the makers represented to be a note, was given. It had a note stamp.—Lord Ellenborough held that as between the original parties it was an agreement, and not a note, and therefore nonsuited the plaintiffs.

(36) Hartley v. Wilkinson, 4 Camp. 127. 4 Maule 25. A note was made payable to Foster or order, for 25*l.* "being the "amount of the purchase-money for a quantity of fir belong-"ing to Mr. Hartley." Before the note was signed, this memorandum was indorsed upon it: "This note is given on condition "that if any dispute shall arise between Mr. Hartley and Lady "Wray respecting the fir, this note to be void." In an action upon this note by indorsee against the maker, Lord Ellenborough thought it not a note within the statute, because its payment depended upon there being no dispute between Mr. Hartley and Lady Wray, and he nonsuited the plaintiff. On a motion for a new trial, the court agreed with him, and refused a rule.

(37) Williamson & al. v. Bennett & al., 2 Campb. N. P. C. 417. The defendants were sued upon the following instrument, which was stamped and declared upon as a promissory note, "Borrowed and received of J. and J. Williamson (the plaintiffs) "the sum of 200*l.* in three draughts, by W. and B. William-

So an order from the (38) owner of a ship to the freighter to pay money *on account of freight* is no bill, because the quantum due for freight may be open to litigation, but such an order from the freighter (39) is, because it is an admission that so much at least is due.

" son, dated as under, payable to us W. Bennett and S. M. (the " defendants) on J. and J. Williamson, which we promise to pay " unto the said J. and J. Williamson, with interest. As witness " our hands this 26th day of August, 1802.

" August 26,	1 draught at 2 months		£120
" ———	1 do.	———	30
" ———	1 do.	———	50
			£200

(Signed by the defendants.)

Lord Ellenborough held that this was not a promissory note. And said there can be no doubt that the money was not payable immediately, and that it was not to be paid at all, unless the draughts were honoured. The plaintiffs were nonsuited.

(38) Banbury v. Lisset, Str. 1211. Gibson drew on the defendants in favour of the plaintiff " on account of freight of the " galley Veale, Edward Champion, and this order shall be your " sufficient discharge for the same." The action was brought against the defendants as acceptors, and they contended it was not a bill of exchange, because it was only payable out of a particular fund; and Lee, C. J. was of that opinion, but he left the point to the jury, who found for the defendants on another ground.

(39) Pierson v. Dunlop, Cowp. 571. M'Lintot freighted a ship of which Nichol was captain, and Pierson owner, and being unable to pay the freight, drew upon Dunlop and Co. in favour of Nichol *on account of freight:* Pierson afterwards sued Dunlop and Co. as acceptors, and though other objections were taken, it was never insisted that this was payable out of a particular fund.

And an order to pay money as (40) *the drawer's quarter's half-pay by advance* before the pay will be due, is a good bill, because it will be payable though the half-pay shall never become due.

So a note to pay a sum of money (41) *being a portion of a value as under deposited in security for the payment hereof according to the receipt in my hands*, or *for value deposited and registered* is a good note, because it is payable at all events.

---

(40) Macleod v. Snee, Lord Raym. 1481. Str. 762. 1 Barnard. 12. Macleod was sued in the Common Pleas as acceptor of a bill of exchange drawn by Dundas and indorsed to the plaintiff, dated 25th of May, 1724, by which Dundas required him one month after date "to pay 9*l*. 10*s*. as his (Dundas's) quarter's half-pay "from the 24th June, 1724, to 25th September following, by "advance," and obtained judgment. Macleod brought a writ of error, and insisted that this was similar to the cases of Jocelin v. Laserre, and Jenney v. Herle, but the whole court was of a contrary opinion; for per cur. this bill was not payable upon a contingency, nor out of a particular fund, but is made payable at all events, and drawn upon the general credit of the drawer, and not out of the half-pay, for it is payable as soon as the quarter begins, and the half-pay was not to be due till three months afterwards.

(41) Haussoullier v. Hartsink, 7 Term. Rep. 733. The defendant issued two notes upon a deposit by one Richardson: one payable to J. S. or bearer, for 25*l*. "being a portion of a "value as under deposited in security for payment hereof ac-"cording to the receipt in our hands," and specifying the particulars of the deposit: the other, payable to J. S. or order "for "value deposited and registered $\frac{A}{V}$." The plaintiff discounted both notes, bona fide, and for a valuable consideration: and on a case reserved the court said they were clearly of opinion, that though as between the original parties to the transaction, the payment of the notes was to be carried to a particular account, yet the notes were payable at all events, and therefore the plaintiff was entitled to recover.

So an order or promise to pay money when (42) J. S. shall come of age, specifying the day when that event is to happen, is a good bill or note, because it is payable though J. S. die in the interim.

And an order or promise (43) to pay within a limited time after a man's death is a good bill or note, because it must become payable at some time or other, though the exact period is uncertain: and if a bill or note be made payable at ever so distant a day, if it be a day that must come, it is no objection to the bill or note (44).

So an order or (45) promise to pay within a

---

(42) Goss v. Nelson, Burr. 226. Action on a note payable to an infant "when he (the infant) shall come of age, to wit, "12th June, 1750;" and it was objected in arrest of judgment, that it was uncertain whether the money would ever have been payable, because the infant might have died under 21, but the court held it a good note, because it was payable at all events on the 12th June, 1750, though the infant should have died before that time.

(43) Cooke v. Colehan, Str. 1217. Willes, 393. On error from the Common Pleas, the court held a note payable six weeks after the death of the defendant's father, a good negotiable note, because there was no contingency, whereby it might never become payable, but it was only uncertain as to the time, which is the case with all bills payable so many days after sight.

(44) Per Willes, Ch. J. in delivering judgment in Colehan v. Cooke, Willes's Rep. 394.

(45) Andrews v. Franklin, Str. 24. A note payable two months after a certain ship (in his majesty's service) should be paid off, was objected to, as depending upon a contingency which might never happen: but per cur. the paying off the ship is a thing of a public nature; judgment for the plaintiff. And in Evans v. Underwood, 1 Wils. 262. where an action was brought by

limited time after the payment of money due from government is a good bill or note, because it is morally certain that such payment will be made.

Sect. 5. — It is not in general essential that a bill or note should be dated.

But negotiable bills or notes, except bank-notes, for between 20*s.* and 5*l.*, if made in England, must. (46)

And notes payable to the bearer on demand must not have the dates printed. (47)

And giving false dates to evade the stamp duties upon draughts on bankers, or upon bills or notes not payable within two months after date, or sixty days after sight, will subject the party to a penalty of 100*l.* (48)

If a bill or note is dated forward, of a day not arrived, and any of the parties die before that day, such deaths will be no bar to the remedy of a bonâ fide holder. (49)

---

an indorsee against the maker upon a note payable on the receipt of the payee's wages from his majesty's ship the Suffolk, the court thought the case like that of Andrews v. Franklin, and after looking into that case *are said* to have given judgment for the plaintiff. Quære tamen, because it was uncertain, though the wages might be paid, whether the maker would receive them.

(46) See ante, p. 11.

(47) See post, — 55 G. 3. c. 184. s. 18.

(48) See post, — 55 G. 3. c. 184. s. 12, 13.

(49) See Pasmore v. North, post.

So if a blank be left for the date, and that date is afterwards filled up, the manner of filling it up will furnish no ground of objection either to the original parties;

Or to the person who filled it up. (50)

Sect. 6.—Bills and notes are either inland or foreign: inland when made and payable within this kingdom; and foreign, when made or payable abroad.

It was once doubted whether notes would be intitled to the aid of 3 & 4 Ann. c. 9. unless they were made within this kingdom, (51) but there have been instances (52) (53) since in which actions have

---

(50) See Usher v. Dauncey, post.

(51) Carr v. Shaw, B. R. H. 39 Geo. 3. In an action on a promissory note made at Philadelphia, the first count of the declaration stated that the defendant, at Philadelphia, in parts beyond the seas, to wit, at London, &c. according to the form of the statute, &c. made his note in writing, &c. There were also the common money counts. The defendant demurred specially to the first count, and pleaded the general issue to the others. On the demurrer the court intimated a strong opinion that the statute did not apply to foreign notes, and advised the plaintiff to amend: but on the general issue Lord Kenyon said, the note, though not within the statute, is evidence to support any of the money counts, and the plaintiff had a verdict at Guildhall, 1st May, 1799.

N. The pleadings are entered as of Michaelmas Term, 39 G. 3. Roll. 1238.

(52) See Pollard v. Herries, 3 Bos. & Pull. 335, where the plaintiffs recovered upon notes made at Paris. See also Splitgerber v. Kohn, post.

been brought upon such notes without exception, and 48 G. 3. c. 149. s. 21. prohibited the negotiation or payment of such notes unless they were stamped, and this prohibition is still continued by 55 G. 3. c. 184. s. 29. as to notes payable to the bearer on demand.

And it is no objection to a bill or note that it was made by a British subject in an enemy's country in time of war, if it do not appear to have been made for any illegal purpose, and was made payable to a neutral. (53)

Or, if made by a British prisoner of war, if made payable or indorsed to an alien enemy. (54)

Inland bills and notes seldom consist of more than one part: foreign bills in general consist of several.

The several parts of a bill are called a set.

Each part contains a condition that it shall be payable only so long as all the others remain unpaid: in other respects all are of the same tenor.

---

(53) Houriet v. Morris, 3 Campb. 303. Payees against maker on note made at Paris in time of war: defendant was a British subject, plaintiffs neutral merchants in Switzerland: the note was given by defendant for watches bought by him in Paris of plaintiffs: it was objected that this was a trading in an enemy's country in time of war, and that a note founded on such trading was not valid: but Lord Ellenborough said, plaintiffs were not enemies, and might legally sell their goods in an enemy's country, and defendant did not appear to have bought them for any illegal purpose. Plaintiffs had a verdict.

(54) See Antoine v. Morshead, and Daubuz v. Morshead, post.

This condition should be inserted in each part, and should in each mention every other part of the set, for if a man with an intention to make a set of three parts should omit the condition in the first, and make the second with a condition mentioning the first only, and in the third alone take notice of the other two (which, by the way, is the mode pointed out by (55) Molloy, (56) Malynes, and (57) Marius) he might perhaps in some cases be obliged to pay each; for it might be questionable if it would be any defence to an action on the second that he had paid the third, or to an action on the first that he had paid either of the others.

But an omission is not, perhaps, material, which upon the face of the condition must necessarily have arisen from a mistake, as if in the enumeration of the several parts one of the intermediate ones were to be omitted, for instance, "Pay this my first of exchange, second and *fourth* not paid."

Where a bill consists of several parts, each ought to be delivered to the person in whose favour it is made, (unless one is forwarded to the drawee for acceptance,) otherwise there may be difficulties in negotiating the bill, or obtaining payment.

---

(55) Book 2. c. 10. s. 14.

(56) Book 3. c. 5. p. 261, 262.

(57) P. 7.

Sect. 7.— A bill or note may fix a particular place for payment.

And where this is what is to be considered as part of the bill or note, it is a variance to omit stating it; (58)

And in an action against the maker of the note, or acceptor of the bill, may make it necessary to allege and prove presentment at that place. (59)

The place is considered part of the instrument where it is incorporated in the body of the bill or note; where it is detached from the body as a memorandum only, not.

Sect. 8.—Bills and notes are made payable to order, or to bearer, or to specified individuals.

A bill or note payable to J. S. or order, is payable to the order of J. S. and negotiable by indorsement. A bill or note payable to J. S. or bearer, is (60) payable to the bearer and negotiable by

(58) Hodge v. Fillis. See post.

(59) Roche v. Campbell. See post.

(60) Grant v. Vaughan Burr. 1516. Vaughan gave Bicknell a draught upon his banker payable " to ship Fortune or bearer." The draught came to the hands of Grant, who sued Vaughan upon it. The defendant contended that this draught was a mere authority to receive the money, and not negotiable, and that point and another being left to the jury, they found for the defendant; but upon an application for a new trial, and cause shewn, the court held clearly that it was negotiable, and a new trial was granted, in which the plaintiff recovered,

delivery; and in the latter case J. S. is a mere cypher.

If a bill or note import to be payable to a person not in esse, or his order, and is issued with an indorsement in blank, purporting to be made by him thereon, it is as against the drawer or maker to be considered as a bill or note(61) payable to

(61) This point has been repeatedly discussed within a few years upon several bills drawn in 1788. A case of the kind had occurred at the London Sittings after Easter Term 1769; Stone v. Freeland, cited 1 H. Bl. 316. in the notes: a bill drawn by Cox on the defendant was made payable to Butler and Co. or their order, and indorsed in their name, and instead of proving that this indorsement was made by Butler and Co., the plaintiff's own witnesses said, they believed it was made by Cox, and though there was a house under the firm of Butler and Co. with which Cox had dealings, it was proved that the bill had never been in their hands, upon which it was contended that the indorsement being fictitious, the plaintiff could not recover; but by Lord Mansfield, "the intent of the bill was only to enable Cox to raise money, and the reason why it was not made payable to his order was, that there would then have been too many payable to his order in circulation at the same time, which would have had the appearance of fictitious credit; names are often used of persons who never existed;" and it appearing that the defendant promised to pay the bill at the time the plaintiff discounted it, the jury upon the footing of that undertaking found a verdict for the plaintiff. As this case however was distinguishable from those on the bills drawn in 1788, on account of the express undertaking to pay the plaintiff, which (as was admitted by Mr. J. Ashhurst, who held a brief in the cause, in 3 Term Rep. 176.) was the ground of the determination, as this was a nisi prius decision only, and as the amount of the bills in 1788 was very considerable, the point was very strongly contested in the actions on those bills. The first case that came before the court was Tatlock v. Harris, 3 Term Rep. 174. It was an action brought upon a bill drawn by the defendant, as

bearer; and so is a bill as against the acceptor, if he knew at the time of his acceptance, that the payee was a fictitious person.

---

one of several partners in a house at Nottingham upon himself in London, payable to Grigson and Co. or order, and purporting to be indorsed by Grigson and Co. and Lewis and Potter; the defendant was sued upon the bill, and the declaration contained counts upon the bill, and counts for money paid and money had and received. It appeared in evidence that there was no such house as that of Grigson and Co.; that the defendant paid the bill to Lewis and Potter, to whom he was indebted, and they gave him credit in account; and that the plaintiffs discounted it for Lewis and Potter: to this evidence the defendant demurred; and after argument and time taken to consider, the court intimated a strong opinion that the plaintiffs might recover on the counts upon the bill: but the ground of their decision was, that he was entitled to recover on the counts for money paid, and money had and received, because the giving the bill was an appropriation of so much money to be paid to the person who should become holder of the bill, and therefore when the plaintiffs discounted it, they paid the money to the use of the defendant, and when Lewis and Potter gave the defendant credit for the value of the bill, that was money had and received to the use of such persons as should afterwards be the holders of the bill.

The next case was that of Vere v. Lewis, 3 Term Rep. 182. which was brought against the defendant as acceptor, and the only difference between that and Tatlock v. Harris was, that there was no evidence to shew that the defendant had received any value for the bill, and that there was strong evidence to shew that the indorsement, in the name of the payee, was made by the defendant; but the court held that the latter circumstance did not vary the question, and that the acceptance was evidence that the defendant had received value from the drawers, and therefore they gave judgment for the plaintiffs without argument. Lord Kenyon, Mr. J. Ashhurst, and Mr. J. Buller, thought also that he was entitled to recover on one of the

It was for some time unsettled whether it was not essential that a bill or note should be payable

---

counts of the declaration, which stated the bill to be payable to bearer.

This case was followed by that of Minet v. Gibson, 3 Term Rep. 481. 1 H. Bl. 569. where a bill drawn by Livesay and Co. on the defendants were made payable to John White, or order, and it was found upon a special verdict, that White was a fictitious person, that his name was indorsed upon the bill by Livesay and Co.; that the defendants knew, when they accepted the *bill*, that no such person as John White, whose indorsement was then upon the bill, existed, and that the indorsement was not made by any person of that name, the court of King's Bench thought this case decided by Vere and Lewis, and gave judgment for the plaintiffs; and on a question from the House of Lords, whether the bill might not be deemed in law to be payable to the bearer, Hotham, Perryn, and Thompson, Barons, and Gould, J. gave it as their opinions that it might; but Eyre, C. B. and Heath, J. differed: after which Lord Kenyon, Lord Loughborough, and Lord Bathurst spoke in favour of the judgment, and Lord Thurlow against it, and the judgment was affirmed without a division.

After the judgment in Minet v. Gibson, in the King's Bench, and before its determination in the House of Lords, came on the case of Collet v. Emmett, 1 H. Bl. 313. where Livesay and Co. (who were authorised by the defendant to draw for him by his writing his name on a piece of blank paper with a shilling bill stamp thereon), made a bill payable to George Chapman, or order, and indorsed it with George Chapman's name; and it appearing that there was no such person as George Chapman, the court of Common Pleas, after two arguments, and time taken to consider, held that the action might fairly be supported on a count that stated the bill to be payable to bearer, and there being such a count in the declaration, they gave the plaintiffs judgment upon it. Vide Bennet v. Farnell, 1 Camp. 180.

either to order, or to (62) bearer, but it is now decided that it is not.

But where the bill or note is payable otherwise than to the bearer, it must contain the name of the payee.

---

(62) Smith v. Kendall, 6 Term Rep. 123. In an action for money paid and lent, the defendant pleaded the statute of limitations, and the plaintiff replied a latitat sued out 26th Sept. 1793. A note was given in evidence dated 25th June, 1787, and payable to the plaintiff three months after date, but it was not payable either to order or to bearer, and the court on consideration held that it was a good note within the statute, that it was entitled to three days' grace, and consequently that the statute of limitations did not begin to run until those three days had expired, which was on 28th September, 1787, and therefore within six years of 26th September, 1993. See also Chadwick v. Allen, ante, p. 5. The old entries also describe the custom upon bills to be to pay the payee without adding any words to make them payable to order or to bearer. Lutw. 231. 277. 891. Vid. 17 Brownl. Rep. 77. Clift. 916.; and see Lord Raym. 1545.

Rex v. Box, 6 Taunt. 325. Indictment for forging a promissory note. The note was as follows: " On demand we pro-
" mise to pay Mesdames S.W. and S.D., stewardesses for
" the time being of the Provident Daughters Society, held at
" the Hope, Smithfield, or their successors in office, 64*l.*, with
" 5*l. per cent.* interest, value received this 7th February, 1815,
" for F.C. and Co. J. Forster." This society was not enrolled according to 33 G. 3. c. 34., so that these payees were not strictly stewardesses, nor could they legally have successors in office, and it was insisted that this was not in law a promissory note: but on a case for the opinion of the twelve judges, they were unanimously of opinion that it was: that it was not essential a note should be negotiable, that the description of stewardesses was one which went to designate the payees, and the note, if genuine, would have enured to them, and the survivor of them, and the executors and administrators of such survivor, and the conviction of the prisoner was held right.

Uncertainty as to the person to whom the payment shall be made will prevent an instrument from being a bill or note, as making it payable to *A.* or *B.* (63)

If a bill or note is issued with a blank for the payee's name, any *bonâ fide* holder may insert his own name as payee. (64)

---

(63) Blankenhagen v. Blundell, 2 Barn. & Ald. 417. Declaration on a note by which it was stated that defendant promised to pay J. P. Dahmer or plaintiffs, or his or their order; another count stated Dahmer to be since dead: each count averred that the note was delivered to plaintiffs, and negatived payment to Dahmer: defendant demurred, and on argument the court were clear this was not a note within the statute, because it was not payable in certain either to Dahmer or the plaintiffs, but the claim of either, or of the indorsee of either, might be defeated by payment to the other; and if it were not within the statute, when issued, subsequent events could not make it so. It was urged, that in legal operation it was payable to Dahmer and plaintiffs, but the court said they could not take that to be its operation as the declaration was framed, and judgment was given for the defendant.

(64) Cruchley v. Clarance, 2 Maule, 90. In an action by the payee of a bill against the drawer, it appeared that defendant drew the bill in Jamaica, and sent it to England with a blank for the payee's name, that it was put into negotiation here, and afterwards paid to the plaintiff for an old debt, without the blanks being filled up: and that he inserted his own name as payee: plaintiff had a verdict; and on motion for nonsuit or new trial, the court held plaintiff warranted in inserting his own name, for by leaving the blank the defendant authorized any *bonâ fide* holder to fill it up, and the rule was refused.

Cruchley v. Mann, 5 Taunt, 529. Plaintiff brought another action on the same bill against the acceptor: one objection was that the blank was filled up without Clarance's authority, and Clarance gave in evidence that he did not authorize the inser-

But until the blank is filled up it is not a bill or note. (65)

Unless perhaps where it may be considered in legal operation as payable to the order of the drawer.

Giving a payee a wrong description, if there is no doubt as to the person, is of no (66) consequence.

Sect. 9. — The (67) name of the person making it must be inserted in the body, or subscribed

---

tion; but it appears that Clarance had passed the bill to Vashon, that Vashon had passed it to plaintiff, and that defendant accepted it under Clarance's eye and at Clarance's instance, after plaintiff's name was inserted; the court was clear Clarance's consent must be implied, and a rule for a new trial was refused.

(65) Rex v. Randall, Trin. 1811. The prisoner was indicted for forging a bill of exchange, the bill was payable to or order (leaving a space for the payee's name), and was in appearance a navy-bill for an officer's wages; the point was saved for the consideration of the judges, whether this could be deemed a bill, there being no payee: it was urged that such a bill authorized any proper holder to fill up the blank as he might choose: but the judges held it was no bill till the blank was filled up, and recommended it to the judge who tried the prisoner to apply to the Crown for his pardon.

(66) See Rex v. Box, ante, p. 29.

(67) Taylor v. Dobbins, Str. 399. The declaration upon a note stated that the defendant wrote it with his own hand, but did not allege that he signed it, and an exception was taken on that ground. Sed per cur. If the defendant wrote it, his subscription to it was unnecessary; it is sufficient if his name appeared in any part. "I, J. S. promise to pay" is as good as "I promise to pay," subscribed J. S.

at the bottom of every bill or note, and every bill or note must be written or signed by the person making it, or some one authorized by him for that purpose.

The clerk, who signs bank notes, need not have authority for that purpose under the common seal. (68)

Elliot v. Cowper, Str. 609. Lord Raym. 1376. 8 Mod. 307. It was objected on demurrer to a declaration on a note, that it alleged only that the defendant made it, but did not state that he signed it; but by the court, if he did not either write or sign it, he did not *make* it, for making implies signing, and making is alleged. Judgment for plaintiff.

Smith v. Jarves, Lord Raym. 1484. The declaration upon a note drawn by Jarves and Baily, stated that Jarves for himself and partner made his note in writing with his own hand subscribed, whereby he promised for himself and partner to pay. It was objected on demurrer, that it was not charged, that Jarves had signed the note for himself and Baily; but the court held the statement shewed that Jarves did sign for himself and Baily, and gave the plaintiff judgment.

Ereskin v. Murray, Lord Raym. 1542. In an action on a bill it was alleged that the plaintiff made his bill in writing, and thereby requested the defendant to pay. It was objected on error, that it did not appear that the plaintiff signed the bill; but it was answered, that the allegation that he made it, and required the defendant to pay, implied that his name was in it, (otherwise he could not request,) and that he or somebody for him wrote it. Judgment for the plaintiff was affirmed.

(68) Rex v. Bigg, 3 P. Will. 419. On an indictment under 8 & 9 W. 3. c. 20. s. 36. for altering and erasing a genuine bank note, it was found upon a special verdict that the person who signed the note was employed by the company to sign notes, but that he had no authority under their common seal: an objection was taken that an authority under their common seal was necessary: many other objections were taken, and what was the opinion of the judges upon each is not stated; but

And now by 1 Geo. 4. c. 92. s. 3. his signature may be impressed by machinery.

The signature to a bill or note must import to bind at all events each person who signs it. A note signed A. B. or else C. D. is not as against C. D. binding as a note. (69)

If a person signs his name upon a blank paper, stamped with a bill-stamp, and delivers it to another person to draw such bill as he may choose thereon, he (70) is the drawer of any bill such person shall draw thereon, to which the stamp is applicable.

Sect. 10.—If there be a subscribing witness to a bill or note, the bill or note cannot be read in evidence unless such witness is produced, or his absence properly accounted for.

Mr. P. Williams, who argued for the prisoner, says the judges were divided, but the majority of the judges held it to be felony, and the prisoner was transported, not executed.

(69) Ferris v. Bond, ante, p. 13.

(70) Collis v. Emett, 1 H. Bl. 313. Emett signed his name upon a blank paper stamped with a shilling bill-stamp, (the highest stamp then in force for bills,) and delivered it to Livesay and Co. that thay might draw thereon such bill as they should please. They drew one for 155*l.* at three months' date, which was duly transferred to Collis and Co., and Collis and Co. sued Emett thereon. A special verdict was found, principally with a view to another point; the court held Emett answerable, and the plaintiffs had judgment. See Russell v. Langstaffe, post. Pasmore v. North, post. Usher v. Dauncey, post.

Sect. 11.—It was for some time matter of controversy whether it was not necessary that a bill or note should import to be for value received, but it is now settled (71) that it need not.

But notes for coals in ships in the port of London must by 3 G. 2. c. 26. s. 7, 8. import to be for value received in coals, and a refusal to insert words to that effect, or taking a note without such words, subjects the buyer and master of the ship to a penalty of 100*l.* (72)

The note however is not, for want of those words, void. (73)

---

(71) White v. Ledwich, B. R. H. 25 G. III. A declaration upon a bill of exchange was demurred to, because it was not stated to have been given for value received, but the court said, it was a settled point, that it was not necessary, and gave judgment for the plaintiff. The same point is ruled in Macleod v. Snee, Lord Raym. 1481. See also Fort. 282. 8 Mod. 267. 1 Barnard. 88. Lutw. 889. 1 Mod. Ent. 310. 1 Show. 497.

(72) By 3 G. 2. c. 26. s. 7. every contractor for coals on board any ship or vessel in the port of London, shall at the time of the delivery of such coals either pay for them in ready money, or for such part as shall not be so paid for, shall give his promissory note or notes for payment thereof, expressing therein the words "value received in coals;" and by s. 8. all lightermen, or other buyers of or contractors for coals, who shall refuse to give their notes for coals to them respectively delivered, and shall refuse to insert the words "value received in coals," and every such master (*i. e.* master of a ship or vessel with coals in the port of London) who shall take any such note from any dealer in coals, in which note the words "value received in coals" are not expressly inserted, such lightermen, buyers of or contractors for coals, and masters, shall, for every such refusal or acceptance, respectively forfeit 100*l.*

(73) Per Holroyd J. 1 Stark. 463.

Sect. 12.—A memorandum on a bill or note before it is issued, may, in some instances, be considered as part of the bill or note, and control its operation.

As a memorandum, that if any dispute shall arise respecting the consideration, the bill or note shall be void. (74)

But a memorandum upon a note to state where it shall be payable, is not. (75)

Nor a memorandum of acceptance on a note payable after sight. (76)

---

(74) See Hartley v. Wilkinson, ante, p. 17.

(75) Exon v. Russell, 4 Maule, 505. At the bottom of a promissory note was written "At Messrs. Brown and Co.'s, bankers, London." In an action against the maker the declaration alleged that defendant made the note, and thereby promised to pay, &c. and made the same payable and to be paid at the house of certain persons described, as Messrs. Brown and Co.'s: there was no averment or proof of presentation at Brown and Co.'s; and on a rule nisi for a nonsuit for want of such proof, and cause shown, the court held that as the "At Messrs. Brown and Co.'s" was a memorandum only and no part of the note, it was a misdescription to state it as part of the legal effect of the note itself to make it payable there, and on that account the rule was made absolute.

(76) Splitgerber v. Kohn, 1 Stark. 125. Indorsee against maker on a note made in Prussia, and payable seven days after sight: in the margin were these words, "Accepted on myself, payable every where" [and these words were on the note when it issued]; it was urged that they altered the nature of the note, and should have been noticed in the declaration; but Lord Ellenborough said they constituted no part of the original instrument; they were merely an acknowledgment of a sight of the note; and though they were contemporaneous with the note, their effect was in point of law subsequent.

Nor is a memorandum by way of direction to the payee's executors, in case of his death. (77)

Nor a memorandum which cannot be read for want of an agreement stamp. (77)

Nor one which has an attesting witness, and cannot be read on account of his absence. (77)

Sect. 13.—The act of drawing a bill implies an undertaking from the drawer to the payee, and every other person to whom the bill may after-

---

(77) Stone v. Metcalfe, 1 Stark. 53. 4 Campb. 217. In an action by payee against maker on a note for 1000*l*. and interest, payable months after date, there appeared to be a memorandum indorsed upon the note, but that memorandum was attested by J. S.: it was urged for defendant that he had a right to have the memorandum read as well as the note: but per Lord Ellenborough, "Plaintiff is entitled to have the note "read, having proved defendant's hand-writing; but the in-"dorsement may be an unconnected instrument." J. S. was then called, and proved the indorsement, which was as follows: "Although the within note is payable in months, my will and desire is that it shall not then be called in, and if defendant shall wish for further time, he shall have it without suit at law until three years after my decease:" it was urged that this indorsement made part of the note, and that neither of them could be read, because, taken together, they required an agreement-stamp. Sed per Lord Ellenborough: "I have on one side "a perfect note, and on the other that which, if stamped, might "have operated as a defeasance, but at which, for want of a "stamp, I cannot look: but if the words were incorporated, "they are words of mere indulgence and favour. As to the "executors, the case might be different." The plaintiff had a verdict.

wards be transferred, that the drawee is a person capable of making himself responsible for its payment, that he shall, if applied to for the purpose, express in writing upon the bill an undertaking to pay it when it shall become payable, and that he shall then pay it: and subjects the drawer on a failure in any of these particulars to an action at the suit of the payee or holder.

The making of a note is an express engagement to the payee, or person to whom it shall be transferred, to pay the money mentioned therein, according to its tenor.

CAP. II.

A BILL or note cannot properly be made or indorsed by, nor can a bill be properly addressed to any person incapable of making himself responsible for the payment, nor can they be properly made payable or indorsed to any person incapable of suing.

Sect. 2.—Therefore a bill or note cannot properly be made or indorsed by, nor can a bill be properly addressed to an infant (1), except perhaps

(1) Williams v. Harrison, Carth. 160. 3 Salk. 197. In an action against the drawer of a bill, the defendant pleaded infancy, and the plaintiff demurred, and the court held clearly without argument, that infancy was a good bar, for the bill was drawn by the defendant as a trader in course of trade, and not for necessaries.

where it is drawn, indorsed, or accepted for necessaries. (2)

But if an infant draw a bill to his own order, and indorse it, and the drawee accept it, the acceptance will bind the drawee, and he will be compellable to pay the indorsee, because, by accepting, he precludes himself from disputing the competence of the drawer. (3)

And the drawing, indorsing, or accepting by an infant, is voidable only, not void (4), and if he ra-

---

(2) Williamson v. Watts, 1 Campb. N. P. C. 552. In an action against the acceptor of a bill, the defendant pleaded infancy, and the plaintiff replied that the bill was accepted for necessaries, on which issue was joined: on opening the case Sir J. Mansfield C. J. said, "This action certainly cannot be maintained. The defendant is allowed to be an infant, and did any one ever hear of an infant being liable as an acceptor of a bill of exchange? The replication is nonsense, and ought to have been demurred to." He said as the point of law was so clear, he felt strongly inclined to nonsuit the plaintiff; but he heard the evidence, and the plaintiff was nonsuited, on proof that the goods, for which the bill had been given, were not necessaries.

(3) Taylor v. Croker, 4 Esq. N. P. C. 187. In an action against the acceptor of a bill, drawn by Eversfield and Jones on the defendant, in their own favour, and indorsed by them to one S. and by him to the plaintiff; it appeared that both the drawers were infants at the time of drawing the bill. But Lord Ellenborough held that though that might have been a good defence had the action been brought againt the drawers themselves, it was no defence in the present action. Verdict for the plaintiff.

(4) Gibbs v. Merrill, 3 Taunt. 307. A bill was accepted by Merrill and Le Blond; Le Blond was an infant. An action being brought against Merrill only, he pleaded that he did not

tify the act after he comes of age, it will bind him.

As an infant is capable of suing (5), he may be a payee or indorsee.

But it may be questionable in some cases, whether payment should not be made to his guardian. (6)

Sect. 3.—Bills or notes cannot properly be made, indorsed, or accepted by a feme covert, un-

---

undertake unless jointly with Le Blond. Replication that he did; plaintiff proved Le Blond's infancy, and defendant proved by Le Blond, that he had never disaffirmed the acceptance. The jury found for the plaintiff; but on a rule nisi for a new trial, and time to consider, the court held Le Blond's acceptance voidable only, not void; and that the issue should have been found for the defendant; they therefore set aside the verdict, but gave the plaintiff leave to amend his replication by stating Le Blond's infancy, and so raising the question whether he was compellable to join him.

(5) See Teed v. Elworthy, 14 East, 210. Warwick v. Bruce, 2 Maule & S. 205. 6 Taunt. 118.

(6) See Pothier pl. 166. who observes that payment to an infant will be no discharge of the debtor, unless it appear that the payment were beneficial to the infant; if the money were applied to his advantage, the payment will be good; if not, as where the infant squanders it, the party paying will not be discharged. So money *lent* to an infant for necessaries, if duly applied, may in equity be recovered from him. Marlow v. Pitfield, 1 P. Williams, 558. Though it is otherwise at law, 1 Salk. 279. 386. But if an executor pay a legacy to an infant, which the infant's father obtains and dissipates, the executor will be answerable to the infant. Philips v. Paget, 2 Atk. 80. See also Pothier on Obligations, part iii. ch. 1. art. 2. s. 1. pl. 504. and s. 2.

less where she acts by authority from her husband (7), or where she resides here, and he is under a civil incapacity of being in this kingdom. (8)

Her living apart from her husband, and having a separate maintenance secured by deed (9), or

---

(7) Barlow v. Bishop, 1 East's Rep. 432. Ann Parry was married, but traded in her own name, with her husband's consent. She became indebted to the plaintiff, and to enable her to pay him, the defendant who knew that she was married, gave her a note payable to her or order. She indorsed it in her own name to the plaintiff, and he brought this action. Lord Kenyon thought it not maintainable, but saved the point; and after a rule nisi for a nonsuit, and cause shewn, he said it was clear that the delivery of the note to the wife vested the interest in the husband; that as he permitted her to trade on her own account, and this was a transaction in the course of that trade, he was not prepared to say that had she indorsed the note in his name, it would not have availed; the jury might have presumed that she was authorized by her husband; but the indorsement being in her own name, it was impossible to say it could pass the husband's interest. Rule absolute.

Cotes v. Davis. 1 Campb. N. P. C. 485. In an action by an indorsee against the maker of a note made payable to "Mrs. "Carter, or order," and indorsed by her in her own name, the defendant offered to show that Mrs. Carter was wife to one Cole; but it being proved that subsequently to the indorsement, and when the note was presented for payment, the defendant had promised to pay it, Lord Ellenborough said the jury might presume that she had authority from her husband to indorse the note, and *that* in the name by which she passed in the world. Verdict for the plaintiff.

(8) Vide Derry v. Duchess of Mazarine, Lord Raym. 147. Salk. 116. Sparrow v. Carruthers cited Blackst. 1197. 1 Term Rep. 6. See also Blackst. 1081, 1082. 1 Term Rep. 9.

(9) Vide Marshall v. Rutton, 8 Term Rep. 545.

her trading, by particular custom, on her own account (10), gives her no capacity to draw, indorse, or accept.

If a bill or note be made payable, or indorsed to a feme covert, whose husband is under no civil incapacity, the wife alone cannot, except as agent to her husband, make it available, or sue upon it; (11)

The husband may.

And he may either negotiate it;

Or sue upon it.

And he may either sue upon it in his own name, and treat it as if it were made payable to himself; (12)

Or sue upon it in the joint names of himself and his wife. (13)

Sect. 4.—If several, who are not partners, join in a note, and it begins with, "I promise," &c. it is several as well as joint, and it will bind each individual separately; (14)

---

(10) Vide Blackst. 1081. Caudell v. Shaw, 4 Term Rep. 361. but see also Lacie v. Phillips, Burr. 1776.

(11) See Barlow v. Bishop, ante, 41.

(12) Arnold v. Revoult, 1 Brod. & Bingh. 443.

(13) Philliskirk v. Pluckwell, 2 Maule, 393. A note to a feme covert; action thereon by her and her husband. Rule nisi for a nonsuit, but on cause shown, the court held that as a note primâ facie imported a consideration according to its tenor, and the wife might have been the meritorious cause of it, or it might have been given for a debt due to her before marriage, the husband might suffer her to join in suing upon it, and the rule was discharged.

(14) Lord Galway v. Matthew, post, 45.

And all jointly. (15)

And it only requires one stamp, if it were the bargain before it was issued that all should join. (15)

But if there were no such bargain, the addition of a fresh signature after it was once issued would make a new stamp necessary. (15)

If a bill or note is payable to several persons, not in partnership, the right to transfer is in all collectively, not (16) in any individually.

And an indorsement by and in the name of one only, will not give the indorsee a right to sue. (16)

---

(15) Clark v. Blackstock, Holt, 474. A note was in this form; "I promise to pay plaintiff or order, 30*l.* with interest, value received; Thos. Jackson, Jno. Blackstock." In an action against Blackstock alone, two objections were made, one that this was the joint note of Jackson and Blackstock; and, secondly, that there should have been an additional stamp for Blackstock's signature; it was ruled that the word "I" made the note several as well as joint; and, secondly, that the necessity of an additional stamp would depend upon this, viz. whether Blackstock's signature was part of the original bargain before plaintiff took the note, or an afterthought, and it appearing to have been part of the original bargain, verdict for plaintiff.

(16) Carvick v. Vickery, Dougl. 2d edit. p. 653. n. 134. A bill was drawn by father and son, who were not partners, payable *to their own order*. The son alone indorsed it, and upon an action by his indorsee against the acceptor, Lord Mansfield thought an indorsement by both parties essential, and nonsuited the plaintiff. A new trial however was afterwards granted, the court, after time taken to consider, being of opinion that by making the bill payable to their own order, the father and son had made themselves partners as to this transaction; but upon

So if a bill is drawn on several persons not connected in partnership, an acceptance by one will bind him, but him (17) only.

Sect. 5. — Each partner has in general a power to bind the partnership, and therefore a bill or note by one, or an indorsement or acceptance by one will in general bind all. (18)

---

the second trial Lord Mansfield said he did not think the question so decided as to preclude evidence which was offered, that by the universal usage and understanding of all the bankers and merchants in London the indorsement was bad, as not being signed by both the payees, and the jury, *unâ voce*, declared that that was the usage and understanding, and without hearing any evidence upon the point they found a verdict for the defendant.

(17) Bull. Nisi Prius, 279. In the case of two joint traders, an acceptance by one will bind both; but if ten merchants employ one factor, and he draw a bill upon them all, and one accept it, this shall only bind him, and not the rest. Mar. 2d ed. 16. Beawes, § 228. 1st ed. p. 444. Molloy, b. 2. c. 10. § 18.

(18) Mason v. Rumsey and another, 1 Campb. N. P. C. 384. A bill was drawn on "Messrs. Rumsey and Co.;" and T. Rumsey, jun. wrote upon it "Accepted, T. Rumsey, sen." The present action was defended by T. Rumsey, jun. who contended that even if he were a partner, (which he denied,) this acceptance would not bind him. Lord Ellenborough told the jury, that if the defendants were partners, they were both bound by this acceptance. He said the word "accepted" alone would have been sufficient, and that the effect could not be altered by the addition of "T. Rumsey, sen." The jury found for the Plaintiff; and on motion afterwards for a new trial, on the ground of the evidence of partnership not having been sufficient, the court held the Chief Justice's direction right, and refused a rule.

And a note by one, importing to be for all, may bind the partnership, though it begin, "I promise." (19)

And a bill or note by one in the partnership-name will, as between them and an innocent holder, bind the partnership, though the partner making it was prohibited from drawing bills or notes. (20)

---

(19) Lord Galway v. Matthew and another, 1 Campb. N. P. C. 403. This was an action against the defendants as surviving partners of T. Whitsmith, on a note drawn thus: "Sixty days after date, I pay Ld. Viscount Galway, or order, 200*l*. value received. For J. Matthew, T. Whitsmith, and T. Smithson (Signed) "J. Matthew." Lord Ellenborough held that it bound the whole firm. S. C. 10 East Rep. 264.

This signature by the one (presuming his authority) is a good signature by all. See Wilks v. Back. 2 East Rep. 142.

(20) Swan and others v. Steele and Wood, 7 East's Rep. 210. The house of Wood and Payne carried on under the same firm and at the same counting-house, two trades, those of wholesale grocers and cotton dealers. The defendant, Steele, was a secret partner in the latter trade, but not in the former. The house was indebted to the plaintiffs, as grocers, and to pay this debt Wood and Payne, without the knowledge of Steele, indorsed to the plaintiffs a bill which they had received on account of the cotton concern. The bill was indorsed in the usual firm of W. and P., and Steele's being a partner was unknown to the plaintiffs. Wood and Payne afterwards became bankrupts, and Payne being dead, this action, by the plaintiffs as indorsees of the bill, was brought against Steele and Wood; and on a case reserved, the only question was, whether the indorsement were good: and the court held the case too clear for argument; and Lord Ellenborough said, that in the absence of all fraud on the part of the indorsee there was no doubt that such indorsement would bind all the partners. Postea to the plaintiffs.

Or though the particular bill or note were a fraud upon the partnership. (21)

But such bills or notes will not bind the partnership as to persons who when they took them knew of the want of authority; (22)

---

(21) Ridley and another v. Taylor, 13 East's Rep. 175. Ord and Ewbank were linen-drapers and partners. The plaintiffs, in Nov. 1806, sold a cargo of coals to Ewbank for 34*l.* 11*s.*, and Ewbank in May following gave them 5*l.* in part payment, and a promissory note for the balance. This note was dishonoured; and in payment of this balance, Ewbank, on the 7th of Nov. 1807, gave the plaintiffs a bill for 40*l.*, dated 20th of October, 1807, drawn and indorsed by him in the partnership name, and accepted by the defendant. The bill was drawn, indorsed, and accepted, before it was produced to the plaintiffs, and it did not appear that they knew that it had been drawn and indorsed by Ewbank. Ewbank afterwards applied to the plaintiffs for the difference between the balance due, and the 40*l.*, but they refused to pay it, until payment of the note. This bill was dishonoured; and the plaintiffs in their account debited Ewbank for the amount. Ord and Ewbank afterwards became bankrupt, and the plaintiffs now sued the defendant as acceptor. A verdict was found for the plaintiff, subject to the opinion of the court of King's Bench on a case, stating these facts. The court held, that in this case, there being no evidence of covin between the plaintiffs and Ewbank to defraud Ord, and no such gross negligence on the part of the plaintiffs in not inquiring whether Ewbank had authority to transfer the bill, as to render the transaction fraudulent, the plaintiffs were entitled to recover: and they held, that Ord or Ewbank might have been called to disprove Ewbank's authority. The plaintiffs had judgment for the amount of Ewbank's debt.

(22) Lord Galway v. Matthew and Smithson, 10 East's Rep. 264. The defendants and Whitehouse (since deceased) were in partnership as brewers. Matthew applied to the plaintiff to lend his acceptance for 200*l.* to enable him to pay excise duties due from the house, and promised in return to

Or of the fraud. (23)

If one partner give a partnership-bill or note for his own private debt without the knowledge of the partnership, it is a fraud upon the partnership. (23)

And though an innocent indorsee may be able to inforce payment the creditor cannot. (23)

And in such case, if an action be brought by such creditor, notice need not be given him that the consideration will be disputed; the nature of the transaction is sufficient notice to him. (23)

---

give the note of the firm payable four days before the acceptance. The plaintiff gave his acceptance, and Matthew drew the note and signed it for himself and partners. He then got the acceptance discounted, and applied 180*l.* in payment of partnership debts, reserving the rest to himself. The plaintiff (after Whitehouse's death) was obliged to take up his acceptance, and now sued the defendants on the note. Matthew suffered judgment by default. But Smithson proved that the plaintiff before he took the note had received notice of an advertisement by him warning persons not to trust Matthew on his account, and that he would no longer be liable for drafts drawn by the other partners on the partnership-account. And Lord Ellenborough held that the plaintiff having taken the note after such warning could not recover, and therefore nonsuited him; and on motion to set aside the nonsuit the court held it right, and refused a rule.

(23) Shirreff v. Wilks and others, 1 East's Rep. 48. In October, 1795, Bishop and Wilks, who were then partners, became indebted to the plaintiffs for goods sold and delivered. Robson became a partner with Bishop and Wilks, in April, 1796, and continued so until the 8th November following, when the partnership was dissolved. On 5th November, 1796, the plaintiffs drew on the partnership for the amount of their demand against Bishop and Wilks, and Bishop accepted the bill in the partnership-firm. The plaintiffs now sued the three

If one of several persons who have been in partnership accept a bill in the partnership-name

---

partners upon this acceptance. Bishop and Robson were outlawed; and Wilks pleaded the general issue. A verdict was found for the plaintiff, subject to the opinion of the court. Lord Kenyon said he did not know how the case came to be reserved, as he had repeatedly decided the same question at the sittings; the propriety of which decisions had not been canvassed. He said, the consideration of the bill was goods sold to Bishop and Wilks only, when Robson was not a partner. "Then the plaintiffs, knowing this, draw the bill on the three partners, and knowingly take an acceptance from one of them, to bind the other two, one of whom, Robson, had no concern with the matter, and was no debtor of theirs; no assent or knowledge on his part being found. The transaction is fraudulent on the face of it." The other judges concurred. Postea to the defendant.

Hope v. Cust, B. R. M. 1774, cit. per Lawrence J. in Shirreff v. Wilks, 1 East's Rep. 53. Fordyce traded on his separate account, as well as in partnership with others, and being indebted to Hope on his separate account, gave him a general guarantie in the partnership-name for his own debt. Lord Mansfield left it to the jury, whether the taking of the guarantie were, in respect of the partners, a fair transaction; or covinous, with sufficient notice to the plaintiff of the injustice and breach of trust Fordyce was guilty of in giving it. The jury found for the defendant.

See also Pinkney v. Hall, 1 Salk. 126. S. C. Ld. Raym. 175., and Wells v. Masterman and another, 2 Esp. N. P. C. 731.

Green v. Deakin, 2 Stark. 348. Hickman owed Green money, and gave him a draft for the amount in the name of himself and his two partners Deakin and Bickley: neither Deakin or Bickley knew of the giving this draft, nor had this been done with their concurrence; Green was not apprized that the other partners were ignorant of the transaction, and it was urged that Deakin should have given notice of his intention to dispute the consideration; sed per Lord Ellenborough, the transaction is intrinsically notice: one partner has no right to bind another without his knowledge by drawing in the partnership-name for his private debt. Nonsuit.

after a dissolution of the partnership, the partnership will not be liable even to a bonâ holder for valuable consideration, if the dissolution took place after the date of the bill and before it became due, and proper means were taken to make the dissolution notorious. (24)

And if a dissolution is agreed upon, a person who knows of it cannot charge the partnership with a subsequent acceptance by one of the partners in the partnership name, unless he can prove that the intention to dissolve was abandoned, or that the acceptance was for a partnership transaction, and free from fraud. (25)

---

(24) Wrightson v. Pullan, 1 Stark. 375. Defendants, Pullan and Hopcroft, had been partners; but on 13th February 1815 their partnership was dissolved, and on 14th February notice thereof was published in the Gazette. After this date Taylor and Son drew upon Pullan and Hopcroft, and antedated the bill to 1st February, 1815. Hopcroft accepted this bill in the partnership name; after which Taylor and Son paid it to plaintiffs for value. It was urged for plaintiffs, that as the bill was dated before the dissolution, and plaintiffs had taken it bonâ fide and for a valuable consideration, plaintiffs were entitled to recover upon it; but Lord Ellenborough held, that as the partnership had been dissolved before the bill was drawn, Pullan could not be charged by the subsequent act of Hopcroft: and the court afterwards agreed with him, and refused a motion for a new trial.

(25) Paterson v. Zachariah, 1 Stark. 71. In an action against A. & B. upon an acceptance by A. in the joint names they having been in partnership, the defence was, that the acceptance was in fraud of B. after a dissolution to which plaintiff was privy; and it was proved, that before the date of the bill plaintiff had, as attorney, prepared a deed of dissolution, and had sent it for

But a dissolution will not protect the retiring partners, if they suffer their names to continue on the partnership premises, and the holder of the bill or note took it bonâ fide, and for value, and without knowledge of the dissolution. (26)

No *banking* partnership in England, if there be more than six partners, can properly draw, accept, or indorse, any bill or note payable at less than six months after the date; for, by the acts for protecting the Bank of England, such partnerships are not at liberty to borrow, owe, or take up any money on their bills or notes payable at demand, or at less than six months from the borrowing thereof. (27)

---

approbation to B.'s attorney; but it did not appear the deed had been executed. Sed, per Lord Ellenborough: — You need not labour this; where an intention to dissolve is made known, and the dissolution is in the course of execution, the burthen is on the other side to shew that the intention has been abandoned. Nonsuit.

(26) Williams v. Keats and Archer, 2 Stark. 290. In an action against defendants as acceptors of a bill, it appeared that they dissolved partnership 18th January, 1817, and that notice thereof was in the preceding night's Gazette; but that the business, (a hatter's,) was carried on as usual by Keats, and that the name, "Keats, Archer, and Co." continued over the door till April; that the bill in question, though dated in December, was not drawn till February; that it was then accepted, in the old partnership name, by Keats; and that plaintiffs took it bonâ fide and for full value in March. Lord Ellenborough thought Archer's permitting his name to remain over the door was notice of a continuance of the partnership; and as there was no proof that plaintiffs knew of its dissolution when they took the bill, they had a right to recover: and they had a verdict accordingly.

(27) 6 Ann. c. 22. § 9. Whereas by an act of parliament

But it has been held that this prohibition

---

made in the eighth year of the reign of his late Majesty King William, intituled, &c., it is amongst other things enacted, That during the continuance of the corporation of the governor and company of the Bank of England, no other bank, or any other corporation, society, fellowship, company, or constitution in the nature of a bank, shall be erected or established, permitted, suffered, countenanced, or allowed by act of parliament within the kingdom, as in and by the said act more at large may appear; nevertheless, since the passing of the said act some corporations, by colour of the charters to them granted, and other great numbers of persons, by pretence of deeds or covenants united together, have presumed to borrow great sums of money, and therewith, contrary to the intent of the said act, to deal as a bank, to the apparent danger of the established credit of the kingdom: now, for preventing of such practice in time to come, and the mischief thence to arise, be it enacted, That during the continuance of the governor and company of the Bank of England, it shall not be lawful for any body politic or corporate whatsoever, erected, or to be erected, other than the said governor and company of the Bank of England, or for other persons whatsoever, united or to be united in covenants or partnership, exceeding the number of six persons, in that part of Great Britain called England, to borrow, owe, or take up, any sum or sums of money on their bills or notes payable at demand, or at less time than six months from the borrowing thereof.—And by 15 Geo. 2. c. 13. § 5. to prevent any doubts that may arise concerning the privilege or power given by former acts of parliament to the said governor and company of exclusive banking, and also in regard to the erecting any other bank or banks by parliament, or restraining other persons from banking, during the continuance of the privilege granted to the governor and company of the Bank of England, it is enacted and declared, That it is the true intent and meaning of this act, that no other bank shall be erected, established, or allowed by parliament; and that it shall not be lawful for any body politic or corporate whatsoever, erected, or to be erected, or for any other persons whatsoever, united or to be united in

does not extend to any but banking partnerships. (28)

At least a common partnership cannot make this a defence against an innocent holder, who was ignorant of what number the firm consisted. (29)

Sect. 6.—Corporations are mentioned in the statute of Anne, as persons who may make or indorse notes, and to whom notes may be payable; and as

---

covenants or partnership, exceeding the number of six persons, in that part of Great Britain called England, to borrow, owe or take up, any sum or sums of money on their bills or notes payable at demand, or at any less time than six months from the borrowing thereof, during the continuance of such said privileges to the said governor and company; who are hereby declared to be and remain a corporation, with the privilege of exclusive banking, as before recited, subject to redemption, on the terms and conditions therein mentioned.

(28) Wigan v. Fowler, 1 Stark. 459. In an action against seven partners, as makers of a promissory note for 1000*l.* payable three months after date, the defence was, that the bank acts made this note void: the number of partners did not appear upon the face of the note, nor was there any evidence that plaintiff knew it. Lord Ellenborough thought at the trial, that the bank acts applied to banking partnerships only, and it was with reluctance he saved the point. On motion to enter a nonsuit, he adhered to his original opinion; and it was noticed that plaintiff did not appear to have known how many partners there were when he took the bill, and the rule was refused.

(29) In Broughton v. Manchester Water Works Company, post, 53, this point was relied upon as forming a distinction between the two cases.

it gives the like remedy to and for corporations and others as upon inland bills of exchange, it implies, that by the custom of merchants they might, in some cases at least, draw, indorse, accept, or sue upon bills of exchange.

But if the being parties to bills or notes were inconsistent with the purpose for which they were incorporated, that inconsistency might be a bar to any remedy by, or through, or against them, on a bill or note.

And English corporations, unless authorized by statute, cannot be parties to bills or notes of less than six months after date. (30)

And this applies to all English corporations; it is not confined to banking corporations. (30)

And where an English corporation is empowered by statute to raise money by notes for a special purpose, if it issue notes at less than six months' date, without stating therein that they were given

(30) Broughton v. the Manchester Water Works Company, 3 Barnw. and Alderson, 1. Action against defendant, as acceptors of two bills of exchange payable at three months after date. Demurrer: and the objection was, that they were not liable; they were incorporated for water-work purposes only. One of their acts authorized them to borrow to a limited extent upon bonds under their common seal; but no other power was expressly given, nor was such power necessary for the purposes for which they were established: and the court thought the bank acts (ante, p. 50) an answer to the action, because the acceptance made them debtors and owe money upon the bills.

for that purpose, the corporation may resist payment, on the ground that they were given for another purpose. (31)

And this will be a defence even against an innocent indorsee. (31)

Sect. 7.—Where a bill or note is drawn by an agent, executor, or trustee, he should take care, if he means to exempt himself from personal responsibility, to use clear and explicit words to shew that intention.

Thus, if a broker sell goods, and draw upon the buyer in favour of his principal, he will be liable upon the bill, if it be dishonoured, unless he use special words to prevent it; (32)

And may be sued there on by his principal. (32)

---

(31) Slark v. Highgate Archway Company, 5 Taunt. 792. Defendants were incorporated by 52 Geo. 3. c 146. (local and personal) and authorized to borrow money to complete their works; they gave a note under their common seal at two months after date for 1000*l.*, payable to Nash or order: it did not import to be for money borrowed to complete their works. Plaintiff sued thereon as indorsee. Defence, that it was given for Nash's accommodation, not to complete their works. Gibbs C. J. thought this no defence against an innocent indorsee who had paid the value, and the plaintiff had a verdict; but on a rule nisi for a new trial, the Court of Common Pleas, without assigning their reasons, granted a new trial.

(32) Lefevre v. Lloyd, 5 Taunt. 749. Defendant, as broker, sold cotton for plaintiff at two months' credit, and drew on the

So if an agent for A. draw upon B. in favour of C., though he direct B. to place the amount to A.'s debit, he will be personally liable to C. if the bill is not paid, though C. knew he was only agent for A., unless he uses proper words to prevent such liability. (33)

So if an agent employed to buy bills get them payable to himself and indorse them generally, he will be liable upon that indorsement even to his own employer (34); to have exempted himself he

---

seller for the amount in favour of plaintiff: the bill being dishonoured, plaintiff sued defendant on the bill; and Gibbs C. J. at the trial, held, that as defendant had put his name upon the bill, however imprudent that was, all the legal consequences of that act attached upon him, and verdict for plaintiff: and on motion for a new trial, the court agreed with him; for by drawing the bill, defendant removed from plaintiff all consideration of the buyer's responsibility. Rule refused.

(33) Leadbitter v. Farrow, Michaelmas, 1816, in B. R. Plaintiff wanted a bill upon London for 50*l*., and sent to defendant, whom he knew to be agent to the Durham Bank at Hexham: defendant drew a bill accordingly, "Pay to the order of Mr. Leadbitter 50*l*., value received, which place to the account of the Durham Bank, as advised C. Farrow. To Messrs. A. and B. London." In an action thereon, the defendant urged that he was not personally liable, or at least that the plaintiff, who knew him to be only agent, could not sue him; but on a case reserved, the court held his signature pledged his own credit, and *that* only, and that he was therefore liable.

(34) Goupy v. Harden, Holt. 342. 2 Marsh. 404. 7 Taunt. 159. Plaintiff employed defendant at a commission of 10*s*. per cent. to procure him bills on Portugal, and to transmit them to him in Paris: defendant got bills payable to his own order, and indorsed them generally, without restriction: plaintiff after-

should have got the bills made payable to his employer, or should have introduced into his indorsement words to exclude his personal responsibility.

So if a man draw a bill or note as executor of J. S., and sign it in terms as such, yet if it is in a form which implies assets, or will procure forbearance, it will bind him personally. (35)

If an executor means to limit his responsibility, he should confine his stipulation, viz. to pay out of the estate; and if an executor indorse, it binds him personally. (36)

---

wards sued him on this indorsement, and defendant insisted that under the circumstances this indorsement did not make him liable to plaintiff; but on rule nisi, to set aside verdict for plaintiff, the court thought it did; for had defendant meant to exclude his liability, he should have given a qualified indorsement; and rule refused.

(35) Childs v. Monins and Bowles, 2 Brod. and Bingh. 460. Defendants signed this note, "As executors to J. S. we severally and jointly promise to pay plaintiff 200*l.* on demand, together with interest:" they were sued thereon, and then contended that it only bound them as executors; but on demurrer, the court were clear it bound them personally. It admitted assets, and tended to procure forbearance, and as a several note from each would bind the executor of whoever died first, and ultimately the executors of both; an effect it would not have, if it bound them as executors only.

(36) King v. Thom, 1 Term Rep. 487. The court held, that upon a bill payable to several as executors, they might sue as executors: and, per Buller J., no inconvenience can arise from their indorsing the bill; for if they indorse, they are liable personally, and not as executors, for their indorsement would not give an action against the effects of the testator,

So if drainage or inclosure commissioners draw upon the banker appointed by the act, they may be personally liable, unless they use proper words to prevent it, though the bill imports to be drawn on the drainage or inclosure account, and directs the money to be placed to their account as commissioners. (37)

So if a bill is addressed to a man as cashier of a particular company, though it direct him to place it to the company's account, an acceptance upon it by him will bind him personally, unless he uses special words to prevent it. (38)

---

(37) Eaton v. Bell, Michaelmas, 1821. 5 Barnw. and Ald. 34. Defendants were inclosure commissioners, and plaintiff the banker under the act; the act authorized the commissioners to raise money by rate, and directed that persons advancing money for the purposes of the act should be repaid with interest out of the monies the commissioners should raise: defendants drew on plaintiff in this form: "Messrs. E.—Pay A. or bearer, 40*l.* on account of the public draining, and place the same to our account as commissioners of the Frodsham inclosure:" Plaintiff sued defendants personally; and Dallas C. J. left it to the jury whether credit was given by plaintiff to defendants personally, or to the fund they had to raise: the jury thought it given to defendants personally; and, on case, the court thought them right, and plaintiff had judgment.

(38) Thomas v. Bishop, Ann. 1 Str. 955. A bill for 200*l.* was drawn upon the defendant by the description of *Mr. H. Bishop, cashier of the York Buildings Company, at their house in Winchester-street, London;* and the bill directed him to place the 200*l.* to the account of the company. The defendant accepted the bill; but on being sued insisted that the acceptance did not bind him personally, and gave in evidence that the letter of advice from the drawer of the bill was sent to the

Sect. 8.—It is no objection to a bill or note, that it is payable or indorsed to a person who at the time it was given was an alien enemy, if it were given to him in his own country by a British subject who was then a prisoner there. (39)

And it is no objection to an action on such a bill, that it is brought as to part in trust for an alien enemy. (40)

So it is no objection to an action on such a bill that it was given whilst an act of parliament was

---

company. But Page J. directed the jury to find for the plaintiff, which they did; and upon a rule to shew cause why there should not be a new trial, the whole court held the direction right: that the addition to the defendant's name was only to describe him with more certainty, and to point out where he was to be found; that the direction to place the money to the account of the company was for the use of the drawee only: and that the letter of advice could not vary the case against an indorsee, (which the plaintiff was,) because an indorsee could only look to the bill itself.

(39) Antoine v. Morshead, 6 Taunt. 237. Sir John Morshead, Tyndall, and Estwick, were prisoners of war at Verdun in France. Sir John Morshead drew bills on defendant, some payable to Tyndall, and some to Estwick; they indorsed them to plaintiff a banker at Verdun. Defendants accepted them; but on being sued thereon at the return of peace, he insisted that the indorsement, as being during war, was void: Gibbs C. J. thought otherwise; and on motion for a new trial, the whole court agreed with him, and the plaintiff recovered.

(40) Daubuz v. Morshead, bart. 6 Taunt. 332. Indorsee against acceptor, on bills drawn by an English prisoner in France in favour of Borau Basti, and indorsed to plaintiff; defence, that plaintiff was only a trustee, except as to a small part, for an alien enemy: but Gibbs C. J. thought plaintiff entitled to a verdict for the whole; and verdict accordingly.

in force which made it penal to pay such bills, if after the act expired there was a promise to pay it. (41)

(41) Duhammel v. Pickering, 2 Stark. 90. Defendant was a prisoner of war in France in 1795, and drew four bills on Wishaw in England, payable to La Tailleur, an alien enemy residing in France: by 34 G. 3. c. 9. § 4. if any person paid any bill drawn in France during the war, he was liable to forfeit double value, and the payment was annulled. On the peace in 1802, defendant wrote to La Tailleur's agent, promising payment; this action was brought by La Tailleur's administrator. It was insisted that the statute was a bar to plaintiff's claim; and Lord Ellenborough said, no doubt the bills were void in their creation as bills to be enforced in this country, but they might constitute the basis of a promise on the return of peace; and he thought the promise in defendant's letter removed all doubt on the subject; and plaintiff had a verdict for principal and interest.

CAP. III.

The paper, parchment, vellum, or other matter, whereon a bill or note made in Great Britain is written, must, except in a few instances, be stamped (1) before the bill or note is written; otherwise

---

(1) The last stamp act, namely, 55 Geo. 3. c. 184. does not in terms require that the paper, &c. shall be stamped before the bill or note is written thereon; but by 31 Geo 3. c. 25. § 19. it is enacted, That all vellum, parchment, and paper, liable to any stamp duty by that act, shall, before any of

the (2) party making, signing, or issuing it, or causing it to be made, signed, or issued, or accept-

---

the matters or things thereby charged shall be engrossed, printed, or written thereupon, be brought to the head office for stamping vellum, parchment or paper ; and the commissioners, by themselves, or by their officers employed under them, shall and may, from time to time, stamp and mark any quantities or parcels of vellum, parchment or paper, before any of the matters or things thereby charged shall be engrossed, printed, or written thereupon, upon payment of the several duties payable for the same by virtue of this act. And no bill of exchange, promissory note, or other note, draught or order, liable to the duties by this act imposed, or any of them, shall be pleaded or given in evidence in any court, or admitted in any court to be good, useful, or available in law or equity, unless the vellum, parchment or paper, on which such bill of exchange, promissory note, or other note, draught or order, shall be engrossed, printed, written or made, shall be stamped or marked with a lawful stamp or mark, to denote the rate or duty as by that act is directed, or some higher rate or duty in that act contained; and it shall not be lawful for the said commissioners, or their officers, to stamp or mark any vellum, parchment or paper, with any stamp or mark directed to be used or provided by virtue of that act, at any time after any bill of exchange, promissory note, or other note, draught or order, shall be engrossed, written, or printed thereon, under any pretence whatever. And by 55 Geo. 3. c. 184. § 3. the commissioners are authorized to do all things necessary for carrying that act into execution, in the *like* manner as former commissioners have been authorized to do, for carrying into execution former acts; and by § 4. all powers, provisions, clauses, regulations and directions, relating to former duties, are extended to the duties by that act imposed. The 34. Geo. 3. c. 32. authorizing the commissioners to stamp bills, &c. after they were drawn on payment of a certain penalty was only a temporary act and has long since expired.

(2) By 55 Geo. 3. c. 184. § 11. it is enacted, That if any person or persons shall make, sign, or issue, or cause to be

ing or paying it, or causing or permitting it to be accepted or paid, will be liable to a penalty of *50l.*, and the bill or note will (3) not be available in law or equity.

And no laches by the holder will make such unstamped bill or note amount to payment of a prior debt (4), even though the bill but for such laches would have been paid. (4)

---

made, signed, or issued, or shall accept or pay, or cause or permit to be accepted or paid, any bill of exchange draught or order or promissory note for the payment of money liable to any of the duties imposed by that act, without the same being duly stamped for denoting the duty thereby charged thereon, he, she, or they, shall, for every such offence forfeit the sum of *50l.*

(3) See 31 Geo. 3. c. 25. § 19. supra, p. 60. and by 55 Geo. 3. c. 184. § 8. All the powers, provisions, clauses, regulations and directions, fines, forfeitures, pains and penalties, contained in and imposed by the several acts of parliament relating to the duties hereby repealed, and the several acts of parliament relating to any prior duties of the same kind and description, shall be of full force and effect, with respect to the duties hereby granted, and to the vellum, parchment, and paper instruments, matters and things charged, or chargeable therein, as far as the same are or shall be applicable, in all cases not hereby expressly provided for; and shall be observed, applied, enforced, and put in execution, for the raising, levying, collecting, and securing of the said duties hereby granted, and otherwise relating thereto, so far as the same shall not be suspended by, and shall be consistent with, the express provisions of this act, as fully and effectually, to all intents and purposes, as if the same had been herein repeated, and specially enacted, with reference to the said duties hereby granted.

(4) Wilson v. Vysar, 4 Taunt. 228. Action for goods sold; defence, payment. Defendant had indorsed to plaintiff a bill for the amount, and plaintiff had neglected to present it for pay-

But an unstamped bill or note may be looked at for a collateral purpose, as to judge whether the party signing it was drunk or sober at the time. (5)

And the forging a bill or note on unstamped paper, or uttering such bill or note with knowledge of its being forged, and with an intent to defraud, is as much an offence as if the bill or note were on paper duly stamped. (6)

---

ment. The bill appeared to be upon a stamp of less than the proper amount, but defendant proved that it would nevertheless have been paid by the acceptor, had it been presented: but Mansfield C. J. held at the trial, that the defect in the stamp precluded the defendant from having this considered as payment; and the court, on motion, concurred; and rule refused.

(5) Gregory v. Frazer, 3 Campb. 454. In an action for money lent, the defence was that defendant was drunk at the time, and imposed on by plaintiff; and plaintiff having produced an unstamped note which defendant gave for the money at the time, it was made a question whether the note could be looked at to strengthen or repel the imputation of drunkenness, and Lord Ellenborough held it might; he said it could not be produced in evidence as a security, or to prove the loan, but he thought it might be looked at as a contemporary writing to prove or disprove the fraud; it was accordingly put in, and having the appearance of being written by a drunken man, verdict for defendant.

The bill was probably looked at at plaintiff's instance.

(6) Rex v. Hawkeswood, Pasch. 1783. The prisoner was convicted of forging a bill of exchange; the bill was on unstamped paper. Buller J. thought the stamp acts mere revenue laws, and that what was forgery before those laws was forgery still; and on the point being saved, the judges all concurred that the want of a stamp was no objection.

See Rex v. Teague, post.

Sect. 2.—A note payable to the bearer on demand, made, or purporting to be made, out of Great Britain, or purporting to be made by or on the behalf of any person resident out of Great Britain, (excepting where made and payable in Ireland only,) (7) cannot be negotiated, circulated, or offered or taken in payment, or offered for payment or paid here, unless it be stamped in like manner as a note of the same tenor and value made in Great Britain, under a penalty upon the party offending therein of 20*l.*

---

(7) By 55 G. 3. c. 184. § 29. it is enacted, That from and after the passing of this act, promissory notes for the payment of money to the bearer on demand, made out of Great Britain, or purporting to be made out of Great Britain, or purporting to be made by or on the behalf of any person or persons resident out of Great Britain, shall not be negotiable, or be negotiated, or circulated, or paid, in Great Britain, whether the same shall be made payable in Great Britain or not, unless the same shall have paid such duty, and be stamped in such manner as the law requires for promissory notes of the like tenor and value made in Great Britain; and if any person or persons shall circulate or negotiate, or offer in payment, or shall receive or take in payment any such promissory note, or shall demand or receive payment of the whole, or any part of the money, mentioned in such promissory note, from or on account of the drawer thereof in Great Britain, the same not being duly stamped as aforesaid; or if any person or persons in Great Britain shall pay, or cause to be paid, the sum of money expressed in any such note, not being duly stamped as aforesaid, or any part thereof, either as drawer thereof, or in pursuance of any nomination or appointment for that purpose therein contained, the person or persons so offending, shall for every such offence forfeit the sum of 20*l.*: Provided always, that this clause shall not extend to promissory notes made and payable only in Ireland.

Before this provision, a note made in (8) any part of the King's foreign dominions, (as Jamaica) where by law a stamp was necessary, could not have been received in evidence here, unless it had such stamp as the law of that country was proved to require.

Sect. 3.—A bill drawn in Ireland with blanks for sum, date, and drawee's name, and transmitted to England to have the blanks filled up, though it may require an Irish stamp, will not require an English one. (9)

---

(8) Alves v. Hodgson, 7 Term Rep. 241. A note was produced in evidence, which had been made in Jamaica; the defendant objected that it ought to have been stamped, and proved the law of Jamaica requiring a stamp. Lord Kenyon thought the objection good, but suffered the plaintiff to take a verdict, with liberty to the defendant to move to enter a nonsuit. In shewing cause against a rule nisi obtained for such purpose, it was urged that the defendant could not avail himself of an objection founded on a revenue law of a foreign country; but Lord Kenyon said, I think we must resort to the laws of the country in which the note was made, and unless it be good there, it is not obligatory in a court of law here. But as the plaintiff might have recovered, without this note, on the quantum meruit, let there be a new trial.

(9) Snaith v. Mingay, 1 Maule and Sel. 87. Bayley and Co. of Waterford, in Ireland, had one partner, Wallace, resident in England, where he carried on a separate trade, and he was restrained by the articles of partnership from drawing bills in the partnership name; they sent him over four signatures made by them as drawers and indorsers on copper-plate impressions, with blanks for dates, sums, and drawee's names; they were to be

Sect. 4.—If a bill upon which a person residing abroad is intended to be drawer, is sketched out and accepted here, and then transmitted to such person abroad that he may sign his name as drawer, this is to be considered a foreign bill, and does not require an English stamp. (10)

And the acceptor is liable upon it though it is unstamped. (10)

Sect. 5.—If upon a bill dated abroad the defence is that it was made in England, and has not an English stamp, that defence ought to be made out

---

used by him in his separate trade, and he filled them up and used them accordingly. They were on Irish stamps only; and in an action upon them against the second indorser, it was objected that they ought to have had English stamps; but on a case reserved, the court thought otherwise; because they were bonâ fide *signed* in Ireland, and therefore were to be considered as *made* there.

(10) Boehm v. Campbell, Gow. 56. In an action by drawer against the guarantee of an acceptor, it appeared that the plaintiff lived at Antwerp; that the whole of the bill, except plaintiff's signature, was written here; that the bill was accepted before plaintiff signed it; that it was then transmitted to plaintiff for his signature, and that he signed it at Antwerp. It had no stamp, and it was urged that it was to be considered as made here, and should have had a British stamp; but Dallas C. J. thought it was to be considered as made where it was drawn, and that it was not to be considered as drawn till the plaintiff signed it; and plaintiff had a verdict.

by distinct evidence, because such conduct to evade the stamp duties would be a very serious offence. (11)

Proof that the drawer was in London so near the date of the bill, that it could not have been drawn on the date at the place from which it is dated, is not sufficient. (11)

Sect. 6. — The following bills and notes need not be stamped, namely,

Bills and notes which are issued by the (12) Bank of England.

Bills drawn pursuant to certain acts of parliament for the (13) pay and expenses of the army and navy.

Bills drawn for the payment of less than forty shillings.

---

(11) Abraham v. Dubois, 4 Campb. 269. Action on bill dated Paris, 1st March; defence, that it was drawn in London, and proof that the drawer was in London 3d March, at eleven in the forenoon. Per Lord Ellenborough: It is not very probable this bill was drawn in Paris 1st March; but if it were proved ever so distinctly, that it was not drawn in Paris 1st March, it would not follow that it was not drawn there at some other time, or that it was drawn in England. Drawing here with a foreign date, to evade the stamp duties, is a very serious offence, and the fact must be made out by distinct evidence. Verdict for plaintiff.

(12) See 55 Geo. 3. c. 184. § 21. The bank is to pay 3500*l.* per million, for the notes and bank-post bills they issue, and at that rate per half million.

(13) See the exemptions from duties on bills, post. p. 71. n.

Notes for one pound, one guinea, two pounds, and two guineas, payable to the bearer on demand, issued by (14) the Bank of Scotland, Royal Bank of Scotland, or the British Linen Company in Scotland.

Notes payable in any other manner than to the bearer on demand, for less than forty shillings.

All draughts or orders for the payment of money to the bearer on demand, drawn upon any (15) banker, or person acting as a banker, and residing or transacting the business of a banker, within ten miles of the place where they are issued, provided they specify such place, and bear date on or before the day on which they are issued, and do not direct payment to be made by bills or notes.

Sect. 7. — And any person, under colour of this last exemption, making or issuing, or causing to be made or issued, any bill, draught or order (16) post-

(14) See 55 Geo. 3. c. 184. § 23.

(15) See the exemptions from duties on bills, post. p. 72. n.

(16) By 55 Geo. 3. c. 184. § 13. For the more effectually preventing of frauds, and evasions of the duties hereby granted on bills of exchange, draughts or orders, for the payment of money, under colour of the exemption in favour of draughts or orders upon bankers, or persons acting as bankers, contained in the schedule hereunto annexed, it is enacted, That if any person or persons shall, after the thirty-first of August, 1815, make and issue, or cause to be made and issued, any bill, draught or order, for the payment of money to the bearer on demand, upon any banker or bankers, or any person or persons acting as a banker or bankers, which shall be dated on any day subsequent to the day on which it shall be

dated, or not falling in every respect within such exemption, and not stamped as a bill of exchange, will be liable to a penalty of 100*l.*; the person knowingly receiving or taking it will be liable to a penalty of 20*l.*; and the banker, or other person, knowingly paying, or causing or permitting it to be paid, will be liable to a penalty of 100*l.*, and will not be allowed the money paid on it in account.

---

issued, or which shall not truly specify and express the place where it shall be issued, or which shall not in every respect fall within the said exemption, unless the same shall be duly stamped as a bill of exchange according to this act, the person or persons so offending, shall, for every such bill, draught or order, forfeit the sum of 100*l.*; and if any person or persons shall knowingly receive or take any such bill, draught or order, in payment of, or as a security for, the sum therein mentioned, he, she, or they, shall, for every such bill, draught or order, forfeit the sum of 20*l.*; and if any banker or bankers, or any person or persons acting as a banker, upon whom any such bill, draught or order shall be drawn, shall pay, or cause or permit to be paid, the sum of money therein expressed, or any part thereof, knowing the same to be post-dated, or knowing that the place where it was issued is not truly specified and set forth therein, or knowing that the same does not, in any other respect, fall within the said exemption, then the banker or bankers, or person or persons so offending, shall, for every such bill, draught or order, forfeit the sum of 100*l.*; and moreover shall not be allowed the money so paid, or any part thereof, in account against the person or persons by or for whom such bill, draught or order, shall be drawn, or his, her, or their executors or administrators, or his, her, or their assignees or creditors, in case of bankruptcy or insolvency, or any other person or persons claiming under him, her, or them.

See Allen v. Keeves, 1 East. Rep. 435. and Whitwell v. Bennett, 3 Bos. and Pull. 559.

Sect. 8.—On other bills and notes, the proper stamps, as regulated by the (17) act of the 55 Geo. 3. c. 184. must denote the payment of the following duties *: that is, an

Inland bill of exchange, draught or order, for the payment to the bearer, or to order, either on demand or otherwise, of any sum of money

	Not exceeding 2 months after date, or 60 days after sight.			*If exceeding* 2 months after date, or 60 days after sight.		
	£	s.	d.	£	s.	d.
Amounting to 40s. and not exceeding *5l. 5s.*	0	1	0	0	1	6
Exceeding *5l. 5s.* and not exceeding 30*l.*	0	1	6	0	2	0

(17) By 55 Geo. 3. c. 184. (the first section of which repeals all former stamp duties on bills and notes) § 2. it is enacted, That there shall be raised, levied, and paid, unto, and for the use of his Majesty, his heirs and successors, in and throughout the whole of Great Britain, for and in respect of the several instruments, matters and things mentioned and described in the schedule thereunto annexed, (except those standing under the head of exemptions,) or for or in respect of the vellum, parchment or paper, upon which such instruments, matters and things, or any of them, shall be written or printed, the several duties or sums of money set down in figures against the same respectively, or otherwise specified and set forth in the same schedule; and that the said schedule, and all the provisions, regulations and directions therein contained, with respect to the said duties, and the instruments, matters and things charged therewith, shall be deemed and taken to be part of that act, and shall be read and construed as if the same had been inserted therein at this place, and shall be applied, observed, and put in execution accordingly.

* See note * in the following page.

	Not exceeding 2 months after date, or 60 days after sight. £	s.	d.	If exceeding 2 months after date, or 60 days after sight. £	s.	d.
Exceeding 30*l.* and not exceeding 40*l.*	0	2	0	0	2	6
Exceeding 40*l.* and not exceeding 50*l.*	0	2	6	0	3	6
Exceeding 50*l.* and not exceeding 100*l.*	0	3	6	0	4	6
Exceeding 100*l.* and not exceeding 200*l.*	0	4	6	0	5	0
Exceeding 200*l.* and not exceeding 300*l.*	0	5	0	0	6	0
Exceeding 300*l.* and not exceeding 500*l.*	0	6	0	0	8	6
Exceeding 500*l.* and not exceeding 1000*l.*	0	8	6	0	12	6
Exceeding 1000*l.* and not exceeding 2000*l.*	0	12	6	0	15	0
Exceeding 2000*l.* and not exceeding 3000*l.*	0	15	0	1	5	0
Exceeding 3000*l.*	1	5	0	1	10	0

* *The Schedule, as far as it relates to bills or notes, is inserted in the text, except the exemptions, which are as follow:*

1. *As to Bills*—" Exemptions from the preceding and all " other stamp duties:

" All bills of exchange, or bank-post bills issued by the " Governor and Company of the bank of England.

" All bills, orders, remittance bills, and remittance certificates " drawn by commissioned officers, masters and surgeons in the " navy, or by any commissioner or commissioners of the navy, " under the authority of 35 Geo. 3. c. 94.

Inland bill, draught or order, for the payment of any sum of money, though not made payable to the bearer or to order, if the same shall be delivered to the payee, or some person on his or her behalf,	The same duty as on a bill of exchange for the like sum payable to bearer or order.

" All bills drawn pursuant to any former act or acts of parlia-" ment, by the commissioners of the navy, or by the commis-" sioners for victualling the navy, or by the commissioners for " managing the transport service, and for taking care of sick " and wounded seamen, upon and payable by the treasurer of " the navy.

" All draughts or orders for the payment of any sum of money " to the bearer on demand, and drawn upon any banker or " bankers, or any person or persons acting as a banker, who " shall reside or transact the business of a banker, within ten " miles of the place where such draughts or orders shall be " issued; provided such place shall be specified in such draughts " or orders; and provided the same shall bear date on or before " the day on which the same thall be issued; and provided the " same do not direct the payment to be made by bills or pro-" missory notes.

" All bills for the pay and allowances of his Majesty's " land forces, or for other expenditures liable to be charged in " the public regimental or district accounts, which shall be " drawn according to the forms now prescribed or hereafter to " be prescribed by his Majesty's orders, by the pay-masters " of regiments or corps, or by the chief pay-master or deputy " pay-master and accountant of the army depot, or by the pay-" masters of recruiting districts, or by the pay-masters of de-" tachments, or by the officer or officers authorized to perform " the duties of the pay-mastership during a vacancy, or the " absence, suspension, or incapacity of any such pay-master as " aforesaid, *save and except such bills as shall be drawn in favour* " *of contractors or others, who furnish bread or forage to his*

Inland bill, draught or order, for the payment of any sum of money, weekly, monthly, or at any other stated periods, if made payable to the bearer or to order, or if delivered to the payee, or some person on his or her behalf; where the total amount of the money thereby made payable shall be specified therein, or can be ascertained therefrom,	The same duty as on a bill payable to bearer or order on demand, for a sum equal to such total amount.

"*Majesty's troops, and who, by their contracts or agreements,* "*shall be liable to pay the stamp duties on the bills given in pay-* "*ment for the articles supplied by them.*

As to Notes —" Exemptions from the duties on promissory "notes:

"All notes promising the payment of any sum or sums of "money, out of any particular fund which may or may not be "available; or upon any condition or contingency, which may "or may not be performed or happen, where the same shall "not be made payable to the bearer or to order; and also "where the same shall be made payable to the bearer or to "order, if the same shall amount to 20*l*. or be indefinite.

"And all other instruments bearing in any degree the form "or style of promissory notes, but which in law shall be deemed "special agreements, except those hereby expressly directed "to be deemed promissory notes.

"*But such of the notes and instruments here exempted from* "*the duty on promissory notes, shall nevertheless be liable to the* "*duty which may attach thereon, as agreements or otherwise.*

"Exemptions from the preceding and all other stamp duties:

"All promissory notes for the payment of money issued by "the Governor and Company of the Bank of England."

And where the total amount of the money thereby made payable shall be indefinite,	The same duty as on a bill on demand for the sum therein expressed only.

And the following instruments shall be deemed and taken to be inland bills, draughts, or orders, for the payment of money, within the intent and meaning of this schedule, viz.

All draughts or orders for the payment of any sum of money, by a bill or promissory note, or for the delivery of any such bill or note, in payment or satisfaction of any sum of money where such draughts or orders shall require the payment or delivery to be made to the bearer or to order, or shall be delivered to the payee, or some person on his or her behalf.

All receipts given by any banker or bankers, or other person or persons for money received, which shall entitle, or be intended to entitle, the person or persons paying the money, or the bearer of such receipts, to receive the like sum from any third person or persons.

And all bills, draughts, or orders for the payment of any sum of money out of any particular fund, which may or may not be available, or upon any condition or contingency, which may or may not be performed or happen; if the same shall be made payable to the bearer or to order, or if the same shall be delivered to the payee, or some person on his or her behalf.

A foreign bill of exchange, (or bill of exchange drawn in, but payable out of, Great Britain,) if drawn singly and not in a set, the same duty as on an inland bill of the same amount and tenor.

Foreign bills of exchange, drawn in sets according to the custom of merchants: for every bill of each set,

	s.	*d.*
Where the sum made payable thereby shall not exceed 100*l.*	1	6
And where it shall exceed 100*l.* and not exceed 200*l.*	3	0
And where it shall exceed 200*l.* and not exceed 500*l.*	4	0
And where it shall exceed 500*l.* and not exceed 1000*l.*	5	0
And where it shall exceed 1000*l.* and not exceed 2000*l.*	7	6
And where it shall exceed 2000*l.* and not 3000*l.*	10	0
And where it shall exceed 3000*l.*	15	0

Promissory note for the payment to *the bearer on demand*, of any sum of money,

	£	*s.*	*d.*
Not exceeding 1*l.* 1*s.*	0	0	5
Exceeding 1*l.* 1*s.* and not exceeding 2*l.* 2*s.*	0	0	10
Exceeding 2*l.* 2*s.* and not exceeding 5*l.* 5*s.*	0	1	3
Exceeding 5*l.* 5*s.* and not exceeding 10*l.*	0	1	9

	£	s.	d.
Exceeding 10*l.* and not exceeding 20*l.*	0	2	0
Exceeding 20*l.* and not exceeding 30*l.*	0	3	0
Exceeding 30*l.* and not exceeding 50*l.*	0	5	0
Exceeding 50*l.* and not exceeding 100*l.*	0	8	6

Which said notes may be re-issued, after payment thereof, as often as shall be thought fit.

Promissory note for the payment, *in any other manner than to the bearer on demand*, of any sum of money

	Not exceeding 2 months after date, or 60 days after sight.			If exceeding 2 months after date, or 60 days after sight, payable to bearer or otherwise.		
	£	s.	d.	£	s.	d.
Amounting to 40*s.* and not exceeding 5*l.* 5*s.*	0	1	0	0	1	6
Exceeding 5*l.* 5*s.* and not exceeding 20*l.*	0	1	6	0	2	0
Exceeding 20*l.* and not exceeding 30*l.*	0	2	0	0	2	6
Exceeding 30*l.* and not exceeding 50*l.*	0	2	6	0	3	6
Exceeding 50*l.* and not exceeding 100*l.*	0	3	6	0	4	6

These Notes are not to be re-issued after being once paid.

Promissory note for the payment *either to the bearer on demand, or in any other manner than to the bearer on demand,* but not exceeding two months after date, or sixty days after sight, of any sum of money

	£	s.	d.	£	s.	d.
Exceeding 100*l.* and not exceeding 200*l.*	0	4	6	0	5	0
Exceeding 200*l.* and not exceeding 300*l.*	0	5	0	0	6	0
Exceeding 300*l.* and not exceeding 500*l.*	0	6	0	0	8	6
Exceeding 500*l.* and not exceeding 1000*l.*	0	8	6	0	12	6
Exceeding 1000*l.* and not exceeding 2000*l.*	0	12	6	0	15	0
Exceeding 2000*l.* and not exceeding 3000*l.*	0	15	0	1	5	0
Exceeding 3000*l.*	1	5	0	1	10	0

These notes are not to be re-issued after being once paid.

Promissory note for the payment of any sum of money by instalments, or for the payment of several sums of money at different days or times, so that the whole of the money to be paid shall be definite and certain	The same duty as on a promissory note, payable in less than 2 months after date, for a sum equal to the whole amount of the money to be paid.

And the following instruments shall be deemed and taken to be promissory notes, within the intent and meaning of this schedule: viz.

All notes promising the payment of any sum or sums of money out of any particular fund which may or may not be available, or upon any condition or contingency which may or may not be performed or happen, if the same shall be made payable to the bearer, or to order, and if the same shall be definite and certain, and not amount in the whole to twenty pounds: where they are not made payable to the bearer, or to order, or where the sum is indefinite, or amounts to 20*l.*, they are exempt from note duties, but liable to such duties as may attach thereon as agreements or otherwise.

And all receipts for money deposited in any bank, or in the hands of any banker or bankers, which shall contain any agreement or memorandum importing that interest shall be paid for the money so deposited.

All other instruments bearing in any degree the form or style of promissory notes, but which in law shall be deemed special agreements, except those expressly directed to be deemed promissory notes, shall be exempt from the duties on notes, but liable to the duties which may attach thereon as agreements or otherwise.

Sect. 9. — Reserving interest from the date of a bill or note will not vary the stamp; the stamp is to be according to the sum due at the time the bill or note is given. (18)

---

(18) Pruessing v. Ing, 4 Barnew. and Ald. 204. In an action on a note at three months for 30*l.*, with interest from the date

Sect. 10. — A note payable two months after sight, if those two months, exclusive of the days of grace, exceed sixty days, requires the same stamp as a bill exceeding sixty days at sight. (19)

A bill payable at sight is not to be considered as a bill payable on demand. (20)

Sect. 11.—And giving a false date so as to make a note or bill, which really exceeds two months

---

thereof, objection was taken at the trial that it was only upon a stamp applicable to notes for a sum not exceeding 30*l.*; whereas this being for 30*l.* and interest, was, in substance, a note for 30*l.* 7*s.* 6*d.* But on motion for nonsuit, the court were of opinion that the stamp was to be regulated by the sum due at the time the note was given, the principal without interest; and rule refused.

(19) Sturdy v. Henderson, 4 Barnew. and Ald. 512. Action on note for 400*l.* payable two months after sight: nonsuit, because it had not a stamp required for note payable at more than sixty days after sight: motion for new trial, on the ground that it was, in substance, at two months after date; for that the drawing it was having sight thereof, and it would be payable without the maker's having further sight thereof. But it being suggested that bank-post bills at seven days' sight, which are really notes, do not become payable till after they have been presented for acceptance, and a further term of seven days and days of grace have elapsed, the court thought this note would require a new presentment for sight, and was therefore properly a note after sight, not after date; and rule refused.

(20) J. Anson v. Thomas, B. R. T. 24 Geo. 3. In an action on an inland bill, the question was, whether it was included under an exception in the Stamp Act of 23 G. 3. c. 49. § 4. in favour of bills payable *on demand*, and the court held it was not, and Buller J. mentioned a case before Willes C. J. in London, in which a jury of merchants was of opinion that the usual days of grace were to be allowed on bills payable at sight.

after date, or sixty days after sight, the appearance as if there were no such excess, subjects to a penalty of 100*l.* unless it have the stamp for such excess. (20)

Sect. 12. — Provided a bill or note bear a stamp of the proper denomination, it is now (21) no ground of objection to it, that it is of greater value than that required by law: nor is it, since 55 Geo. 3., though it have a stamp of a different denomination, unless such stamp is specially appropriated to some

---

(20) By 55 G. 3. c. 184. § 12. it is enacted, That if any person or persons shall make and issue, or cause to be made and issued, any bill of exchange, draught or order, or promissory note, for the payment of money at any time after date or sight, which shall bear date subsequent to the day on which it shall be issued, so that it shall not in fact become payable in two months if made payable after date, or in sixty days if made payable after sight next after the day on which it shall be issued, unless the same shall be stamped for denoting the duty thereby imposed on a bill of exchange and promissory note for the payment of money at any time exceeding two months after date or sixty days after sight, he, she or they shall, for every such bill, draught, order or note, forfeit the sum of one hundred pounds.

(21) By 43 G. 3. c. 127. § 6. it is enacted, That every instrument, matter or thing, although stamped or impressed with any stamp of greater value than the stamp required by law, shall be valid and effectual; provided such stamp shall be of the denomination required by law for such instrument, matter or thing, any statute, law or usage to the contrary notwithstanding.

N. See the cases of Farr v. Price, 1 East. Rep. 55., and Taylor v. Hague, 2 East. Rep. 414., in which stamps were objected to on the ground which this act has now removed; see also Chamberlain v. Porter, 1 New Rep. 30.

other instrument, by having its name on the face thereof. (22)

And where a bill or note is upon a stamp so specially appropriated, it may, perhaps, be stamped under 37 G. 3. c. 136. § 5. on payment of the duty and 40*s.* penalty before it has become payable, and on payment of the duty and 10*l.* afterwards. (23)

---

(22) By 55 Geo. 3. c. 184. § 10. it is enacted, That from and after the passing of this act, all instruments for or upon which any stamp or stamps shall have been used of an improper denomination or rate of duty, but of equal or greater value in the whole with or than the stamp or stamps which ought regularly to have been used thereon, shall, nevertheless, be deemed valid and effectual in the law; except in cases where the stamp or stamps used on such instruments shall have been specially appropriated to any other instrument by having its name on the face thereof.

(23) By 37 Geo. 3. c. 136. § 5. (incorporated with 48 Geo. 3. c. 149. by § 3. and 8. of that act) after reciting that part of 31 Geo. 3. c. 25. § 19. which declares that it shall not be lawful for the commissioners to stamp any vellum, &c. after any bill, &c. is written thereon, it is enacted, That it shall and may be lawful for any person or persons who shall be the holder or holders of any bill of exchange, promissory note, or other note, draught, or order, made after the passing of that act, and liable to any stamp duty by virtue of the said recited act, which shall be stamped with a stamp of a different denomination than is required by the said act, if the same shall be of equal or superior value to the stamp required, to produce the same, or cause the same to be produced, within the respective times thereinafter mentioned, to the commissioners appointed to manage the said duties, at the head office of stamps in Middlesex, or to such officer or officers as the said commissioners, or the major part of them, shall, by writing under their hands, appoint for such purpose; and it shall and may be lawful for such commissioners to direct the proper officer or officers, and such officer

Sect. 13.—The paper, &c. on which a bill or note is written (though it might formerly have been stamped at any time, on paying a penalty), ought not *now*, excepting in the case above mentioned,

---

or officers, is and are hereby required, upon payment of the duty payable on such vellum, parchment or paper, by the said recited act, and such penalty as is thereinafter mentioned, over and above the said duty, to mark or stamp such bill of exchange, promissory note, or other note, draught or order, with the proper mark or stamp, and to give a receipt for the duty and penalty so paid, on the back of such bill of exchange, promissory note, or other note, draught or order so stamped; and every such bill of exchange, promissory note, or other note, draught or order so stamped, shall have, and be deemed of, the like force and validity in the law, as if the same had been duly stamped, according to the directions of the said recited act; and all and every person or persons procuring such bill of exchange, promissory note, or other note, draught or order, to be stamped as directed by this act, shall be, and is and are, hereby indemnified, freed and discharged, from and against all penalties and forfeitures incurred by reason of such bill of exchange, promissory note, or other note, draught or order, not having been duly stamped, according to the directions of the said act."

And by s. 6. it is enacted, "That if any such bill of exchange, promissory note, or other note, draught or order, shall be produced to the said commissioners before the same shall be payable, according to the tenor and effect thereof, the same shall be stamped, on payment of the said duty, and the penalty of 40*s.*; but in case such bill of exchange, promissory note, or other note, draught or order, shall be payable, according to the tenor and effect thereof, before the production thereof to the siad commissioners, for the purpose before mentioned, then the same shall not be stamped, unless on payment of the duty, and the sum of ten pounds for the said penalty."

to be stamped after it is issued; but if it is, the (24) court will allow no evidence to prove *when* it was stamped, at least against a person who might not know but that it was stamped when it was issued.

Sect. 14.—Notes payable to the bearer on demand for any sum not exceeding 100*l.* duly stamped according to 55 Geo. 3. c. 184., (25) may be re-

---

(24) Wright v. Riley, Peake, 173. In an action by the indorsee of a bill dated 9th September, 1791, the bill when produced appeared to be properly stamped, but the defendant proved that it was not stamped until some time after it was drawn; Lord Kenyon however held, "That though the commissioners might have exceeded their authority in stamping it against the positive directions of the act, it became a valid instrument when stamped, and a judge at nisi prius could not enquire how and at what time it was stamped; that great inconvenience might arise, and a great check might be put upon paper credit, if the objection were allowed, because it would be impossible for a man taking a bill in the ordinary course of business if it was not unstamped when he took it, to know whether it was stamped before it was issued." The plaintiff had a verdict.

(25) By 55 Geo. 3. c. 184. s. 14., it is enacted, "That from and after the 31st day of August, 1815, it shall be lawful for any banker or bankers, or other person or persons who shall have made and issued any promissory notes for payment to the bearer on demand, of any sum of money not exceeding 100*l.* each, duly stamped according to the directions of this act, to re-issue the same from time to time after payment thereof, as often as he, she, or they shall think fit, without being liable to pay any further duty in respect thereof; and that all promissory notes so to be re-issued as aforesaid, shall be good and valid, and as available in the law to all intents and purposes as they were upon the first issuing thereof."

issued after payment, as often as may be thought fit, without a new stamp; so as such issuing is by the same persons by whom they were originally issued, or some or one of them; or, if they were originally issued by partners, by some one or more of the original partners, either alone, or jointly with some one or more additional partners; and if such notes were at first made payable elsewhere than where they were drawn, an alteration as to the house or place of payment will be immaterial. (26)

But no persons are at liberty to issue such re-issuable notes, unless they take out a licence yearly for that purpose. (27)

---

(26) By 55 Geo. 3. c. 184. s. 15., "No promissory note for the payment to the bearer on demand, of any sum of money not exceeding 100*l.*, which shall have been made and issued by any bankers or other persons in partnership, and for which the proper stamp duty shall have been once paid according to the provisions of this act, shall be deemed liable to the payment of any further duty, although the same shall be re-issued by and as the note of some only of the persons who originally made and issued the same, or by and as the note of any one or more of the persons who originally made and issued the same, and any other person or persons in partnership with him or them jointly, nor although such note (if made payable at any other than the place where drawn) shall be re-issued with any alteration therein, only of the house or place at which the same shall have been at first made payable."

(27) By 55 G. 3. c. 184. s. 24., it shall not be lawful for any banker or bankers, or other person or persons (except the governor and company of the bank of England), to issue any promissory, notes for money payable to the bearer on demand, hereby charged with a duty and allowed to be re-issued

And where they issue notes in several towns or places, they must in general have a distinct licence for each town or place. (28)

---

without taking out a licence yearly for that purpose, which licence shall be granted by two or more commissioners of stamps for the time being, or by some person authorized in that behalf by the said commissioners, or the major part of them, on payment of the duty charged thereon in the schedule hereunto annexed; and a separate and distinct licence shall be taken out, for or in respect of every town or place where any such promissory notes shall be issued by, or by any agent or agents for or on account of, any banker or bankers, or other person or persons; and every such licence shall specify the proper name or names and place or places of abode of the person or persons, or the proper name and description of any body corporate to whom the same shall be granted, and also the name of the town or place where, and the name of the bank, as well as the partnership or other name, style, or firm, under which such notes are to be issued; and where any such licence shall be granted to persons in partnership, the same shall specify and set forth the names and places of abode of all the persons concerned in the partnership, whether all their names shall appear on the promissory notes to be issued by them, or not; and in default thereof, such licence shall be absolutely void; and every such licence which shall be granted between the 10th day of October and the 11th day of November in any year, shall be dated on the 11th day of October; and every such licence, which shall be granted at any other time, shall be dated on the day on which the same shall be granted; and every such licence respectively shall have effect and continue in force from the day of the date thereof, until the 10th day of October following, both inclusive.

(28) By 55 Geo. 3. c. 184. s. 26., " Where any banker or bankers, person or persons, applying for a licence under this act, would, under the act of the forty-eighth year of his Majesty's reign, have been entitled to have two or more towns or places in England included in one licence if this act had not been made, such banker or bankers, person or persons, shall have and be entitled to the like privilege under this act."

Except that houses which had established branch banks or agents elsewhere than where they had their chief establishment before 10th October, 1808, may include the places where such branch banks or agents were established in the licence for the place where they have their chief establishment; and that houses in Scotland who issue notes in more than four towns or places, need only take out four distinct licences. (29)

And the issuing re-issuable notes without a licence for the purpose, is subject to a penalty of 100*l.* (30)

And re-issuing notes or bills which ought not to be re-issued, subjects the person re-issuing them

---

(29) By 55 Geo. 3. c. 184. s. 25., "No banker or bankers, person or persons, shall be obliged to take out more than four licences in all for any number of towns or places in Scotland; and in case any banker or bankers, person or persons, shall issue such promissory notes as aforesaid, by themselves or their agents, at more than four different towns or places in Scotland, then after taking out three distinct licences for three such towns or places, such banker or bankers, person or persons, shall be entitled to have all the rest of such towns or places included in a fourth licence."

(30) By 55 Geo. 3. c. 184. s. 27., "If any banker or bankers, or other person or persons (except the governor and company of the bank of England), shall issue or cause to be issued by any agent, any promissory note for money payable to the bearer on demand, hereby charged with a duty and allowed to be re-issued as aforesaid, without being licensed so to do in the manner aforesaid, or at any other town or place, or under any other name, style, or firm than shall be specified in his or their licence, the banker or bankers, or other person or persons so offending, shall, for every such offence, forfeit the sum of one hundred pounds."

to a penalty of 50*l.* and the duty; and any person knowingly taking them to a penalty of 20*l.* (31)

---

(31) By 55 G. 3. c. 184. s. 19., "All promissory notes hereby allowed to continue re-issuable for a limited period, but not afterwards, shall, upon the payment thereof at any time after the expiration of such period; and all promissory notes, bills of exchange, drafts or orders for money, not hereby allowed to be re-issued, shall, upon any payment thereof, be deemed and taken respectively to be thereupon wholly discharged, vacated, and satisfied, and shall be no longer negotiable or available in any manner whatsoever, but shall be forthwith cancelled by the person or persons paying the same; and if any person or persons shall re-issue, or cause or permit to be re-issued, any promissory note hereby allowed to be re-issued for a limited period, as aforesaid, at any time after the expiration of the term or period allowed for that purpose; or if any person or persons shall re-issue, or cause or permit to be re-issued, any promissory note, bill of exchange, draft or order for money, not hereby allowed to be re-issued, at any time after the payment thereof; or if any person or persons paying or causing to be paid any such note, bill, draft, or order, as aforesaid, shall refuse or neglect to cancel the same according to the directions of this act, then, and in either of those cases, the person or persons so offending, shall, for every such note, bill, draft, or order as aforesaid, forfeit the sum of fifty pounds; and in case of any such note, bill, draft, or order being re-issued contrary to the intent and meaning of this act, the person or persons re-issuing the same, or causing or permitting the same to be re-issued, shall also be answerable and accountable to his Majesty, his heirs and successors, for a further duty in respect of every such note, bill, draft, or order of such and the same amount as would have been chargeable thereon in case the same had been then issued for the first time, and so from time to time as often as the same shall be so re-issued; which further duty shall and may be sued for and recovered accordingly, as a debt to his Majesty, his heirs and successors; and if any person or persons shall receive or take any such note, bill, draft or order, in

But a licence for a partnership will continue in force for issuing notes under the same firm till the 10th of October inclusive, after its date, notwithstanding an alteration in the partnership. (32)

Re-issuable notes must not have the date printed thereon under a penalty of *50l.* (33)

---

payment of or as a security for the sum therein expressed, knowing the same to be re-issued contrary to the intent and meaning of this act, he, she, or they shall, for every such note, bill, draft, or order, forfeit the sum of twenty pounds."

(32) By 55 Geo. 3. c. 184. s. 28., "Where any such licence as aforesaid shall be granted to any persons in partnership, the same shall continue in force for the issuing of promissory notes duly stamped, under the name, style, or firm therein specified, until the tenth day of October inclusive, following the date thereof, notwithstanding any alteration in the partnership."

(33) By 55 Geo. 3. c. 184. s. 18., "It shall not be lawful for any banker or bankers, or other person or persons, to issue any promissory note for the payment of money to the bearer on demand, liable to any of the duties imposed by this act, with the date printed thereon; and if any banker or bankers, or other person or persons, shall issue or cause to be issued any such promissory note with the date printed therein, he or they shall for every such promissory note so issued, forfeit the sum of fifty pounds."

CAP. IV.

IF a bill or note is altered in a material part (though by consent of all parties) after it has once issued, it requires (1) a new stamp;

Unless such alteration is to correct a mistake, and merely to make the bill what it was originally intended to have been, for in such case a new stamp is not necessary. (2)

---

(1) Wilson v. Justice, 1796. A bill of nine months after date was, by consent of all parties, a fortnight after it had been delivered to the payee, altered to ten months after date. Lord Kenyon held a new stamp necessary, and nonsuited the plaintiff.

Bowman v. Nicoll, 5 Term Rep. 537. A bill dated 2d September, and payable twenty-one days after date, was, by consent of the acceptor, altered to fifty-one days after date: on 30th September it was with the like consent, and whilst it remained in the drawer's hands, restored to twenty-one days, but the date was altered to September 14th. Lord Kenyon nonsuited, and the court held the nonsuit right.

(2) Kershaw v. Cox, 3 Esp. N. P. C. 246. In an action on a bill, it appeared that the defendant, who was the payee, had *indorsed* the bill to one K., by whom it was passed to the plaintiffs; that they, on discovering that the words, "or order," had been omitted, returned it the day after it was drawn, and the drawer, with the consent of the defendant, then inserted those words. Le Blanc, J. held that no new stamp was necessary; that this

Where an alteration will vacate a bill or note, it will have that effect, though it is made by a mere stranger. (3)

And such alteration not only makes a new stamp necessary, but vacates the bill or note, (independently of the stamp laws) except as between the parties consenting to such alteration.

---

was not a new instrument, as in Bowman v. Nicholl, but merely a correction of a mistake, and in furtherance of the original intention of the parties; and the plaintiffs had a verdict. A new trial was afterwards moved for, but the court refused a rule. See 10 East. Rep. 437.

Jacob v. Hart, 2 Stark. 45. In an action on a bill drawn by A. on B., payable to C. or order, B. discovered, when it was in C.'s hands, that by mistake the date was March instead of April, and C. altered it. Some time after B. had accepted it, C. added on the bill, payable at Mr. J.'s, St. Mary Axe; that was the proper place. Lord Ellenborough held both alterations immaterial, and the plaintiff had a verdict.

(3) Master v. Miller, 4 Term Rep. 320. 2 H. Bl. 141. In an action by indorsees against the acceptor of a bill, payable three months after date, to Wilkinson and Cooke, the declaration had one count upon the bill as dated the 20th March, and another as dated the 26th March. The jury found a special verdict, stating that the bill was drawn and dated the 26th March; that it was accepted; and that afterwards, and whilst it remained in the hands of Wilkinson and Cooke, the date was altered from the 26th to the 20th March, without the defendant's knowledge, and by some person unknown to the jury. That after such alteration it was endorsed for a valuable consideration by Wilkinson and Cooke to the plaintiffs. After two arguments, Lord Kenyon, Ashhurst, and Grose, Js. held, that the alteration, though by a stranger, vacated the bill; Buller, J. differed; but on error, the whole court was so clear that it was vacated, that they would not hear a second argument, and judgment for the defendant was affirmed. See Henfree v. Bromley, 6 East. Rep. 309.

Altering the (4) date, or sum, or (4) time for payment; or inserting words, rendering a bill or note (5) negotiable, which was not so originally; or inserting words in a bill or note originally expressed to be for value received generally, stating such value to have been received on a (6) parti-

---

(4) Walton v. Hastings, 4 Campb. 223. 1 Stark. 215. A bill drawn by Brooks in favour of plaintiff was dated 5th July. An agent of plaintiffs presented it for acceptance, and defendant, the drawee, desired to have the date altered to the 10th, which was done accordingly, and then defendant accepted it. Lord Ellenborough held that as the bill was issued before this alteration was made, and was a perfect available instrument, the alteration made a new stamp necessary, and nonsuit.

Outhwaite v. Luntley, 4 Campb. 179. A bill drawn 5th March was indorsed to J. S., who left it for acceptance. The drawees altered the date to 15th March, and then accepted it. In an action on the bill by indorsee against indorser, it was argued that this alteration vacated the bill. Lord Ellenborough was of that opinion, because the bill was a perfect instrument when issued to the indorsee, the alteration might embarrass parties who would expect notice or payment according to the original date, and the alteration made it a new bill, and made a new stamp necessary.

See Wilson v. Justice, and Bowman v. Nicholl, ante, p. 89. and Cardwell v. Martin, infra, p. 94. As to acceptances varying from the tenor of the bill, see Chapter VI.

(5) See Kershaw v. Cox, ante, p. 89. n. (2.) In Knill v. Williams, 10 East's Rep. 437, Le Blanc, J. said, that Kershaw, and Cox could only be supported on the ground that the alteration was merely the correction of a mistake, for the alteration was a very material one.

(6) Knill v. Williams, 10 East. Rep. 431. This was an action on a note, by which, nine months after date, the defendant promised to pay to the plaintiff, or order, 100*l.* for value received, *for the good-will of the lease and trade of Mr. F. Knill,*

cular account, is a material alteration, and makes a new stamp necessary.

But inserting a mere memorandum to say where the bill or note is to be payable, if it give a right direction in that respect, is not. (7)

But altering an acceptance, so as to give an unwarranted place for payment, vacates the acceptance. (8)

---

deceased. It appeared at the trial before Le Blanc J., at Hereford, that the words in Italics were added, by consent of both parties, on the day after the note had been signed and delivered to the plaintiff, without any new stamp being impressed upon it; upon this the plaintiff was nonsuited, and on a rule nisi to set aside the nonsuit, the whole court held that the alteration was material, and therefore discharged the rule.

(7) Trapp v. Spearman, 3 Esp. N. P. C. 57. In an action on a bill by an indorsee against the acceptor, the defence was, that the bill had been altered, by the insertion of the words, "When due, at the Cross Keys, Black Friars Road." But Lord Kenyon held that the alteration was immaterial, and the plaintiff had a verdict.

Marson v. Petit, 1 Campb. N. P. C. 82. n. Indorsee against acceptor of a bill; after acceptance, the drawer, without the consent or knowledge of the defendant, wrote under his name, Prescott and Co. Lord Ellenborough held it immaterial.

(8) Tidmarsh v. Grover, 1 Maul. and Sel. 735. Defendant accepted a bill so as to make it payable at Bloxam and Co.'s: Bloxam and Co. failed, and the holder, without defendant's knowledge or consent, struck out their names, and substituted Esdaile and Co.'s. On point reserved whether this alteration vacated the acceptance, the whole court held it did, and plaintiff was nonsuited.

Cowie v. Halsall, 4 Barnew. and Ald. 197. In an action by indorsee of a bill against the acceptor, it appeared that the acceptance was general, and that the drawer, without the defendant's knowledge, added to it "Payable at Mr. B.'s, Chis-

And altering the place where a bill or note is payable, if for purpose of fraud, may be a capital forgery. (9)

Sect. 2. — A bill or note is, primâ facie, to be considered as issued as soon as it is passed away by the drawer or maker, (10) or accepted by the drawee; (11)

Not before. (12)

---

well Street;" and on the ground that this was a material alteration and vacated the acceptance, verdict for defendant: A motion was made for a new trial, but the court thought the verdict right, for this alteration would lead to a presentment at B.'s, not at defendant's, and the bill might be treated as dishonoured, and defendant be arrested thereon, without any presentment where he would expect it, and a rule was refused.

(9) Rex v. Treble, 2 Taunt. 328. Kellaway issued ten pound notes payable at Fordingbridge, or at Wilkinson and Co.'s London: these notes were re-issuable, several of them were paid in town, and stolen on their way back to Fordingbridge: Wilkinson and Co. failed, and the prisoner, who had got one of these notes, covered the names of Wilkinson and Co. with a small piece of paper containing the names of Ramsbottom and Co. and re-issued the note: he was indicted for forgery and convicted, and on argument before the twelve judges this was held a forgery, for substituting a solvent house as one of the places of payment instead of an insolvent: one varied the credit of the note, and though Kellaway by the real note answered for no payment in London, but at Wilkinson and Co.'s, this alteration made him answerable for it at Ramsbottom's.

(10) See Walton v. Hastings, ante, p. 91. Outhwaite v. Luntly, ante, p. 91. Knill v. Williams, ante p. 91.

(11) See Tidmarsh v. Grover, and Cowie v. Halsall, ante, p. 92.

(12) Kennerly v. Nash, 1 Stark. 452. Maules drew a bill upon Nash at three months, payable to his (Maule's) order, and

If two persons exchange acceptances, each bill is to be considered as issued, and any alteration afterwards will make new stamps necessary. (13)

But a bill is not to be considered as issued, so as to make a new stamp necessary, until it is in the hands of some one who is entitled to make a claim thereon; (14)

Though it is accepted and indorsed; (14)

And an alteration thereon without the knowledge of acceptor or indorser, though it will entitle them to consider their acceptance or indorsement vacated if they do not assent thereto, will be binding upon them if they assent. (14)

---

sent it to Nash for acceptance: Nash sent it back to Maule, and desired him to let the bill be at four months instead of three: Maule assented, and the bill was altered accordingly. On question whether this made a new stamp necessary, Lord Ellenborough held it did not, and the plaintiff had a verdict.

(13) Cardwell v. Martin, 9 East. Rep. 190. On the 3d of June, 1807, the defendant and Giles and Co. exchanged acceptances; on the 23d, before either of the bills had been passed away, they altered the dates to the 23d; the bills were payable at a certain period after date. Lord Ellenborough thought a new stamp necessary, and nonsuited the plaintiff, with liberty to move to set aside the nonsuit: on motion accordingly, the whole court thought that the exchange of acceptances was a negotiation of each bill, and that the subsequent alteration rendered a new stamp necessary. Rule refused.

N. Each bill was payable to the drawer's order, and the plaintiff was a bonâ fide indorsee.

(14) Downes v. Richardson, B. R. Easter Term, 1822. Upon an issue from chancery, on the question whether Thompson, as acceptor of a bill of exchange, was indebted thereon to Downes, an indorsee; it appeared in evidence that the bill was drawn by

Sect. 3.—If the date of a bill appear upon production to have been altered, and such alteration is in the hand-writing of the acceptor, the holder must prove that such alteration was made before the bill was parted with by the drawer. (15)

But proof that it was in the drawer's hands after it was accepted, will be primâ facie evidence for that purpose. (15)

Raines to his own order upon Thompson, accepted by Thompson and indorsed by Raines and Lachlan; that its date was the 6th March; that Raines, Thompson and Lachlan were in the habit of putting their names for each other upon bills, and that Thompson and Lachlan put their names upon this bill to enable Raines to pass it: Raines put it into the hands of an agent, and he could not pass it till 10th April, when he paid it for value to Howell, who passed it for value to plaintiff. Before it was paid to Howell, the date was altered to the 16th of March: Thompson did not know of this alteration till after the bill was paid to Howell, but as soon as he knew of it he assented to it. It was urged for defendant, that this alteration made a new stamp necessary; but upon a case reserved, the court thought otherwise; for though the bill had names upon it, so as to give it the semblance of an available bill before it was paid to Howell, it was not in fact an available bill till that payment; no person could have made a claim upon it, and if not, it was not to be considered as issued till that period, and then the alteration was in time; and though Thompson would not have been bound by the bill in its altered state had he not assented to the alteration but might have insisted that the alteration cancelled his acceptance, his subsequent assent bound him, and revived and continued his acceptance.

(15) Johnson v. Duke of Marlborough, 2 Stark. 313. In action by indorsee against acceptor on bill payable to the drawer's order, the bill on production appeared to have been dated originally 29th December, 1816, but the date was altered

If the bill is put into an agent's hands to pay away, and it is left in doubt whether the date was altered before he paid it away or afterwards, it will not be sufficient. (16)

---

to 29th January, 1817, and the alteration, which was immediately above the acceptance, was proved to be in defendant's handwriting. Abbot J. intimated, that he must have proof that the alteration was made before the drawer indorsed away the bill, for otherwise a new stamp would have been necessary. Proof was then given that the bill was in the drawer's hands after defendant had accepted it, and that was considered primâ facie proof that it had not been previously negotiated.

(16) In Downes v. Richardson, ante p. 94. it was at first left in doubt when the date was altered, whether before or after the payment to Howell, and then the court inclined against the plaintiff; it was afterwards ascertained that the alteration was before that payment.

CAP. V.

Bills or notes payable to order, or to bearer, or containing any words to make them assignable, may be assigned so as to give the assignee a right upon the bill or note against all the antecedent parties; and bills or notes containing no words to make them assignable may, where the stamp laws do not prevent it, be assigned so as to give the assignee a right upon them against the assignor, but (1) not so as to give him a right against any of the antecedent parties.

Bills and notes are assigned either by delivery only, or by indorsement and delivery. Bills and notes whilst payable to order are assignable by the latter mode only; bills and notes payable to bearer, and bills and notes originally payable to order, and indorsed as (2) they may be so as to be payable to the bearer, by either.

On a transfer by delivery only, without indorse ment, the person making it ceases to (3) be a party to the bill or note; on a transfer by indorse-

(1) Hill v. Lewis, Salk. 132. Moor drew one note payable to the defendant, or his order, and another payable to him generally, without any words to make it assignable; the defendant indorsed them to Zouch, and Zouch to the plaintiff; the first objection was that the plaintiff had been guilty of laches, but the jury thought he had not: and it was then urged that the second note was not assignable; and Holt, C. J. agreed that the indorsement of this note did not make him that drew it chargeable to the indorsee, for the words "*or to his order*" give authority to assign it by indorsement; but the indorsement of a note which has not these words is good so as to make the indorser chargeable to the indorsee.

(2) See post, p. 100.

(3) Vide Ld. Raym. 442. 774. 929, 930. 12 Mod. 203. 241. 408 517. 521. Salk. 124. 128. — 3 Salk. 68. Comb. 57.

ment, he (4) is, according to the legal operation, a new drawer.

Upon bills and notes for the payment of less than *5l.* the indorsement (5) must be attested by one subscribing witness.

No particular (6) words are essential to an indorsement; the mere signature (7) of the indorser is in general sufficient.

But the indorsement of a bill or note for the payment of less than five pounds must (8) mention the name and place of abode of the indorsee, and bear date at or before the time of making it.

A promise to indorse, though on sufficient consideration, cannot be treated as an actual indorsement. (9)

---

(4) Smallwood v. Vernon, Str. 478. In an action against the indorser of a note, the declaration stated that he became chargeable according to the tenor of the indorsement: and it was objected that the indorsement might appoint the payment at a time different from that mentioned in the note; sed per cur. if it did, it would charge the indorser, for every indorsement is the same as making a new note. Vide 2 Show. 501. Comb. 32. Skinn. 255, 256. 342. 411. 3 Mod. 87. 12 Mod. 36. Ld. Raym. 181. 444. 744. Salk. 125. 132, 133. 3 Salk. 68. Str. 442. 479. 1 Atk. 282. 2 Atk. 182. Burr. 670. 675. Dougl. 613.

(5) Vide 17 G. 3. c. 30. s. 1. ante p. 9.

(6) Vide Holt. 117. Ld. Raym. 176. 810.

(7) Vide 12 Mod. 192. 244. Salk. 126. 128. 130. Ld. Raym. 444.

(8) Vide 17 G. 3. c. 30. s. 1. ante p. 9.

(9) Moxon v. Pulling, 4 Camp. 50. Defendant had accepted a bill, he could not pay, and referred the holder to one May, to whom he said he had lent the acceptance. May proposed that plaintiff should take an acceptance of Hullett and Co., and

Nor will it preclude the party from proving that an indorsement afterwards in his name is a forgery. (9)

But delivery without indorsement, where indorsement is essential, and where it is omitted by mistake, will entitle the party to call for an indorsement afterwards; (10)

And if the party who ought to have made it afterwards become bankrupt, will prevent his assignees from claiming the bill or note. (10)

An indorsement which mentions the name of the person in whose favour it is made, is called a full indorsement; an indorsement which does not, a blank one.

A blank indorsement, so long as it continues blank, makes a bill or note payable to the (11)

---

that defendant should indorse it: defendant agreed, and said he would go and indorse it. Four days afterwards May sent plaintiff Hullett and Co.'s acceptance, with an indorsement in defendant's name; and plaintiff gave up defendant's acceptance: the indorsement in defendant's name was a forgery, and defendant being sued as indorser, Lord Ellenborough said, "You cannot establish any agency to indorse: when the promise was given, the bill does not appear to have existed, and all was *in fieri*: defendant might repent and refuse to indorse; he may be liable for breach of promise, but cannot be sued as indorser." Nonsuit.

(10) See Smith v. Pickering, post. 114.

(11) Peacock v. Rhodes, Dougl. 611—633. A bill was drawn by the defendant, payable to Ingham or order. Ingham indorsed it in blank, after which it was stolen; the plaintiff took it *bonâ fide*, and paid a valuable consideration for it, and acceptance and payment being refused, gave notice to the defendant, and brought this action. A case was reserved for the opinion of the court, and it was contended that this bill was

bearer, but the holder may write over it what he pleases.

And the holder, by writing a direction over the indorsement, ordering the money to be paid to particular persons without adding his own name, does (12) not become an indorser.

As long however as the first indorsement continues blank, the (13) bill or note as against the

---

not to be considered as payable to bearer, and that the plaintiff had no better right upon it than the person of whom he took it; but the court said there was no difference between a note indorsed in blank, and one payable to bearer, and the plaintiff had judgment. Francis v. Mott, N. P. before Lord Mansfield, cited Dougl. 612. was a similar case, and the attorney-general, who was for the defendant, after attempting unsuccessfully to show that the plaintiff *knew* the bill was obtained unfairly, gave up the cause.

(12) Vincent and another v. Horlock and another, 1 Campb. N. P. C. 442. In an action against the defendants as indorsers of a bill, it appeared that the payee had indorsed it in blank to the defendants, and that they had written over the payee's signature, " Pay the contents to Vincent and Co." Lord Ellenborough was clearly of opinion that this was not an indorsement by the defendants; and the plaintiffs were nonsuited.

(13) Smith v. Clark, Peake, 225. A bill was indorsed in blank by the payee, and after some other indorsements was indorsed to Jackson or order; Jackson sent it to Muir and Atkinson, but did not indorse it, and Muir and Atkinson discounted it with the plaintiffs: the plaintiff struck out all the indorsements except the first, which continued blank. This was an action against the acceptor, and it was objected, that the plaintiffs could not recover without an indorsement by Jackson; but Ld. Kenyon held otherwise, and the plaintiffs recovered. The plaintiffs afterwards proved that Jackson desired Muir and Atkinson to discount this bill, but Ld. Kenyon thought the plaintiff's case made out without this evidence.

payee, the drawer, and acceptor, is assignable by mere delivery, notwithstanding it may have upon it subsequent full indorsements.

A full indorsement may restrain the negotiability of a bill or note.

An indorsement is restrictive, which has express words making it so, or is made in favour of a person who cannot make a transfer.

Thus an indorsement in these words, "Pay the "contents to I. S. only," "to I. S. (14) for my use;" or (at least when addressed to the drawee) (15)

---

(14) Per Wilmot J. Burr. 1227. Blackst. 299. The payee may check the currency of a bill or note by giving a bare authority to receive the money; as "Pay to A. for my use;" and per Lord Hardwicke in Snee v. Prescott, 1 Atk. 249. Bills and notes are frequently indorsed in this manner, "Pray pay the "money to my use," in order to prevent their being filled up with such an indorsement as passes the interest.

(15) Ancher v. Bank of England, Dougl. 615. 637. A bill was drawn by the plaintiffs upon Claus Heide and Co. payable to Jens Mœstue or order. Mœstue indorsed it to this effect: "The within must be credited to Captain M. L. Dahl, value in account," and sent it to Claus Heide and Co. who credited Dahl for the amount, and gave notice to Dahl and the plaintiffs that they had done so; an indorsement by Dahl was afterwards forged upon the bill, and the bank discounted it. Claus Heide and Co. having become insolvent, Fulgberg paid it for the honour of the plaintiffs, and upon the ground that the indorsement had restrained the negotiability of the bill, they brought an action for money had and received against the bank: Lord Mansfield directed a nonsuit, but upon a rule to shew cause why there should not be a new trial, and cause shewn, Lord Mansfield, Willes, and Ashhurst, Js. thought the indorsement restrictive, and that the plaintiffs were entitled to recover; but Buller J. thought otherwise; upon which Lord Mansfield said,

"the within must be credited to I. S.," is restrictive.

An indorsement, "Pay the contents to A. B. on my being gazetted ensign in a given time" is restrictive, and will give no subsequent indorsee a right, unless he is so gazetted. (16)

An indorsement, "Pay to A. or order, for account of B.," will not prevent A. from indorsing for value, if it be under circumstances which may induce a belief that such value is to be applied to B.'s use; (17)

---

the whole turned on the question, whether the bill continued negotiable? and if they altered their opinion, they would mention the case again; but it never was mentioned afterwards, and upon a new trial Lord Mansfield directed the jury to find for the plaintiffs, which they did.

(16) Robertson v. Kensington, 4 Taunt. 30. Bill payable to plaintiff or order: he indorsed it, "Pay the within to Clerk and Ross, or order, upon my name appearing in the Gazette as ensign in any regiment of the line between the 1st and 64th, if within two months from this date:" the bill was at forty-five days after date: defendants accepted it after it was so indorsed; Clerk and Ross indorsed it over, and after passing through several hands it came to the bank, and them defendants paid: plaintiff's name was never in the Gazette, and he therefore insisted the payment by defendants was wrongful, and that he was entitled to the money. He accordingly brought an action, and on a case reserved the court was of that opinion, and decided for the plaintiff.

(17) Treuttel v. Barandon, 8 Taunt. 100. Two bills were indorsed "Pay to J. P. De Roure, Esq. or order, for account of Messrs. Treuttel and Wurtz:" De Roure indorsed them, and gave them to defendants as a security on his own account: he was indebted to them at the time to more than the value of the bills, and they afterwards advanced him money on these bills: De Roure failed, and Treuttel and Wurtz brought trover for

But it will from indorsing by way of pledge for the private debt of A; (17)

Or for advances to A. on his own account.

But an indorsement is not restrictive, merely because it expresses what is the consideration for it.

Therefore this indorsement, "Pay the contents to I. S., being part of the consideration in a certain deed of assignment, executed by the said I. S. to the indorser and others," is (18) not restrictive.

And the (19) mere omission of words to give a

---

the bills. Gibbs C. J. thought this indorsement sufficiently intimated that the bills were not the property of De Roure, and under his direction, verdict for plaintiffs: and on rule nisi for new trial, the court thought, that though he might not be restricted from discounting, and might pass a good title to a person who might suppose they were passed to the use of plaintiffs, he could not pledge them on his own account, and rule discharged.

(18) R. Potts v. Reed, 6 Esp. N. P. C. 57.

(19) Moore v. Manning, Com. 311. A note was drawn by the defendant payable to Statham or order; Statham indorsed it to Witherhead, but did not add "or to his order," and Witherhead indorsed it to the plaintiff. The defendant contended, that as there were no express words to authorize Witherhead to assign it, he had no such power, but the whole court resolved, that as the bill was at first assignable by Statham as being payable to him or order, and as all Statham's interest was transferred to Witherhead, the right of assigning it was transferred also, and the plaintiff had judgment.

Acheson v. Fountain, Str. 557. Bull. N. P. 275. A bill was payable to Abercrombie or order, and he indorsed it thus, "Pray pay the contents to Louisa Acheson." This being stated in the declaration as an indorsement to Acheson or order, it was objected that it was a fatal variance; but upon

power of transfer, will not make an indorsement restrictive.

A restrictive indorsement precludes the person in whose favour it is made from making a transfer so as to give a right of action against either the person making it, or any of the antecedent parties, and if payment is made to the person to whom such transfer is made, the party paying may, under circumstances, be liable to pay the money a second time (20), or the person receiving it may be liable to refund. (21)

An (22) indorsement cannot be made for the

---

consideration the whole court was of opinion against the objection, because this was the legal import of the indorsement, and Louisa Acheson was authorized by it to make an indorsement over.

Edie v. East India Company, Blackst. 295. Burr. 1216. A foreign bill drawn upon the East India Company was payable to Campbell or order; Campbell indorsed it to Ogilby, but did not insert the words "or order," or any similar words in the indorsement; Ogilby indorsed it to the plaintiffs. It was insisted, that under the indorsement to Ogilby he had no authority to indorse it over, and upon that ground the jury found for the defendants; but upon a rule to shew cause why there should not be a new trial, and cause shewn, the court was clear, that as the bill was originally in its nature negotiable, it continued so in the hands of Ogilby, and that his indorsement was good; and a new trial was granted.

(20) Vide Robertson v. Kensington, ante p. 103. note.

(21) Vide Ancher v. Bank of England, ante p. 102. note.

(22) Hawkins v. Cardy, Ld. Raym. 360. Carth. 466. 12 Mod. 213. Salk. 65. In an action upon a bill drawn by the defendant for 46*l*. 19*s*. payable to Blackman or order, the declaration stated that Blackman indorsed 43*l*. 4*s*. of it to the plaintiff; the defendant pleaded an insufficient plea, upon which the plaintiff

transfer of less than the full sum appearing to be due upon the bill or note.

Sect. 2. — A transfer by indorsement will convey no title, except against the person making it, unless it is made by him who has a right to make the transfer: a transfer by delivery may.

Therefore in case of a loss by theft or accident, if the bill or note be assignable by mere delivery, the thief or finder may (23) confer a title by trans-

---

demurred; but the whole court held the declaration bad, because the bill could not be indorsed for less than all the money due thereon, and the plaintiff discontinued his action. And per Gould, J. in Johnson v. Kennion, 2 Wils. 262. where the drawer of a bill has paid part, you may indorse it over for the residue; otherwise not, because it would subject him to a variety of actions.

(23) Anon. Ld. Raym. 738. Salk. 126. 3 Salk. 71. B. lost a bank bill payable to A. or bearer; C. found it, and assigned it for a valuable consideration to D. who got a new bill for it from the bank. Trover was then brought against D. for the first bill, but by Holt, C. J. " the action will not lie against *him*, because he took it for a valuable consideration, though it would against C., as he had no title; but payment to C. would have indemnified the bank."

Miller v. Race, Burr. 452. A bank note payable to William Fenney, or bearer, was stolen out of the mail in the night of the 11th of December, 1756, and on the 12th came to the hands of the plaintiff for a full and valuable consideration, in the usual course of his business, and without any knowledge that it had been taken out of the mail; he afterwards presented it at the bank for payment, and the defendant, being one of the clerks, stopped it, upon which an action of trover was brought; and upon a case reserved upon the point, whether the plaintiff had

ferring it; if it be assignable by indorsement only, he (24) cannot.

---

a sufficient property in the note to entitle him to recover, the court was clear in opinion that he had, and that the action was well brought. Vide Lawson and others v. Weston and others, 4 Esp. N. P. C. 56.

Grant v. Vaughan, Burr. 1516. Vaughan gave Bicknell a draught upon his banker payable to "Ship Fortune, or bearer." Bicknell lost it, and the plaintiff afterwards took it, bonâ fide, in the course of trade, and paid a valuable consideration for it: the banker refused to pay it, upon which the plaintiff brought this action against Vaughan. Lord Mansfield left it to the jury to consider, 1st, whether the plaintiff came to the possession of the bill fairly and bonâ fide; and 2dly, whether such draught was in fact and practice negotiable; and the jury found for the defendant: but upon an application for a new trial, and cause shewn against it, the Court was clear that the second point ought not to have been left to the jury, because it was clear that such draughts were negotiable, and if the jury thought the plaintiff took the note fairly and bonâ fide, of which there appeared to be no doubt, he was entitled to recover. A new trial was accordingly granted, in which the plaintiff recovered the money. Peacock v. Rhodes, Dougl. 611. 633. ante, p. 100. note (11).

By 9 & 10 W. 3. c. 17. § 3. "If any inland bill be lost, or miscarry within the time limited for its payment, the drawer shall, on security given upon request to indemnify him if such bill shall be found again, give another bill of the same tenor with the first." And it should seem that the equity of this statute would comprehend indorsements also, and that the 3 & 4 Anne, c. 9. (which gives the like remedies upon notes as were then in use on inland bills) would extend it to notes. See Walmsley v. Child, 1 Ves. Sen. 341. and see post, Chap. IX., in what cases an action may be maintained, where a bill or note has been lost.

(24) In this case, however, it is adviseable for the loser, in order to guard against the forgery of his indorsement, to give immediate notice of the loss to all the antecedent parties, and if

If a bill or note transferable by delivery be lost, the loser should give immediate notice thereof to the drawee, or persons who are to pay it. (25)

And if such persons afterwards pay it to a person who has not taken it *bonâ fide* or paid value for it, they will be responsible to the loser. (25)

The right to transfer a bill or note is in the payee, or in the person to whom it has been transferred from him.

And if a bill or note be deposited with a banker for a particular purpose, and is indorsed so as to give him the right to transfer it, and he (26) (27) nego-

---

payment has been made before such notice could be given, to apprise the payee thereof without delay.

See the case of Smith and another v. Shepherd, in Chitty on Bills.

(25) Lovell v. Martin, 4 Taunt. 799. Plaintiff lost a bill accepted payable at defendant's, and immediately gave notice thereof to the acceptor, and the acceptor communicated the notice to defendants with a request that they would not pay or discount the bill: they afterwards (probably from inadvertence) discounted it for one Powell, who had it from a child who picked it up: when due they wrote a receipt upon it, and debited the acceptor with the amount. Plaintiff brought trover, and there being no proof that Powell took it bonâ fide or paid value, verdict for plaintiff. Rule nisi for nonsuit on the ground that plaintiff had not demanded the bill of defendants, and without such demand trover would not lie: but the court held the writing a receipt upon it, and debiting the acceptor with the amount, was a conversion; and rule discharged.

(26) Bolton v. Puller, 1 Bos. and Pull. 539. Forbes and Gregory, traders in London, were also partners in the house of Caldwell and Co. in Liverpool. Bolton dealt with Caldwell and Co. and they prevailed with the house in London to let him make his bills payable there; Bolton kept no account but with the

tiate, or (27) pledge it; such negociation or pledging, although it may amount to a gross breach of

---

house at Liverpool; and they kept the account with the house in London; and the payments on Bolton's bills, when made, were carried by the house in London to *their* account with the house in Liverpool; and by the house at Liverpool to their account with Bolton. In Feb. 1793, he accepted bills payable at the house in London, to the value of 19,702*l.*; and to enable the Liverpool house to provide for their payment, he indorsed to them (among other bills) a bill for 4000*l.* and another for 398*l.* These two bills they remitted generally, with many others, to Forbes and Gregory, to whom they were considerably indebted; but before the latter bill arrived, both houses became bankrupt. The acceptances were payable before the indorsed bills. Bolton was obliged to pay all his own acceptances; and the assignees of Forbes and Gregory having refused to deliver up these bills, he brought trover for them. A special verdict was found: and after two arguments, the court were unanimously of opinion, that the assignees were entitled to keep the bills. They admitted, that as Forbes and Gregory were partners in the Liverpool house, they were to be considered as privy to the fact that the bills had been indorsed to that house to enable it to provide for Bolton's acceptances; but they held that the application which had been made of these bills, was the very thing which Bolton intended; and that therefore the privity of the London house in the agreement made between him and the house at Liverpool, could have no effect on the transaction, which, *as between the two houses, had undoubtedly changed the property in the bills:* that for the purpose of providing for Bolton's acceptances, the house at Liverpool was intitled to deal with the bills as it thought fit; that they had therefore a right to remit them to Forbes and Gregory; and as they were indebted to Forbes and Gregory in more than the amount, the assignees of Forbes and Gregory were intitled to keep them. Judgment for the defendants.

(27) Collins v. Martin, 1 Bos. and Pull. 648. The plaintiff sent bills indorsed in blank to Messrs. Nightingales, to receive

trust, and defeat the purpose for which the deposit was made, will, as between the person who made the deposit and an innocent holder of the bill or note, be binding upon the former.

An indorsement by a person of the same name with the person entitled to transfer it is (28) void

---

the money upon them: they borrowed money of the defendants, and pledged these bills as a security. They afterwards became bankrupt, and the plaintiff brought trover for the bills. There being no evidence that the defendants knew under what circumstances the bills had been left with Messrs. N., or how the plaintiff's account (he being in cash) stood with them, Eyre C. J. thought the action would not lie, and nonsuited the plaintiff. On a rule nisi to set aside the nonsuit, it was urged that though the Messrs. N. might have negotiated the bills, they could not pledge them; but after consideration, the court was unanimous, that they had the power of binding the plaintiff as well by pledging as negotiating the bills, of which they were enabled to hold themselves out to the world as the absolute owners. Rule discharged.

(28) Mead v. Young, 4 Term Rep. 28. A bill payable to Henry Davis or order, was sent by the post, and got into the hands of a wrong Henry Davis, who indorsed it to the plaintiff: there was no description of Henry Davis in the bill, or addition to his name, nor was any fraud imputable to the plaintiff. This was an action against the acceptor, and on his offering evidence to shew that the Henry Davis who indorsed the bill was not the person in whose favour it was drawn, Lord Kenyon was of opinion that the evidence was inadmissible, and he retained that opinion after cause shewn against an application for a new trial; but Ashhurst, Buller, and Grose, Js. held, that unless the indorsement was made by the person to whom the bill was really payable, it was a forgery, and could confer no title, and that therefore it was competent for the defendant to shew that the person who indorsed the bill was not the person in whose favour it was made, and a new trial was accordingly granted.

(except against the person indorsing it, and the subsequent indorsers), though the person entitled to transfer it was not particularly described upon the bill or note.

On a bill or note payable to A. for the use of B., the (29) right to transfer is in A.

On a bill or note payable to *several persons*, not in partnership, the right to transfer it is in all collectively, not (30) in any individually.

If the right to transfer a bill or note be in a feme sole, and she marry, it (31) devolves upon her husband.

---

(29) Evans v. Cramlington, Carth. 5. 2 Vent. 307. Skinn. 264. A bill was payable "to Price or order, for the use of Calvert." Price indorsed it to Evans, after which an extent issued against Calvert, and the money due upon it was seized to the use of the King. These facts appearing upon the pleadings, two points were made upon demurrer; the one, whether Calvert had such an interest in the money as might be extended; and the other, whether Price had power to indorse the bill, or whether he had only a bare authority to receive the money for the use of Calvert; and the Court of King's Bench, and afterwards the Exchequer Chamber, held that Calvert had not such an interest as could be extended, and that Price had power to indorse the bill, and judgment was given for the plaintiff.

(30) See Carvick v. Vickery, ante p. 43.

(31) Connor v. Martin, Str. 516. cited 3 Wils. 5. A bill was made payable to Susan Connor, or order, while she was sole: she married, and during her coverture indorsed it to the plaintiff, and upon demurrer and argument the Court of Common Pleas held, that the feme covert could not assign the note, because by the marriage it became the sole right and property of the husband; and by Parker C. J. in Miles v. Williams, 10 Mod. 246.

If a bill or note be made payable to a feme covert, the right to transfer it is in the husband; the wife cannot transfer unless as agent to him.

But if she do, and the husband promise to pay, it will be evidence (32) that she had authority from her husband to transfer.

If a bill be payable to an infant, an indorsement by him will convey (33) no interest, as against himself; but if he draw the bill, it may against the acceptor. (33)

If the person who has the right to transfer a bill or note die, it (34) devolves upon his personal

---

if a note be payable to a feme sole or order, and she marries, her husband is the proper person to indorse it.

M'Neilage v. Holloway, 1 Barnw. and Ald. 218. A bill was payable to a feme sole or order; she married before it became due; her husband brought an action upon it in his own name; and on a rule to shew cause why the judgment should not be arrested on the ground that the wife should have joined in the action, the court held that as this was a negotiable security, the marriage transferred the property to the husband, and entitled him, if he thought fit, to sue alone.

(32) See Cotes v. Davis, ante, p. 41.

(33) See Taylor v. Croker, 4 Esp. N. P. C. 187. post.

(34) Rawlinson v. Stone, 3 Wils. 1. Str. 1260. 2 Barnes, 137. A note was payable to A. B. or order: A. B. died intestate, and his administrator indorsed it to the plaintiff. These facts appearing upon the declaration, the defendant demurred, and contended that the personal representative of the payee had no power to indorse a note; but the Court of Common Pleas, after three arguments; and the Court of King's Bench, upon error brought, were unanimously of opinion that he had; and each court said, it was every day's practice, and the constant usage for executors and administrators to indorse bills and notes payable to the order of their testators or intestates.

representative; if he becomes bankrupt, and he holds the bill or note in his own right, on his assignees.

And if the right to a bill or note be in several partners, and some of them become bankrupt, and afterwards indorse it, such indorsement, though made to a creditor of the partnership, will confer (35) no title on the indorsee.

And if the creditor receive the money due upon the bill or note, the solvent partners, together with the assignees of the bankrupts, (35) may recover back the money so received.

---

(35) Thomason and others v. Frere and others, 10 East's Rep. 418. Thomason, Underhill, and Guest, were partners in trade at Birmingham; and being debtors to the defendants to the amount of 1800*l.*, and creditors upon Gamble and Co. for 1450*l.*, Underhill and Guest, on the 11th October 1807 without the consent or knowledge of Thomason, (who was abroad,) indorsed to the defendants a bill drawn by the firm of Thomason, Underhill, and Guest, upon, and accepted by, the agents of Gamble and Co. for this 1450*l.* Underhill and Guest had, on the 7th October 1807 committed acts of bankruptcy; upon which separate commissions issued on the 19th. The bill for 1450*l.* became due on the 6th December, and was then paid. And to recover this money the present action was brought by Thomason, and the assignees of Underhill and Guest. The house of Thomason, Underhill, and Guest was still indebted to the defendants beyond the amount of the sum now sought to be recovered. — The plaintiffs were nonsuited. But on a rule nisi for a new trial, the court (Lord Ellenborough C. J. absente) held that the indorsement, having been made after an act of bankruptcy, though before the issuing of the commission and for the purpose of paying a partnership debt, was invalid; and they inclined to think that, this action being

But if a man holds a bill or note, not in his own right, but as a trustee, his bankruptcy will not pass the right to transfer to his assignees. (36)

And if partners hold a bill or note, as trustees, the bankruptcy of one of them will not preclude him and the others from transferring it. (36)

If the person who has a right to indorse a bill or note, deliver it over to another for a valuable consideration, and forget to indorse it, he (37) may

---

brought to recover the money received on the bill, which had been thus wrongfully indorsed, the defendants had no right to set off their demand upon the firm, against this claim by Thomason and the assignees. Rule absolute.

(36) Ramsbottom and others v. Cator, 1 Stark. 228. J. and M. Hervy were partners as bankers; defendant delivered them a bill that they might get it discounted; they passed it to plaintiffs, their bankers; but before they did so, J. H. committed an act of bankruptcy, upon which a commission afterwards issued: it was urged for defendant that the bankruptcy of J. H. destroyed his and his partner's right to pass away the bill; but Lord Ellenborough held, that as the Herveys held it upon a special trust, to get it discounted, and not in their own right, no interest in it passed to the assignees of J. H., and though he doubted whether plaintiffs had an interest beyond what the Herveys had, he allowed them to take a verdict, and gave the defendant leave to take the opinion of the court upon the point.—But the defendant did not move it.

(37) Smith and another v. Pickering, Peake, N. P. C. 50. Richardson and Hill drew a bill on the defendant, payable to their own order, which the defendant accepted. The drawers delivered this bill to the plaintiffs for a valuable consideration, but forgot to indorse it. They afterwards became bankrupts, and then indorsed it. The plaintiffs, as indorsees, now sued the defendant as acceptor. Lord Kenyon was clearly of opinion that the indorsement was good, and the plaintiffs had a verdict.

indorse it after he has become a bankrupt, and the right in it will pass to the person to whom he so delivered it.

So the right to indorse will not devolve upon a bankrupt's assignees, if (38) neither he or they would have any right to demand payment.

Therefore if a bankrupt draw a bill payable to his own order, having at the time (38) no effects in the hands of the drawee; or if, having effects, he draw it for a sum (39) exceeding their amount,

(38) Arden v. Watkins, 3 East's Rep. 317. On the 5th of October, 1801, Lewis Jones committed an act of bankruptcy, on which a commission issued on the 31st December, 1801. On the 4th of December, 1801, he drew a bill on Watkins for 100*l.* payable to his own order, and indorsed it to the plaintiff, who paid him the full value. Watkins owed Jones nothing, but accepted the bill to enable him to raise money upon it, and Jones deposited a lease with him as an indemnity: the assignees insisted upon a restoration of the lease, and Watkins refused to pay the bill. — Action on the bill and reference. The arbitrator awarded against Watkins, but stated the facts specially, to enable him to take the opinion of the court. After a rule nisi to set aside the award, cause shewn, and time taken to consider, the court was clear that the defendant was liable: that as Jones had no effects in Watkins's hand, no right to indorse devolved on his assignees, and that therefore his indorsement was effectual, and transferred the property to the plaintiff. Rule discharged.

(39) Willis v. Freeman and another, 12 East's Rep. 656. In an action by the indorsee of a bill against the acceptors, a verdict was found for the plaintiff, subject to the opinion of the court upon a case. The case stated, that Anderson, the drawer, being indebted to the plaintiff in more than 2000*l.* and being insolvent, proposed to pay the plaintiff a composition of 13*s.* 6*d.* in the pound, together with the costs of an action

and the bill be accepted for his accommodation; his indorsement will, in the former case, confer a good title as to the whole sum mentioned in the bill; and in the latter, as to such sum as is not covered by the effects.

So if a trader get a bill by fraud, and become bankrupt, the bill will belong, not to his assignees, (40) but to the person from whom he obtained it;

---

which had been brought by the plaintiff against him, by a bill upon the defendants. This proposal being acceded to, Anderson applied to the defendants to accept a bill for 1400*l.* *for his accommodation.* The defendants accepted the bill, drawn on the 5th of July, and payable on the 10th of November 1809, having in their hands effects of Anderson's to the amount of 888*l.* 16*s.* 8*d.* Anderson had committed a secret act of bankruptcy on the 7th of March 1809, upon which a commission issued on the 25th of July. The Court of King's Bench held, that to the extent of 888*l.* 16*s.* 8*d.* the defendants had a right to resist payment on the ground of their being answerable for that amount to the assignees, to whom these funds devolved upon the act of bankruptcy; and that therefore the indorsement by Anderson to that extent was inoperative: but as to the surplus (511*l.* 3*s.* 8*d.*) for which the acceptance was accommodation, the case of Arden v. Watkins was in point to shew that the indorsement was valid. And they held that the law in this respect had not been altered by the 49th Geo. 3. c.121. §8. They therefore ordered the verdict to be entered for this reduced sum of 511*l.* 3*s.* 4*d.*

(40) Gladstone v. Hadwen, 1 Maule, 517. Sill and Co. got bills from Hadwen under colour of giving him a security upon some coffee to which however they had no title: on being pressed by Hadwen, they promised to return him the bills, which were on their way from London to Liverpool; but before they arrived, Sill and Co. committed acts of bankruptcy upon which a commission afterwards issued: when the bills arrived,

at least if he promised, before he became bankrupt, to return it.

So if a banker who has a lien on a bill or note for his general balance, delivers it to his customer when it is due, that he may obtain payment, and the customer become bankrupt, the bill or note will nevertheless belong not to the assignees but to the banker. (41)

If a bill or note is made payable to a person who is merely an agent in the transaction, if he indorse generally, without using words to prevent his liability, he will be bound personally. (42)

If an executor or administrator indorse, he binds himself personally, not the assets in his hands. (43)

---

they were delivered to Hadwen, upon which Sill and Co's. assignees brought trover; but on case and time to consider, the court held that they could not sue for what a court of equity would not have allowed them to keep; and that as Hadwen would never have parted with the bills but for a false pretence and fraud, a court of equity would have compelled the assignees, who claimed under Sill and Co., had they got the bills, to have delivered them up to Hadwen.

(41) Bruce v. Hurley, 1 Stark. 23. Young and Co. bankers at Taunton, sent to plaintiffs, their town bankers, a note of defendant's at two months after date. The day before it became due plaintiffs sent it to Young and Co. at Taunton, that they might obtain payment from defendant; defendant did not pay it, and whilst the bill was in their hands, Young and Co. became bankrupts. Young and Co. had overdrawn plaintiffs, and plaintiffs sued defendant on this note; and as plaintiffs only sent the note to Young and Co. that they might obtain payment for plaintiffs and act as their agents in that respect, Lord Ellenborough held plaintiffs entitled to recover, and they had a verdict accordingly.

(42) See Goupy v. Harden, ante, p. 55.

(43) See King v. Thom. ante, p. 56.

Sect. 3.—The transfer of a bill or note may be made either before the expiration of the time limited for its payment, or, unless (44) the sum payable thereby be under five pounds, (45) afterwards.

But a man who takes a bill after it is due, takes it subject to all the objections and equities to which it was liable in the hands of the person from whom he takes it. (46)

---

(44) Vide 17 Geo. 3. c. 30. § 1. ante, p. 9.

(45) Dehers v. Harriott, 1 Show. 163. A bill was indorsed to the plaintiff after it was due, and he had judgment without any objection on this ground.

Mutford v. Walcott, Lord Raym. 575. Holt C. J. said, he remembered a case where a bill was negotiated after the day of payment, and he had all the eminent merchants in London with him at his chambers, and they all held it to be very common, and usual, and a very good practice.

(46) Taylor v. Mather, B. R. E. 27 Geo. 3. 3 Term Rep. 83 n. Indorsee of a note against the maker. It appeared to have been indorsed after it was due, and there were many circumstances which led the court and jury to conclude it had been unfairly obtained, upon which the jury found for the defendant. A new trial was refused upon the merits, and per Buller J. "It has never been determined that a bill or note is not negotiable after it is due, but if there are any circumstances of fraud in the transaction, and it is indorsed to the plaintiff after it is due, I have always left it to the jury upon the slightest circumstance to presume that the indorsee was acquainted with the fraud." The rest of the court concurred in this opinion.

Brown v. Davies, 3 Term Rep. 80. Davies drew a note payable to Sandall or order; Sandall indorsed it to Taddy, and he had it presented, and noted for non-payment. Davies then paid the money to Sandall, and he took up the note from Taddy, but instead of returning the note to Davies, indorsed it to Brown.

And if such person were agent only, to receive the money for his principal, the person to whom he passes it will be accountable to the principal for whatever he receives thereon, whether it be money,

Or a new bill. (47)

Brown thereupon sued Davies, and on Davies's offering to prove these facts, Lord Kenyon thought they would not amount to a defence, unless it could be proved that Brown knew them when he took the note, and he rejected the evidence; but upon a rule nisi for a new trial, and cause shewn, Lord Kenyon said, he thought there ought to be further enquiry; it did not strike him at the trial that the note had been noted before Brown took it, and that that circumstance ought to have awakened Brown's suspicion. Ashhurst and Buller Js. thought that the party taking a note after it was due, was to be considered as taking it on the credit of the person from whom he received it, and that whatever would be a defence against the giver would be a defence against the receiver; upon which Lord Kenyon said, he agreed with that, if the note appeared on the face of it to have been dishonoured, or if knowledge could be brought home to the indorsee that it had been so; but otherwise he was not prepared to go that length. Grose J. said, if collusion could be proved between the defendant and Sandall, the defendant would not be entitled to insist on the objection; but as the case then stood he thought there ought to be a new trial. Rule absolute.

(47) Lee v. Zagury, 8 Taunt. 114. Sebag had a bill accepted by defendant, over due; he sent it to White, that White's correspondent might get the amount for Sebag: White's correspondent indorsed it to Vidal for a debt he owed Vidal, and Vidal not being able to obtain the money, got a new bill from defendant for the amount, and indorsed it to plaintiffs as his agents. Sebag gave defendant notice not to pay this bill, and an action being brought thereon, the defence was, that plaintiffs were mere agents for Vidal, and that as Vidal took the first bill after it was due, he stood in the place of White; and as White would

And an order from the principal to prohibit payment of such new bill, will be a bar to any action at the suit of the person to whom the first bill was passed. (48)

It has been held however, that a man who takes a bill after it is due, will stand in the same situation as if he had taken it before, if he held it for value before it was due, and it is re-delivered to him for the same value afterwards; (48)

As if a banker's customer deposits a bill with him for value before it is due, gets it from him again before it is due, and again deposits it with him for value after it is dishonoured. (48)

---

have been accountable to Sebag for whatever he received in respect of the first bill, Vidal was equally so accountable; and then the second bill was, as against Vidal, the property of Sebag, and Sebag's prohibition to defendant not to pay the second bill, was an answer to the action upon it. Gibbs C. J. was of this opinion, and left it to the jury whether plaintiffs were not mere agents to Vidal, and whether the second bill was not the property of Sebag. The jury found for defendants; and on rule nisi to enter verdict for plaintiffs, the other judges agreed with Gibbs C. J. and rule discharged.

(48) Bosanquet v. Dudman, 1 Stark, 1. Clarkson and Co. banked with plaintiffs, and deposited a bill with them as a security for their engagements on behalf of Clarkson and Co., but before it became due Clarkson and Co. got it back from plaintiffs. After it was dishonoured Clarkson and Co. re-delivered it to plaintiffs, but in the interim Clarkson and Co. bought a ship from the drawer, for whose accommodation defendants had accepted, and agreed to give up this bill in part payment, so that Clarkson and Co. could not have sued upon the bill; but Lord Ellenborough held, that when the bill was returned to plaintiffs they returned to their former right, and were not affected by what Clarkson and Co. had done; and verdict for plaintiffs.

So if a bill or note is returned to an indorser after it becomes due, and he pays the amount, he will be entitled to recover the full amount from the antecedent parties, though some of these parties had lodged securities with the person who held the bill when it became due, and part of the amount had been paid on the sesecurities; (49)

At least if such indorser did not know when he took up the bill, that such securities had been so lodged. (49)

And though a man who takes a bill after it is due, takes it subject to the objections to which it was liable in the hands of the person from whom he took it, he is not subjected to every description of evidence to which that person would be liable; (50) therefore, though the entries in that person's

---

(49) Buzzard v. Flecknoe, 1 Stark. 333. Plaintiffs indorsed two bills to Lord; Lord held them three months after they fell due, and then called on plaintiffs, who took them up. In the interim Lord had received another bill from the drawer as a collateral security, but plaintiffs did not appear to have known that fact; that bill was afterwards satisfied, and plaintiffs having brought this action against the acceptor, he insisted that the amount of that bill ought to be deducted on the ground that plaintiffs stood in the situation of Lord; but Lord Ellenborough thought otherwise, because plaintiffs' title did not first commence after the bill became due, but was referable to their prior holding; had they been discharged from the bills, they might have stood in the situation of new holders. Verdict for the whole amount.

(50) Collenridge v. Farquharson, 1 Stark. 259. In an action by indorsee against indorser, it appeared that one Powell was holder when the bill became due, and that he had afterwards

books, if made at the time of passing the bill and accompanying that act, might be evidence against him, yet entries which cannot be proved to have been so made, and might have been made afterwards, are not. (50)

And though a bill be indorsed over *before* the time appointed for its payment, yet if acceptance has been previously refused, the indorsee (51) will

---

indorsed the bill to plaintiff there being accounts between defendant and Powell, which would have regulated the extent to which Powell could have recovered. Defendant offered in evidence Powell's books, to shew how those accounts stood, and insisted that whatever would have been evidence against Powell would be evidence against plaintiff; but Lord Ellenborough held, that though an entry by Powell at the time and accompanying the act would have been evidence, an entry not accompanying the act and which might have been made afterwards for the very purpose of being used in evidence was not, and the plaintiff had a verdict.

(51) Crossley v. Ham. 13 East. Rep. 498. The defendant for the accommodation of Clark, indorsed two bills drawn by Clark in America, upon Dickinson and Co. in London, for 450*l.* each, in favour of the defendant, dated 10th of February, 1804, and payable 60 days after sight. These bills were paid over by Clark to Parry, in February, 1804. The defendant, Parry and Clark, then, and until after the 14th of April, 1808, resided in America. On the 1st of March, Parry indorsed and remitted the bills to his agents in London, with directions to make a payment to the plaintiff, to whom he then, and still, was indebted. On the 26th of April, the bills were presented for acceptance, dishonoured, and protested for non-acceptance; and notice thereof was given to the defendant. The plaintiff having been advised of the remittance by a letter from Parry, dated on the 12th of April, applied to Parry's agents for 450*l.*; and on the 6th of June they delivered one of the bills to the plaintiff, apprising him of its dishonour, and that therefore he took the

be liable to the same objections as might have been taken against his indorser, if he take the bill with a knowledge of its having been dishonoured;

And if the bill be noted for non acceptance, he must be taken to have this knowledge.

But if he take the bill without this knowledge, and be a bonâ fide holder for a valuable consideration, he will not be liable to the objection. (52)

---

bill, subject to all its infirmities. The bill became due on the 29th of June, and payment being refused, this action was brought. The defendant, however, produced at the trial an instrument signed by Parry, dated 14th of April, 1804, by which he agreed that the defendant, on paying one of the bills in London, should be exonerated from paying the other; and the defendant proved his having, on the 2d of July, paid one of the bills, which then remained in the hands of Parry's agents, who delivered it upon payment. This agreement was, until the 2nd of July, unknown to the plaintiff and Parry's agents. A verdict was found for the plaintiff, and a case reserved for the opinion of the court. The court (Le Blanc J. absente) held that the plaintiff, having taken this bill after its dishonour, had taken it with all its infirmities, and subject therefore to the agreement between Parry and the defendant. Postea to the defendant.

(52) Dunn v. O'Keefe, (6 Taunt. 305.) 5 Maule. 282. Action on bill drawn by defendants on Ricketts and Co. payable to Sinclair or order, and by him indorsed to plaintiff; breach for non-acceptance; plea, that before indorsement to plaintiff, Sinclair presented it for acceptance, that acceptance was refused, and notice thereof not given to defendants; replication, that it was not so presented, and verdict inde that it was, but non obstante veredicto, judgment for plaintiff. On error it was urged that the presentment by Sinclair, and want of notice inde, discharged defendants entirely from the bill; but the court held,

And if the holder's immediate indorser might have recovered upon a bill or note, it is no defence to an action by the holder that an (53) antecedent party would have been precluded from recovering upon it.

The rule as to bills and notes when taken after they are due, is in general applicable also to (54) checks upon bankers.

But it will not apply to such checks where they appear to have been issued long after their date. (54)

---

it did not discharge him against an innocent indorsee, who took the bill for a valuable consideration before the time appointed for its payment; and as it was not alleged in the plea that plaintiff knew of the prior dishonour, or that it was indorsed to him after it was due, or that he did not give value for it, judgment affirmed.

(53) Chalmers v. Lanion, 1 Campb. N. P. C. 383. To an action by the indorsees against the acceptor of a bill, one ground of defence was, that the bill had been accepted for a debt contracted in a smuggling transaction, and that though it had been indorsed for value before it became due to a bonâ fide holder, yet that it had been indorsed by him to the plaintiffs after it was due; and it was contended that having been so indorsed to the plaintiffs, it was competent to the defendant to set up the illegality of the consideration as a defence, in like manner as if the action had been brought by the payee. But Lord Ellenborough held, that if the plaintiff's indorser might have maintained an action upon the bill, the circumstance of the indorsement to them having been made after the bill had become due, was insufficient to let in the proposed defence. And the court of King's Bench concurred in opinion with his lordship.

(54) Boehm v. Sterling, 7 Term Rep. 423. Muilman lent the defendant his acceptance for 2444*l*. 14*s*. at three months, and the defendant gave Muilman a check upon his banker for the amount, dated 17th of Feb. 1796. The year was perhaps

A bill or note cannot be (55) indorsed or negotiated after it has been once paid, if such indorse-

---

intended for 1797. On the 20th of January Muilman gave this check to the plaintiff in payment of an old debt. Muilman died before his acceptance became due, and the defendant was obliged to take it up. In an action upon the check, the defendant urged that Muilman could not have sued him upon this check, and that therefore the plaintiff could not, because he took it so many months after it was dated. Lord Kenyon left it to the jury whether the plaintiff took it bonâ fide, and without knowing the circumstances under which Muilman held it. They found for the plaintiff. And on a rule nisi for a new trial, and cause shewn, Lord Kenyon admitted that it was to be considered as a rule that the person who takes a bill after it is due, is subject to the same equity as the party from whom he took it, though the bill did not appear upon the face of it to have been dishonoured; and he thought there was no distinction in this respect between checks upon bankers and bills of exchange; but as the defendant had not issued this check until nine months after it was dated, he thought it was not competent to him to object to the time when the Plaintiff took it; the other judges agreed that the rule mentioned by Lord Kenyon was to be considered as settled, but for the reasons given by Lord Kenyon that it did not bear upon this case. Rule discharged.

R. acc. Tinson v. Francis, 1 Campb. N. P. C. 19.

(55) Beck v. Robley, B. R. Tr. 14 Geo. 3. cited 1 H. Blackst. 89 n. Brown drew a bill upon Robley, which Robley accepted, payable to Hodgson or order; Robley did not pay it when it was presented, upon which Brown took it up; Brown afterwards indorsed it to Beck, and Beck brought an action upon it against Robley; but the jury thought that when Brown took up the bill, its negotiability ceased, and found for the defendant; and on a rule nisi for a new trial, the court thought the jury right, and Lord Mansfield said, "When a draught is given payable to A. or order, the purpose is, that it shall be paid to A. or order; and when it comes back unpaid, and is taken up by the drawer, it ceases to be a bill. If it were negotiable here, Hodgson would be liable, for which there is no colour."

ment or negotiation would make any of the parties liable who would otherwise be discharged.

But an indorser who pays a bill, may indorse or negotiate it, because his indorsement or negotiation will make no person liable but himself, and those whom he might sue. (56)

And if a bill or note is paid before it is due, and nothing done upon it to mark such payment, an indorsement afterwards before the time it would have become due, will give the indorsee, if he take it bonâ fide and for a valuable consideration, the same right as if there had been no such payment. (57)

---

(56) Callow v. Lawrence, 3 Maule. 95. Pywell drew on defendant, payable to his own order, and indorsed to Taylor; defendant accepted the bill, but did not pay it; Pywell took it up, and indorsed it to plaintiff. It was urged, that after Pywell had once paid it he could not indorse it, its negotiability was at an end; but on cause shewn the court were clear that Pywell's payment did not terminate its negotiability, because his indorsement would make no person liable but himself and defendant, and defendant had never been discharged. Rule discharged.

(57) Burridge v. Manners, 3 Campb. 194. Four days before a note became due, some person went to the banker's where it lay, and paid it, and carried it away; it was not cancelled, nor any minute made upon it to denote such payment; within the four days it was indorsed bonâ fide, and for valuable consideration, to plaintiff, and in an action by him against the payee this payment was relied on, and it was urged that after payment it could not be negotiated; sed per Lord Ellenborough, that means payment in due course, not payment by anticipation; had the note been due before plaintiff took it, he would have taken it with all its infirmities, but here was nothing to awaken his suspicion; this payment does not extinguish it more than discount-

If a (58) man indorse a bill or note before the sum or time of payment be mentioned therein, he will be precluded from saying that his indorsement was prior to the completion or issuing of the bill or note, and this though the holder knew when he took it in what state the bill was at the time of the indorsement.

And if a man indorse a bill or note with blanks for sum and date, and die before they are filled up,

---

ing would; whilst its time is running, it remains negotiable. Verdict for plaintiff.

(58) Russel v. Langstaff, Dougl. 496. 514. The defendant, to accommodate Galley, indorsed his name on five copper-plate checks, made in the form of promissory notes, but in blank, without any sums, dates, or times of payment being mentioned therein, and delivered them to Galley; Galley filled them up as he thought fit, and the plaintiff discounted them; the plaintiff knew the notes were blank at the time of the indorsement; Galley not paying them when they became due, the plaintiff brought this action. Hotham, B. before whom the cause was tried, was of opinion, that as the notes were incomplete when the defendant indorsed them, no subsequent act of Galley could make them otherwise, because that would alter the effect of the defendant's indorsement, and he accordingly directed a verdict for the defendant; but upon an application for a new trial, and cause shewn, Mr. Wallace, the attorney-general, gave up the point, though Mr. Lee afterwards argued it, and Lord Mansfield said, "Nothing is so clear as the point; the indorsement on a blank note is a letter of credit for an indefinite sum; the defendant said, trust Galley to any amount, and I will be his security; it does not lie in his mouth to say, the indorsements were not regular." A new trial was accordingly granted, and a verdict having been found for the plaintiff in a similar action before Lord Mansfield, the defendant submitted in this, without going to a second trial.

the person filling them up can make no objection on account of his previous death. (59)

And if a bill or note be post-dated (as in most cases it (60) may be) an indorsement before the date (61) will entitle the indorsee to sue the drawer

---

(59) Usher v. Dauncey, 4 Camp. 97. F. D. and three others were partners, and used to draw bills, with blanks for sums and date, to raise money: F. D. drew one 28th February to his own order, and indorsed it in blank, and died 15th March: 22d April the clerk to the surviving partners inserted as the date 27th Feb., and as the sum of 1574*l.* and an agent of theirs got it discounted: in an action thereon against the surviving partners, it was urged, that F. D.'s death countermanded all authority in the clerk to fill up a bill with his name to it, and that the bill was therefore void: but Lord Ellenborough thought the clerk's authority emanated from all the partners, and that when he filled up the bill on account of their survivors and for their use, he acted as their agent and bound them, and that the case was within the principles of Russel v. Langstaffe. The plaintiff had a verdict, and the court of king's bench refused to set it aside.

(60) See ante, p. 21.

(61) Passmore v. North, 13 East. Rep. 517. The defendant, on the 4th of May, 1810, drew a bill for 200*l.* on Brook and Co., dated the 11th of May, 1810, payable to Totty or order, sixty-five days after date. On the 5th of May, Totty indorsed this bill to the plaintiff for a valuable consideration; and on the same day died. After the 4th, and before the 11th of May, the defendant received effects of Totty's to the amount of about 130*l.* to answer this bill. On the 12th of May, the defendant advised the drawees of the bill having been drawn, and of Totty's death, and desired them not to accept or pay the bill. Acceptance and payment were accordingly refused: and this action was brought against the drawer. A verdict was found for the plaintiff, subject to the opinion of the court of king's bench, on a case reserved. The court, after adverting to the 17 G. 3. c. 30. as to bills for less than 5*l.*, and to the 48 G. 3.

or maker, although the indorser die before the date of the bill or note.

Upon the transfer of a bill drawn in sets, each part must be delivered to the person in whose favour the transfer is made; otherwise the same inconveniences may follow, which would ensue upon a neglect to deliver each of them to the payee.

The indorsement of a bill or note, implies an undertaking from the indorser to the person in whose favour it is made, and to every other person to whom the bill or note may afterwards be transferred, exactly similar to that which is implied by drawing a bill, except that in the case of a note, the stipulations with respect to the drawer's responsibility and undertaking do not apply; and a transfer by delivery only, if made on account of an antecedent debt, implies a similar undertaking from the person making it, to the person in whose favour it is made.

And a transfer by delivery, where the bill or note is sold, may imply that it is a genuine bill. (62)

---

c. 149. as to post-dating draughts upon bankers, held clearly, that the plaintiff was entitled to recover for the whole amount of the bill; and he had judgment accordingly.

(62) Jones v. Ryde, 5 Taunt. 488. 1 Marshall, 157. Defendant sold plaintiff a navy bill as and for a bill of 1800*l.*, which it imported to be: it turned out that the bill was issued for 800*l.* only, and had afterwards been altered. Government paid the 800*l.* only, and plaintiff who had parted with the bill, paid his vendee the 1000*l.* and called upon defendant to reimburse him;

defendant refused, and plaintiff sued him: it was urged for defendant, that both parties were equally innocent; but the court held, that as defendant took upon himself to sell as a bill for 1800*l.* what in fact was a bill for 800*l.*, the consideration pro tanto had failed, and plaintiff was entitled to recover it back. In Bruce v. Bruce, 1 Marshall, 165. the same point was decided upon a victualling bill.

CAP. VI.

THE doctrine of acceptances applies chiefly to bills; for a note may (1) in general be considered, on comparison with a bill, as accepted when it issues.

But on notes payable a limited time after sight, an acceptance is necessary to fix the time of their becoming due.

(1) D. acc. 2 Bl. Comm. 470.

An acceptance is an engagement to pay a bill according to the tenor of the acceptance, and a general acceptance is an engagement to pay according to the tenor of the bill.

This engagement is made by the drawee of the bill or some (2) other person, to the (3) drawer or

---

(2) Mutford v. Walcott, Lord Raym. 575. 12 Mod. 410. Com. 76. per Holt, C. J. "If A. draws a bill on B. and B. will not accept, and C. offers to accept for the honour of the drawer, the holder need not acquiesce, but if he does, C. is bound." And per Lord Mansfield and Yates, J. in Pillans v. Van Mierop, Burr. 1672, 1674. an acceptance for the honour of the drawer will bind the acceptor.

(3) Pillans and another v. Van Mierop, Burr. 1663. White drew on the plaintiffs at Rotterdam for 800*l*., and proposed to give them credit upon the defendant's house in London; the plaintiffs paid White's bill, and wrote to the defendants to know, "Whether they would accept such bills as they, the plaintiffs, should draw in about a month upon them for 800*l*. on White's credit." The defendants answered, that they would, but White having failed before the month elapsed, the defendants wrote to the plaintiffs not to draw. The plaintiffs did however draw, and on the defendant's refusal to pay the bills, brought this action. The jury found a verdict for the defendants, but upon an application for a new trial, as upon a verdict against evidence, and two arguments upon it, the court was unanimous that the defendant's letter was a virtual acceptance of such bills as the plaintiff should draw to the amount of 800*l*. and the rule was made absolute. See Johnson v. Collings, post. p. 144.

Pierson v. Dunlop and others, Cowp. 571. M'Lintot drew upon the defendants in favour of Nicholl, and gave Nicholl a navy bill assigned to the Defendants as a security till the bill of exchange should be accepted; both bills were sent by Nicholl to the defendants, who said, the bill of exchange would not be accepted till the navy bill was paid, but they would receive the money on the navy bill; and they wrote to M'Lintot, saying his

some of the other parties, and might heretofore have been made upon any bill foreign or inland,

---

bill would receive due honour, but it was drawn too short, being payable before the navy bill: they afterwards received the money on the navy bill, but refused to pay the bill of exchange, upon which this action was brought: the plaintiff obtained a verdict, but the defendants had a rule to shew cause why there should not be a new trial, and insisted that the letter to M'Lintot, upon which the jury had in some measure relied, was no acceptance; but on cause shewn, Lord Mansfield said, "I consider what the defendants did as an acceptance; it has been truly said, as a general rule, that the mere answer of a merchant to the drawer of a bill, saying he will duly honour it, is no acceptance, unless accompanied with circumstances which may induce a third person to take the bill by indorsement, if there are any such circumstances, it may amount to an acceptance, though contained in a letter to the drawer; in this case, there is great reason to say, that what the defendants did was equivalent to an acceptance; there may be a conditional as well as an absolute acceptance, what then is the declaration by the defendants, but an undertaking that the bill should be accepted when the navy bill was paid; afterwards he writes this letter, which is an admission he looked to the navy bill as the fund out of which the bill of exchange was to be paid." A new trial was refused.

Mason v. Hunt, Dougl. 284. 297. Rowland Hunt in Dominica, wrote a letter to his partner Thomas Hunt in London, stating that he had agreed that Thomas should accept bills for 3600*l.* upon certain conditions; it was doubtful whether those conditions had been performed, but at all events it was clear that the obligation created by this letter was waived; an action was however brought against the Hunts, and after a verdict for the defendants, and an application for a new trial, upon which the court took time to consider, Lord Mansfield said "There is no doubt but an agreement to accept may amount to an acceptance, and it may be couched in such terms as to put a third person in a better situation than the drawer."

before the (4) bill was drawn or (5) afterwards, and either verbally (6) or in writing: but now by

---

Powell v. Monnier, 1 Atk. 611. Newburgh drew upon Monnier for 50*l.* and sent him a letter of advice, and Monnier wrote for answer that the bill should be duly honoured and placed to Newburgh's debit. A bill in chancery was afterwards filed against Monnier's executrix, upon the ground that this letter amounted to an acceptance; and Lord Hardwicke thought it clear that it did, and decreed payment. (See Wynne v. Raikes, post. p. 145. n. (34.)

(4) Vide Pillans v. Van Mierop, and Mason v. Hunt, ante p. 132, 133. But see also Johnson v. Collis, post. p. 144.

(5) Vide Powel v. Monnier, supra.

(6) Cox v. Coleman, M. 6 Geo. 2. cited arguendo Ann. 75. A foreign bill drawn on defendant was protested for non-acceptance and returned, and afterwards defendant told the plaintiff, "If the bill comes back, I will pay it;" and this was held a good acceptance.

Lumley v. Palmer, Str. 1000. Ann. 74. In an action against the defendant as acceptor of a bill, the acceptance appeared to be by parol only, which Lord Hardwicke, C. J. ruled to be sufficient; but Eyre, C. J. of Common Pleas, having ruled it otherwise in Rex v. Meggott, H. 7 Geo. 2. because of the proviso in 3 & 4 Ann. c. 9. s. 5. "that no acceptance of any inland bill shall be sufficient to charge any person whatsoever, unless the same be under-written or indorsed in writing thereupon," an application was made for a new trial, and the court to settle the point ordered it to be argued; upon the argument the court held Lord Hardwicke's direction right, on the ground that the statute of Ann was intended to give a holder additional remedies, not to deprive him of any he before had; and Eyre, C. J. waived his opinion, and agreed with the court of King's Bench; and this determination is referred to and approved of in Julian v. Shobrooke, 2 Wils. 9. Powell v. Monnier, 1 Atk. 612, and in Pillans v. Van Mierop, Burr. 1662, Lord Mansfield says, a verbal acceptance is binding; and in Sproat v. Matthews

1 & 2 Geo. 4. c. 78. s. 2., which operates from 1st August, 1821, every acceptance of an inland bill must be in writing upon the bill, or if there be several parts of the bill, on one of such parts. (7)

An acceptance is also either absolute or (8) conditional, and either according to, or (9) varying from, the tenor of the bill.

---

1 Term Rep. 182. it was taken for granted by the court and bar that a parol acceptance was good. See also Str. 817.

(7) By 1 & 2 Geo. 4. c. 78. s. 2. After 1st August 1821., no acceptance of any inland bill of exchange shall be sufficient to charge any person, unless such acceptance be in writing on such bill; or, if there be more than one part of such bill, on one of the said parts.

(8) Smith v. Abbott, Str. 1152. Defendant accepted a bill *to pay when goods consigned to him were sold;* he sold the goods, and on being sued upon his acceptance, insisted in arrest of judgment that it was not binding, because it was conditional; but the court, on consideration, held, that though the plaintiff might have refused to take it, and have protested the bill, yet as he did take it, it was binding on the defendant.

Julian v. Shobrooke, 2 Wils. 9. The defendant accepted a bill to pay, *when in cash for the cargo of the ship Thetis;* and on being sued, moved in arrest of judgment that a conditional acceptance was not good; but the court held otherwise, and over-ruled the objection.

Pierson v. Dunlop, Cowp. 571. ante, p. 132. An answer that the bill would not be accepted till a navy bill was paid, was held a conditional acceptance, to pay when the navy bill should be discharged.

(9) Wegerstoffe v. Keene, Str. 214. A foreign bill for 127*l.* 18*s.* 4*d.* was drawn on the defendant, and he accepted it to pay 100*l.* part thereof; he was sued upon this acceptance, and on demurrer to the replication, insisted that a partial acceptance

An acceptance is seldom made before the bill is drawn by any other person than the drawee; afterwards for the purpose either of promoting the negotiation of a bill where the drawee's credit is suspected, or to save the reputation and prevent the suing of some of the parties where the drawee either cannot be found, is not capable of making himself responsible, or refuses acceptance, it is not uncommon; and it is called an acceptance for the honour of the (10) person on whose account it is made, and enures to the benefit of all the parties subsequent to that person.

Such acceptances for honour as are made with

---

was not good within the custom of merchants; but the court held otherwise, and judgment was given for the plaintiff.

Walker v. Atwood, 11. Mod. 190. A bill was drawn on the defendant 8th of April, and no time fixed for its payment; it was presented to defendant 18th of April, and he accepted it to pay 8th of September; this being stated in the declaration, the defendant demurred, and insisted that as no time was prescribed for the payment, the bill was payable at sight, and then a promise to pay two or three months after sight was not an acceptance within the custom of merchants; but the court held it was an acceptance within the custom, and the demurrer was over-ruled.

Petit v. Benson, Comb. 452. A bill was accepted to be paid, half in money and half in bills; and the question was, whether there could be a qualification of an acceptance; and it was proved by divers merchants that there might, for he that might refuse the bill totally might accept it in part; but that the holder was not bound to acquiesce in such acceptance.

(10) Vide Lutw. 899. Beawes, s. 34. 1st. ed. p. 418. s. 40, 42. 1st ed. p. 419.

the former view, are considered as made on account of the person in possession of the bill at the time they are made, and such as are made with the latter, unless they declare the contrary, on account of the drawer.

Acceptances for honour may be made by the drawee, or any other person. Thus, if a bill be drawn by A. on account of B., and the drawee be unwilling to accept on account of B., he (11) may accept for the honour of A. and on his account.

So the drawee may accept for the honour of an indorser.

And if the drawee refuse acceptance, or if he accept and afterwards abscond, or (12) become bankrupt, any other person may accept for the honour of the drawer or of an indorser.

But after a general acceptance by the drawee, another person (13) cannot make a second acceptance in order to guaranty the acceptor's credit.

If however such second acceptance be written on the bill, the party for whose benefit it is made

---

(11) Beawes, § 33. 2d ed. p. 421. Marius, 21.

(12) See ex parte Wackerbarth, 5 Ves. 574. and infra, n. (15.)

(13) Jackson v. Hudson, 2 Campb. N. P. C. 447. This was an action on a bill drawn by the plaintiff on I. Irving, and accepted by him; and under his acceptance the defendant wrote "accepted, Jos. Hudson, payable at, &c." The defendant was sued as acceptor. The plaintiff offered to prove that he had had dealings with Irving, and had refused to trust him further,

(14) may sue the person who made it, as upon a collateral undertaking to guaranty the payment of the bill, if it has the stamp proper for such an undertaking.

A person who accepts for honour, is only liable if the original drawee does not pay. (14)

And to charge such acceptor, there must be a presentment for payment to such original drawee. (14)

And if the acceptor for honour pay, he is (15)

---

unless the defendant would become his surety; and that the defendant, in order to guaranty Irving's credit, wrote this acceptance on the bill. Lord Ellenborough said, that this was neither an acceptance by the drawee, nor by a person for the honour of the drawer: but that it was a collateral undertaking that the bill should be paid, and ought to have been declared upon as such. Nonsuit.

It seems, however, that after an acceptance supra protest for the honour of one party, there may be a similar acceptance for the honour of another. Beawes, § 72. 2d ed. p. 422.

(14) Hoare v. Cazenove, 16 East. 391. A foreign bill was drawn on Penn & Hanbury; they refused acceptance, and it was protested for non-acceptance. Defendant accepted it for the honour of the first indorsers; but did not pay: action inde, defence, that it had not been presented for payment when due to Penn & Hanbury, nor protested for non-payment by them; and on case and time to consider, the court held such payment and protest essential, because they considered defendant's acceptance as conditional if Penn & Hanbury did not pay; and Penn & Hanbury might have funds when the bill became due, though they had none before.

(15) Beawes, § 47. 49. 2d. ed. p. 422. and see ex parte Wackerbarth, 5 Ves. 574. The acceptor of a bill having become bankrupt, and the holders having protested it for better security,

entitled to have recourse for repayment to the person for whose honour he made the acceptance, and to all other parties who are liable to that person.

An acceptance of this description is not made on a foreign bill until after a (16) protest (either for non-acceptance, or (where the acceptor absconds or becomes bankrupt) for want of better security), and from this circumstance it is called an acceptance *supra protest*.

If a bill is drawn on several partners, an acceptance by one, though in his own name only, will bind (17) all; but if drawn on several persons not connected in partnership, an acceptance by one will bind him, but him (17) only.

And if an acceptance by one of several partners be a fraud on the others; or if the one has no authority to bind the others by accepting bills;

Christen and Bowen accepted it for the honour of the drawers; and having paid it, now claimed to be entitled to dividends out of the bankrupt's estate. The chancellor said, that he had spoken to persons in trade on the subject, and that the result was, that the person accepting for the honour of the drawer had a right to come upon the acceptor. He said, however, that the justice of the case required that they should go in the first place against the drawer, if the acceptor had no effects, and directed an inquiry to be made whether the original acceptor or Christen and Bowen had effects of the drawers in hand.

(16) Beawes, 2d ed. p. 421. Marius, p. 21. See Evans on Bills of Exchange, p. 35.

(17) See ante, p. 44. note (17).

a person who is (18) privy to such fraud, or who (18) has received notice of such want of authority, cannot, by taking such acceptance, acquire a right to sue the partnership.

On a bill drawn upon a man by the description of servant, a general acceptance will (19) bind him personally.

An acceptance after the bill is drawn may be made even after (20) the time appointed for its payment.

In such case an acceptance to pay according to the tenor, will (21) be considered as a general acceptance to pay upon demand.

Upon the acceptance of a bill payable at a given time after sight, if the words of acceptance and

---

(18) See ante, c. 2. p. 45. to 50.

(19) See Thomas v. Bishop, ante, p. 57. n. (38.)

(20) Jackson v. Piggot, Lord Raym. 364. Salk. 127. Carth. 450. 12 Mod. 212. In an action against the acceptor of a bill, the declaration stated, that it was dated 25th March, 1696, payable one month after date, and that in April, 1697, it was shewn to the defendant, and he promised to pay it according to its tenor and effect; after verdict for the plaintiff, it was moved in arrest of judgment, that the promise was void, because as the day of payment was past at the time of the acceptance, it was impossible to pay the bill according to its tenor and effect; but it was answered for the plaintiff, that it amounted to a promise to pay generally; and of that opinion was the court, and they accordingly gave judgment for the plaintiff.

Mutford v. Walcot, Lord Raym. 574. Salk. 129. 12 Mod. 410. Com. 75. is precisely to the same effect.

(21) Vide Jackson v. Piggott, and Mutford v. Walcot, supra.

the date are in one hand-writing, and the drawee's name under it in the drawee's, the presumption is that the words of acceptance and the date were either upon the bill when he signed his name, or put there afterwards with his consent, because that is the usual course. (22)

A written acceptance is either made upon the bill or (23) elsewhere.

On a written acceptance by the drawee, his name need not appear; and any words written by him upon the bill, not putting a direct negative upon its request, as, "accepted," (24) "presented," "seen," (24) "the day of the month," or a

---

(22) Glossop v. Jacob, 4 Campb. 227. 1 Stark. 70. Action against acceptor on bill payable sixty days after sight; the acceptance was, "Accepted, 25th October, 1814. B. Jacob." The signature only was Jacob's; whose the other words were did not appear: but it was proved to be usual for a clerk to write "accepted," and the date, and for the drawee then to subscribe his name; and Lord Ellenborough, on objection, said he should leave it to the jury to presume the words were written with defendant's privity when he accepted the bill, unless defendant could give some other date to the transaction. The jury presumed accordingly, and verdict for plaintiff.

(23) Vide Pillans v. Van Mierop, Mason v. Hunt, Powell v. Monnier, and Pierson v. Dunlop, ante, p. 132, 133, 134.

(24) Anon. Comb. 401. per Holt, C. J. If the drawee underwrites a bill "presented such a day, or only the day of the month," it is such an acknowledgment of the bill as amounts to an acceptance; and this was declared by the jury to be the common practice.

Powell v. Monnier, 1 Atk. 611. A bill was sent by the post to the drawee for acceptance; he entered it in his bill-book

(25) direction to a third person to pay it, is primâ facie a complete acceptance.

It has indeed been said, (26) that an express refusal to accept, written on a bill, is an acceptance; but this is not the case, unless it is accompanied with a conduct which shows an intent to create a belief that it is accepted.

On a written acceptance on the bill by any other person than the drawee, it should seem essential that his name should appear.

A promise to accept an existing bill, if made

(which was his practice with all bills he received whether he meant to accept them or not), wrote upon it the number of the entry, and kept it ten days; on the tenth he wrote upon it the day of the month, and returned it, saying he could not accept it; and per Lord Hardwicke, "It has been said to be the custom of merchants, that if a man underwrites any thing, be it what it may, it amounts to an acceptance; but if there were nothing more than this in the case, I should think it of little avail to charge the defendant;" but he decided that a letter the drawee had written, amounted to an acceptance. Vide ante, p. 134.

(25) Moor v. Whitby, B. R. Tr. 10 Geo. 3. Bull. ni. pri. 270. A bill drawn by Newton on Whitby, was presented for acceptance, and Whitby wrote upon it, "Mr. Jackson, please to pay this note, and place it to Mr. Newton's account. R. Whitby." It was insisted that this was no acceptance, but merely a direction to Jackson to pay it out of a particular fund, and if there was no fund there was to be no payment; sed per cur. this is a direction to Jackson to pay the money, and it signifies not to what account it is to be placed; that is between Jackson and Whitby only, this is clearly an acceptance.

(26) In Ann. 75. is this note: "Underwriting or indorsing a bill thus, 'I will not accept this bill,' is held by the custom of

upon an (27) executed consideration, or if it (28) influence any person to take or retain the bill, is where 1 & 2 Geo. 4. c. 78. s. 2. does not apply a complete acceptance as to the person to whom the promise is made in the one case, and the person influenced in the other, and as to all the subsequent parties in each.

---

merchants a good acceptance;" but by Lord Mansfield in Peach v. Kay, in sittings after Trinity Term, 1781. "It was held by all the judges that an express refusal to accept, written on the bill, where the drawee apprized the party who took it away what he had written, was no acceptance; but if the drawee had intended it as a surprize upon the party, and to make him consider it as an acceptance, they seemed to think it might have been otherwise.

(27) Vide Pillans v. Van Mierop, ante, p. 132.

(28) Vide Pierson v. Dunlop, and Mason v. Hunt, ante, p. 132.

Clarke and others v. Cock, 4 East's Rep. 57. Woodward authorized the defendant to receive certain African bills, of which he sent him a list, and apprized him that he had drawn upon him for the amount. The defendant, by letter, acknowledged the receipt of the list, and assured Woodward that the bills he had drawn on him "should meet with due honour." The plaintiffs, who were Woodward's bankers, and greatly in advance to him, having refused to give him further credit, he indorsed to them the bills which he had so drawn upon the defendant, and at the same time either communicated the purport of the defendant's letter or else represented his having made an absolute promise to accept, but did not shew the letter itself: and the plaintiffs, on the faith of defendant's promise, advanced to Woodward the full amount of the bills. The defendant afterwards wrote to Woodward, that the African bills had been attached, and Woodward in answer desired them to refuse acceptance of the bills drawn on him. The defendant did in fact receive the amount

But a promise to accept a bill to be afterwards drawn, is (29) no acceptance of the bill when drawn unless some person be thereby (30) induced to take or retain the bill; and indeed it may be doubted, whether in any case, a promise to accept

---

of the African bills before the bills drawn on him became due; but this amount was afterwards attached in his hands, and upon that attachment he paid over the money so received. This action was brought against the defendant as acceptor of the bills drawn by Woodward; a verdict was found for the plaintiffs, subject to the opinion of the court. The court held that this was a good acceptance, and that the subsequent circumstances had not done it away; and therefore awarded the postea to the plaintiff. Lawrence, J. said the defendant might have resisted the attachment on the ground of his acceptances, which would have been a defence to him.

(29) Johnson v. Collings, 1 East's Rep. 98. Collings owed Ruff 23*l.* 10*s.* 6*d.* Ruff applied for payment, and Collings said that if Ruff would draw for it at two months he would pay it. Ruff drew accordingly, and indorsed the bill to the plaintiff, but did not mention to him Colling's promise. The plaintiff now sued Collings, on the ground, that his promise to Ruff was virtually an acceptance. But Le Blanc J. thought that as it was not made to a third person, nor with circumstances which might induce a third person to take the bill, it was no acceptance, and nonsuited the plaintiff. On a rule nisi for a new trial, and cause shewn, the whole court thought it no acceptance: and Lord Kenyon thought that the admitting a promise to accept, made before the existence of the bill, to operate as an actual acceptance of it afterwards, even though a third person were thereby induced to take the bill, was carrying the doctrine of implied acceptances to the utmost verge of the law, and he doubted whether it did not go beyond the proper boundary. Rule discharged.

(30) Vide Pierson v. Dunlop, and Mason v. Hunt, ante, p. 133. and Johnson v. Collings, supra.

a non-existing bill, would (31) now be considered as an acceptance of the bill when drawn.

And a promise to accept, made upon an executory consideration, is in no case (32) binding so long as such consideration remains executory, unless it influence some person to take or retain the bill.

A promise in a letter that a bill then drawn (33) " shall meet with due honour; or that the writer will (34) " accept or certainly pay" it, is, where 1 & 2 G. 4. c. 78. does not apply, an acceptance.

---

(31) Vide Johnson v. Collings, ante, p. 144. n. (29).

(32) In Pillans v. Van Mierop, ante, p. 132. n. (3). Burr. 1666. Lord Mansfield says, " It was argued upon at the trial, that this imported to be a credit given to the plaintiffs in prospect of a *future* credit to be given by them to White, and this credit might well be countermanded before the advancement of any money, AND THIS IS SO."

(33) See Clarke v. Cock, ante, p. 143. n. (28), and Pierson v. Dunlop, ante, p. 132. n. (3).

(34) Wynne v. Raikes, 5 East's Rep. 514. On 9th Nov. 1801, Brown in America, drew on the defendants in London, a bill for 500*l.* at sixty days after sight; and on the same day wrote to them, that he had valued on them for 5,548*l.* by divers bills, of which he requested their acceptance. The bill for 500*l.* which was one of those bills, was indorsed by the payees to the plaintiffs in London, for a valuable consideration. On 2d Jan. 1802, the plaintiffs, on receiving the bill, presented it for acceptance, which was refused. On 13th January, 1802, the defendants wrote to Brown, stating, that as their prospects of security had improved, they would " accept or certainly pay all the bills which had then appeared." The bill for 500*l.* had so appeared. This letter was received by Brown in America on 19th March, 1802. The plaintiffs presented the bill for payment on 6th March, sixty-three days after the presentment

And this, although the letter was not received until (35) after the bill had become due; and although no person has been (35) induced by such promise, to take the bill.

But to make a promise, in a letter to the drawer, where the bill is payable to a third person, amount to an acceptance, it ought to be in terms which do not admit of doubt. (36)

An answer in reply to a letter of advice from the drawer desiring it may be honoured, that the bill shall have attention, will not, in general, amount to an acceptance. (36)

And it will make no difference though this answer is communicated to an indorsee before he takes the bill. (36)

---

for acceptance, and on payment being refused, brought this action on the bill. At the time when the bill was drawn, Brown was indebted to the defendants, and still continued to be so, to the amount of 5,000*l.* A verdict was found for the plaintiffs subject to the opinion of the Court of King's Bench. The court held that the case of Powell v. Monnier was in point; that this was a good acceptance. Postea to the plaintiffs.

(35) See Wynne v. Raikes, preceding note.

(36) Rees v. Warwick, 2 Barnew. 113. 2 Stark. 411. Action against defendant as acceptor of a bill drawn by Denison and Co., to the order of Johnson and Co., dated 3d May; 4th May, Denison and Co. wrote to defendant, "We yesterday valued on you, favour Johnson and Co. for 100*l.*, which please to honour:" defendant answered, "Your bill 100*l.* &c. shall have attention." This letter was shewn by Denison and Co. to Johnson and Co., and by them before he took the bill to plaintiff; it was insisted this amounted to an acceptance: Bayley J. thought not; but it being suggested that in the

But if, by the course of dealing between the parties, these words are considered as an acceptance, they will have that effect.

So in cases not within 1 & 2 G. 4., a verbal promise to accept, though the party expressly defer a written acceptance, as where he says, "Leave the bill and I will accept it," is a (37) complete acceptance. And a verbal promise to accept a returned bill when it shall come back, is binding (38) if it do come back.

Saying, "Send the bill to my counting house, and I will give directions for its being accepted," is not of itself an acceptance; the bill must be sent to the counting house. (39)

---

dealings between these parties, these words had that meaning; other letters from defendants were read in evidence, but they did not prove the point: the jury intimated their opinion that these words, per se, did not amount to an acceptance; and nonsuit, with liberty to plaintiff to move to enter a verdict; motion accordingly; but the court were also of opinion that these words by no means imported an unequivocal acceptance of the bill, and as the jury were of that opinion in this case, the nonsuit was right.

(37) D. Molloy, B. 2. c. 10. § 20. Mar. 2d ed. 17.

(38) Cox v. Coleman, ante, p. 134. note (6).

(39) Anderson v. Hick, 3 Campb. 179. Acceptance being refused by the drawees, the holder remonstrated with the managing partner, who said, "If you will send it to the counting-house again, I will give directions for its being accepted." In an action against the drawees as acceptors, it was urged that without proof of the bill's being again sent to the counting-house, this answer was an acceptance. Sed per Lord Ellenborough, it was only a conditional promise to accept, and could not operate as an acceptance till the bill was sent back.

An answer by the drawee when a bill is called for, " there is your bill, it is all right," is no (40) acceptance.

Saying, when a bill is presented for payment, " that it will be paid," if said with reference to immediate payment, will not amount to an acceptance, if the person, who brought the bill, declines the immediate payment (41) because he makes an ulterior demand.

Especially if the drawee has before refused to accept. (41)

---

(40) Powell v. Jones, Espinasse, 17. In an action against the defendant as acceptor of a bill, the only evidence to prove the acceptance was, that when the bill was called for, he returned it, and said, " There is your bill, it is all right." Lord Kenyon though these words could by no implication amount to an acceptance, and nonsuited the plaintiff. Vide ante, p. 142. note (26).

(41) Anderson v. Heath, Trin. 1815, 4 Maule, 303. A bill for 2000*l*. at sixty days' sight was presented to defendants, the drawees, 2d August, 1814, for acceptance, which they refused, and it was protested. At the end of the sixty days, 4th October, it was brought for payment, and one of defendants said, " This bill will be paid; but we cannot allow you for a duplicate protest," which was charged, and he was about to pay the bill; but the clerk who brought it said, " he could not receive the payment without all the charges, without further orders;" and he went away for instructions: he returned in half an hour; but in the interim defendants had learnt the drawer had failed, and they refused payment. An action was brought on the ground that the saying, " the bill would be paid," was an acceptance; but, on case, the court held it was not; it was said alio intuito, acceptance did not enter into the contemplation of either party at the time; they thought of immediate, not future, payment; defendants did not think of giving a pledge, nor the clerk of receiving one. Nonsuit.

In cases to which 1 & 2 G. 4. does not apply, the drawee's keeping a bill presented for acceptance, (42) may amount to an acceptance;

---

(42) Harvey v. Martin, King's Bench, sittings after Michaelmas Term, 1806. In an action by the payee and holder of a bill against the defendant as acceptor, it appeared that the bill was drawn in Guernsey, where the drawer and the plaintiff resided, on the defendant, who lived in Cornwall, dated 13th March, 1805, at three months; within a fortnight after it was drawn, the plaintiff sent it to the defendant, desiring him to accept it, and remit it to S. Dobree, the plaintiff's correspondent in London. On 13th April, 1805, the plaintiff, finding that the bill had not been sent to S. Dobree, wrote to the defendant requesting him to accept and send it, stating, that though he considered the keeping the bill as tantamount to an acceptance, yet that it was not the same to him, as S. Dobree would not give him credit for it until he received it accepted. The defendant, however, did not accept the bill, or remit it, or give any notice of his refusal so to do. On 1st of June the defendant signed a letter, admitting that he had kept the bill, though told by the plaintiff that he considered his doing so as tantamount to an acceptance, "as he intended to have paid it," but having no effects of the drawer's, he refused to pay: and on 4th July, when the bill was protested for nonpayment, he said he had neglected to write an acceptance upon it, thinking it of no consequence, "as he meant to pay it." Lord Ellenborough referred to a MS. case of Trimmer v. Oddie, mentioned post, p. 161., in which Lord Kenyon expressed an opinion, that a mere keeping of a bill was an acceptance; and said he inclined to entertain the same opinion; but should leave that question to the jury on the custom. Gibbs, however, for the defendant, admitting that he could not answer the case, a verdict was found for the plaintiff. And on an application to Lord Ellenborough to certify for a special jury, his lordship refused, saying that this was a clear case; but that if it had not been attended with such strong admissions on the part of the defendant, but had been a mere case of a bill kept by the drawee,

And so may his destroying it.

But if there is a refusal to accept, and the holder submits to that refusal, but omits taking the bill away, a subsequent destruction by the drawee is not necessarily an acceptance. (43)

---

he should have thought it a fit case for a special jury to decide, whether such detention of the bill amounted to an acceptance.

See Scaccia de Commerciis and Cambio, fol. 383, num. 335., who, in enumerating the different acceptances, mentions that which is made "tacite per receptionem, et *detentionem* literarum." See also Pothier Contrat de Change, part 1. c. 3. § 3. p. 39, who observes, that the ordonnance having directed that an acceptance should be in writing, had rendered inadmissible the "*acceptation tacite*" resulting from the drawee's having received and retained the bill.

(43) Jeune v. Ward, 1 Barnew. 653. 2 Stark. 326. Godfrey was entitled to a 200*l.* legacy under a will, to which defendant was an executor, and he drew upon defendant for 150*l.* at sight in favour of plaintiff, who was a creditor: the bill was drawn 28th May; on 29th plaintiff went to defendant, who lived in the country, and left the bill for acceptance: in June plaintiff wrote to defendant's solicitor, Egerton, saying defendant had refused to accept the bill, desiring his assistance to get payment from the drawer: Egerton apprised him when the legacy was to be paid, and Godfrey having received it without paying plaintiff, plaintiff applied to defendant to return the bill, to which defendant replied, that having also been applied to by Godfrey's mother to send it her, he had, to avoid trouble, destroyed it. Plaintiff brought an action on the ground that the destruction was tantamount to an acceptance; and of that opinion was Lord Ellenborough, and verdict for plaintiff. On rule nisi for a new trial, and cause shewn, Lord Ellenborough retained his opinion; and Holroyd J. thought, that in general destruction was equivalent to acceptance, but as there was a refusal to accept, and plaintiff seemed to consider defendant not liable in June,

If a bill is sent by the post to the drawee for acceptance, and that has been the course between the holder and drawee, a neglect by the drawee to return it for ten or twelve days whilst he is waiting to see if the drawer sends him funds, is no acceptance. (44)

Though he keeps it at the instance of the drawer on a promise from him of funds. (44)

At least, it is not, if by the course of dealing between the holder and the drawee, the former is apprised that the latter will accept, without delay, when he has funds, and that he will not accept without. (44)

A fortiori the holder cannot insist upon it as an acceptance, if he makes no remonstrance on account of the delay whilst the bill is kept, or when it is returned unaccepted. (44)

And query whether, when the holder sends the bill by post to the drawee and thereby makes him his agent, whether any neglect by the drawee will have any other effect than that of subjecting the drawee to a special action for the negligence. (44)

---

he thought there ought to be a new trial, to put the facts upon the record: Bayley and Abbot Js. thought, under the circumstances, the destruction was no acceptance; and rule absolute. Bayley J. doubted whether, in any case, destruction would do more than subject to an action of trover.

(44) Mason and others v. Barff, M. 59 G. 3. 2 Barnew. 26. Brankstone used to draw on defendants for wool he sent them: August 1814, plaintiff, who used to discount the bills, sent one

By the usage of trade, a banker in London will not render himself responsible by retaining a check drawn on him, (45) provided he return it

---

by letter to defendants, and defendants returned it accepted, but said, it would be well for the future if plaintiffs would enquire whether the wools were delivered to the carrier, and the invoices and the carrier's acknowledgment sent, and in such case the bills would be accepted without delay: 25th February, plaintiffs sent another bill for acceptance, which arrived 27th; but defendants not having received remittance of the invoice, &c. omitted returning it till 8th March, and then sent a letter to say they could not accept because they had not received the invoice, &c., and said they had kept it during the interval on a promise from Brankstone that the invoice should be sent: this letter arrived 11th March, on which day, before its arrival, plaintiffs sent another bill for acceptance, making no mention of the other bill: defendants kept both bills till 25th March, and then sent back both unaccepted. Plaintiffs insisted their conduct amounted to an acceptance of both, and they brought an action on the case; but on argument, the court was clear against plaintiffs, for as they knew the bills would be accepted without delay if the invoices, &c. were sent, they must have concluded, from the delay, that defendants were waiting for them: that their making no remonstrance when they wrote on 11th March, implied that they so considered it, and their making no reply to the letter of the 8th of March, shewed that they did not then consider silence as an acceptance, and had they meant so to consider it, they should at once have written to say so to defendants, because that would have prevented his keeping the second bill, and would have put him upon getting funds for the first. Nonsuit.

(45) Fernandez v. Glynn, 1 Campb. N. P. C. 426. n. In this case it was decided, that by the custom in London, a banker might return a check at any time before five o'clock of the day on which it was drawn. And although the check had been cancelled by mistake, yet having been returned within the time, the banker was holden to be discharged.

at any time before five o'clock in the evening of the day on which it is drawn.

An acceptance to pay when remitted for, is (46) a conditional acceptance.

So an answer by a drawee who lived in London, that a ship was consigned to him and a person in Bristol, and that till he should know to which port the ship would come he could not accept, connected with a subsequent answer that the bill was a good one, and would be paid though the ship should be lost, was (47) held a conditional acceptance

---

(46) Banbury v. Lissett, Str. 1211. The drawee accepted a bill "*for Lissett and Galley, of Leghorn, to pay as remitted from thence at usance,*" and it was objected, in an action against him, that there was no evidence to shew he had a remittance, and that his acceptance was conditional only. Lee C. J. declared he so understood it; but he left it to the jury, and they found for the defendant upon another point, and gave no opinion upon this.

(47) This was the case of Sproat v. Matthews, 1 Term Rep. 182. The ship did arrive at London, and the defendant disposed of the cargo; but it appearing that upon the defendant's answer that the bill would be paid though the ship should be lost, the plaintiff noted the bill for non-acceptance, Buller J. held that the acceptance was conditional only, and that the noting shewed the plaintiff did not choose to take it, and he directed a nonsuit; and upon a rule to shew cause why there should not be a new trial, the court, viz. Willes, Ashhurst, and Buller, Js. concurred that the acceptance was conditional only, but Willes J. thought if there were a doubt whether it was conditional, or whether the plaintiff had precluded himself from insisting upon it, all the facts should have been left to the jury, and he was therefore of opinion that the nonsuit should be set aside; but the other judges thought differently, and the rule was discharged.

only; it being clear that the drawee looked for an opportunity of reimbursing himself, and had three events in contemplation,—the ship's arrival at Bristol, her arrival at London, and her loss; in the two latter he should have the opportunity, and therefore accepted; in the former he should not, and did not accept.

But an answer by the drawee, that he would pay if I. S. would not, but that he must first apply to him, not that he thought he would pay, but because he judged it right to put him to the trial, with an assurance to the holder that he might rest satisfied of the payment, was, before 1 and 2 G. 4. held (48) an absolute acceptance.

---

(48) Wilkinson v. Lutwidge, Str. 648. Two bills drawn on the defendant were sent to him by the plaintiff's agent for acceptance, and he wrote for answer, "The two bills which you sent me, I will pay if the owners of the Queen Anne do not: and they living in Dublin must first apply to them: I hope to have their answer in a week or ten days. I do not expect they will pay them, but I judge it proper to take their answer before I do, which I request you will acquaint Mr. Wilkinson with, and that he may rest satisfied of the payment." He afterwards wrote, "I have not had an opportunity of sending the bills to the owners of the Queen Anne, but will take the first opportunity, and shall then remit to the gentlemen concerned, according to my promise." One of the bills he paid, but being sued upon the other, he contended that his acceptance was conditional only, to pay if the owners of the Queen Anne did not; but Raymond C. J. held it an absolute acceptance, and that the attempt to procure payment from the owners of the Queen Anne was to be made by him, and was wholly for his benefit and accommodation, but that the plaintiff was to have his money at all events. The jury found accordingly for the plaintiff.

If a man purposes making a conditional acceptance only, and commits that acceptance to writing, he should be careful to express the conditions therein; for it may at least be doubted whether parol evidence of such conditions would be admissible; if it were, the onus of proving them would be upon the acceptor, and the proof would be of no avail if the holder, or any person under whom he claims, took the bill without notice of such conditions, and gave a valuable consideration for it.

A conditional acceptance becomes absolute, as soon as its conditions are performed.

Thus an answer by the drawee, that he could not accept until a navy bill should be paid, was thought (49) to operate as an absolute acceptance upon the payment of the navy bill.

So an answer that the bill would not be accepted till certain goods against which it was drawn arrived, was held virtually an acceptance when they did arrive, and were received. (50)

---

(49) Pierson v. Dunlop, ante, p. 132.

(50) Miln v. Prest, Holt, 181. 4 Camp. 393. Indorsee against defendant as acceptor, and question whether what defendant had written or said amounted to an acceptance. The drawer bought wheat for defendant, and in a letter to him defendant said he would accept bills for it when they received notice that the wheat was shipped; this letter had been shewn to plaintiff, (before he took the bill;) when the bill was presented for acceptance, defendant said he would not accept till the wheat arrived; the wheat afterwards arrived, and defendant accepted it and sold it; Gibbs C. J. was clear that the letter would have been no acceptance, had it not been shewn to plaintiff; but he

But if the drawee says he cannot accept without further directions from I. S., and I. S. afterwards desires him to accept, and draw upon A. B. for the amount, the (51) mere drawing upon A. B. will not make this an acceptance, although the actual payment of the bill upon him may.

An acceptance varying from the tenor differs from it either in the (52) sum, the (53) time, the (54) place, or (55) mode of payment.

---

said a conditional acceptance was valid if the conditions were performed; this wheat arrived, and defendant had it and sold it; and he was clear what defendant had done was equivalent to an acceptance, and verdict for plaintiff.

(51) Smith and another v. Nissen and another, 1 Term Rep. 269. Taubert ordered goods of the defendants, and desired them to draw on the plaintiffs for the amount, which they did; the plaintiffs wrote two letters to the defendants, one saying they could not accept, because the defendants had sent more goods than were ordered, but that they had written to Taubert for further directions; the other saying they had written to Taubert and were waiting his answer before they could accept, but had desired the holder to keep the bill; in the mean time, Taubert desired the Plaintiffs to accept, and draw on Goverts for the amount; they accordingly drew on Goverts, who refused to accept, and upon that they paid the bill for the honour of the defendants, and brought an action against them for money paid; the plaintiffs had a verdict, but the defendants moved for a new trial, on the ground that the drawing on Goverts was an acceptance of the bill drawn by the defendants. Sed per cur. What the plaintiffs did, did not amount to an acceptance, for they never meant to make themselves liable, unless the bill they drew was accepted and paid, and a rule was refused.

(52) Vide Wegersloffe v. Keene, ante, p. 135. note (9).

(53) Vide Walker v. Atwood, ante, p. 136. note (9).

Paton v. Winter, 1 Taunt. 420. The drawee altered the time of payment of a bill from one month to two, and accepted it;

The effect of accepting a bill in such way as to make it payable at a bankers, or elsewhere than at the drawee's residence or place of business, (56) has of late been matter of great controversy and difference of opinion, but the point is now settled by 1 and 2 G. 4. c. 78. (57)

By that statute, if the acceptance merely makes it payable at a particular house, without any further expression in such acceptance, it is to be deemed a general acceptance. (57)

If it make it payable at that house *only*, a qualified one. (57)

Though any acceptance varying from the tenor bind the person making it, the holder of a bill is

---

the holder kept it the two months and then presented it for payment; the court held that this was an acquiescence in the alteration, and the holder having brought an action on the case against the acceptor for having mutilated the bill, they directed a nonsuit.

(54) Bishop v. Chitty, and Smith v. De la Fontane, post.

(55) Vide Petit v. Benson, ante, p. 136. note (9).

(56) See post.

(57) By 1 and 2 G. 4. c. 78. After 1st August, 1821, if any person shall accept a bill of exchange, payable at the house of a banker or other place, without further expression in his acceptance, such acceptance shall be deemed and taken to be, to all intents and purposes, a general acceptance of such bill; but if the acceptor shall in his acceptance express that he accepts the bill payable at a banker's house or other place only, and not otherwise or elsewhere, such acceptance shall be a qualified acceptance of such bill, and the acceptor shall not be liable to pay the said bill, except in default of payment when such payment shall have been first duly demanded at such banker's house or other place.

entitled from the undertaking of the drawer and indorsers to expect an absolute acceptance by the drawee, (58) (or if there be several not connected in partnership by (59) each,) for the payment of the full (60) sum of money mentioned therein (61) according to its tenor, specifying (62) (if none be mentioned for the purpose) a place for its payment, and (63) expressing, if the bill be payable within a limited time after sight, the time of its presentment for acceptance; and may reject any other.

If upon the offer of any other acceptance the holder does any act expressing a refusal to take it, as if he gives notice to any of the antecedent parties generally that acceptance is refused, or notes the bill for non-acceptance, the offer (64) is not binding.

---

(58) Mar. 2d ed. 22.

(59) Molloy, B. 2. c. 10. § 18, 19. Mar. 2d ed. 16.

(60) Molloy, B. 2. c. 10. § 20. Mar. 2d. ed. 17. Beawes, § 218. p. 443.

(61) Molloy, B. 2. c. 10. § 28. Mar. 2d ed. 21. Beawes, § 221. p. 444.

See Boehm v. Garcias, 1 Campb. 425. where Lord Ellenborough held that the holder was not bound to take an acceptance to pay in a different kind of currency from that mentioned in the bill.

(62) Mutford v. Walcot, Lord Raym. 575. per Holt C. J. "If a bill be payable at London, and the person on whom it is drawn accept it, but names no house where he will pay it, the party that has the bill is not bound to be satisfied with this acceptance."

(63) Beawes, p. 452. Where a bill is drawn payable at so many days' sight, the acceptance must express the day it is made.

(64) Sproat v. Matthews, ante p. 153. note (47), and Bentinck v. Dorrien, post. p. 162. note (71).

There is a case (65) however in which it has been supposed to have been decided, that if the holder strikes out an acceptance which varies from the tenor of the bill, and substitutes an acceptance according to the tenor, he may afterwards restore the acceptance he struck out, and that such acceptance will continue binding, but it has (66) been doubted whether the determination went farther than to decide that the alteration in the acceptance (though it annulled the acceptance and discharged the acceptor) did not leave the bill in statu quo as to the other parties.

An alteration in a material point certainly vacates an acceptance. (67)

---

(65) Price v. Shute, Beawes, § 222. 1st ed. p. 444. Moll. B. 2. c. 10. § 28. A bill was drawn payable the 1st of January, and the drawee accepted it to pay the 1st of March: the holder struck out the 1st of March, and substituted the 1st of January, and sent the bill for payment on that day, which the acceptor refused: the holder then struck out the 1st of January and restored the 1st of March, and in an action on this bill, the question was, Whether these alterations did not destroy the bill? And Pemberton, C. J. ruled that they did not.

(66) In Master v. Miller, 4 Term Rep. 330. Lord Kenyon, in commenting on the case of Price v. Shute, observes, that the books do not say against whom the action was brought; and it could not have been against the acceptor, because his acceptance was struck out by the party himself who brought the action; and he concludes, "that on the person to whom the bill was directed refusing to accept the bill as it was originally drawn, the holder resorted to the drawer;" however Buller, J. 4 Term Rep. 336., says he cannot consider this case in any other light than as an action against the acceptor, because the books only state what passed between the holder and the acceptor.

(67) Tidmarsh v. Grover, 1 Maule 735. Defendant accepted

And an alteration by substituting or adding a new place for payment is an alteration in a material point. (67)

An acceptance once completed and issued (68) cannot be revoked.

And there are cases (69) in which it was held,

---

a bill "payable at Bloxham and Co's." Bloxham and Co. failed; the holder struck out their names, and without defendant's knowledge or consent inserted "Esdailes."—The point was reserved whether this alteration vacated the acceptance, and the court held it did, and ordered a nonsuit to be entered.

Cowie v. Halsall, 4. Barnew. and Ald. 197. Indorsee against acceptor. It appeared that the acceptance was general, and that the drawer, without the acceptor's knowledge, added to the acceptance "payable at Mr. B.'s, Chiswell-street," and on the ground that this was a material alteration, and vacated the acceptance, verdict for defendant. Motion for a new trial; but the court thought the verdict right, for this alteration would lead to a presentment at B.'s, not at defendant's, and the bill might be treated as dishonoured, and defendant be arrested thereon, without any presentment where defendant would expect it; and rule refused.

(68) See Marius, p. 20. and the cases mentioned in the two next notes.

(69) Thornton and another v. Dick and another, 4 Esp. N. P. C. 270. A bill was drawn on the defendants, payable three months after sight, was, on the 1st of October, left with them by the plaintiffs for acceptance. It was not called for until the 11th; when it appeared that the words, "Accepted the 1st of Oct. 1799. Q. Dick and Co." had been written upon the bill, and afterwards nearly obliterated by ink. The words however were still legible. At the time of drawing the bill the defendants were in advance to the drawer. The plaintiffs, as indorsees, sued the defendants as acceptors. The acceptance and subsequent cancellation were admitted: and the only question was, whether the cancellation, having been made before

that if the drawee wrote an acceptance upon a bill he could not afterwards cancel it, though he

---

the re-delivery of the bill, had discharged the acceptor. Lord Ellenborough said, that if a party once accepted a bill he had done the act, and could not retract; and that there was no difference in point of legal effect, whether the bill were payable after sight or after date. Verdict for the Plaintiffs. — Trimmer v. Oddie was cited: in that case however the declaration contained counts against the drawee for having mutilated the bill.

Trimmer v. Oddie, 1800. A bill was left for acceptance and accepted, but the acceptance was afterwards cut off, and the bill returned in that mutilated state. Lord Kenyon was clearly of opinion, that the acceptance once made could not be revoked, and that the acceptor was still bound. This case was cited in Bentinck v. Dorrien, 6 East. Rep. 200., and the Hamburgh ordinance was referred to as having been recognized by Lord Kenyon to be the law of merchants here: and Lord Ellenborough said, "The rule is certainly laid down in the Hamburgh ordinance as stated, that an acceptance once made cannot be revoked; though, to be sure, that leaves the question open as to what is an acceptance, whether it be perfected before the delivery of the bill." And Lawrence J. in the case last mentioned, 6 East. Rep. 201., said, "When the general question shall arise, it will be worth considering how that which is not communicated to the holder, can be considered as an acceptance while it is yet in the hands of the drawee; and where he obliterates it before any communication made to the holder." From this it would appear, that Mr. J. Lawrence had taken the same view of this question as Pothier, who cites from La Serra, ch. 10. a case where the holder of a bill having left it for acceptance, the drawee, before he returned it, cancelled an acceptance which he had written and signed upon it, and it was adjudged that this acceptance was annulled; and observes, "La raison est, que le concours de volontés qui forme un "contrat, est un concours de volontes que les parties se sont "reciproquement déclarées; sans cela, la volonté d'une partie "ne peut acquérir de droit à l'autre partie, ni par conséquent "être irrévocable. Suivant ces principes, pour que le contrat

cancelled it whilst the bill remained in his possession, and before it had been called for by the holder. But the contrary has since (70) been decided.

And before this decision it was adjudged, that if upon such a cancellation, the holder noted the bill for non-acceptance, he (71) precluded himself from insisting that the acceptance was binding.

" entre le propriétaire de la lettre et celui sur qui elle est tirée, " soit parfait, il ne suffit pas que celui-ci ait eu pendant quelque " temps la volonté d'accepter la lettre, et qu'il ait écrit au bas " qu'il l'acceptoit ; tant qu'il n'a pas déclaré cette volonté au " porteur, le contrat n'est pas parfait ; il peut changer de " volonté, et rayer son acceptation." — Traté du Contrat de Change, part 1. ch. iii. § 3. pl. 44. — See also Emerigon Traité des Assurances, ch. ii. § 4. p. 45., who observes, that La Serra " pose en maxime, que tant que l'acceptant est maitre de sa " signature, c'est-à-dire, qu'il n'a pas délivré la lettre de change, " il peut rayer son acceptation." — See also Stevenson on Bills, p. 162—164.

(70) Cox v. Troy, 5 Barnew. and Ald. 474. A bill on defendant and Co. for 938*l*. 16*s*. 10*d*., payable sixty-one days after sight, was put into their bill box for acceptance the 24th of May, 1820; they wrote an acceptance upon it, and dated it 24th May, 1820; the bill was not called for till the 27th of May, and before that time the acceptance was erased by inking it over: when, or by whom that was done, did not appear. Plaintiffs brought an action on the ground that the writing the acceptance bound the drawee, and that he could not afterwards cancel his acceptance: but on case, the court were clear the acceptance might be cancelled at any time before it was delivered out by the drawee, and they ordered the postea to be delivered to the defendant. Plaintiff had leave to turn the case into a special verdict. See also ante, p. 160. note (2.)

(71) Bentinck v. Dorrien and another, 6 East. 199. This action which was by an indorsee against the defendants as acceptors of a bill, was referred ; and the arbitrator, after reciting

And if an acceptance is struck out before a bill left for acceptance is called for, the drawee is not compellable to shew in evidence why it was struck out, or when, or by whom. (72)

And it makes no difference though the bill is left beyond the usual time with the drawee, if the delay is imputable not to the drawee but to the holder.

The obligation also of a complete acceptance may be (73) waived.

---

in his award that the plaintiff on the 31st of May, left the bill with the defendants for acceptance, that they signed an acceptance thereon, but that, on the 1st of June, and *before the bill was called for*, they cancelled that acceptance, and that the plaintiff thereupon noted the bill for non-acceptance, declared himself to be of opinion, that by such noting the plaintiff had precluded himself from insisting that the defendants had bound themselves to pay the bill, and therefore awarded in favour of the Defendants. A rule nisi was obtained for setting aside this award, on the ground that the acceptance was irrevocable. But after cause shewn, the court held that whether such acceptance could or could not be revoked, the plaintiff had, at all events, by noting the bill for non-acceptance, precluded himself from contending that the acceptance was valid. Rule discharged. See Sproat v. Matthews, ante, p. 153. note (47).

(72) See Cox. v. Troy, ante p. 162.

(73) Vide Walpole v. Pulteney, and Black v. Peele, post. p. 164., and Mason v. Hunt, post. p. 165. note (76); — and in Dingwall v. Dunster, post. p. 169. note (84), the whole court held, that though nothing short of an express agreement would discharge the acceptor, an express agreement would.

Whatley v. Tricker, 1 Campb. 35. The indorsees of a bill, knowing that it had been accepted for the accommodation of the drawer, and possessing goods of the drawer's, from the produce of which they expected payment, said, (at a meeting of

further trouble, is an express waiver*; the receipt
This waiver may be either expressed or implied.

An (74) agreement to consider an acceptance as at an end, or a (75) message to the acceptor upon an accommodation bill, that the business was settled with the drawer, and he need give himself no

---

the acceptors' creditors) that "they looked to the drawer, and should not come upon the acceptors." In consequence of which the latter assigned their property for the benefit of their creditors, and paid them 15*s.* in the pound. The drawer's goods however proved to be of little value, and he became insolvent, upon which the indorsees sued the acceptors. Lord Ellenborough said, that if the plaintiff's language amounted to an unconditional renunciation of all claim upon the acceptors, whereby the latter had entered into the arrangement with their creditors, the acceptors were discharged; if only to a conditional promise, not to resort to the acceptors, if satisfied elsewhere, they were not. The jury found for the plaintiffs.

(74) Walpole v. Pulteney, cited Dougl. 236, 237—248, 249. Walpole held a bill accepted by Pulteney, but agreed to consider his acceptance as at an end, and wrote in his bill-book, opposite the entry of this bill, "Mr. Pulteney's acceptance at an end." Walpole kept the bill from 1772 to 1775, without calling upon Pulteney, and then brought this action. The jury found a verdict for the plaintiff; but the court of exchequer thought the verdict wrong, and granted a new trial, upon which the jury found for the defendant.

(75) Black v. Peele, cit. Dougl. 236, 237—248, 249. Black arrested Peele as acceptor of a bill drawn by Dallas, but on finding that the acceptance was an accommodation one, his attorney took a security from Dallas, and sent word to Peele that he had settled with Dallas, and that Peele need give himself no further trouble; Dallas afterwards became bankrupt, upon which Black again sued Peele; but it was held, that as Black had in express words discharged Peele, the action could not be maintained.

(76) of the known consideration of the acceptance, an implied one.

But a declaration by the holder that he should look to the drawer for payment, and that he wanted no more of the acceptor than another debt, not connected with the bill, will not be sufficient to discharge the acceptor. (77)

Though in consequence of that declaration, the acceptor pays the other debt. (77)

---

(76) Mason v. Hunt, Dougl. 284. 297. ante p. 133. note (3). Rowland Hunt agreed that his partner, Thomas Hunt, should, on consignment of a cargo, and an order for its insurance, accept bills for 3,600*l*. The cargo was consigned, the order for insurance given, and Thomas Hunt effected the insurance, but he refused to accept the bills; after some negociation, the plaintiff being the holder, signed a memorandum, by which, after stating that the consignment had been made on account of the bills, and that the Hunts, being apprehensive that the net proceeds might not be sufficient to discharge them, had refused to accept, he accepted the bill of lading and policy, and undertook to apply the net proceeds, when in cash, as far as they would go, to the credit of the payee, in part payment of the bills; the plaintiff afterwards sued the Hunts; and insisted that Rowland Hunt's agreement was an acceptance: but after a verdict for the defendant, and time taken to consider upon a rule to shew cause why there should not be a new trial, the whole court was clear that by the memorandum the plaintiff had waived all right to insist on Rowland Hunt's agreement, for it was obvious that the whole consideration of the acceptance was the consignment, upon which there would be a commission, and the policy, and these the plaintiff had taken to himself.

(77) Parker v. Leigh, 2 Stark. 228. In an action against the acceptor on a bill for 300*l*., the defendant proved that he

If the holder of a bill receives a part of the money from the drawer, and takes a promise from him upon the back of the bill for the payment of the residue at an enlarged time, it (78) is for a jury to say whether this is not a waiver of the acceptance.

---

owed plaintiff 700*l.*, or warrants of attorney, and that plaintiff had said, that as to the 300*l.* bill, he should look to the drawer for that, and that he wanted no more from defendant than what was included in the warrants of attorney, and that in consequence of this declaration, defendant paid plaintiff what was included in the warrants of attorney; but Lord Ellenborough held, that as plaintiff had not expressly renounced all claim upon this acceptance, it continued binding, and the plaintiff had a verdict.

(78) Ellis v. Galindo, B.R.M. 24 Geo. 3. cited Dougl. 250. note. James Galindo drew upon his brother for 30*l.* in favour of the plaintiff; when the bill became due James paid the plaintiff 3*l.* 15*s.* 4*d.* and indorsed a promise to pay the remainder in three months. Three years elapsed, and then the plaintiff sued the drawee upon his acceptance. Lord Mansfield thought the defendant discharged, and nonsuited the plaintiff. An application was made for a new trial, when Lord Mansfield said, he thought the case did not interfere with that of Dingwall v. Dunster, but a rule to shew cause was granted: after cause was shewn, Lord Mansfield said, "The doubt is, whether the question should not have been left to the jury, it being a question of intention arising out of the circumstances." Willes J. thought it should have been left to the jury; and per Buller J. "I rather think the case should have gone to the jury; but I am not therefore of opinion that there ought to be a new trial; the indorsement could not have been meant as an additional security, for the drawer was equally liable before. I should have left the question to the jury, but with very strong observations; and as the demand is so small, I do not think there ought to be a new trial." Rule discharged.

Where a bill has been accepted for the mere accommodation of the drawer, it has been held, that if the holder, knowing that circumstance, give time to the drawer, he (79) will discharge the acceptor.

But this has been doubted. (80) (81) (82)

Especially if the holder when he took the bill, did not know it was an accommodation acceptance. (81)

---

(79) Laxton v. Peat, 2 Campb. N. P. C. 185. The holder of a bill, knowing that it had been accepted for the accommodation of the drawer, received part payment from the drawer, and gave him time for payment of the remainder; he now sued the acceptor; but Lord Ellenborough held, that the acceptor was a mere surety, and by time having been given to the principal, was discharged. Nonsuit.

(80) Raggett v. Axmore, 4 Taunt. 730. In an action against the acceptor of a bill, motion for new trial, on the ground that it was an accommodation acceptance, and that the holder had given time to the drawer. Sed per Mansfield C. J. there was no sufficient evidence that it was an accommodation acceptance; nevertheless, excepting in the case in Campbell, it never was known that any thing passing between other parties could discharge an acceptor; but it is unnecessary to decide that question.

(81) Fentum v. Pocock, 5 Taunt. 192. Indorsee against acceptor, on bill drawn by Beazley. Defence, that plaintiff had taken a cognovit from Beazley, payable at a future day, without defendant's privity or consent; that defendant's was a mere accommodation acceptance, and that plaintiff knew it was so when he took the cognovit from Beazley: Mansfield C. J. thought this no answer to the action; and verdict for plaintiff. On rule nisi for nonsuit, and cause shewn, two cases were cited in which Lord Ellenborough, under similar circumstances, held the acceptor discharged; but the court thought those cases wrong; and rule discharged. Mansfield C. J. noticed that plaintiff did not know, when he took the bill, that it was an accommodation acceptance, but he disclaimed proceeding on that ground.

Or if it were duly presented, when due, to the acceptor, and he promised payment. (82)

Telling an accommodation acceptor that he shall not be troubled about the bill, will not discharge him, though the party knew him to be an accommodation acceptor only, if such party held for value. (83)

But a neglect to call upon an acceptor, or an indulgence to any of the other parties, though for

---

(82) Kerrison v. Cooke, 3. Campb. 362. Indorsee against acceptor. Defence, that it was an accommodation acceptance to accommodate the drawer, that plaintiff knew it, and that on the bill's becoming due, plaintiff gave time to the drawer without the concurrence of defendant; and Laxton v. Peat was cited as in point: when the bill was due it was presented to defendant, and he promised payment; per Gibbs J. "Grave doubts have been entertained of Laxton v. Peat, and this case may be distinguished from it; here payment is demanded of defendant, and he promises payment. I think the giving time under these circumstances to the drawer did not discharge the acceptor." Verdict for plaintiff.

Sed vide Adams v. Gregg—the next case.

(83) Adams v. Gregg, 2 Stark. 531. Defendant accepted a bill to accommodate Holmes, and plaintiff knew it; Holmes paid it to plaintiff for an old debt; when it became due defendant could not pay it, and one Jones gave plaintiff the amount, on a stipulation that he should, if necessary, stand in plaintiff's situation. Defendant asked Jones to give up the bill, which he refused, but he said defendant should not be troubled about it. Jones afterwards sued defendant in plaintiff's name; defendant insisted she was discharged. Abbott C. J. seemed to think she would have been, had Jones given time to the drawer, or disabled himself for a moment from suing him; but he thought Jones's declaration that defendant should not be troubled, no discharge, and plaintiff had a verdict.

ever so long a time, shall (84) not be considered as a waiver.

If the holder of a bill agree not to sue the acceptor, upon his making an affidavit that the acceptance is a forgery, he will be (85) precluded from

---

(84) Dingwall v. Dunster, Dougl. 235. 247. Dunster lent Wheate his acceptance, which became due 13th December, 1774; it was then in the hands of Dingwall, but he finding that Wheate was the real debtor, wrote to his attorney in February and November, 1775, for payment, received interest upon the bill from Wheate, and suffered several years to elapse without calling on Dunster; on 13th of February, 1775, Dunster wrote to thank Dingwall for not proceeding against him, and said he had been informed by a person Dingwall had sent, that Wheate had taken up the bill; but Dingwall took no notice of this letter: he aftewards sued Dunster, for whom the jury found; but upon a rule to shew cause why there should not be a new trial, the whole court held there was nothing in the plaintiff's conduct to discharge Dunster; that it meant nothing more than an indulgence to him and that he would try to recover from the drawer if he could; but by Lord Mansfield, no use had been made of the defendant's letter; probably the fact did not warrant him in asserting that a person the plaintiff sent had told him Wheate had taken up the bill; had the plaintiff by any thing in his conduct, confirmed him in such a belief, it might have altered the case.

Anderson v. Cleveland, 13 East's Rep. 430. n. In an action by an indorsee against the acceptor of a bill, no demand was proved till three months after the bill was due, and when the drawer had become insolvent. But by Lord Mansfield, the acceptor of a bill, or maker of a note, always remains liable. The acceptance is proof of having assets in his hands, and he ought never to part with them, unless he be sure that the bill is paid by the drawer.

(85) Stevens v. Thacker, Peake, N. P. C. 187. The plaintiff, who was indorsee of a bill, presented it to the defendant, as acceptor, for payment. The defendant said the acceptance was

suing him, if such affidavit be made and sworn, though it be false.

---

a forgery, and offered to make an affidavit that he had never accepted the bill. The plaintiff at first agreed not to sue him, if he would make such affidavit; but being afterwards convinced that the defendant had accepted the bill, refused to receive the affidavit, and brought this action. The affidavit had been engrossed, but not sworn. It was urged, that the plaintiff could not recede from his agreement. But Lord Kenyon said, that had the affidavit been sworn, he should have held that the defendant had discharged himself from this action, though such affidavit had been false. But not having been sworn, the defendant was still liable, unless he could prove the acceptance a forgery. Verdict for the plaintiff.

CAP. VII.

THE receipt of a bill or note implies an undertaking from the receiver to (1) every party to the

(1) Vide post, p. 231 to 243.

bill or note who would be entitled to bring an action on paying it, to (2) present in proper time the one, where necessary, for acceptance, and each for payment, to (3) allow no extra time for payment, and to give (4) notice without delay to such person of a failure in the attempt to procure a proper acceptance or payment ; and a (5) default in any of these respects will discharge such person from all responsibility on account of a non-acceptance or non-payment, and unless (6) the bill or note were on an improper stamp, make it (7) operate as a satisfaction of any debt or demand for which it was given.

---

(2) Vide post, p. 182 to 186.

(3) Vide Tindal v. Brown, post, p. 207. note (74).

(4) Vide post p. 205 to 243.

(5) Vide post, p. 205 to 243.

Syderbottom v. Smith, Str. 649. In an action against the indorser of a note, Eyre, C. J. of the Common Pleas, directed the jury to find for the defendant, because the plaintiff had not proved diligence to get the money from the maker; being of *the old* opinion that the indorser only warrants upon default of the maker.

Gee v. Brown, Str. 792. The holder of an inland bill gave the acceptor time, by intervals, from 14th of May, when the bill became due, to 7th of June, and then sued the drawer; but there being no notice to him, Eyre C. J. held the loss ought to fall on the plaintiff.

(6) See Wilson v. Visar, ante, p. 62.

(7) By 3 and 4 Ann. c. 9. § 7. It is enacted, that if any person doth accept any such bill of exchange, for and in satisfaction of any former debt, or sum of money formerly due unto him, the same shall be accounted and esteemed a full and

The presentment is to be made where the bill or note is payable.

If the drawee or maker cannot be found at the place where the bill or note is payable, and it appears that he never lived there, or has (8) absconded, the bill or note is to be considered as dishonoured, especially if he cannot be heard of at any of the banking-houses there; (9) if he has only removed, the holder (10) must endeavour to find out to what place he has removed, and make the presentment there.

If on a presentment it appears that the drawee or maker is dead, the holder (11) should enquire

---

complete payment of such debt, if such person accepting of any such bill for his debt, doth not take his due course to obtain payment thereof, by endeavouring to get the same accepted and paid, and make his protest as aforesaid, either for non-acceptance or non-payment thereof.

(8) Anon. Lord Raym. 743. "The custom of merchants is, that if B., upon whom a bill of exchange is drawn, absconds before the day of payment, the man to whom it is payable may protest it, to have better security for the payment, and to give notice to the drawer of the absconding of B." Proved by merchants at Guildhall, Tr. 6 W. and M., before Treby C. J.

(9) See Hardy v. Woodroffe, post.

(10) Collins v. Butler, Str. 1087. The maker of a note shut up his house before the note became due, and in an action against an indorser, the question was, whether the plaintiff had shewn sufficient in proving that the house was shut up? and Lee C. J. thought not, but that he should have given in evidence that he enquired after the maker, or attempted to find him out. Vide Bateman v. Joseph, p. 228. n. (105).

(11) Molloy, B. 2. c. 10. § 34. "If a bill be accepted, and

after his personal representative, and if he lives within a reasonable distance, present the bill or note to him.

If, in the absence of a drawee, a bill has been accepted by his agent, and at the time when the bill becomes due, the drawee be still absent, presentment for payment (12) should be made to such agent.

If a bill or note is made payable at a banker's, it is (13) sufficient to present it for payment at the banker's, and if the banker is himself the holder, it is (13) sufficient for him to see whether he has effects in hand.

If a bill or note is made payable at a particular house, that house is the proper place at which to make the presentment, whether such house be mentioned in the body of the bill or note, or

---

the party dies, yet there must be a demand made of his executors or administrators; and in default of payment, a protest must be made."

(12) See Philips v. Astling, post, p. 232.

(13) Saunderson and others v. Judge, 2 H. Bl. 509. A note made payable at the plaintiffs' was indorsed to them; when it became due, the maker having no effects in their hands, they wrote to one of the indorsers to say it was not honoured, and afterwards brought an action against him; but it appearing that they had made no demand on the maker, they were non-suited; on shewing cause however against a rule for a new trial, the court held, that it was sufficient to present the note where the maker made it payable, and as the persons at whose house it was made payable were themselves the holders, it was sufficient for them to refer to their books, and see whether they had effects in hand; and a new trial was granted.

in a marginal note only, or in the acceptance only. (14)

And if such house be mentioned in the body of a note, a presentment there is necessary even to charge the maker. (15)

---

(14) Ambrose v. Hopwood, 2 Taunt. 61. In an action against the drawer of a bill, the declaration stated the bill to have been accepted by the drawee, payable at Messrs. Freeman's and Co., No. 6. Church-street, Bermondsey, Southwark, and averred that the bill was in due manner presented to them for payment, not saying in *Church-Street*, &c. and dishonoured. On special demurrer for other causes (which were abandoned) it was contended that there was no due averment of a presentment for payment, and that this objection, which was *not one of the causes* assigned, went to the substance of the case. The court held the objection fatal, but permitted the plaintiff to amend on payment of costs.

See Garnett v. Woodcock, 1 Stark. 475.

(15) Sanderson v. Bowes and others, B. R. M. 52 Geo. III. In an action on twelve country bank notes, for 1*l.* 1*s.* each, issued by the defendants from their banking-house at Workington, the declaration contained a count upon each note, stating that the defendants made a certain promissory note, " and thereby, on demand, promised to pay at the banking-house at Workington, to one R. N. or bearer," the sum of 1*l.* 1*s.*; and that thereby the defendants became liable, and promised to pay, according to the tenor and effect of the note. There was, however, no averment of a presentment for, or demand of, payment at the banking house; but only the usual allegation, that the defendants, " although often requested," (without saying where) had refused to pay. To these counts there was a general demurrer and joinder; and after argument, the court held, that there being no privity between these parties but in respect of the note, and that being a contract to pay at a particular place, a demand of payment at that place was in the nature of a condition precedent to the plaintiff's right to recover; and there

And so it is if it be printed on the note, though by way of memorandum only. (16)

---

being no averment of such demand, the defendants were entitled to judgment; and they gave judgment accordingly.

Dickinson v. Bowes, 16 East. 110. Action against the makers on fifty-six guinea notes; they were dated Workington Bank, and ran thus: "On demand I promise to pay at the banking-house here to R. W. or bearer, the sum of one guinea, value received." Proof was given that thirty-two were presented for payment at the banking-house at Workington, and payment refused; but there was no such proof as to the other twenty-four, and on point saved, the court held that plaintiff could only recover in respect of the thirty-two, and judgment accordingly.

Howe v. Bowes, 16 East. 112. Action on a similar note for five guineas against the makers, instead of averring presentment plaintiff alleged that defendants became insolvent, and ceased and wholly declined and refused to pay at the banking-house aforesaid, the sum specified in any note issued by them, and he proved that the shop was shut up and no notes paid there for some time before the action; the jury considered this proof as making out the averment, and verdict for plaintiff: and on rule nisi to set aside the verdict, and cause shewn, the court thought the verdict right; the shutting up the shop was in substance a refusal to make any payments there, and rule discharged. But on error, the Exchequer chamber thought the allegations in the declaration not sufficient to excuse a presentment, and reversed the judgment, 5 Taunt. 30.

(16) Trecothick v. Edwin, 1 Stark. 468. The whole of a note, except the names of parties, sum, and date, was printed; and at the bottom was printed, "at Barclay, Tritton, and Co.'s." In an action against the maker, a question was made whether it was necessary to prove a presentment at Barclay and Co.'s; and Lord Ellenborough held it was, because the stipulation being printed, must have been on the note at the time the note was made, and was to be considered part of the note. The proof was then given, and the plaintiff had a verdict.

And if such house be mentioned in an acceptance, and the acceptance makes the bill payable there *and not otherwise or elsewhere*, a presentment there will be necessary to charge the acceptor. (17)

---

(17) See 1 and 2 Geo. 4. ante, p. 157.

Callaghan v. Aylett, 3 Taunt. 397., 2 Campb. 549. In an action against the acceptor of a bill, it appeared that the bill was accepted, payable at Messrs. Ramsbottoms', bankers, London; and two objections were taken to the plaintiff's right to recover; first, that there was a variance between the acceptance proved, which was a special one, and that averred in the declaration, which was general; and secondly, that there was no proof of a presentment for payment at the place where the bill, by the acceptance, had been made payable. A verdict was found for the plaintiff, subject to the opinion of the court upon these points, which were reserved. A rule nisi to set aside this verdict and enter a nonsuit, was obtained; and after cause shewn, the court (Mansfield C. J. absente) held, that the place where a bill is made payable must be considered as part of the contract between the acceptor and the holder; that this was a special and qualified acceptance, binding the acceptor to pay at Ramsbottom's, and not universally. They said, it seemed fair that when a party had provided funds at his banker's for the due satisfaction of a bill, he should be allowed to protect himself from the risk of being arrested upon it by a malicious creditor. They referred to Parker v. Gordon, 7 East, 385., and said it could make no difference (for this purpose) whether the action were against the drawer or acceptor. Rule absolute.

Gammon v. Schmoll, 5 Taunt. 344. Bill directed to defendant, Bath: the declaration alleged that he accepted it, "payable at Batson's, London;" there was no averment of a presentment at Batson's. Demurrer on that ground; and after argument, the court held the averment essential, and the declaration, for want of it, bad.

But where a particular house is mentioned in a note by way of marginal memorandum only, presentment at that house may not be necessary to charge the maker; (18)

Nor is it, (since 1 & 2 Geo. 4. c. 78., on acceptances made after 1st August, 1821,) to charge an acceptor, where the acceptance mentions that house without further expressions to make it the exclusive place of payment. (19)

Rowe v. Young, 2 Brod. 165. Bill directed to defendant at Torpoint, Devon: the declaration alleged that he accepted it, payable at Sir John Perring and Co.'s, bankers, London: the action was by an indorsee; and on error, objection that there was no averment of presentment at Sir John Perring's, and the House of Lords held the objection fatal; and judgment for plaintiff below reversed.

(18) In Wild v. Rennards, 1 Campb. N. P. C. 425. n. Bayley J. held, that if a promissory note be made payable at a particular place, there is no necessity for proving, in an action against the maker, that it has been presented there for payment. And upon this case being cited in Sanderson v. Bowes, Bayley J. said, that as far as he could recollect, the place was not incorporated with the body of the note; it was only mentioned in a memorandum at the bottom. And in Callaghan v. Aylett, 2 Campb. N. P. C. 551., and Sanderson v. Judge, 2 H. Bl. 509., the same distinction is taken.

Price v. Mitchell, 4 Campb. 200. At the bottom of a note was written, "At Vere and Co.'s, 77, Lombard-street." In an action against the maker, it was urged that plaintiff ought to prove a presentment at Vere and Co.'s; but as the direction was only at the foot of the note, and not part of the note, Gibbs C. J. thought otherwise, and the plaintiff had a verdict.

(19) See 1 and 2 Geo. 4. ante p. 157.

Fenton v. Goundry, 13 East's Rep. 459. Drawer against acceptor of a bill. The declaration stated, that the defendant

And where a bill is so accepted as to make it necessary even to charge the acceptor that it should be presented for payment at a particular place, a neglect to present it there the very day it becomes due will not discharge the acceptor, unless the money is lost in consequence of such neglect. (20)

If the money is lost in consequence, it may. (20)

---

accepted the bill, payable at Sykes and Co.'s, and thereby became liable and promised to pay according to the tenor and effect of the bill and of his acceptance. There was no averment of a presentment for payment at Sykes and Co.'s, nor of any demand upon the defendant other than the common allegation that the defendant, "although often requested," had not paid the bill. The defendant demurred specially, and assigned for cause, the want of an averment of a due presentment for payment. And after argument, the court (Le Blanc J. absente) held, that the place mentioned in the acceptance was only an intimation to the holder where the acceptor was to be found; that it formed no part of the contract that the bill should be presented there; and that the acceptance, though stated to be payable at a particular place, bound the party to pay the bill generally and universally. The court, however, being desirous of looking into the case of Callaghan v. Aylett, which was cited, gave judgment nisi for the plaintiff; but they did not mention the case again in the course of the term, and the judgment therefore stood for the plaintiff.

Head v. Sewell, Holt, 363. Action against acceptor on acceptance payable at Messrs. Harrison's, Picket-street. Gibbs C. J. held proof of presentment at that place not necessary.

(20) Rhodes v. Gent, 5 Barnew. 244. In an action on an acceptance, payable, when due, at Messrs. P. and H.'s. bankers, London, it was proved that the bill was presented for payment at Messrs. P. and H.'s, but that such presentment was not until several days after the bill became due. Abbot C. J. thought

If a check upon a banker be lodged with another banker, a presentment by the letter at the clearing house is (21) sufficient.

A presentment should be made at a seasonable time.

If by the known custom of any place, bills and notes are only payable within limited hours, a presentment *there* out of those hours is unreasonable.

And so is a presentment out of the hours of business to a person of a particular description, as a (22) banker in a place where, by the known

---

the plaintiff nevertheless entitled to a verdict; and on motion to set aside the verdict, all the judges in court, viz. Abbott C.J., and Holroyd and Best Js., held, that as the bill had been presented at the banker's, and the non-payment arose not because the bankers had failed, but from some other cause, and the acceptor was not prejudiced by the postponement of the presentment, such postponement was no defence to him; and a rule was refused.

(21) See Robson v. Bennett, post, p. 195. n. (47)

(22) Parker v. Gordon, 7 East's Rep. 385. The drawee accepted the bill, payable at Davison and Co.'s, his bankers; at the part of the town where Davison and Co. lived, bankers shut up at six o'clock. The bill was not presented for payment until after six, when the shop was shut up, and the clerks gone. In an action against the drawer, Lord Ellenborough held that this was not a good presentment, and nonsuited the plaintiff: and on motion for a new trial, the court held, that if a party took an acceptance payable at a banker's, he bound himself to present the bill during the banking hours; and therefore rule refused.

N. Lawrence and Le Blanc Js. said, the holder was not bound to take such an acceptance.

custom of that place, all persons of his description begin and leave off business at stated hours.

But to an acceptor not so circumstanced (23),

Elford v. Tred, 1 Maule and Selw. 28. The drawee accepted a bill, payable at his banker's, Hodsoll and Co.; the only evidence of a presentment was by a notary's clerk, between half after six and seven in the evening: the banking-house was then shut, and the answer at the private door was "no orders." Lord Ellenborough allowed plaintiff to take a verdict, with liberty to defendant to move to enter a nonsuit; rule nisi: and on cause shewn, the court thought this presentment too late; that it furnished no ground for presuming that there had been a prior presentment by the holder within the banking-hours; but that plaintiff might have an opportunity of proving such a presentment, they allowed him to have a new trial on his paying the costs.

(23) Barclay v. Bailey, 2 Campb. N. P. C. 527. This was an action against the drawer of a bill. At eight o'clock in the evening of the day on which it became due, it was presented at the house of the acceptor in London, for payment; and the answer given was, that the acceptor had become bankrupt, and had removed into another quarter of the town. It was, however, proved that a person had been stationed at the house from nine o'clock till four, for the purpose of taking up this bill, but that it was not presented within those hours. Lord Ellenborough held, that the acceptor being a common trader, not a banker, the presentment was good; and said, that eight o'clock in the evening, could not be considered an unseasonable hour for demanding payment at the house of a private merchant who had accepted a bill. Verdict for the plaintiff.

Morgan v. Davison, 1 Stark. 114. A bill made payable at Herring & Co.'s (not bankers), Copthall-court, was presented there between six and seven in the evening the day it became due; there was only a girl there, who was left to take care of the counting-house. In action by indorsee against drawer, Lord Ellenborough held this a sufficient presentment, the hour being one at which the holder might reasonably expect to find the party in his counting-house.

eight o'clock in the evening is not an unseasonable hour for making a presentment for payment.

And no objection can be made to a presentment on the ground of its being at an unseasonable hour if a person is stationed there at the time to give an answer. (24)

Therefore a presentment at a banker's out of the usual hours will be unobjectionable, if the banker or any agent on his behalf, is there at the time of such presentment. (24)

A presentment for acceptance is not (25) neces-

---

(24) Garnett v. Woodcock, 1 Stark. 476. In an action against the acceptor, on a bill made payable in London, and accepted payable at Dennison and Co.'s, plaintiff proved a presentment at Dennison and Co.'s between seven and eight o'clock in the evening, and that a boy returned for answer "no orders." It was insisted that this presentment, being at a London banker's, was at an unseasonable hour; but Lord Ellenborough said, if the banker appointed a person to attend to give an answer, a presentment at any time whilst that person was in attendance would be sufficient. Plaintiff had a verdict, and a rule to set it aside was refused.

(25) Molloy, B. 2. c. 10. § 16. "If a bill is drawn upon a merchant in London, payable to I. S. at double usance, I. S. is not bound in strictness of law to procure an acceptance, but only to tender the bill when the money is due."

Beawes, § 266. p. 453. "There is no obligation to procure acceptance to a bill payable at a day certain, as the time goes on, whether accepted or not; but it is otherwise with bills payable at so many days sight." See also Mar. 12, 13. and Blesard v. Hirst, and Goodall v. Dolley, post.

Indeed in all cases where a bill is remitted to a factor or agent, it may be his duty to apply for an acceptance, and he may be answerable for any loss his principal may suffer by a neglect; but this neglect does not affect the bill, if payable otherwise

sary, except upon bills payable within a limited time after sight.

No (26) certain time is fixed within which this presentment must be made, but it should (27) be made within a reasonable time.

What shall be deemed a reasonable time must depend upon the particular circumstances of each case.

Keeping it a whole day, exclusive of the day of receiving it, without negotiating it or sending it for acceptance, is not necessarily an unreasonable delay. (28)

No delay warranted by the common course of business is improper, nor is any delay which is occasioned by keeping the bill in (29) circulation at a distance from the place where it is payable; but a delay by locking it up for any length of time (30) is.

---

than after sight, nor the principal's right thereon. Vide Beawes, § 49. p. 420. Mar. 12, 13.

(26) Per Eyre C. J. and Heath J. H. Bl. 569, 570.

(27) Per Eyre C. J. 2 H. Bl. 569.

(28) Fry v. Hill, 7 Taunt. 397. Plaintiff took a bill at Windsor on Friday, payable in London a month after sight. What he did with it did not appear, but it was not presented for acceptance till Tuesday: it was left to the jury whether there was a default to present within a reasonable time, and they found for plaintiff; and on motion for new trial, the court said, it would still be a question for the jury whether there had been a presentment in reasonable time; and as they had passed their judgment on that point, rule refused.

(29) See ante, n. (27)

(30) Per Buller J. 2 H. Bl. 170. See Muilman v. D'Eguino, infra, note (31)

If a bill payable abroad at a certain time after sight is taken in a course of negotiation (31), it is

---

(31) Muilman v. D'Eguino, 2 H. Bl. 565. In debt on bond conditioned to pay certain bills drawn on India at sixty days after sight, in case they should be returned protested, defendant pleaded that they were not presented for acceptance within a reasonable time after the drawing: it appeared that they were drawn 5th of March, 1793; that they were indorsed on that day by defendant to plaintiffs, who procured them for a house at Paris; that plaintiffs sent immediate advice to the house at Paris, and on receiving their directions on 30th of April, sent them to India, where they arrived the 3d of October; on the 5th of October, the holder wrote to the drawee, who was from home, desiring him to accept the bills, and on the 17th of October, he sent an answer of refusal; some of the bills were thereupon protested 29th of October, and the rest 18th of November. Eyre C. J. left the case to the jury, but told them, he thought the bills had been sent to India in time, as they were put up here for negotiation, and were therefore liable to be delayed, and that they were presented in India in time after their arrival. The jury found for the plaintiff; and on a rule to shew cause why there should not be a new trial, and cause shewn, the court was satisfied with the verdict, and plaintiff had judgment. Eyre C. J. said, " It is not necessary to lay down any new rule as to bills of exchange payable at sight, or within a given time afterwards; if it were, I should feel great anxiety not to clog the negotiation of bills circumstanced like these. It would be a very serious and difficult thing to say, that a person buying a foreign bill, in the way these were bought, should be obliged to transmit it by the first opportunity to the place of its destination. There would also be a great difficulty in saying *at what time* such a bill should be presented for acceptance. The courts have been very cautious in fixing any time for presenting for acceptance an inland bill, payable at a certain period after sight, and it seems to me more necessary to be cautious with respect to a foreign bill payable in that manner I think, indeed, the holder is bound to present the bill in reasonable time, in order that the period may commence from

not necessary to send it by the first opportunity to the place where it is payable.

---

which the payment is to take place; but the question, what is reasonable time, must depend on the particular circumstances of the case; and it must always be for the jury to determine whether any laches are imputable to the plaintiff." Per Buller J. "The only rule I know of, which can be applied to the case of bills of exchange, is, *that due diligence must be used.* Due diligence is the only thing to be looked at, whether the bill be foreign or inland, and whether it be payable at sight, at so many days after, or in any other manner. But I think a rule may thus far be laid down as to laches, with regard to bills payable at sight, or a certain time after sight, namely, that they ought to be put in circulation; and if a bill drawn at three days sight were kept out in that way for a year, I cannot say there would be laches; but if instead of putting it in circulation, the holder were to lock it up for any length of time, I should say that he would be guilty of laches, but farther than this, no rule can be laid down." Per Heath J. "No rule can be laid down as to the time for presenting bills payable at sight, or at a given time afterwards. In the French ordinances of 1673, in Postlethwaite and Marius, it is said, 'That a bill payable at sight *or at will* is the same thing.'"

Goupy v. Harden, Holt, 342. 7 Taunt. 159. 2 Marsh. 454. A bill drawn in London 12th May, 1815, at thirty days after sight, on a house at Lisbon, was remitted by defendant to plaintiff at Paris. Plaintiff indorsed it to a house at Genoa; they negotiated it, and it was not till 22d August that it reached Lisbon, and was presented for acceptance; before that time, viz., on 15th July, the drawer failed, and on that account acceptance was refused. It was urged for defendant, that it was unwarrantable in plaintiff to send the bill to Genoa, instead of transmitting it to Lisbon for acceptance: but Gibbs C. J. thought otherwise; and the jury said such a bill might be sent round the world before it was presented for acceptance, and found for the plaintiff. On motion for a new trial, Gibbs C. J. relied upon Muilman v. D'Eguino, in which, he said, the point had been deliberately considered, and he was clearly of opinion

Upon a presentment for acceptance, the bill should be left with the drawee (32) twenty-four hours, unless in the interim he either accepts or declares a resolution not to accept.

But a bill or note must not be left (unless it is paid) on a presentment for payment; if it be, the presentment is (33) not considered as made until the money is called for.

The time when a presentment for payment must be made, depends upon the time when the bill or note is payable.

A bill or note payable on demand must not be kept locked up; if it be, the loss will fall on the holder. (34)

---

that the plaintiff had not taken the risk upon himself by sending the bill into circulation; and the jury having been of opinion that the bill had been presented in reasonable time, a rule was refused.

(32) Vide Mar. 2d ed. 16. Moll. b. 3. c. 5. § 1. Lord Raym. 281.

(33) Hayward v. Bank of England, Str. 550. Hayward kept cash at the bank, and paid in a banker's note; the runner to the bank left it the next morning, and called for the money in the afternoon, but in the interval the banker had stopped; and though this appeared to be the usual practice at the bank, King C. J. said, it was dangerous to suffer persons to deal with notes in that manner, and that the Common Pleas were of that opinion in the like case; and he directed the jury to find for the plaintiff, which they did. Sed vide Turner v. Mead, and Hoar v. Da Costa, post, p. 191.

(34) Breching v. ———— Holt, 315. Plaintiff took of defendant at Tunbridge, on the 5th, before the Maidstone post went out, a 20*l*. Maidstone bank note, payable on demand; he kept it till the morning of the 7th, and then sent it by the

And it will be no excuse that it would not have been paid had it been presented sooner. (34)

A bill or note payable on demand, is payable immediately upon presentment; and unless put into circulation must be presented within a reasonable time after the receipt.

It has (35) not been expressly decided whether what shall be considered as a reasonable time is to be taken as a question of fact for the determination of the jury, or as a question of law for the determination of the court. In Darbishire v. Parker (36), Lawrence J. intimated very decidedly

---

carrier who reached Maidstone at nine in the morning of the 7th; the post of the 6th reached Maidstone an hour sooner; the bank did not open that day: Gibbs C. J. held there were laches in plaintiff, and he directed a nonsuit.

(35) See ante, Muilman v. De Eguino, p. 184. note (31) Tindall v. Brown, post, p. 207. note (74), Appleton v. Sweetapple, post, p. 192. note (43). Hankey v. Trotman, post, p. 193. note (45), and Hilton v. Shepherd, Hopes v. Alder, and Darbishire v. Parker, infra, note (36).

(36) Whether it is the province of the judge, or of the jury, to decide upon the reasonableness of notice, has never been expressly determined. In Tindal v. Brown, post, p. 207. note (74), Lord Mansfield considered it as a question partly of fact and partly of law: Ashhurst and Buller Js. as a question of law. In the two cases of Hilton v. Shepherd, and Hopes v. Alder, 6 East's Rep. pp. 14. 16. note, Lord Kenyon considered it as a question for the jury, under all the circumstances of accident, necessity, and the like. But the judgment of Lawrence J. in Darbishire v. Parker, shews it was his decided opinion that it was an inference of law, to be drawn by the court from the facts, which (as in all other cases) were to be found by the jury.

that it was a question of law for the judges, and

Darbishire and another v. Parker, 6 East's Rep. 3. The plaintiffs received at Manchester notice of the dishonour of a bill, between eight and nine o'clock in the morning of the 12th of August. The post from Manchester to Liverpool, where the drawer resided, set off between twelve and one o'clock at noon. They, however, sent no notice by the post of that, or the next day, but sent it by a private hand on the 13th, by which it was delivered about nine o'clock at night, two hours later than it would have arrived had it been sent by the post. Lord Ellenborough left it to the jury, whether reasonable notice had been given, and they found for the plaintiffs. A new trial was moved for, on the ground of a misdirection, and a rule nisi granted. The court, without entering into the general question, held that the case deserved reconsideration; inasmuch as the plaintiffs appeared, at all events, to have been guilty of laches, whether the notice should have been sent by the post of the 12th or by that of the next day, having failed in doing either. Rule absolute. In this case, Lawrence, J. on the general question, whether reasonable notice be a question of law or of fact, said, "It must be recollected, that the facts stated in the report of Tindal v. Brown were afterwards found in a special verdict, in which the jury did not find whether the notice were reasonable or not; on which special verdict this court gave judgment for the plaintiff, and that judgment was unanimously confirmed in the Exchequer Chamber. But if reasonable notice were a question of fact and not of law, I am at a loss to know how those judgments are to be sustained; for the jury did not find the fact of reasonable notice, but left that as a question of law to be inferred from all the circumstances. But if it were a question of fact, there ought to have been a venire de novo in that case." In Ball v. Wardell, Willes, 204, 6. where a custom was pleaded for the inhabitants of a town to walk and ride over a certain close of the plaintiff's at all *seasonable* times, what was to be deemed a *seasonable* time was considered to be a question of law, arising out of all the circumstances; of which Lord C. J. Willes, says, "the court were the proper judges, as in the

yet in many instances since it has been treated as a question of fact for the jury. (37)

Upon a bill or note payable on demand or at sight, and given for cash by a person who makes the profit by the money on such bills or notes a source of his livelihood, it is difficult to say what length of time such person shall be entitled to consider unreasonable; but upon such bills or notes

---

case of *reasonable time*, reasonable fines," &c. " For," he adds, " what is contrary to reason cannot be consonant to law, which is founded on reason; and therefore the reasonableness in these and the like cases depends on the law, and is to be decided by the judges." And in the same case he says, " issues may be joined on things which are partly matters of fact, and partly matters of law; and then, when the evidence is given at the trial, the judge must direct the jury how the law is; and if they find contrary to such direction, it is a sufficient reason for a new trial.

See also Anderson v. Royal Exchange Assurance Company, 7 East's Rep. 43., in which Lord Ellenborough, in speaking of the time within which the assured may abandon the property insured, says, " an abandonment must be made within a reasonable time; and I rather conceive that it is the province of the judge to direct the jury as to what is a reasonable time under the circumstances." See also Bateman v. Joseph, post. See also Co. Litt. 56. *b.* " Reasonable time shall be adjudged by the discretion of the justices before whom the cause dependeth: and so it is of reasonable fines, customs, and services, upon the true state of the case depending before them; for reasonableness in these cases belongeth to the knowledge of the law, and therefore to be decided by the justices." " For nothing that is contrary to reason is consonant to law."

(37) See Fry v. Hill, ante, p. 183. note (28). and Goupy v. Harden, ante, p. 185.

given by way of payment, or paid into a banker's, any time beyond what the common course of business warrants (38), is.

Upon a bill or note of this kind given by way of payment, the course of business seemed formerly to allow the party to keep it, if it was payable in the place where it was given, until the (39) morn-

---

(38) See Turner v. Mead, infra, note (39).

(39) Ward v. Evans, Ld. Raym. 928. A banker's note was paid to the plaintiff's servant at noon, and presented for payment the next morning, at which time the banker stopped payment. On a case reserved, the court held it was presented in time; and judgment was given for the plaintiff.

Moor v. Warren, Str. 415. The defendant gave the plaintiff a banker's note at two o'clock in the afternoon, and he tendered it for payment the next morning at nine: the banker stopped a quarter of an hour before; and Pratt C. J. told the jury the loss should fall on the defendant, there being no laches in the plaintiff, who had demanded the money as soon as was usual in the course of dealing, and that keeping the note till next morning, could not be construed giving a new credit to the banker; and the jury found for the plaintiff. In Holmes v. Barry, Str. 415. the circumstances were the same; and King C. J. of the Common Pleas, gave a similar direction, and the jury found accordingly.

Fletcher v. Sandys, Str. 1248. A banker's note was paid to the plaintiff after dinner, and he sent it for payment the next morning, but the banker had stopped payment; and Lee C. J. ruled that there were no laches in the plaintiff, and that in all these cases there must be a reasonable time allowed, consistent with the nature of circulating paper.

Turner and others v. Mead, Str. 416. The defendants paid the Sword Blade Company (the plaintiffs) two banker's notes at three o'clock in the afternoon; and the next morning their servant left them at the banker's, in order to call for the money

ing of the next day of business after its receipt, and till the next post, if payable elsewhere; but (40) not longer.

---

in the evening, it then being the custom with the plaintiffs and the bank to send out their notes in the morning and to call for the money in the afternoon. The plaintiffs' servant called for the money between four and five in the afternoon, and the banker had just stopped payment; and because the plaintiffs had done nothing more than was usual in leaving the notes in the morning without taking the money, Pratt C. J. directed the jury to find for them, which they did.

Hoar v. Da Costa, Str. 910. The defendant paid the plaintiff a banker's note at twelve: he put it into the bank at one, and at ten the next morning the runner from the bank carried it with other notes, and left them, as was then usual, to call again for the money: he called at eleven, and was told the banker's servant was gone to the bank: he called again at two, when the banker said he was going to stop, and refused payment; but he paid small notes till four o'clock. The defendant gave notice to the plaintiff the next morning: the question was, whether this note was payment to the plaintiff. It was insisted for the defendant, that if the note had been tendered by itself it would have been paid; and for the plaintiff, that if there had been no demand there would have been no laches, being within a day after the receipt. Raymond C. J. said there was no standing rule, and left it to the jury, who found for the plaintiff.

(40) Manwaring v. Harrison, Str. 508. On Saturday the 17th of September, about two o'clock, Harrison gave Manwaring a banker's note, dated the 5th of September, and payable to Harrison or order on demand; Manwaring paid it away the same afternoon to J. S., and he presented it for payment on the Tuesday morning as soon as the shop was open: but the banker stopped payment at that time. Manwaring paid the money to J. S., and brought this action to recover it from Harrison. Pratt C.J. left it to the jury, whether there had been any neglect; and observed, that as Harrison had kept it eleven days, he probably would not have demanded payment sooner than

Thus where a note of this kind, payable in London, was given there in the morning, a presentment the next morning was held (41) sufficiently early; a presentment at two the next afternoon too (42) late.

In (43) a later modern case, where a similar note was given in London at one, and not presented

---

J. S. did. The jury wished to leave it to the court whether there had been a reasonable time: but the Chief Justice told them they were the judges of that; upon which they found for the defendant, and gave it as their opinion, that a person who did not demand a banker's note in two days, took the credit on himself.

East India Company v. Chitty, Str. 1175. At half past eleven in the morning of the 18th of January, the defendant paid the East India Company's cashier a banker's note, and they did not send it for payment till the next day at two, at which time the banker stopped payment. The question was, who should bear the loss? and upon examining the merchants, it was held, that the company had made it their own by not sending it out the afternoon they received it, or at furthest the next morning; and the jury found accordingly for the defendant.

(41) Ward v. Evans, Moore v. Warren, Holmes v. Barry, Fletcher v. Sandys, ante, p. 190. note (39).

(42) East India Company v. Chitty, supra.

(43) Appleton v. Sweetapple, B. R. M. 23 Geo. 3. A bill payable in London on demand was given to the plaintiff in London at one o'clock in the afternoon, and he did not present it till the next morning; the question was, whether he presented it in time? Lord Mansfield left the point to the jury, who found for the defendant; but the court granted a new trial, because the question was a matter of law upon which the judge should have decided; the jury found again for the defendant, but against the judge's direction; a second new trial was granted, and the jury again found for the defendant; and then the court refused to interfere.

till the next morning, two juries held the delay unreasonable, but it was against the opinion of the court.

But in a very recent case, where such a note payable in London was given in the country, it was held that the person receiving it was not bound to send it to London till the following day. (44)

And that the person receiving it in London was not bound to present it till the next day. (44)

A bill or note of this kind, given by way of payment to a banker, must (45) be presented by him

---

(44) Williams v. Smith, Pasch. 1819, 2 Barnew. and Ald. 496. At 10 o'clock on Friday morning, defendant paid plaintiff at Wantage, (eighteen miles from Newbury,) 450*l.* in Newbury bank notes, payable at Newbury or London: plaintiff sent them to the Wantage bank the same day, to remit to London, but they declined on account of the risk, and halves of them were sent to London by Saturday's coach, and the other halves by Sunday's post: they were presented for payment on the Tuesday, but no Newbury notes were paid in London after the Monday, nor at Newbury after the Saturday. Newbury is a two-days' post from Wantage, and the post for London leaves Wantage at half after five in the evening; on case, it was urged for defendant, that plaintiff should have sent the notes to London by the Friday's post, or if not that they should have been presented for payment the day they arrived in London, in either of which cases they would have been paid; but the court held, plaintiff had till the day after they were received, i. e. till Saturday, to send them to London, and the banker there had till the day after he received them, i. e. till Tuesday, to present them, and postea to plaintiff.

(45) Hankey v. Trotman, Blackst. 1. The plaintiff was a banker, and had a bill on the defendant, for which the defendant paid him a draught upon another banker at twelve at noon, and the plaintiff got it marked for acceptance that night; be-

as soon as if it had been paid into his hands by a customer.

And it has been held that a bill or note of this kind if payable at the place where the banker lives, must be presented the next time the banker's clerk goes (45) his rounds.

But if a London banker receive a check by the general post, he is not bound to present it for payment (46) until the following day.

---

fore the next morning the banker on whom it was drawn stopped. The question was, whether the plaintiff or defendant should bear the loss? The jury found a verdict for the defendant, and upon a rule to shew cause why there should not be a new trial, and cause shewn, the court (Wright J. dubitante) held that it was a question of fact, whether the plaintiff had sufficient time for receiving the money, of which the jury were the proper judges; and the verdict stood.

But see the cases of Rickford v. Ridge, and Robson v. Bennett, in the two following notes. In the last-mentioned case, Mansfield C. J. said, that Hankey v. Trotman had been overruled by Appleton v. Sweetapple. See 2 Taunt. 394.

(46) Rickford and others v. Ridge, 2 Campb. N. P. C. 537. The plaintiffs, bankers at Aylesbury, gave the defendant cash for a check upon Smith and Co., bankers in London; and in an action to recover this money, it appeared that they took the check on the 13th of June, but instead of sending it to London by the post of that day, which they might have done, they sent it by a morning coach on the 14th; and their bankers, to whom it was directed, received it between three and four o'clock on the same day, and presented it at Smith's house at noon on the 15th, when payment was refused. It was proved that bankers to the west of St. Paul's, where the plaintiffs' bankers resided, sent out checks and bills for payment only once in the day, and that generally before the arrival of the post; and therefore such as arrived by the post on one day generally remained with them

And where a person in London received a check upon a London banker between one and two o'clock, and lodged it soon after four with his banker, and the latter presented it between five and six, and got it marked as a good check, and the next day at noon presented it for payment at the clearing house; the court held that there had been no unreasonable delay, either by the (47) holder in not presenting it for payment on the first day, which he might have done, or by his (47) banker in pre-

---

until the following morning; so that had this check arrived by the post on the 14th, it would not have been presented until the 15th. The question therefore was, whether such practice were reasonable. It was admitted that a different practice prevailed to the east of St. Paul's. Lord Ellenborough said he could not hear of any arbitrary distinction between one part of the city and another. That in towns where posts arrived at different hours, it would be impossible, or at least unreasonable, to require that bankers should present bills and checks on the same day on which they were received. That the practice here proved, that checks received in the course of one day should be presented on the following day, appeared to him to be subservient to general convenience, and consistent with the law merchant, which merely required checks to be presented with reasonable diligence. Verdict for the plaintiffs.

(47) Robson v. Bennett, 2 Taunt. 388. On the 11th of September, between one and two o'clock, the defendants gave the plaintiffs a check upon Bloxam and Co., their bankers, in payment for goods. The plaintiffs lodged the check with Messrs. Harrisons, their bankers, a few minutes after four; and they presented it between five and six to Bloxam and Co., who marked it as good. It was proved to be the usage among London bankers, not to pay any check presented by or on behalf of another banker after four o'clock, but merely to mark it if good, and pay it the next day at the clearing house. On the 12th at

senting it at the clearing house only, on the following day at noon: it being proved to be the usage among such bankers, not to pay checks presented by one banker to another after four o'clock, but only to mark them if good, and to pay them the next day at the clearing house.

If a man takes a bill on the eve of its becoming due, and it is payable at a distant place, he must not keep it by him so as to prevent its being presented for payment on the day it becomes due. (48)

And if he takes it so near the time of its becoming due, that it will be impossible to present it on the day it becomes due, he must lose no time in forwarding it, or putting it into circulation, so that it may be presented without delay. (48)

---

noon, Harrisons' clerk took this check to the clearing house; but no person attended for Bloxam and Co., who stopped payment at nine on that morning, and the check was therefore treated as dishonoured. The plaintiffs in going with the check to Harrisons' passed Bloxam's house. On a case stating these facts, the court held, that there had been no laches in the plaintiffs in not presenting the check to Bloxam and Co. on the 11th for payment; or in his bankers in not presenting it at the banking house, but merely at the clearing house; and therefore gave judgment for the plaintiffs.

See also Reynolds v. Chettle, 2 Campb. N. P. C. 596.

(48) Anderton v. Beck, 16 East. 248. 26th December plaintiff received in Yorkshire a bill payable in London, 28th; he kept it till the 29th, and then sent it to the Lincoln bank, who forwarded it to London without delay, and it was received in London and presented for payment 2d January; plaintiff had no correspondent in London; the bill was dishonoured, and in an action for goods sold, the question was, whether this bill was payment? Bayley J. thought it was, and verdict for defendant;

If a bill is payable at either of two places, the person taking it has the option at which to present it; and it cannot be imputed as laches in him that he presented it at the most distant, and that if he had presented it at the other it would have been paid. (49)

A (50) bill or (51) note importing to be payable

---

and on motion to enter verdict for plaintiff, the court held, that as plaintiff submitted to take this bill, he was bound to use due diligence in presenting it, and that he had been guilty of laches in keeping it from the 26th to the 29th; he might have sent it off the 27th or 28th. Rule refused.

(49) Beeching v. Gower, Holt. 313. Plaintiff took of defendant at Tunbridge, on 5th March, a 10*l*. Kentish bank note, payable on demand at Maidstone or at Messrs. Ramsbottom's, London. Plaintiff sent the note to London the same day, and it was presented at Ramsbottom's on the 6th, but they ceased paying that day; the Kentish bank paid all the 6th, so that had it been sent to Maidstone it would have been paid: defendant insisted that plaintiff ought to have sent it to Maidstone, which was nearer, and where plaintiff had a clerk; Gibbs C. J. was clear that as the note was payable at either place, plaintiff had his option at which to present it; and verdict for plaintiff.

(50) Colman v. Sayer, 1 Barnard. B. R. 303. In an action upon an inland bill payable six days after sight, one question was, whether three days grace are allowed where a bill is payable at certain days after sight, as well as where it is payable upon sight? and Raymond C. J. said they were allowable in one case as well as in the other. Another question was, whether they were allowable upon inland as well as upon foreign bills? and the common serjeant and foreman of the jury said it was the constant practice in the city to allow them in both cases; upon which Raymond C. J. said he would not alter it; but the plaintiff was nonsuited on another point.

(51) Brown v. Harraden, 4 Term Rep. 148. In an action on

within a limited time after a certain event, or (52) at sight, is not in fact payable until (53) two days after the expiration of that time, nor unless the third be a day of public rest, until (53) three.

These extra days are called days of grace.

Different (54) countries vary in the number of days allowed by way of grace; and in two cases

---

a note dated the 13th of September 1789, and payable the 2d of November, the declaration stated a presentment and refusal on the 2d of November. The Defendant pleaded a tender on the 5th, and the plaintiff replied a bill of Middlesex sued out the 4th: rejoinder, that defendant was not liable to pay the note at the time the bill of Middlesex was sued out, and surrejoinder that he was. Demurrer and joinder. The question therefore was, whether three days' grace were to be allowed on promissory notes? and after argument the court was unanimous that they were. The same point was taken for granted in Smith v. Kendall, ante, p. 29, note (62). See Dexlaux v. Hood, Bull. Ni. Pr. 274. Ward v. Honeywood, Dougl. 62. May v. Cooper, Fort. 376.

(52) See Coleman v. Sayer, ante, note (50), and in Janson v. Thomas, ante, p. 79, note (20), Buller J. mentioned a case before Willes C. J. in London, in which a jury of merchants was of opinion that the usual days of grace were to be allowed on bills payable at sight. But see Poth. pl. 12. 172. 198.

(53) Tassell v. Lewis, Lord Raym. 743. "In case of foreign bills of exchange, the custom is, that three days are allowed for the payment of them; but if it happens that the last of the three days is a Sunday, or great holiday, as Christmas day, &c. upon which no money used to be paid, there the party ought to demand the money upon the second day, otherwise it will be at his own peril. Merchants in evidence swore this to be the custom of merchants, and it was approved by Holt C. J. See also 2 Bl. Com. 469. Mar. 2d ed. 25.

(54) Beawes, § 260. 1st ed. p. 449. The number allowed by the Hamburgh ordinance, art. 16., is twelve.

some years ago it was proved (55), that at Hamburgh the holder of a bill is not bound to present it until the eleventh day after the time limited for its payment, where the eleventh is a post day; that if the eleventh be not a post day, he must present it the next preceding post day; but that (56) if

(55) Goldsmith and another v. Shee, C. P. cor. Lord Eldon, 20th of December, 1799. A bill for 500*l.* drawn on Katter at Hamburgh, at three usances, was dated the 25th of June, 1799; it was presented for payment on the 4th of October, which was a post day. In an action by the indorsees against the payee, the defence was, that the presentment was improper: but it was proved in evidence as the settled usage at Hamburgh, that although it is usual to pay bills on the day they become due, the holder may, if he pleases, keep them a certain number of days, called respite days; and that the number of respite days is eleven where the eleventh is a post day; but where the eleventh is not a post day, the respite days extend to the preceding post day only, the holder being obliged at his peril to protest, and send off the protest by the eleventh day. Verdict for the plaintiffs.

But this is not consistent with the Hamburgh ordinance, art. 17; in which it is stated that the holders may postpone the protest until the twelfth day, if it be not a Sunday or holiday.

(56) Goldsmith and another v. Bland and another, C. P. cor. Lord Eldon, 1st of March, 1800. A bill for 998*l.* 9*s.* 9*d.* drawn on Treviramus of Bremen, but payable in Hamburgh at three months, was dated the 15th of June, 1799; it was not presented or protested until the 26th of September, which was not a post day: another bill for 261*l.* 7*s.* 2*d.* addressed to Voeg, in Lubeck, payable in Hamburgh, at three months, was dated the 26th of June, 1799; it was not presented or protested until 7th of October, which was not a post day. In an action on these bills against the defendants as indorsers, it was proved that it was optional in the holder of a bill at Hamburgh, whether he would present and protest it on the post day before the eleventh day after the day limited for its payment, the eleventh

the drawee reside not at Hamburgh, but at Lubeck or Bremen, or other places near Hamburgh, and in daily intercourse with it, the holder need not present it until the eleventh day, although the eleventh be not a post day.

In this country, upon the last day of grace, and within a reasonable time before the expiration of that day, a bill or note must be presented for payment.

But if the holder makes a second presentment on that day, the drawer or maker is (57) entitled to insist on paying it when such presentment is made, without paying the fees of noting or protesting, notwithstanding such presentment is made after the banking hours, and for the purpose of noting and protesting.

A presentment on the second day of grace, where the third is not a day of public rest, is a (58) nullity.

---

not being a post day, or whether he would keep it until the eleventh: and one witness proved, that where the drawee lived at Lubeck or Bremen, it was the constant usage to keep the bill until the eleventh, whether it was a post day or not, there being posts from Lubeck and Bremen to Hamburgh every day. Verdict for the plaintiffs for 1633*l*. See the preceding note.

(57) Leftley v. Mills, post. p. 213. note (83).

(58) Wiffen v. Roberts, Espinasse, 261. A bill was dated 1st November, 1798, and payable three months after date: in an action against the drawer, it appeared that the only presentment for payment was on the 3d of February, which was only the second day of grace, and the day following was not a day of public rest; and Lord Kenyon held, that the non-payment by the acceptor the day before the bill became regularly due, was not such a default in him as could authorise the holder to have recourse to the drawer, and the plaintiff was nonsuited.

Upon a bill or note payable within a limited time after sight, the time must be computed from its (59) presentment for acceptance; and upon a bill or note payable within a limited time after the date, where it has no date, from (60) the day it issued.

The calculation of the time depends upon the different modes of computing time.

All places with which we are in the habit of negotiating bills compute their time, as we do, (except that Russia adheres to the old style) by years reckoned in a series from the birth of our Saviour, and divided each into twelve months, and 365 (or in every fourth year 366) days.

Upon a bill drawn at a place using one style, and payable at a place using the other, if the time is to be reckoned from the date, it shall be computed according to the style of the place at which it was drawn; otherwise according to (61) the style

---

(59) Beawes, § 252. 1st ed. p. 447.; but Mar. 2d ed. p. 19. says from the day of acceptance, or protest for non-acceptance. By the Hamburgh ordinance, art. 26. "If a bill of exchange, at or after sight, should not be accepted immediately on its being presented, but it should be done afterwards, such acceptance is to be considered as made on the first day of *presentment.*" Pothier, pl. 13. says, from the day of presentment *and* acceptance. See Campbell v. French, 6 Term Rep. 200.

(60) Armitt v. Breame, Lord Raym. 1076. An award which directed the removal of some scaffolds within fifty-eight days from the date of the award, had no date; and an objection being taken upon this ground, the court said that the time was to be computed from the delivery.

(61) Vide Mar. 2d ed. p. 25. Beawes, § 251. 1st ed. p. 447.

of the place where it is payable; and in the former case the date (62) must be reduced or carried forward to the style of the place where the bill is payable, and the time reckoned from thence.

Thus on a bill dated the 1st of March, old style, and payable here one month after date, the time must be computed from the corresponding day of February, new style; and on a bill dated the 19th of February, new style, and payable at Petersburgh one month after date, from the corresponding day of March, old style.

Where the time after the expiration of which a bill or note imports to be payable is limited by months, it is to be computed by (63) calendar, not lunar months.

Thus on a bill or note payable one month after date, and dated the 1st of January, the (64) month will not expire till the 1st of February.

Where the time is computed by days, the day on which the event happens is to be (65) excluded.

---

(62) Mar. 2d ed. p. 22.

(63) Mar. 2d ed. p. 19.

(64) Vide Mar. 2d ed. p. 24. Beawes, § 253. 1st ed. p. 447.

(65) Bellasis v. Hester, Lord Raym. 280. Lutw. 1591. Upon a bill payable ten days after sight, Treby C.J. was of opinion, that the day on which the bill was seen by the drawee was not to be reckoned one of the ten, because then a bill payable one day after sight would be payable the day it was seen; but Powell and Neville Js. held the contrary, and judgment was given according to their opinion. However, in May v. Cooper, Fort. 376., the court seemed to consider a note payable ten days

Thus on a bill or note payable ten days after date, dated the 1st of January, the time does not expire until the 11th.

Instead of an express limitation by years, months or days, we continually find the time on bills drawn or payable at Amsterdam, Rotterdam, Hamburg, Altona, Paris, or any place in France, Cadiz, Madrid, Bilboa, Leghorn, Genoa, or Venice, limited by *the usance*, that is, the usage between those places and this country; because, in the infancy of bills, all bills between this country and any of those places respectively were usually made payable after the same interval.

An usance between this kingdom and Amsterdam, Rotterdam, Hamburg, Altona, Paris, or any place in France, is one calendar month from the date of the bill; an usance between us and Cadiz, Madrid, or Bilboa, two; an usance between us and Leghorn, Genoa, or Venice, three.

A double usance is double the accustomed time; an half usance, half.

Where it is necessary to divide a month upon an half usance, which is the case where the usance is either one month or three, the division, (66) not-

---

after date, and dated the 21st July, as payable the 31st (not allowing, however, any days of grace); and in Coleman v. Sayer, 1 Barnard. B. R. 303., in an action upon a bill payable six days after sight, one question was, whether the day of sight was to be reckoned one of the six? and Raymond C. J. said it was not; and the modern practice is conformable to his opinion.

(66) Mar. 2d ed. p. 23.

withstanding the difference in the length of months, contains fifteen days.

The bankruptcy or known insolvency of the drawee or maker is no (67) excuse for a neglect to make a presentment, or to give notice;

---

(67) In Russel v. Langstaffe, Dougl. 497. 515. Lee said, arguendo, that it had frequently been ruled by Lord Mansfield at Guildhall, that it is not an excuse for not making a demand on a note or bill, or for not giving notice of non-payment, that the drawer or acceptor has become a bankrupt, as many means may remain of obtaining payment by the assistance of friends, or otherwise; and Lord Mansfield, who was in court, did not deny the assertion: this dictum was also referred to, arguendo, in Bickerdike v. Bollman, 1 Term Rep. 408.

Esdaile & al. v. Sowerby & al. 11 East. Rep. 114. In an action by the indorsees of a bill drawn by Cheetham on Hill in favour of the defendants, and by them indorsed to the plaintiffs, a verdict was found for the plaintiffs, and a case reserved. The bill, which was payable in London, became due on Saturday the 20th of February, when it was presented for payment, and dishonoured. By mistake, notice of non-payment was not given to the defendants, who resided at Liverpool, until the 27th of February, whereas it ought to have been given on the 24th, and they refused payment on the ground of this laches. Before the bill became due, the drawer had stopped payment and become bankrupt, and the acceptor was insolvent. The drawer had himself apprized the defendants of his situation at the time of his stopping payment, and that this bill would not be paid; and they knew that the acceptor had no funds but such as the drawer furnished him with: and on the 25th of February they admitted to the plaintiff's agent that they knew of the insolvency of the drawer and acceptor. It was contended that notice of the dishonour was unnecessary; but the court was clear that the insolvency of the drawer and acceptor, and the knowledge of it, did not dispense with the necessity of giving notice of the dishonour of the bill to the defendants. Postea to the defendants. See also Smith v. Beckett, and Brown v. Massey, post.

Nor is a general ceasing to pay. (68)

Sect. 2.—Notice (69) must be given of a failure in the attempt to procure an acceptance, though the application for such acceptance might have been unnecessary; otherwise the person guilty of the neglect may lose his remedy upon the bill.

But such neglect will be no bar to a subsequent indorsee, if he took the bill before it became due, and gave value for it, and was ignorant that acceptance had been refused. (70)

---

(68) See Howe v. Bowes, ante, p. 176.

(69) Vide Blesard v. Hirst, and Goodall v. Dolley, post.

(70) O'Keefe v. Dunn, 6 Taunt. 305. (1815. Trin.) A bill at one month after date was drawn by defendants, payable to Sinclair, or order: Sinclair presented it for acceptance, and acceptance was refused, but no notice was given to defendants: Sinclair indorsed the bill to plaintiff for a valuable consideration, before the month from the date expired, but plaintiff had no notice of the prior refusal to accept: when the bill became due it was duly presented for payment, payment was refused, and notice thereof given to defendants. Action inde: defendants pleaded the presentment for acceptance by Sinclair, the refusal and want of notice thereof; plaintiff traversed the presentment and refusal, and after verdict thereon for defendants, rule nisi to enter judgment for plaintiff non obstante veredicto: after cause shewn, and time to consider, Gibbs C. J., Heath and Dallas, against Chambre J., were of opinion that plaintiff was entitled to judgment; that the bill did not necessarily require presentment for acceptance; that defendants therefore had not, by the nature of the instrument, stipulated for such presentment; but that, on the contrary, they had, by its form, agreed that it should be negotiable till the period for payment arrived; that an innocent in-

So if the drawee offer a partial or conditional acceptance, or an acceptance at an extended period, or if any other person offer an absolute one, though the holder may be willing to acquiesce in such acceptance, he must (71) give notice.

In that case, however, if he wishes to have the power of availing himself of it, he should mention in his notice the acceptance offered; for a notice generally of non-acceptance shews (72) he did not acquiesce in such offer.

A neglect to give notice, upon the refusal of any thing more than a conditional acceptance, is done away by the completion of those conditions before the bill becomes payable; and a neglect, upon the refusal of any thing more than a partial acceptance, discharges the persons entitled to it only from their responsibility as to the payment of the residue.

The notice must come from the (73) holder, or

---

dorsee therefore might be deluded, and the negotiation of such bills defeated, if his remedy were to be destroyed by a fact of which he had no notice, and as to which there was nothing to raise a suspicion. Rule absolute. And on error, the judgment was affirmed in the king's bench. Ante, Dunn v. O'Keefe, p. 123.

(71) Vide Mar. 4th ed. p. 21. Beawes, § 221. 2d ed. p. 445.

(72) Vide Sproat v. Matthews, ante, p. 153. note (47).

(73) Ex parte Barclay, 7 Ves. 597. Barclay was indorsee and holder of two bills drawn by Kemp upon Dearlow, and indorsed by Clay to Barclay. These bills were dishonoured, of which Clay gave notice to Kemp; and on petition by Barclay to be allowed to prove these bills under a commission of bankruptcy issued against Kemp, one question was, whether this notice from Clay, and not from Barclay the holder, were suf-

some party entitled to call for payment or reimbursement; and though there is no prescribed form for it, ought to import that (74) the person to whom

---

ficient. And Lord Eldon C.J., after referring to Tindal v. Brown, held that the notice ought to have come from the holder, and dismissed the petition. See Jameson v. Swinton, post.

(74) Tindal v. Brown, 1 Term Rep. 167. 186. A note which became due on the 5th of October, was presented at ten in the morning, and the maker not being at home, word was left for him where it lay; the holder sent again on the 6th, when the maker promised to take it up within the banking hours, which were from nine to four; on the 7th, the holder sent again to the maker, and the note not being paid, gave notice to the defendant, who was an indorser, but the defendant said he had made it his own; the maker had told defendant on the 6th, that he could not pay it, and desired the defendant would: all the parties lived at Bristol. The jury found for the plaintiff; but upon a rule to shew cause why there should not be a new trial, and cause shewn, the court granted a new trial. Lord Mansfield said, "What is reasonable notice is a question partly of fact, and partly of law: it may depend in some measure on facts; such as the distance at which the parties live, the course of the post, &c.; but wherever a rule can be laid down with respect to this reasonableness, *that* should be decided by the court, and adhered to for the sake of certainty." Per Willes J. "New credit was given to the maker, and I cannot consider notice from the maker equal to notice from the holder." Ashhurst J. "The reasonableness ought to be settled as a question of law; the next day at the most is as long as is necessary in a case like this; if the parties live at a small distance, this is a sufficient time; if at a greater, they should write by the next post. Notice means something more than knowledge, because it is competent to the holder to give credit to the maker: it is not enough to say that the maker does not intend to pay, but that the holder does not intend to give credit; the party ought to know whether the holder intends to give credit to the maker, or to resort to him." Per Buller J. "*When* the post goes out, is a matter of fact; when that is established, it is a matter of

it is given is considered liable, and that payment from him is expected.

It has indeed been held, that notice from the acceptor to the drawer that he had not been able to pay it, and that it was then in plaintiff's hands, was sufficient; but that might, perhaps, have been on the ground that the acceptor wrote for the plaintiff, and as his agent. (75)

A notice from the holder or any other party will enure to the benefit of every other party who stands between the person giving the notice and the person to whom it is given. (76)

---

law, what notice is reasonable; as to giving time, the holder does it at his peril, and that is enough to decide the case; the purpose of giving notice is to let the party know that he is looked to for payment, that he may have his remedy over by an early application; if it shews that the holder has given time, it discharges the party: it ought to purport that the holder looks to him for payment, and a notice from another person cannot be sufficient; it must come from the holder." Upon the second trial there was contradictory evidence whether the notice from the maker was on the sixth or the seventh, and the jury found again for the plaintiff; but the court said it was a verdict against law, and granted another new trial.

(75) Rosher v. Kieran, 4 Campb. 87. Indorsees of bill against drawer, and the question was, whether defendant had had due notice of the bill's dishonour? It was proved, that, on the day the bill became due, the acceptor wrote to defendant that he had not been able to pay the bill, and that it was in plaintiff's hands: Lord Ellenborough held this sufficient, and verdict for plaintiff. See Stewart v. Kennet, 2 Campb. 177.

(76) Wilson v. Swabey, 1 Stark. 34. In an action by indorsee of a bill against the drawer, it appeared that notice was communicated to Lewis, an indorser, the day after the bill became due, and that Lewis gave defendant notice the next day: it was

Therefore a notice from the last indorsee to the drawer, will operate as a notice from each indorser.

It is nevertheless prudent in each party who receives a notice, to give immediate notice to those parties against whom he may have right to claim; for the holder may have omitted notice to some of them, and that will be no protection (77); or there may be difficulties in proving such notice.

Though a holder, or any other party, gives no notice but to the person of whom he took the bill, yet if notice is communicated without laches to the prior parties, he may avail himself of such communication, and sue any of such prior parties; it is no objection in such case that there was no notice immediately from the plaintiff to the defendant. (78)

To give this notice, in the case of a foreign bill, effect, it is (79) necessary that a minute of the

---

objected, that plaintiff had not given defendant notice: but Lord Ellenborough said, notice from any person who was party to the bill was sufficient, and plaintiff had a verdict.

(77) Edwards v. Dick, 4 Barnew. 212. In an action by indorsee against drawer, it appeared that the acceptor made the bill payable at a particular place, and it did not appear that plaintiff had given the acceptor notice of its dishonour: but on motion for nonsuit on that ground, the court held it sufficient in order to warrant a suit against defendant, that notice was given to him; he could not object that a third person had not had notice: if he was entitled to a remedy over against the acceptor, he should have given him notice. Rule refused.

(78) See note (76).

(79) Rogers v. Stephens, 2 Term Rep. 713. In an action against the drawer of a foreign bill, it appeared that the bill had been noted for non-acceptance, but there was no protest,

non-acceptance or non-payment, and a solemn declaration on the part of the holder against any loss to be sustained thereby, (which minute and declaration is called a protest) should be made out by a notary public, or if there be no such notary in or near the place where the bill is payable, by an inhabitant in the presence of two witnesses; and in some cases a copy, or some other memorial of it, should accompany the notice.

Such protest may also be made on the (80) non-

---

and this was pressed as a ground for a nonsuit. Lord Kenyon admitted the objection, but upon the other circumstances thought this a case in which a protest was not necessary. See post, p. 234. note (117).

Gale v. Walsh, 5 Term Rep. 239. In an action against the drawer of a foreign bill, it was reserved as a point whether it was necessary to prove a protest; and the court thought it so clear upon the motion to enter a nonsuit, that they suggested to the plaintiff's counsel the expediency of making the rule absolute in the first instance; and upon their acquiescence it was accordingly done; they afterwards however wished to have it opened, upon an idea that the drawer had no effects in the hands of the drawee, but it appearing upon the report that that idea was not founded, the rule stood. And in Brough v. Parkins, Lord Raym. 993. 6 Mod. 80. Salk. 131. Holt C. J. says, "A protest on a foreign bill is part of the custom." See also Orr. v. Maginnis, post.

(80) By 3 & 4 Anne, c. 9. § 4. Whereas by an act of parliament in the 9th year of the reign of his late majesty King William the Third, intituled, "An act for the better payment of inland bills of exchange," it is, among other things, enacted, "that from and after presentation and acceptance of the said bill or bills of exchange, (which acceptance shall be by the underwriting the same under the party's hand so accepting, and after the expiration of three days after the said bill or bills shall become due, the party to whom the said bill or bills are

acceptance of an inland bill, if such bill is for the payment of *5l.*, or upwards, within a limited time after date, and the value is expressed therein to have been received, or (81) after an acceptance written on such a bill, for its non-payment.

---

made payable, his servant, agent or assigns, may, and shall cause the same bill or bills to be protested in manner as in the said act is enacted; and whereas by there being no provision made therein for protesting such bill or bills, in case the party on whom the same are or shall be drawn refuse to accept the same, by underwriting the same under his hand, all merchants, and others, do refuse to underwrite such bill or bills, or make any other than a promissory acceptance, by which means the effect and good intent of the said act in that behalf is wholly evaded, and no bill or bills can be protested before or for want of such acceptance by underwriting the same as aforesaid;" it is enacted, that from and after the first day of May, 1705, in case, upon presenting of any such bill or bills of exchange, the party or parties, on whom the same shall be drawn, shall refuse to accept the same, by underwriting the same as aforesaid, the party to whom the said bill or bills are made payable, his servant, agent or assigns, may and shall cause the said bill or bills to be protested for non-acceptance, as in case of foreign bills of exchange; for which protest there shall be paid two shillings, and no more.

(81) By 9 & 10 W. 3. c. 17. § 1. "Whereas great damages and other inconveniences do frequently happen in the course of trade and commerce, by reason of delays of payment, and other neglects on inland bills of exchange in this kingdom;" it is enacted, that from and after the 24th day of June, 1698, all and every bill or bills of exchange drawn in, or dated at and from any trading city or town, or any other place in the kingdom of England, dominion of Wales, or town of Berwick upon Tweed, of the sum of *5l.* sterling or upwards, upon any person or persons of or in London, or any other trading city, town, or any other place (in which said bill or bills of exchange shall be acknowledged and expressed the said value to be received) and

But (82) if a man draw or indorse a bill on this country abroad, and afterwards comes here, a

---

is and shall be drawn payable at a certain number of days, weeks or months after date thereof, that from and after presentation and acceptance of the said bill or bills of exchange, (which acceptance shall be by the underwriting the same under the party's hand so accepting) and after the expiration of three days after the said bill or bills shall become due, the party to whom the said bill or bills are made payable, his servant, agent or assigns, may and shall cause the said bill or bills to be protested by a notary public, and in default of such notary public, by any other substantial person of the city, town or place, in the presence of two or more credible witnesses, refusal or neglect being first made of due payment of the same; which protest shall be made and written under a fair written copy of the said bill of exchange, in the words or form following:

Know all men, that I, A. B., on the day of at the usual place of abode of the said have demanded payment of the bill, of the which the above is the copy, which the said did not pay, wherefore I the said do hereby protest the said bill. Dated this day of

(82) Cromwell v. Hynson, 2 Esp. N. P. C. 511. Indorsee against the indorser of a foreign bill. When the indorsement was made, Hynson (a master of a ship) was in Jamaica where the bill was drawn, but his residence was at Stepney. The bill was presented for acceptance, dishonoured and protested; and then sent to Hynson's house for payment, with notice of non-acceptance. Hynson was not then in England, but the bill was shewn to his wife, and the circumstances stated to her. It was urged, 1st, that notice should have been sent to Jamaica. 2dly, that the demand on the wife was not sufficient; and, 3dly, that a copy of the protest should have been sent with the notice; but Lord Kenyon overruled all the objections, and the plaintiff had a verdict.

Robins v. Gibson, 3 Campb. 334. 1 Maule, 288. Indorsee of bill drawn at Buenos Ayres against drawer; before the notice to him here need not be accompanied by the protest, or any memorial of it.

At least he cannot object to such notice, unless he applied for the protest on receiving the notice.

And a (83) protest cannot properly be made on any other inland bills.

---

bill became due defendant returned to this country: the bill was dishonoured, and notice thereof left at his house, but no notice given of its being protested: Lord Ellenborough held the notice sufficient; and on motion for new trial, the court agreed with him: Lord Ellenborough said, it did not appear that defendant requested to have the protest; he had notice of the bill's dishonour, and as circumstances alter, the rule respecting notice changes; if the party is abroad he cannot know of the protest but by having it: being here, he might have inquired to ascertain that fact. Rule refused.

(83) Leftley v. Mills, 4 Term Rep. 170. An inland bill for 20*l.* 7*s.* payable 14 days after sight, became due 24th April, 1790. A banker's clerk called with it for payment in the morning, and the acceptor not being at home, left word where it lay; after six, another of the clerks, who was a notary, noted it, and between seven and eight the first clerk went with it again. The acceptor tendered him the amount of the bill, and sixpence over; but he insisted on 2*s.* 6*d.* for the noting, and *that* sum not being paid, an action was brought against the acceptor, who pleaded the tender. Lord Kenyon thought a tender of the amount of the bill at any time of the day it was payable, was sufficient; upon which the jury found a verdict for the defendant. A rule to shew cause why there should not be a new trial, was afterwards granted; and upon cause shewn Lord Kenyon thought the acceptor had till the last minute of the day of grace to pay the bill, and that it could not be noted or protested till the following day. Buller J. thought they were payable any time of the last day of grace upon demand, so as such demand was made within reasonable hours; and that they

And a protest upon an inland bill is never necessary where (84) the bill is for the payment of less than 20*l.*; and on such as are for the payment of more, though the 3d & 4th Ann. c. 9. s. 5. contain words which primâ facie import that a neglect to (85)

---

might be protested on that day. Grose J. declined giving any opinion on these points; but the whole court concurred, that the bill in question could not be noted, because it was payable within a limited time after sight, and the statute authorizes the noting of such inland bills only as are payable after date. Lord Kenyon also thought that the sixpence tendered was sufficient for the noting, and the rule was discharged.

(84) By 3 & 4 Anne, c. 9. § 6. it is provided, that no such protest shall be necessary, either for non-acceptance or non-payment of any inland bill of exchange, unless the value be acknowledged and expressed in such bill to be received, and unless such bill be drawn for the payment of 20*l.* sterling or upwards; and that the protest hereby required for non-acceptance shall be made by such persons as are appointed by the act of 9 & 10 W. 3. c. 17. to protest inland bills of exchange for non-payment thereof.

(85) Brough v. Parkins, Tr. 2 Anne, Lord Raym. 992. 6 Mod. 80. Salk. 131. In an action against the drawer of an inland bill, it was insisted upon for error, that it did not appear by the declaration, that the bill had been protested; sed per Holt, C. J. "on an inland bill no protest was necessary by the common law, and the statute does not destroy or take away the party's action where there is no protest; nor is the want of a protest any bar of the action; but the act seems only to take away from the plaintiff his interest and damages where he has not made a protest, or to give the drawers a remedy against him by way of action for their costs and damages" — and the judgment was affirmed.

Harris v. Benson, Tr. 5 G. 2. Str. 910. In an action against the drawer of an inland bill after an acceptance, Raymond, C. J. ruled, that for want of a protest according to 9 & 10 W. 3. c. 17. the drawer could not be charged with interest. In Lumprocure it would preclude the holder from recovering against the persons entitled to notice any

---

ley v. Palmer, Ann. 77. Lord Hardwicke says, "At common law there was no way to charge the drawer of an inland bill with interest and costs after a protest; and therefore the first act was made, that after acceptance by underwriting, these bills might be protested for non-payment, and that thereon interest and charges should be paid by the drawer from the time of the protest, the statute does not say the original sum, for that is recoverable without protest, but interest and charges."

Windle v. Andrews, B. R. Trin. 59 G. 3. 2 Barnew. 696. In an action against the drawer of an inland bill, in which the requisites specified in 3 & 4 Ann. c. 9. § 6. occurred, rule nisi to strike out the interest from the verdict, on the ground that there had been no protest; but on cause shewn, the court held the want of a protest no ground for disallowing interest where notice of the dishonour of the bill had been duly given; that the object of 9 & 10 W. 3., and 3 & 4 Ann. c. 9. § 4. was to give interest damages and costs in cases in which it was supposed they were not recoverable at common law, not to deprive a plaintiff of them in any case in which the common law would give them; that the 5th section, which contained the words of deprivation, was by way of proviso only, to qualify the additional benefit that statute and the statute of William were supposed for the first time to give; that the proviso in the 8th section contained words to secure to a plaintiff all his common law rights, and that the right to damages was a common law right; that it was upon this principle only that the constant allowance of interest where there was no protest could be explained; that the 5th section contained words to annul parol acceptances; and in Rex v. Meggott, Hil. 7 Geo. 2. ante, p. 134. Eyre C. J. of K. B. held that they had that effect; that this notion was corrected in Lumley v. Palmer, ante, p. 134. in Mich. Term 8 Geo. 2. upon the principle now adopted by the court, that the 5th section of 3 & 4 Ann. c. 9. deprived a party of no remedy he had at common law; that that case

special damages or costs occasioned by the non-acceptance or non-payment and interest, yet it hath not generally that effect. (86)

A protest may (87) also be made on the non-payment of coal notes, given pursuant to 3 Geo. 2, c. 26. § 7.

---

must be considered as having virtually overruled Harris v. Benson, which was in Tr. 5 Geo. 2., and that from that time, for any thing which appeared to the contrary, parol acceptances had been held binding, and interest had been allowed against the drawers and indorsers of all inland bills though no instance could be shewn in which any such bill had been protested.

(86) By 3 & 4 Anne, c. 9. § 5. it is provided, that if such (see § 4. ante, p. 210.) bill be not accepted by such under writing, or indorsement in writing, no drawer of any such inland bill shall be liable to pay any costs, damages, or interest thereupon, unless such protest be made for the non-acceptance thereof, and within 14 days after such protest the same be sent, or otherwise notice thereof be given to the party from whom such bill was received, or left in writing at the place of his or her usual abode: and if such bill be accepted, and not paid before the expiration of three days after the said bill shall become due and payable, then no drawer of such bill shall be compellable to pay any costs, damages, or interest thereupon, unless a protest be made and sent, or notice thereof be given, in manner and form above-mentioned. Nevertheless every drawer of such bill shall be liable to make payment of costs, damages, and interest upon such inland bill, if any one protest be made of non-acceptance or non-payment thereof, and notice thereof be sent, given, or left as aforesaid.

(87) By 3 Geo. 2. c. 26. § 7., be it enacted, That from and after the 24th day of June, 1730, all lightermen and other buyers of, or contractors for, coals on board of any ship or vessel in the port of London, shall, at the time of the delivery of such coals, either pay for the same in ready money, or for

A foreign bill should be noted for non-acceptance or non-payment on the (88) day on which acceptance or payment is refused; but it would

---

such part thereof as shall not be so paid shall give their respective promissory note or notes of their hands for payment thereof, expressing therein the words *value received in coals*, payable at such day or days, time or times, as shall for that purpose be agreed upon between such lighterman or other buyer of or contractor for coals, and the master or owner of such ship or vessel, or his agent or factor on his behalf; and that all such notes, in case of non-payment at the respective days and times therein mentioned, shall and may be protested or noted in such manner as inland bills of exchange may now be; and in default of such protesting or noting by any indorsee, and notice thereof given by such indorsee to the respective indorser or indorsers, within twenty days after such failure of payment, such respective indorser or indorsers, to whom such notice shall not be given, shall not be chargeable with or liable to answer or pay such sum of money, as shall be mentioned to be payable in or by such note or notes, nor any part thereof; any law, usage, or custom to the contrary thereof notwithstanding.

(88) In Buller's Nisi Prius, 272. it is said, "The use of noting is, that it should be done the very day of refusal, and the protest may be drawn any day after by the notary, and be dated of the day the noting was made." See Chitty on Bills, 163—4.

In Leftley v. Mills, 4 Term Rep. 174., Buller J. says, "With regard to Foreign bills of exchange, all the books agree that the protest must be made on the last day of grace." This however is not said with reference to any distinction between the time of noting the bill, and that of formally drawing up the protest! but merely, as furnishing an argument, to shew within what time payment must be made; and the argument is equally conclusive, whether the party have the power of noting or of protesting the bill on the last day of grace. Indeed the noting is in effect an incipient protest.

seem that the protest (89) may be formally drawn up at any future period, provided that, in the event of a suit, it be drawn up before the commencement of such suit.

A protest for (90) non-acceptance of an inland bill may be made in like manner as for non-acceptance of a Foreign bill; but a protest for (91) non-payment of an inland bill cannot be made until the day after such bill has become due.

---

(89) Chaters v. Bell, 4 Esp. N. P. C. 48. In an action by an indorsee against an indorser of a foreign bill, it appeared that the bill became due on the 24th of April, when payment was demanded and refused, and the bill noted for non-payment. Regular notice of the dishonour was given to the defendant, but he refused payment because there was no protest. On 14th of May, the protest was formally drawn up, and this action was afterwards brought. Lord Kenyon said, "He was of opinion, that if the bill was regularly presented and noted at the time, the protest might be made at any future period." A verdict was found for the plaintiff, but the point was reserved: and on the case coming on to be tried again on a venire facias de novo before Lord Ellenborough, his lordship expressed his concurrence with the opinion of Lord Kenyon. See the preceding note.

Mr. Selwyn, in his abridgment of the Law of Nisi Prius, 379. says, That a case was reserved in Chaters v. Bell, for the opinion of the court, and that the court, after argument, conceiving the question to be of great importance, directed it to be turned into a special verdict; but that the sum in dispute being small, and the parties unwilling to incur the expence of a special verdict, the recommendation of the court was not attended to, and the case was not mentioned again.

(90) See 3 & 4 Ann. c. 9. § 4. ante, p. 210. n. (80).

(91) See 9 & 10 W. 3. c. 17. § 1. ante, p. 211. n. (81). which enables persons to make such protests "after the *expiration* of three days" after the bill has become due.

A notice the day the bill or note becomes due, is not too soon; for though payment may still be made within the day, non-payment on presentment is a dishonour. (92)

To such of the parties as reside in the place where the presentment was made, the notice must be given at the farthest, by the expiration of the (93) day following the failure; to those who reside elsewhere, by (94) the post of that or the next post day.

---

(92) Burridge v. Manners, 3 Campb. 193. Indorsee of note against payee; the note was presented the forenoon of the day it became due, when payment was refused, and in the afternoon of that day plaintiff sent notice of its dishonour to defendant; it was urged that this notice was too soon, because the maker had the whole day to pay the note; but Lord Ellenborough thought it a sufficient notice, for as soon as the maker refused payment the note was dishonoured. The plaintiff had a verdict.

(93) Tindal v. Brown, ante, p. 207. note (74). Muilman v. D'Eguino, ante, p. 184. note (31).

Smith v. Mullet, 2 Campb. N. P. C. 208. In an action against an indorser of a bill, the only question was, whether the plaintiff had given due notice of its dishonour to one Aylett, his immediate indorser. All the parties resided in London: the bill became due and was dishonoured on the 19th of May, a Saturday. The holder (who had received it from the plaintiff) gave notice to the plaintiff on the Monday; and Plaintiff sent notice to Aylett on Tuesday, by the twopenny post, but so late that it did not reach Aylett till Wednesday. Lord Ellenborough said, he thought there could be no rule more convenient than that where all the parties resided in London each should have a day to give notice; here a day had been lost. He therefore nonsuited the plaintiff.

(94) Malynes, B. 3. c. 6. § 1. 1st ed. p. 265. Mar. 2d ed. p. 24.

Each party has a day for giving notice. (95)

And he will be entitled to the whole day, though the post by which he is to send it, goes out within the day. (95)

Therefore, where the notice is to be sent by the post, it will be sufficient if it is sent by the post of the following day. (95)

Where a party receives notice on a Sunday, he is in the same situation as if it did not reach him till the Monday; he is not bound to pay it any attention till the Monday; (95)

And has the whole of Monday for the purpose. (95)

---

(95) Bray v. Hadwen, 5 Maule, 68. Plaintiffs paid into their Bankers at Launceston a bill on London. On Sunday morning, 17th July, about half after eight, the Launceston bankers received a letter from London announcing its dishonour; Monday evening they put into the post a letter to plaintiffs at Tavistock to give them notice; that post did not leave Launceston till twelve on Tuesday; a post left Launceston for Tavistock at twelve on Monday. Plaintiffs forwarded notice without delay to the person who indorsed the bill to them, and that person immediately forwarded notice to defendant, who was an earlier indorser. Two queries were made; one, whether the Launceston bankers were not bound to have sent notice to plaintiff by Monday's post; and, secondly, whether plaintiff should not have given notice immediately to defendant, and not have left it to the later indorser to give that notice: Graham B. overruled both objections, and verdict for plaintiff: and on motion for new trial, the court held it was now the settled rule that each party was entitled to an entire day for the purpose of giving notice, and that the Launceston bankers therefore were not bound to send their notice by the Monday's post, but had the whole of Monday to put in their letter; and

So if the day on which notice ought thus to be given be a (96) day of public rest, as Christmas-day or Good Friday, or a day of (97) similar sanctity according to the religion of the party bound to give notice, the notice need not be given until the following day.

If the holder of a bill or note place it in the hands of his banker, the banker is only bound to

---

that, as there was no delay in transmitting notice to defendant, he could not protect himself on the ground of want of notice, and rule refused.

Wright v. Shawcross, 2 Barnew. 501. Plaintiff received notice by a letter on a Sunday of the dishonour of a bill; he did not send notice to defendant till Tuesday's post, which set out in the evening; he might have sent it in the evening of Monday by the Monday's post. But on motion for new trial, after verdict for plaintiff, the court held plaintiff was not bound to open the letter till Monday, nor bound to send notice till the Tuesday, and therefore rule refused.

(96) See Smith v. Mullet, ante, p. 219, and Haynes v. Birks, and Scott v. Lifford, post, p. 223. note (98). See also Tassell v. Lewis, ante, p. 198. note (53), and 39 & 40 Geo. 3. c. 42. enacting, that with respect to noting and protesting bills and notes which become due on Good Friday, that day shall be considered like a Sunday or Christmas-day.

(97) Lindo v. Unsworth, 2 Campb. N. P. C. 602. Notice of the dishonour of a bill was sent to the plaintiff in London, on the 8th of October; but he being a Jew, and the 8th of October being the day of the greatest Jewish festival throughout the year, on which all Jews are prohibited from attending to secular affairs, gave no notice by the post of that day to the defendant, who lived at Lancaster, but sent it to him by the post of the 9th. Lord Ellenborough held, that the plaintiff was excused by his religion from giving notice on the 8th; and that the notice sent by the post on the 9th was sufficient. The plaintiff had a verdict.

give notice of its dishonour to his customer, in like manner as if he were himself the holder, and his customer were the party next entitled to notice. (98)

And the customer has the like time to communicate such notice, as if he had received it from a holder. (98)

And therefore by thus placing a bill or note in a banker's hands, the number of persons from whom notice must pass, is increased by one. (98)

Thus notice sent by a London banker to a London customer, the day after the dishonour, (98) is in time; and if the customer communicate that notice the day following, that (98) will be in time also.

---

(98) Haynes v. Birks, 3 Bos. and Pull. 599. In an action against the indorser of a bill, it appeared that the bill, which had been indorsed in blank and deposited by the plaintiff in the hands of his bankers, became due on Saturday, October 1st. On that day, at two o'clock, it was presented for payment by the bankers, and payment being refused, it was again presented between nine and ten at night by a notary, and again dishonoured; the bankers sent the bill, and notice of its dishonour, to the plaintiff on the Monday, and the plaintiff gave notice to the defendant on Tuesday, about noon: the plaintiff lived at Knightsbridge, and the defendant in Tottenham-court-road. The only question was, whether this notice was sufficient. A verdict was found for the plaintiff, with liberty to defendant to move to enter a nonsuit. On motion accordingly, it was urged that the bankers were to be considered as the agents of the plaintiff, and that the defendant was entitled to the same notice as if the bill had remained in the plaintiff's hands: but the court thought that reasonable diligence had been used, and therefore refused a rule. Lord Alvanley, however, said, that

It is no excuse for not giving notice the next day after a party receives one, that he received his notice earlier than the preceding parties were bound to give it; and that he gave notice within what would have been proper time if each preceding party had taken all the time the law allowed him. The time is to be calculated according to the

---

if a bill be returned to a banker, he is bound to give notice to his principal that very day, if he can do so by using ordinary diligence.

Scott v. Lifford, 9 East's Rep. 347. A bill due on the 4th of June, was presented on that day, by Down and Co. the plaintiff's bankers, who lived in London; the plaintiff lived in London also, and they gave him notice on the 5th. The defendant (the drawer) lived at Shadwell; and on the 6th the plaintiff sent notice to him by the twopenny post. Lord Ellenborough left it to the jury, whether the plaintiff had communicated the notice in reasonable time; and they thought he had. And on a motion for a new trial, Lord Ellenborough said, he could not say that the plaintiff, omissis omnibus aliis negotiis, was bound to post off immediately with notice; it was sufficient if reasonable diligence had been used. The court thought the verdict right, and refused a rule.

Langdale v. Trimmer, 15 East. 291. Plaintiff paid a note into Drummonds, his bankers; it became due 25th February, was presented and dishonoured; they presented it again the 26th a little before five, and payment being again refused, they gave notice directly to plaintiff, who lived in Holborn; by the next day's post, plaintiff gave notice to defendant who lived at Farnham. Lord Ellenborough thought both notices in time, and after verdict for plaintiff and motion for a new trial, the court agreed with him; they thought the banker was to be considered as a distinct holder, not as identified with his customer, and that the banker had till the next day to give notice to his customer, and the customer till the day following; and the rule was refused.

period when the party in fact received his notice. (99)

Nor is it any excuse that there are several intervening parties between him who gives the notice and defendant to whom it is given; and that if the notice had been passed through those intervening parties, and each had taken the time the law allows, the defendant would not have had the notice sooner. (99)

Sending a verbal notice to a merchant's counting-house (100) is sufficient; and if no person be there in the ordinary hours of business, it is (100) not necessary to leave or send a written one.

---

(99) Turner v. Leech, 4 Barnew. 451. Plaintiff was the eleventh indorser to a bill, defendant the 8th; plaintiff indorsed it to Bennett, Bennett to Fletcher, Fletcher to Hordem, and Hordem to Sansom, and Co.; it was dishonoured Saturday, 30th August, and on Monday, 1st September, Sansom gave notice to Hordem; this reached Hordem the 2d, and the same day he gave notice to Fletcher; Fletcher sent notice to Bennett on the third, and this notice reached Bennett on the 4th; he did nothing till the 8th, and then he gave notice to plaintiff, who paid the bill. Plaintiff sued defendant, and on case plaintiff urged that Bennett's laches had not discharged defendant, because defendant had notice as soon as he would, had each party between him and Sansom taken the time the law allowed them; but the court was clear that defendant was discharged, and judgment for defendant.

(100) Goldsmith and al. v. Bland and al. at Guildhall, cor. Lord Eldon, 1 March, 1800. The plaintiffs sued the defendants as indorsers of two foreign bills, and to prove notice the plaintiffs shewed that they sent a clerk to the defendants' counting-house, near the exchange, between four and five o'clock in the afternoon; nobody was in the counting-house; the clerk

Sending a verbal notice to a man's place of business, at a time when he or some of his people might reasonably be expected there, is sufficient; it is not necessary to leave or send a written notice, or to send to the house where he lives. (101)

---

saw a servant girl at the house, who said, that nobody was in the way, and he returned, having left no message with her. Lord Eldon told the jury, that if they thought the defendants ought to have had somebody in the counting house at the time, he was of opinion, that the plaintiffs had done all that was necessary by sending their clerk; that the notice was in law sufficient, if the time was regular, whether the defendants were solvent at the time or not. The jury thought that the defendants ought to have had somebody in the counting house at the time, and that the plaintiffs had done all that was necessary. Verdict for the plaintiffs for 1633*l.*

(101) Cross v. Smith, 1 Maule, 545. Smith and Co. had a bill for 3176*l.* drawn by Fea and Co. accepted by Tuke, payable at Smith, Payne and Smith's, due 12th of April, 1810; this bill they remitted to Smith, Payne and Smith, their correspondents. Tuke banked with Smith and Co.; 6th of April Tuke directed Smith and Co. to write to Smith, Payne and Smith, not to pay this bill; they did so, and when the bill was due it was protested, and sent to Smith and Co. at Hull. Fea and Co. had a counting-house at Hull, where they were merchants, and one lived within a mile, and the other within ten of Hull. The morning after Smith and Co. received the bill, their clerk went to give notice, and called at the counting-house of Fea and Co. about half after ten; he found the outward door open, the inner one locked; he knocked so that he must have been heard had any one been there; waited two or three minutes and went away; on his return he saw Fea and Co.'s attorney, and told him. The next morning he went again at the same hour, but with no better success. No written notice was left, nor was any notice sent to the residence of any of the partners. Fea

But telling a man's attorney that a bill is dishonoured, is no notice, unless the attorney has more than the usual powers. (101)

Though the indorser of a bill receive directions from the acceptor, to send word to the house at which it is payable to forbid its payment, and he does so, he is not bound to give any notice

---

and Co. became bankrupts, and their assignees insisted that Smith and Co. had made this bill their own, and were not entitled to carry it to the debit of Fea and Co.; first, because they ought to have given notice of the directions they received from Tuke, to prevent payment by Smith, Payne and Smith; and secondly, because calling at the counting-house without leaving a written notice, and without sending one to the residence of some one of the partners, was not sufficient notice of the bill's dishonour. On case, and time to consider, the court thought the notice to the attorney nothing, because he was not the proper person to receive such a notice; but they held, that Smith and Co. were not bound to give notice of the directions they had received, and that it would have been a breach of confidence in them to have done so; and they held, that going to the counting-house at a time it should have been open, was sufficient; and that it was not necessary to leave a written notice, or to send to the residence of any of the parties; postea to defendants.

Bancroft v. Hall, Holt, 476. Indorsee of bill against drawer. Plaintiff received notice of the bill's dishonour at Manchester, 24th of May; the same day he sent a letter by a private hand to his agent at Liverpool, to give defendant notice; the agent called at defendant's counting-house about six or seven, p.m., but the counting-house was shut up, and defendant did not receive notice till the morning of the 27th, Monday. Two points were ruled, — that sending by a private hand to an agent to give notice was sufficient; secondly, that it was sufficient for the agent to take the ordinary mode to give notice; the ordinary time of shutting was eight or nine.

of those directions to any of the parties to the bill. (101)

And he is entitled to act as though he had received no such directions. (101)

And it is the same if the holder of the bill receive those directions.

Sending (102) notice by the post is sufficient though it is not received; and where there is no post, it is sufficient to send by the ordinary mode of conveyance.

Therefore in the case of a foreign bill it (103) is sufficient to send it by the first regular ship bound for the place to which it is to be sent; and (103) it is no objection, that if sent by a ship

---

102) Saunderson v. Judge, ante, p. 174. note (13). The holder of a note wrote to the defendant, who was one of the indorsers, to say it was dishonoured, and put the letter in the post, but there was no evidence that it ever reached the defendant, and the court held, that sending the letter by the post was quite sufficient. S. P. Kuth, v. Weston, 3 Esp. N. P. C. 54. See also Scott v. Lifford, 9 East's Rep. 347. and 1 Campb. N. P. C. 246. In this case the parties lived in London and its vicinity, within reach of the twopenny post; and notice of the dishonour of a bill was sent by that conveyance, and the court of king's bench held that it was sufficient. The notice however must appear to have been put in in due time, Hilton v. Fairclough, 2. Campb. 633.

(103) Muilman v. D'Eguino, ante, p. 184. note (31). To debt on bond conditioned to pay certain bills drawn on India at sixty days' sight, in case they should be returned protested; defendant pleaded that he had not notice so soon as he should have had. It appeared that notice was sent by the first English ships, but that by the accidental conveyance of a foreign ship not bound for England, and by which the holder wrote to Eng-

bound elsewhere, it would by accident have arrived sooner, though the holder wrote other letters by that ship to the place to which the notice was to be sent.

And it is not essential the notice should be sent by the post where there is one; sending to an agent by a private conveyance, that he may give the notice, will be sufficient, if the agent give the notice, or take due steps for the purpose, without delay. (104)

And it will be of no consequence though the notice by the agent is not quite so early as notice by the post would have been. (104)

Where it is not known where a party lives, due diligence must in general be used to find out. (105) (106)

---

land upon other matters, notice might have been sent sooner, and would have arrived sooner; but Eyre C. J. told the jury, that notice by the first regular ships bound for England was sufficient, and that it was not necessary to send notice by the chance conveyance of a foreign ship. The jury found for the plaintiff, and the court was satisfied with the verdict, and refused a new trial.

(104) See Bancroft v. Holt, ante, p. 226.

(105) Bateman v. Joseph, 12 East's Rep. 433. In an action by an indorsee against the payee and first indorser of a bill, it appeared that the plaintiff received notice of its dishonour on the 30th of September, in time to have given notice to the defendant on that day; he gave no notice however until the 4th of October; to excuse which, his clerk proved that the plaintiff did not know the defendant's residence until that day. Lord Ellenborough left it to the jury, whether the plaintiff had used due diligence to find the defendant's residence. They

And where such diligence is unsuccessful, it will excuse want of notice. (105)

But merely enquiring at the house where a bill is payable, is not due diligence for finding out an indorser. (106)

Inquiry should be made of some of the other parties to the bill or note, and of persons of the same name. (106)

Calling on the last indorser, and last but one, the day after the bill becomes due, to know where the drawer lives, and on his not being in the way calling again the next day, and then giving the drawer notice, may be sufficient. (107)

---

found for the plaintiff; and on motion for a new trial, the court refused the rule, saying, whether due notice had been given was a question of law; but whether due diligence had been used to discover the place of residence of a person entitled to notice, was a question of fact.

(106) Beveridge v. Burgis, 3 Campb. 262. In an action by the indorsee of a bill against the indorser, the excuse for not giving notice to defendant was, that plaintiff did not know his residence, but the only enquiry he proved was at the house where the bill was made payable. Sed per Lord Ellenborough, how could he expect information there? he might have enquired of other parties to the bill, or of persons of the same name in the directory: ignorance may excuse notice, but reasonable diligence must be used to obtain knowledge. Nonsuit.

(107) Browning v. Kinnier, Gow. 81. Defendant indorsed to Newman, Newman to Maberly, Maberly to Chesterman, and Chesterman to plaintiff; the bill became due 23d November; on the 24th plaintiff applied to Chesterman to know where defendant lived; Chesterman could not tell, and referred him to Maberly; he called on Maberly at 4 p.m., but Maberly not being at home, he did not repeat his call till the next morning,

But if a party when he passes a bill or note declines saying where he lives, and undertakes to call upon the acceptor to see if the bill is paid, he cannot complain of want of notice. (108)

Notice to one of several partners, is notice to all: and when a bill has been drawn by a firm upon one of the partners, and by him accepted and dishonoured, it is (109) unnecessary to give notice of such dishonour to the firm; for this must necessarily be known to one of them, and the knowledge of one is the knowledge of all.

If the holder gives due notice of the bill's dishonour, but intimates that he expects it will be paid in a given time, and that he will keep it that time without putting more expense upon it unless the person written to objects, it will be no answer to an action afterwards against the person written

---

and then Maberly gave him the information, and he gave defendant notice. Dallas C. J. thought reasonable diligence had been used, but he left the question to the jury, who were of the same opinion.

(108) Phipson v. Kneller, 4 Campb. 285. 1 Stark. 116. Plaintiff, the holder of a bill, asked defendant, the drawer, where he lived; he said, he had no regular residence, but lived amongst his friends, and he would call himself upon the acceptor, and see if the bill was paid. Lord Ellenborough held that this dispensed with all notice, and threw it upon defendant to enquire; and plaintiff had a verdict.

(109) See Porthouse v. Parker and another, post, in which Lord Ellenborough held that the plaintiff was not bound to prove that the defendants had received express notice of the dishonour of the bill, assigning the reason mentioned in the text.

to, that he had no notice upon the expiration of the extended time of non-payment. (110)

The law does not require a second notice when the extended time expires. (110)

But if the party written to, sustain any damage from not having such notice, he may perhaps be entitled to bring an action on that account. (110)

The (111) drawer of a bill, and every indorser of a bill or note, is, primâ facie, to be presumed entitled to bring an action on paying it, and therefore entitled to insist on a want of notice, or on a

---

(110) Foster v. Jurdison, 16 East. 105. Indorsee against drawer. When payment was refused, plaintiffs apprised defendants thereof, but added, they had reason to believe a friend would advance the money for the acceptor in a few days, that they would therefore hold it till the end of the week without putting more expense upon it, unless they heard from defendant to the contrary; the bill was not paid, but no further application was made to defendant for near two months: action, and Wood B. being of opinion that plaintiff should have given a second notice at the end of the week, and the jury thinking that certain circumstances proved, did not amount to a waiver of the want of such notice, verdict for defendant: but on rule nisi for a new trial, and cause shewn, the court thought plaintiffs had done all the law merchant required by giving one notice, that they then, at the highest, made themselves agents for defendants, to endeavour to get payment, and if any damage resulted to defendant for want of notice, it might perhaps entitle him to call on defendant as his agent by action, but that it was no defence to the action. Rule absolute.

(111) Vide Bickerdike v. Bolman, post, p. 237. note (119); and Rogers v. Stephens, post, p. 234. note (117).

neglect to make a proper presentment, but the (112) contrary may be proved.

And a surety, though not a party to a bill or note, may be discharged by want of notice and neglect to present, if it is probable he would otherwise have been safe. (113)

As if the parties who ought to have paid were solvent when the bill or note became due, and have failed since. (113)

---

(112) Bickerdike v. Bolman, post, p. 237. note (119); Rogers v. Stephens, post, p. 234. note (117); and Goodall v. Dolley, post, p. 236. note (118).

(113) Philips v. Astling, 2 Taunt. 206. The declaration stated, that in consideration that the plaintiff would sell and deliver to Davenport and Finney certain goods, to be paid for by a bill to be drawn by Davenport and Finney on Houghton at six months, the defendants undertook to guaranty the payment of such bill. It then averred delivery of the goods, acceptance of the bill, its presentment for payment, and dishonour. At the trial, it appeared that Houghton was at sea when the bill became due, which was on the 14th of July, 1808; but that he had an agent residing in London, authorised to accept bills, and who had accepted this. That no presentment for payment was made to this agent when the bill became due. That on the 16th of July, the plaintiff gave Davenport and Finney notice that the bill remained unpaid, but no notice was given to the defendants. In February, 1809, Davenport and Finney became insolvent, and Houghton was declared a bankrupt in July, 1809, after which payment was demanded of the defendants. A verdict was found for the plaintiff, but the court, upon a rule nisi for a nonsuit, after referring to Warrington v. Furbor (infra), said, that here the insolvency of the drawers and the bankruptcy of the acceptor, did not happen until long after the bill became due, and that for any thing that appeared, if the money had been demanded either of the drawer or acceptor, the bill might have been paid: but that

But a person not party to a bill or note, cannot complain of laches or want of notice, unless he can shew it has done him prejudice. (114)

Therefore he cannot complain if the person who ought to have paid the bill or note were insolvent when it should have been paid. (114)

---

the necessary steps not having been taken to obtain payment from the parties who were liable upon the bill, and solvent, the guarantee must be discharged, and therefore they made the rule absolute.

(114) Warrington and another v. Furbor and another, 8 East. Rep. 242. The plaintiffs guarantied the payment of the price, to the extent of 1000*l.*, of goods to be sold by one Martin to the defendants, at six months' credit. The goods were furnished, and the defendants accepted a bill at six months, for the value. This bill became due on the 3d of December, 1801; but on the preceding 21st of November the defendants became bankrupts. The plaintiffs were therefore obliged to pay the 1000*l.* and now brought this action to recover the same. It was objected that the plaintiffs had not proved a presentment of the bill to the defendants for payment, without which, it was urged, that Martin could not have recovered against the plaintiffs, and therefore that the latter had paid the money in their own wrong. Lord Ellenborough held the proof unnecessary; this not being an action on the bill, and the defendants having been recently stripped of all their property; and the plaintiffs had a verdict; and on rule nisi to set it aside, and cause shewn, the court held the verdict right: and Lawrence J. said, the guarantees were not prevented from shewing that they ought not to have been called upon at all, for that the principal debtors could have paid the bill if demanded of them. Rule discharged.

Swinyard v. Bowes, 5 Maule, 62. Action for goods sold. Defence, that plaintiff had drawn on Chesner, a debtor of defendant, for the amount, and had given defendant no notice of the dishonour of that bill; Chesner was bankrupt the week after the bill became due, and was not in a condition in the

And in an action on a bond from the drawer or indorser of a bill, conditioned to pay it in a limited time after it becomes due, if the acceptor does not, it is no defence that the bill was not duly presented for payment. (115)

Or that due notice of its dishonour was not given to the defendant. (115)

Payment of (116) part, or (117) a promise to

---

interim to pay it. Bayley J. thought the defendant not within the custom of merchants, because he was not party to the bill; and as he did not appear to have been prejudiced by the want of notice, the not giving it him furnished no ground of defence; and on motion for new trial, the court thought him right, and rule refused.

(115) Murray v. King, 5 Barnew. 165. In an action against the payee of a bill, on a bond from him and the drawer to pay the bill in a month after it became due, if the acceptor did not, defendant pleaded that the bill was not duly presented for payment, and secondly, that defendant had not due notice of its dishonour. Plaintiff replied, that the acceptance was a forgery; and defendant rejoined, that he did not know it when the bill became due. Plaintiff demurred, and on argument the court held the pleas bad, for the condition was silent as to the presentment and notice; and had it been intended that a neglect as to presentment or notice should have avoided the bond, the obligors should have taken care to have had words to express that intention.

(116) Vaughan v. Fuller, Str. 1246. Was an action against the indorser of a note, and it being proved that the defendant had paid part, Lee C. J. held, that *that* made the proof of a demand upon the maker unnecessary. See Lundie v. Robertson, Horford v. Wilson, Gibbon v. Coggon, and Potter v. Rayworth, post.

(117) Rogers v. Stephens, 2 Term Rep. 713. In an action against the drawer of a foreign bill, an objection was taken that there was no protest; but it appearing that the defendant had

pay after full notice of the default, sufficiently evinces that the party could not have sued on

---

no effects in the hands of the drawees when the bill was drawn, or afterwards, and that on being pressed for payment by the plaintiff's agent after the bill was dishonoured, he had said, it must be paid; Lord Kenyon thought a protest or notice unnecessary; and directed the jury to find for the plaintiff, which they did: a rule was afterwards granted, to shew cause why there should not be a new trial, and it was stated *then*, and upon the shewing cause that the defendant had really been prejudiced by the want of notice to the amount of the bill, that he had advanced money to one Calvert to the amount before the bill was drawn, that Calvert desired him to draw on the drawees as Calvert's agents, that he did so on a supposition that Calvert had effects in their hands; that he afterwards settled with Calvert, and upon a reliance that the bill was paid, delivered him up effects to more than the value of the bill, and that Calvert was since insolvent; that the defendant was prepared with evidence to this effect, but that Lord Kenyon delivered it as his opinion, that it did not make a protest or notice necessary; Lord Kenyon did not recollect that this evidence was offered, but he and all the court thought it answered by the defendant's admission that the bill must be paid, because that was an admission that the plaintiff had a right to resort to him upon the bill, and that he had received no damage by the want of notice, and was a promise to pay. The rule was discharged.

Anson v. Bailey, Bull. Nisi Prius, 276. The indorsee of a note presented it for payment, but the maker pretended that the payee had promised not to indorse it over without acquainting him, and so put off the indorsee from time to time for three weeks; at the end of that period the indorsee wrote twice to the payee, stating what he had done, and the maker's excuse; the payee answered, that when he came to town he would set the matter right; and upon an action by the indorsee against the payee, the jury found for the plaintiff, though the maker became bankrupt before the second letter was written, and though he continued solvent for three weeks after the note was due.

paying the bill or note, and consequently that he cannot insist on want of notice, or of a neglect to present; a payment or promise without notice of the default does (118) not.

Wilkes v. Jacks, Peake, 202. In an action against Jacks as indorser of a bill drawn by Vaughan on Eustace and Holland, it appeared that notice had not been given to the defendant, upon which the plaintiff offered to shew that Vaughan had no effects in the hands of Eustace and Holland; sed per Lord Kenyon, "That circumstance will not avail plaintiff; the rule extends only to actions brought against the drawer; the indorser is in all cases entitled to notice, for he has no concern with the accounts between the drawer and the drawee." The plaintiff then proved a letter from the defendant acknowledging the debt, and promising to pay, and upon *that* he had a verdict.

(118) Blesard v. Hirst and another, Burr. 2670. The defendants indorsed a bill to the plaintiff, and he indorsed it over; his indorsee presented it for acceptance a month before it was due, and acceptance was refused; it was afterwards presented for payment, and payment was refused, of which notice was given to the defendants, but they had no notice of the refusal to accept. The drawer was a bankrupt before the bill was due, but he continued in credit three weeks after the presentment for acceptance. Three days after the notice, one of the defendants called on the plaintiff at Bradford, on his way to Leeds, and said he would take up the bill as he returned; but on his return he said he was advised he was not bound to do it, upon which this action was brought; and on a case reserved the court held, that though the holder might not have been obliged to present the bill for acceptance, yet as he did he ought to have given notice of the refusal, and that by not doing so he had taken the risk upon himself, and notwithstanding the promise of one of them the defendants had judgment.

Goodall v. Dolley, 1 Term Rep. 712. A bill drawn in favour of the defendant, payable the 11th of January, 1787, was presented for acceptance by the plaintiffs the 8th of November,

Proof that the drawer had no effects nor any ground to expect any in the hands of the drawee from the time the bill was drawn until it became payable, and that he had no other valid foundation to expect payment by the drawee is (119)

1786, when acceptance was refused: they gave no notice to the defendant till the 6th of January, and then did not say when the bill was presented; upon which the defendant proposed paying by instalments, but the plaintiffs rejected that offer, and brought this action. Heath J. thought the defendant discharged for want of notice, and that his offer to pay being made under an ignorance of the circumstances was not binding, and the jury, under his direction, found a verdict for the defendant. Upon cause shewn against a rule for a new trial, the court thought the direction and verdict right, and discharged the rule.

See Lundie v. Robertson, Horford v. Wilson, Gibbon v. Coggon, and Potter v. Rayworth, post.

(119) Rogers v. Stephens, ante, p. 234. note (117).

Bickerdike and another, assignees of Reichard, v. Bollman, 1 Term Rep. 405. The only question upon a case reserved was, whether a bill the bankrupt had drawn in favour of the petitioning creditor, upon a man who then, and from that time till the bill became due, was one of the bankrupt's creditors, had discharged so much of the petitioning creditor's debt, no notice having been given of its dishonour to the bankrupt? and the court, after argument, were of opinion it had not, because the reason why notice is in general necessary, is that the drawer may without delay withdraw his effects from the drawee, and that no injury may happen to him from the want of notice; but where the drawer has no effects in the hands of the drawee he cannot be injured, and is not entitled to any notice.

Goodall v. Dolley, ante, p. 236. note (118). In this case upon the application for a new trial, the plaintiff's counsel offered an affidavit that the drawer had no effects in the hands of the drawee, but the court thought *that* made no difference, the action being brought against the payee, but by Buller J.

sufficient, at least primâ facie, to shew, that the drawer would be entitled to bring no action on paying the bill, and has therefore no right to insist on the want of notice, &c. and it (120) has

---

"Had the action been against the drawer I should have been willing to let in the affidavit; that would be like the case of Bickerdike v. Bollman: if the drawer has no effects in the hands of the drawee he cannot be injured by want of notice."

Legge v. Thorpe, 12 East's Rep. 171. This was an action by an indorsee against the drawer of a foreign bill drawn upon C. B. Wyatt, payable one month after sight, of which acceptance had been refused. The declaration negatived effects in the hands of the drawee, or any consideration for the bill. It appeared at the trial that the defendant had no effects in Wyatt's hands, and that the latter had therefore refused acceptance; but that Wyatt was one of the executors of Weeks, and that Weeks's executors had desired the defendant to employ the payee of this bill to do some carpenter's work on Weeks's property, and the defendant therefore drew this bill on Wyatt to settle with the payee. Wyatt denied that he had assets to pay the bill. The only question was, whether a protest for non-acceptance were necessary. Lord Ellenborough thought not, and a verdict was given for the plaintiff, but the point was reserved; and on a rule nisi for a nonsuit, and cause shewn, the whole court held that this case was governed by those of Bickerdike v. Bollman, and Rogers v. Stephens, and discharged the rule.

(120) In Rogers v. Stephens, ante, p. 234. note (117), Mr. J. Ashhurst said, "Admitting the proof offered had been given, I do not think it clear it would take the case out of the common rule; for the law being now established, that notice to the drawer of a non-acceptance is not necessary where he has no effects in the hands of the drawee; when the plaintiff found the drawees of this bill had none of the defendant's effects in their hands, he knew he was not bound by law to give the defendant notice; he was not bound to take cognizance of any private transaction between the drawer and a third person not appearing on the face of the bill."

been doubted whether the drawer would be at liberty to shew the contrary.

It is no excuse for not giving notice to the drawer that he had no effects in the drawee's hands when the bill was drawn or became due, if he had effects on their way to the drawee. (121)

Unless the drawer gets back those effects, and would stand indebted in the amount to the drawee, if the drawee paid the bill. (121)

It is no excuse for not giving notice to the drawer that he had no effects in the drawee's hands, if the drawer would be entitled on taking up the bill to sue either the acceptor; (122)

Or any other party; (122)

As if he and the acceptor lent their names to the payee or a subsequent indorsee. (122)

---

(121) Rucker v. Hiller, 3 Campb. 217. 16 East, 43. In an action by the indorsee of a bill against the drawer, it appeared that the drawer had no effects in the drawee's hands, but that he had shipped goods which were on their way to the drawee: the drawee refused to accept, but no notice thereof was given to the drawer; and it was insisted, that as the drawee had not received effects, defendant was not entitled to notice: Lord Ellenborough thought otherwise, as the drawer was in expectation that the goods he had shipped would reach the drawee; and nonsuit: on motion to set aside the nonsuit, it did not appear but that the drawer might have been prejudiced by want of notice, and the rule refused.

(122) Corey v. Scott, 3 Barnew. 619. Indorsee against drawer, on bill drawn by defendant on Gordon, and accepted by him, payable to defendant, indorsed by him to Lough, and by Lough to plaintiff; no evidence of notice to defendant; excuse that defendant had no effects in Gordon's hands; answer, that Lough was to provide for the payment, and that Gordon,

It is no excuse for not giving notice to the drawer that he had in fact no funds in the hands of the drawee if he had made a provision to have such funds there, and might reasonably expect they were there. (123)

As if he drew upon a cargo he shipped for this kingdom, and such cargo was in the hands of a broker, who was to pay the proceeds to the drawee. (123)

If the drawer had effects in the hands of the drawee at the time when the bill was drawn, it has been held he (124) is entitled to notice of non-

---

and defendant Scott both lent their names to accommodate him. Abbot C. J. thought this rebutted the excuse from want of effects; and nonsuit: and on rule nisi to enter verdict for plaintiff, and cause shewn, the court were clear defendant was entitled to notice, for had he taken up the bill he might certainly have sued Lough, if not Gordon: he was, therefore, in a situation in which want of notice might have hurt him, and if so he was entitled to notice; and rule discharged.

(123) Robins v. Gibson, 3 Campb. 334. To excuse want of notice to the drawer of a foreign bill, the drawee proved that he had in fact no funds of the drawer in his hands from the time the bill was given till its becoming due: but he said the bill was drawn on a cargo shipped by the drawer for England, that the cargo was in the hands of a broker for sale, and when it was sold, the proceeds were to be paid to him to answer the bill; and Lord Ellenborough held, that under these circumstances, as the bill was drawn on expected funds, the drawer was entitled to notice: plaintiff then proved notice, and had a verdict.

And see 1 Bos. and Pull. 655; and 12 East, 175.

(124) Orr and others v. Maginnis, 7 East. Rep. 359. In an action by the payees against the drawer of a foreign bill, payable at ninety days after sight, the declaration averred present-

acceptance; although at the time when the bill was presented for acceptance, and from thence until presentment for payment, he had not any.

So if he had effects in the hands of the drawee, when the bill was presented for acceptance, it has been held he will be entitled to notice of non-acceptance (125), although he was indebted to the drawee greatly beyond the amount of such effects.

---

ment for acceptance and refusal, presentment for payment and refusal, and protest for non-payment; it then averred, that at the time of making the bill, and from thence until presentment for payment, the defendant had no effects in the hands of the drawees. At the trial it appeared, that at the time of *drawing* the bill, the defendant had effects in the hands of the drawees, but to what amount did not appear: but that when the bill was presented for acceptance, and thence until presentment for payment, he had not any. The bill was only noted for non-acceptance, but was protested for non-payment: no notice of non-acceptance was given to the defendant. The plaintiffs had paid the amount of the bill to an indorsee. They were non-suited for want of proving protest for, and notice of, non-acceptance. On motion to set aside the nonsuit, Bickerdike and Bollman, and other cases, were cited to shew that no notice, and therefore no protest, was necessary. But Lord Ellenborough said, that that case went on the ground that there were no effects in the hands of the drawee at the time when the bill was drawn; and the other cases followed on the same ground; but that no case had extended the exemption to cases where the drawee had effects of the drawer's in his hands at the time when the bill was drawn, though the balance might vary afterwards, and be turned into the opposite scale. Rule refused.

(125) Blackhan v. Doren, 2 Campb. N. P. C. 503. This was an action against the drawer of a bill for 250*l.* payable after sight; of which acceptance had been refused; and to excuse the want of notice of non-acceptance, it was proved that when the bill was presented, though the drawer had effects in the

Notice to the drawer is not necessary, though he had supplied the drawee with goods, if those goods were supplied upon a credit which had not expired, and the drawer could entertain no reasonable expectation that the drawee would pay the bill; (126)

And could have no remedy against him for not doing so. (126)

The drawer is entitled to notice, though he had no effects in the hands of the drawee at the time the bill was drawn, or at the time it was accepted, if he had before it became due. (127) (128)

---

hands of the drawees to the amount of 1500*l.*, yet that he owed them 10,000*l.* or 11,000*l.* And that they had appropriated the effects to go in satisfaction of this debt. This appropriation, however, was without the defendant's privity. Lord Ellenborough held, that a notice was necessary, and nonsuited the plaintiff.

(126) Claridge v. Dalton, 4 Maule, 226. Defendant drew upon Pickford for 300*l.* at two months after date: defendant had supplied Pickford with goods to the amount of 200*l.*, and between June and September he supplied him with 70*l.* worth more; but, according to their course of dealing, the goods were to be paid for by acceptance at the end of the year. Defendant being sued by an indorsee, insisted upon want of notice: but on point saved, the court held, that under the circumstances, as he had no ground for expecting that Pickford would pay the bill, and as notice could have done him no service, he had no right to object to the want of it; and rule nisi for nonsuit discharged.

(127) Hammond v. Dufresne, 3 Campb. 145. Action against drawer on bill for 301*l.*: proof, that at the time the bill was drawn and accepted, defendant had no effects in the hands of the drawees; but it appearing, that before the bill became due he paid 400*l.* for them, Lord Ellenborough held want of notice not excused; and nonsuit.

And it has been held that the drawer is entitled to notice, if he has any effects in the hands of the drawee at the time the bill becomes due. (128)

Though such effects are not equal to the sum in the bill. (128)

And if there are several bills in the hands of the same owner becoming due on different days, the drawer is entitled to notice as to each, though the effects in the drawee's hands are not equal to any of the bills. (128)

And a neglect to give notice will discharge the drawer as to all. (128)

It is no excuse for not giving notice to the drawer that the bill, before it became due, had been accidentally destroyed, and that he had refused to give a new bill according to 9 & 10 W. 3. c. 17. (128)

The drawee's insolvency is no excuse for not giving notice. (128.)

---

(128) Thackray v. Blackett, 3 Campb. 164. Plaintiff had two bills for 1833*l.* each, drawn by defendant on Preston and Co., due the 13th and 20th of April, 1810; they were accepted, but before they became due they were, by mistake, destroyed by Preston and Co.: plaintiff applied to defendant for new bills in their stead, according to 9 & 10 W. 3. c. 17. but defendant would not give them. Preston and Co. became insolvent before April, 1810, owing defendant 1000*l.*: the bills had been drawn for defendant's accommodation, but during their currency defendant came under engagement for Preston and Co., which created the debt from them of 1000*l.* On the 13th and 20th of April, 1810, payment of each sum was demanded of Preston and Co. and refused, but no notice thereof was given to defendant. Lord Ellenborough thought defendant entitled to

Though notice to the drawer may be dispensed with, where it is shewn he had no effects in the hands of the drawee, or any right to expect payment by him, yet evidence (129) cannot be received for the purpose of shewing that the drawer has not, from the insolvency of the drawee, or other causes, been prejudiced by the want of such notice.

It is no excuse for not presenting a bill in due time, and giving notice to the drawer that the acceptor had told the drawer he could not take up the bill and the drawer must, and that the acceptor had given the drawer part of the amount for that purpose. (130)

But the money so given may be recovered by the holder of the bill against the drawer as money had and received to the holder's use. (130)

---

notice as to each sum, and discharged by want thereof as to each, and nonsuited plaintiff, and B. R. refused to set aside the nonsuit.

(129) Dennis v. Morrice, 3 Esp. N. P. C. 158. In an action on a bill, brought by an indorsee against the drawer, it appeared that no notice had been given to the defendant of non-payment by the acceptor: to excuse which the plaintiff offered to prove, that, in fact, the defendant had not been prejudiced by the want of such notice. But Lord Kenyon said, the only case in which notice is dispensed with, is where the drawer had no effects in the hands of the drawee. This would be extending the rule still further than ever has been done, and opening new sources of litigation, in investigating whether, in fact, the drawer did receive a prejudice from the want of notice or not. He rejected the evidence, and non-suited the plaintiff.

(130) Baker v. Birch, 3 Campb. 107. In an action against the drawer of a bill for 23*l.*, it appeared, that before it became

It is (131) no excuse for not giving notice to the drawer, that on an apprehension that the bill would be dishonoured, he lodged other money,

---

due the acceptor told defendant he could not pay it, but defendant must, and that he gave him five guineas towards it; but the bill was not presented for payment till some days after it became due, nor was proper notice given of its dishonour; and Lord Ellenborough held defendant discharged upon the bill for want of notice, but he thought plaintiff entitled to recover the five guineas as so much money received to his use; and verdict accordingly.

(131) Clegg. v. Cotton, 3 Bos. and Pull. 239. Indorsees against the drawer of a bill. The bill was drawn in America on Cullen, of Liverpool, in favour of Miller and Robertson, and by them indorsed to Booth and Co., and it afterwards came to the plaintiff's hands. It was dated in 1794, and drawn at ninety days' sight. In 1800, the defendant having other effects of Cullen's in his hands, deposited them with Miller and Robertson and Booth and Co., on an undertaking from them that they would return these effects whenever it should appear that they were exonerated from this bill. Cullen afterwards became bankrupt: the defendant was arrested, and then said that he should apply to Cullen's assignees to bail him, for he had lodged property in America to answer the bill, and if he was discharged by want of notice, he should pay it over to them. Acceptance and payment were both refused, but no notice was ever given of it to the defendant. Chambre J. nonsuited the plaintiff on the ground that the defendant was discharged for want of notice: and on rule nisi to set aside the nonsuit, and cause shewn, the court held, that the special circumstances did not excuse the want of notice; that there was no fraud in the defendant, which was the ground of the rule for dispensing with notice; and that when Miller and Robertson, and Booth and Co. were exonerated, which they also were by want of notice, the money deposited with them belonged to Cullen's assignees. Rule discharged.

N. It did not appear that the defendant had got back the property which he deposited, but that circumstance was not relied on.

which he had of the drawee's, in the hands of the indorser, on an undertaking by the indorser, that he would return it whenever it should appear that he was exonerated from the bill; for his having other money of the drawee's does not entitle him to apply it to the dishonoured bill, unless he has due notice of the dishonour.

Nor (132) is it any excuse for not giving notice, &c. to the drawer of a bill, if he had effects in the hands of the drawee, that the drawee represented to the drawer when the bill was drawn, that he should not be able to provide for it, and that the drawer thereby understood that he should have to provide for it.

It is no excuse for not presenting for payment, that defendant, the drawer, told the holder the day the bill was due that he hoped the bill would be paid, and he would see what he could do, and endeavour to provide effects; (133)

And though the drawee said the preceding day that he had no effects. (133)

---

(132) Staples v. Okines, Esp. 332. In an action against the drawer of a bill, the defence was want of notice; the Plaintiff thereupon called the acceptor, who proved that when the bill was drawn he was indebted to the defendant in more than the amount of the bill, but that he then represented to the defendant that it would not be in his power to provide for the bill when it should become due, and that it was therefore then understood between them, that the defendant should provide for it, and it was contended that this superseded the necessity of giving the defendant notice; but Lord Kenyon held it did not, and nonsuited the plaintiff.

(133) Prideaux v. Collier, 2 Stark. 57. In an action against

If the drawer had no effects in the hands of the drawee, it does (134) not entitle him to notice that the payee had, except the bill is drawn to accommodate the payee.

But proof that the drawer had no effects in the hands of the drawee, or any ground to expect payment by him, is no evidence that the payee or any of the indorsers could not have brought an action on paying the bill, and therefore does not excuse the want of notice to them. (135)

If the payee of a note lend his name merely to

---

the drawer on a bill due 23d May, it appeared that plaintiff, the holder, applied to the drawee the 22d, and received for answer that he had no effects, but the drawer would probably provide them: the next day plaintiff saw the drawer, who said he hoped the bill would be paid, he would see what he could do, and endeavour to provide effects: plaintiff did not present the bill that day, and on question whether his neglect was excused, Lord Ellenborough held it was not, and plaintiff was nonsuited.

(134) Walwyn v. St. Quintin, 1 Bos. and Pull. 652. In an action by indorsee against the drawer of a bill, it appeared to have been drawn to accommodate the payee, who had placed securities to raise money in the hands of the drawee. The defendants had no effects in the hands of the drawee; and no notice having been given to him of the dishonour of the bill, the question was, whether that were made necessary by the payee's having effects in the hands of the drawee. Eyre C. J. directed a verdict for the defendant, with liberty to the plaintiff to move to enter a verdict for him. After rule nisi accordingly, cause shewn, and time taken to consider, the court held, that the defendant was not entitled to notice. But postea to the plaintiff on another ground.

(135) Goodall v. Dolley, ante, p. 236. note (118); Wilks v. Jackson, ante 236. note (117).

give it credit, and to enable the maker to raise money upon it, and knows at the time that the maker is insolvent, it has been holden that he (136) is not entitled to notice, and that it (136) is no

---

(136) De Berdt. v. Atkinson, 2 H. Bl. 336. In an action against the payee of a note, it appeared that the note was not presented for payment till the day after it became due, and that no notice was given to the defendant till five days after such presentment; but it also appearing that the defendant gave no value for the note, that he lent his name merely to give it credit, and that he knew at the time that the maker was insolvent, Eyre C. J. directed the jury to find for the plaintiff, which they did. A rule to shew cause why there should not be a new trial was afterwards granted, and upon cause shewn, per Eyre C. J. " If the maker is not known to be insolvent, insolvency will not excuse the want of an early demand; but knowledge excludes all presumption, which would otherwise arise; here the money was to be raised upon the defendant's credit; he meant to guarantee the payment, and no loss could happen to him from the want of notice." And per Buller J. " The general rule is only applicable to fair transactions, where the bill or note has been given for value in the ordinary course of trade, it is said insolvency does not take away the necessity of notice; that is true where value has been given, but no further; here the defendant lent his name merely to give credit to the note, and was not an indorser in the common course of business." Heath and Rooke, Js. concurring, the rule was discharged.

The court appears to have proceeded upon a misapplication of the rule which obtains as to accommodation acceptances; in those cases the drawer, being himself the real debtor, acquires no right of action against the acceptor, by paying the bill, and suffers no injury from want of notice of non-payment by the acceptor. But in this case the maker was the real debtor, and the payee a mere surety, having a clear right of action against the maker, upon paying the note; and therefore entitled to notice to enable him to exert that right.

defence for him that the note was not properly presented for payment.

But inasmuch as the payee, in that case, would, upon paying the note, have a clear right of action upon the note, against the maker, it would seem that he is entitled to notice of the dishonour, or to make non-presentment in time a ground of defence; and it was soon afterwards held, that where the payee of a note lent his name merely to guarantee a debt from the maker, and expected it would not be paid, and had desired the banker at whose house it was payable to send it to him and he would pay it, he was discharged by a neglect to present in proper time (137); and in a later

---

(137) Nicholson v. Gouthit, 2 H. Bl. 609. Gouthit and Burton undertook to guarantee an instalment on the debts of Greens, and for that purpose Greens drew notes payable to Gouthit at Drury and Co.'s, which Gouthit and Burton indorsed, after which they were delivered to the creditors. Before they became due Gouthit enquired at Drury and Co.'s if they had any effects, and on their saying they had not, he desired them to send the notes to him, and he would pay them; many notes were accordingly presented and paid, but the note in question not being presented till three days after it was due, Gouthit refused to pay it. Burton had supplied him with money to take up all the notes, but as this was not presented when due, he had returned the money destined to pay it. An action was brought against Gouthit, and upon the trial, Eyre C. J. thought, as he knew the note would not be paid at Drury and Co.'s, and had provided money for it, and as his indorsement was by way of guarantee, he was not injured by the delay; and that the request to send the notes to him was either a waiver of notice, or notice by anticipation; but on a rule nisi to enter a nonsuit, and cause shewn, though he thought the justice was clearly with

case, where the name was lent to give the maker credit with his bankers, the court thought notice to the payee essential. (138)

And in a (139) subsequent case, where a bill was

---

the plaintiff, he thought he could not recover, for though the indorsement was by way of guarantee, it was liable to all the legal consequences of an indorsement, and Gouthit's promise to pay was only to pay such as should be duly presented at Drury's. Heath and Rooke, Js. were of the same opinion, and the rule was made absolute.

(138) Smith and others v. Beckett, 13 East. Rep. 187. In an action against the payee and indorser of a note, drawn by Canning, dated the 28th of October, 1809, and payable on demand; it appeared that the defendant had lent his name to this, and other notes, merely to enable Canning to obtain credit with the plaintiffs, his bankers, he having then lately stopped payment, which was well known to all the parties. The plaintiffs made advances for six months upon these notes, which advances they afterwards renewed without any communication with the defendant. On the 28th of May, 1810, Canning became bankrupt, and payment of him was afterwards demanded and refused; but no notice of this dishonour was given to the plaintiffs. Lord Ellenborough thought a notice necessary, and therefore nonsuited the plaintiffs. And on a motion to set aside the nonsuit, De Berdt v. Atkinson was cited; but the court held clearly that a notice was necessary, especially as the advances had been renewed without the defendant's knowledge. Rule refused.

(139) Brown v. Maffey, 15 East. 216. Action on a bill drawn by Whitmarsh on J. and H. Neale, payable to Fiander or order, indorsed by Fiander to the defendant, by the defendant to Cosier, by Cosier to Wood, and by Wood to the plaintiff. The bill was drawn for Wood's accommodation, and all the prior names were lent to him. It did not appear that the defendant knew that any name was lent, excepting his own. The bill was dishonoured, but notice of the dishonour was not sent to the defendant. Bayley J. thought the notice necessary;

drawn for the accommodation of a remote indorsee, and the names of all the prior parties were lent to him, it was holden, in an action against one of those parties, an indorser, that the latter was entitled to notice of the dishonour of the bill, because, upon paying it, he would be entitled to sue such indorsee for repayment.

But if the payee of a note lends his name, and takes effects of the drawer to answer it (140), he is not entitled to notice, because he is the proper person to pay it, and would be entitled to no remedy over on making the payment.

It is no excuse for not giving notice to the payee, that the drawer and drawee are non-existing persons, and that their names were used for the purpose of fraud, unless the payee was privy to the fraud; (141)

---

because, if the defendant had paid the bill, he would have been entitled at least to have sued Wood, and therefore non-suited the plaintiff. A rule nisi was granted to set aside the nonsuit, and De Berdt v. Atkinson, and Sisson v. Tomlinson, 1 Selwyn's Ni. Pri. 357. n. were cited, but on cause shewn, the court thought it clear that the defendant was entitled to notice. Rule discharged.

(140) Corney v. Da Costa, Espinasse, 302. Da Costa and Co. compounded with their creditors, and to secure the composition drew notes in favour of the defendant, which he indorsed to the creditors. The defendant took effects of Da Costa and Co. at the time to the amount of the composition; and an action being brought against him upon one of these indorsements, he insisted that he had no notice of the non-payment of the note until five weeks after it was due; but Buller J. held he was not entitled to notice, and the plaintiff had a verdict.

(141) Leach v. Hewitt, 4 Taunt. 731. Cattle drew a bill in

So it is no excuse that there was a parol agreement between plaintiff and defendant, that payment should not be demanded till certain estates were sold. (142)

Upon an acceptance payable at a banker's, notice of non-payment need not be given to the acceptor, for he makes the bankers his agents; presentment to them is presentment to him, and refusal by them is refusal by him; (143)

Especially where what he has in their hands when the bill becomes due is so much below the amount of the bill, that he could have no reasonable expectation they would pay it. (143)

And it makes no difference, though he had enough in their hands when the bill was drawn. (143)

---

the name of Rogers, Crooke and Co. upon Rogers and Co., 83, Lombard Street, payable to defendant or order, and got defendant to indorse it: there were no such houses as Rogers, Crooke and Co., or Rogers and Co., but Cattle used those names for the purpose of fraud. Action against defendant by a bonâ fide holder; defence, want of notice: Mansfield C. J. told the jury, that if defendant was a party to the fraud, he was not entitled to notice, but if he acted innocently, he was: the jury thought he acted innocently, and nonsuit: and on motion for new trial, the court held him entitled to notice, and rule discharged.

(142) Tree v. Hawkins, post.

(143) Smith v. Thatcher, 4 Barnew, 200. Drawer against acceptor on a bill for 300*l*., accepted, payable at Messrs. Coutts and Co.'s: no proof was given of notice to defendant when the bill was dishonoured; but it appeared, that though he had 712*l*. at Coutts's when the bill was drawn, he had only 41*l*. when the bill became due, and on the ground of the inadequacy of that sum to pay the bill, Bayley J. directed a verdict for plaintiff.

So upon a note payable at a banker's, notice of non-payment need not be given to the maker. (144)

A person who has been once discharged by laches from his liability on a bill or note, is always discharged. And therefore where two or more parties to a bill or note have been so discharged, but one of them, not knowing of the laches, pays it, he pays it in his own wrong, and (145) cannot recover the money from another of such parties.

On motion for a new trial, Abbot C. J. expressed a strong doubt whether notice need, in any case, be given to the acceptor, because the banker was his agent; but he and the other Judges held, that where the effects were insufficient, as here, notice was not necessary. Rule refused.

Treacher v. Hinton, 4 Barnew, 413. Indorsee against acceptor, on bill addressed to defendant at Plymouth, and accepted by him, payable at Sir John Lubbock and Co.'s, bankers, London. Plaintiff proved the acceptance, and presentment at Sir John Lubbock's, but there being no evidence of notice to defendant of the bill's dishonour, Abbot C. J. nonsuited plaintiff, with leave to move to enter a verdict for plaintiff: rule nisi accordingly; and on cause shewn, the court thought the notice not necessary; that the acceptance was not a cheque upon the banker, but merely made the banker the acceptor's agent, and then it was his duty to see that his agent did his duty.

(144) Pearse v. Pemberthy, 3 Campb. 261. Action against the maker of a note payable at Were, Bruce and Co.'s: the place of payment being a material part of the instrument, it was urged that defendant should have had notice of the note's dishonour, for the answer being "not sufficient effects," shewed there were some effects there. Lord Ellenborough thought notice unnecessary, and verdict for plaintiff.

(145) Roscoe v. Hardy, 12 East. Rep. 434. Acceptance of a bill was refused; of this however the holders gave no notice, but when the bill became due, again presented it for payment, and that being refused, they called upon the plaintiff, an indorser,

for payment, and he, being ignorant of their laches, paid it. He now sued the defendant as his indorser, who set up the laches of the holders as a defence; and the plaintiff was nonsuited. On motion to set aside this nonsuit, it was urged, that the plaintiff ought not to be prejudiced by the laches of subsequent holders, of which he was ignorant, without the means of information. But the court held that his ignorance, which had prevented his availing himself of this laches as a defence, could not alter or revive the liability of the defendant, who had been discharged by the same laches.

CAP. VIII.

PAYMENT should be made to the (1) proprietor of the bill or note, or to some person authorised by him to receive payment.

If the proprietor die, payment should be made to his (2) personal representative; if he become bankrupt to his assignees; if he be an infant, to his guardian; and payment to the (3) infant him-

(1) Pothier, pl. 164.

(2) A bonâ fide payment of a debt to a person who has the probate of a will purporting to be the creditor's, will discharge the debtor, if the creditor be dead, though the will afterwards turn out to be a forgery, and the probate be annulled on that ground; because such payment is made on the authority of the probate: but it is otherwise (per Ashhurst and Buller Js.) if the creditor be living, because in such case the probate is a mere nullity. Allen v. Dundas, 3 Term. Rep. 125.

(3) See Pothier, pl. 166., and ante.

self, may be good; at least if it be beneficial to him.

In the case of a married woman, payment should be made to (4) her husband.

Payment *to* a bankrupt will be (5) good, if made bonâ fide, and without notice of the bankruptcy: and accepting a bill drawn by a trader, after a secret act of bankruptcy (6), will be protected as much as payment, though the bill do not become due until it is notorious that a commission against him has issued. The acceptance, which creates an obligation to pay, is within the protection of 1 Jac. 1. as much as actual payment.

---

(4) See Connor v. Martin, ante, p. 111. n. (31), and Barlow v. Bishop, ante, p. 41. n. (7)

(5) By 1 Jac. 1. c. 15. § 14. it is provided "That no debtor of the bankrupt be hereby endangered for the payment of his or her debt, truly and bonâ fide, to any such bankrupt, before such time as he shall understand or know that he is become a bankrupt."

(6) Wilkins v. Casey, 7 Term Rep. 711. A factor was indebted to his principal in 222*l.* 18*s.*; the principal committed an act of bankruptcy, and drew on his factor for 222*l.* 18*s.*; the factor did not know of the act of bankruptcy, and accepted the bills: before they became due, a commission issued, notwithstanding which the factor paid them; the assignees sued the factor for the 222*l.* 18*s.*; and on a case reserved, insisted that though the statute (1 Jac. 1. c. 15.) would protect a *payment* before notice of the bankruptcy, it would not a mere acceptance. Sed per Lord Kenyon, the statute ought to receive a liberal construction; giving goods in exchange would have been a payment, though not in money; and so is giving an acceptance, if the bill be paid when due. The other judges concurred, and the plaintiff had judgment.

And payment to a bankrupt, or accepting on his account, even after a commission issued, will be as much protected as a payment before, if the party paying or accepting knew nothing, and had not the means of knowing, of such commission. (7)

And payments *to* a bankrupt are entitled to a different consideration from payments *by*; vacating the former makes the party pay twice, vacating the latter only puts one creditor on the same footing with the rest.

Payment *by* a bankrupt to a bonâ fide creditor in respect of a (8) bill really and bonâ fide drawn, negotiated, or accepted by the bankrupt in the (9) usual and ordinary course of trade and dealing,

---

(7) Sowerby v. Brooks, 4 Barnew. and Ald. 523. On 7th October a commission issued against Carbutt, but it was not gazetted till 5th November. 30th October Sowerby accepted a bill drawn on him by Carbutt for 95*l*. 4*s*., a sum he owed Carbutt; he had no reason to suppose at that time that the commission had issued, or that Carbutt was a banker or insolvent. Carbutt's assignees sued Sowerby for the old debt, and he relied on his acceptance, which he paid when due, as a discharge: the court of common pleas thought it no discharge, on the ground that the issuing of the commission was notice to all the world of the bankruptcy; but the facts being stated in a special verdict, the court of king's bench on error thought otherwise, and reversed the judgment.

(8) See 19 Geo. 2. c. 32. § 1. post, p. 258. n. (10). The statute only mentions bills; whether it may be construed to extend to notes, has not been decided. See Harwood v. Lomas, infra.

(9) Harwood and another v. Lomas, 11 East's Rep. 127. Odell being indebted to the defendant in 400*l*., gave him,

will be (10) valid; provided the party paid be ignorant of the bankruptcy or insolvency of the bankrupt.

---

in August, 1805, his note for that sum, payable at twelve months, with interest half yearly. Part only of the money being paid, the defendant, in 1806, arrested Odell for the residue, and in Hilary Term, 1807, obtained judgment, which was affirmed on error the 5th of February, 1808; and the next day (the 6th of February) Odell paid the amount of the damages, interest, and costs. Odell had committed an act of bankruptcy on the 27th of January, 1808; on which a commission issued dated the 19th of February, 1808. In an action by his assignees to recover this money, the only question was, whether the payments by the bankrupt were protected by the 19 Geo. 2. c. 32. The court inclined to think that it was incumbent on the party receiving the money to shew that the payment was protected by the statute. But it being admitted that the note had been given for the balance of an account stated, consisting (inter alia) of money lent to the bankrupt, the court, without expressing any opinion as to whether the statute could be construed to extend to notes, held that this note could not be said to have been given in the ordinary course of trade and dealing. Postea to the plaintiffs.

(10) By 19 Geo. 2. c. 32. § 1. it is enacted, "That from and after the 29th of October, 1746, no person who is or shall be really and bonâ fide a creditor of any bankrupt, for or in respect of goods really and bonâ fide sold to such bankrupt, or for or in respect of any bill or bills of exchange really and bonâ fide drawn, negotiated, or accepted by such bankrupt, in the usual or ordinary course of trade and dealing, shall be liable to refund or repay to the assignee or assignees of such bankrupt's estate, any money, which before the suing forth of such commission, was really and bonâ fide, and in the usual and ordinary course of trade and dealing, received by such person of any such bankrupt, before such time as the person receiving the same shall know, understand, or have notice that he is become a bankrupt, or that he is in insolvent circumstances."

The statute giving this protection to payments by bankrupts, mentions bills, but is silent as to notes.

Whether it extends to notes has not been decided; and it is in terms confined to bills drawn, &c. in the usual and ordinary course of trade.

But all payments *by* and *to* any bankrupt bonâ fide made more than two calendar months before the date of his commission, will, notwithstanding any prior act of bankruptcy, be (11) good; provided the party so paid or paying, had not any notice of such prior act of bankruptcy, or that the bankrupt was insolvent, or had stopped payment.

After a foreign bill has been protested for non-payment, any person may pay it (under protest) for the (12) honour of the drawer or of an indorser; and he is entitled to demand repayment not only from the person for whose honour he made

---

(11) By 46 Geo. 3. c. 135. § 1. it is enacted, "That in all cases of commissions of bankrupt hereafter to be issued, all conveyances by, all payments by and to, and all contracts and other dealings and transactions by and with, any bankrupt bonâ fide made or entered into more than two calendar months before the date of such commission, shall, notwithstanding any prior act of bankruptcy committed by such bankrupt, be good and effectual to all intents and purposes whatsoever, in like manner as if no such prior act of bankruptcy had been committed; provided the person or persons so dealing with such bankrupt had not at the time of such conveyance, payment, contract, dealing or transaction, any notice of any prior act of bankruptcy by such bankrupt committed, or that he was insolvent or had stopped payment."

(12) Beawes, 2d ed. pl. 50. and vide ante, p. 138.

the payment, but from (13) all other parties who are liable to that person.

Payment of a bill or note should not be made (14) *before* it has become due;

If it be, it is at the peril of the person paying.

A check upon a banker was lost, and paid to a stranger the day before it *bore date;* the banker was obliged to repay the money to the loser. (15)

---

(13) Beawes, 2d ed. pl. 57., vide ante, p. 138., and Mertens v. Winnington, post, p. 263. n. (3), Hall v. Pitfield, post, p. 263. n. (4), and ex parte Lambert, post, p. 263. n. (5).

(14) Marius, 4th ed. p. 31., who observes, that if the drawee pay a bill before it has become due, and it appear that the payee was merely the factor or agent of the person who delivered it to him, and that person countermand the payment before the maturity of the bill, but after such payment by the drawee the latter may be obliged to repay the money."

(15) See Da Silva v. Fuller, Chitty, 2d ed. 112. n.

CAP. IX.

UPON a non-acceptance or non-payment, the holder of a bill or note may sue all the persons liable to him on account of such non-acceptance or non-payment, and he may sue them either at the same time or successively.

An indorser, an acceptor for the honour of an indorser or drawer, or the (1) drawer, is, after payment by him, holder; but he holds in his original capacity, not (2) as upon a transfer from the person he has paid.

---

(1) Louviere v. Laubray, 10 Mod. 36. The plaintiff drew a bill upon the defendant, which the defendant accepted, but afterwards refused to pay; upon this the bill was indorsed to the plaintiff, and the question was, Whether he could maintain an action as indorsee? and, per Parker C. J., upon evidence that he had effects in the hands of the defendant enough to answer the bill, and consequently that the acceptance was not upon the honour of the plaintiff, the action is well brought, but if there were no effects, the action would not lie; and the plaintiff recovered.

Symonds v. Parminter, 1 Wils. 185. 4 Bro. Parl. Cas. 604. The plaintiff drew a bill upon the defendant to the order of Cleer and Co., which the defendant accepted, but did not pay; the plaintiff paid it, and brought this action. The declaration stated that the plaintiff drew the bill; that the defendant accepted it, but did not pay it; that the plaintiff became liable, and paid it; by reason whereof the defendant became liable, and promised. The defendant demurred, and afterwards moved in arrest of judgment, and contended that the action would not lie; but the court, after two arguments upon the demurrer, and one on the motion in arrest of judgment, were of opinion that it would, and judgment was given for the plaintiff. The defendant brought a writ of error in parliament, but did not appear at the bar to support it, and the judgment was affirmed.

(2) Bishop v. Hayward, 4 Term Rep. 470. The plaintiff declared upon a note payable to himself or order, indorsed by him to the defendant, and by the defendant indorsed back again to him, and obtained a verdict; a rule was granted to shew cause why the judgment should not be arrested, on the ground that according to the statement in the declaration the plaintiff would be liable upon his indorsement to pay the defendant the

So the bail of any of the parties who are sued, or (3) any persons who pay the bill or note on account of any of the parties, become, on payment, holders; and they hold as upon a transfer from the person for whom they made the payment, not (4) as upon a transfer from the person they have paid.

And they stand, with respect to other parties to the bill or note, in the situation of the party for whom they made the payment, and consequently unless he could have sued upon the bill or note, they (5) cannot.

---

sum for which the verdict was given; and upon cause shewn, the court held the objection good, because as the plaintiff had not stated it to be otherwise, his indorsement was to be considered as a legal existing indorsement: had any circumstances existed which exempted the plaintiff from answering upon his indorsement to the defendant, they should have been disclosed on the record. And see Louviere v. Laubray, ante, p. 262. note (1)

(3) Mertens v. Winnington, Espinasse, 112. A bill was drawn by the defendant, and indorsed by Burton Forbes and Gregory; the plaintiff paid it for the honour of Burton Forbes and Gregory, and brought this action against the defendant as drawer; the defendant contended that a person who paid for the honour of one of the parties could only sue that party; but Lord Kenyon said, "he was to be considered as an indorsee paying full value for the bill," and he directed the jury to find for the plaintiff.

(4) Hall v. Pitfield, B. R. H. 17 Geo. 2. The indorsee of a note sued the maker, and on payment by his bail permitted them to sue the indorser in his (the indorsee's) name, but the court held that the payment by the bail discharged the indorser, and that the action could not be maintained.

(5) Ex parte Lambert, 13 Ves. 179. Adams and Co. drew

An action (6) may be brought for non-acceptance before the expiration of the time limited by a bill for its payment.

And such action may be brought against an (7) indorser, as well as against the drawer.

---

two bills on Lane and Co., which the latter accepted. Lambert took up both these bills for the honour of the drawers. A commission of bankruptcy afterwards issued against the acceptors, and the drawers also failed: Lambert received a dividend upon the bills from the estate of the drawers, and claimed the balance from the estate of the acceptors. But it being proved that the drawers had no effects in the hands of the acceptors, and that the acceptances were for the accommodation of the drawers, the claim was rejected; and upon petition, the Lord Chancellor said that Lambert could not make a title stronger than that of the drawers, nor oust the assignees of the defence which they would have had against them. Petition dismissed.

(6) Bright v. Purrier, Bull. Nisi Prius, 269. A Foreign bill payable 120 days after sight was presented for acceptance, but acceptance being refused, the holder brought an action immediately against the drawer; the defendant objected that he was not liable till the expiration of the 120 days, and offered to call witnesses to prove that such was the custom of merchants; but Lord Mansfield said the law was clearly otherwise, and refused to hear the evidence; so the plaintiff recovered.

Milford v. Mayor, Dougl. 55. The defendant drew a bill of exchange, which the drawee refused to accept, upon which the plaintiff arrested him before the bill became due; these facts appearing upon the affidavit to hold to bail, a rule was obtained to shew cause why the defendant should not be discharged; but upon shewing cause, Buller J. said, it is settled that if a bill is not accepted, an action will lie immediately against the drawer, because his undertaking that the drawee shall give him credit is not performed; there have been many actions of this sort;" and Willes and Ashhurst Js. concurring, the rule was discharged.

(7) Ballingalls v. Gloster, 3 East. Rep. 481. John Gloster

All the antecedent parties are liable to the holder on account of a non-acceptance or non-payment; and if the bill or note was transferred to him for a precedent consideration by delivery, the person who delivered it is also liable to be sued for such consideration.

If the holder sues all the persons liable at the same time, it was at one time (8) supposed that the court or a judge would not stay proceedings in any one action but upon payment of the money recoverable in that, and the costs in such of the rest in which judgment had not been obtained; but it is

---

drew a bill on Jackson, payable to Anthony Gloster's order, and the latter indorsed it to the plaintiffs. Jackson refused acceptance, on which the plaintiffs immediately sued Anthony Gloster, without waiting until the bill, which was drawn at 90 days' sight, would have been due. The plaintiffs had a verdict, with liberty to the defendant to move for a nonsuit. On rule nisi accordingly, it was urged that an indorser stood in a situation different from that of a drawer; and that although a drawer might be sued immediately on non-acceptance, an indorser could not until the expiration of the time limited for the payment of the bill; but the court was clear that the case of an indorser was not distinguishable from that of a drawer, and that every indorser was a new drawer. Rule discharged.

(8) Golding v. Grace, Blackst. 749. The indorser of a bill obtained a rule nisi to stay proceedings on payment of the debt and the costs of the writ; the plaintiff insisted that he was entitled to be paid for drawing declarations against the defendant and the drawer; and it was agreed, that if any was to be paid for, the plaintiff was entitled to be paid for both; but the court held that the application to pay debt and costs was made so early, that the plaintiff was only entitled to the costs of the writ.

now settled that in the (9) case of a regular bill, where the acceptor is the proper person to provide for payment; he is the only person against whom the plaintiff is entitled to the costs of *all* the actions, and that each of the other parties is entitled to a stay of proceedings upon paying the debt and the costs in the action against him.

The maker of a note stands in this respect in the condition of the acceptor of a bill.

And where it appears that some of the actions are friendly and collusive, not to obtain payment but to increase costs; it is probable the costs of those actions would not be included.

Though the holder may recover judgments in all the actions, he (10) can only once recover the sum payable by the bill or note, and the costs; and if he rejects a tender of such sum and costs,

---

(9) Smith v. Woodcock, Same v. Dudley, 4 Term Rep. 691. The holder of a bill brought actions against the acceptor, the drawer, and two indorsers; the drawer and one of the indorsers obtained a rule nisi to stay proceedings against them on payment of the bill and costs of the actions against *them*: the plaintiff insisted that the costs of the other actions should be also paid: sed per cur. "that is only necessary where the application comes from the acceptor, who is the original defaulter, and against whom all the costs occasioned by his default may be recovered." Rule absolute.

(10) Ex parte Wildman, 2 Vez. 115. per Lord Hardwicke, "In cases of bills of exchange or promissory notes, where there is a drawer and indorser, perhaps more than one judgment is against all, but there can be but one satisfaction.

the (11) court will make an order to restrain him from taking out execution.

If the holder at first sue some only of the persons liable, he may at any time before satisfaction sue all or any of the rest.

And the difference between extinguishment and satisfaction is to be remembered; the holder's claim upon a bill or note may be extinguished as to some parties, and remain entire as to others; if his claim is satisfied as to any, it is satisfied as to all.

Taking security of a higher description, as a bond or judgment, for the money due upon a bill or note, extinguishes the holder's claim upon the bill or note, as against the party giving that security (12): it does not satisfy it.

So obtaining judgment on a bill or note is an extinguishment as between the parties, not a satisfaction.

But taking a warrant of attorney to enter up judgment, is not, unless judgment is actually entered up, even an extinguishment. (13)

---

(11) Windham v. Withers, Str. 515. The plaintiff having obtained judgments against the drawer and indorser of a note, the principal in one, and the costs in both were offered him, which he refused; and the court granted a rule to restrain him from taking out execution, and intimated that they would have punished him, had he taken out execution upon both judgments.

(12) Bac. Abr. tit. Extinguishment, D. vol. iii. p. 106.

(13) R. Norris v. Aylett, 2 Campb. 329.

Obtaining (14) a judgment is no satisfaction, even as to the parties subsequent to him against whom the judgment is obtained.

And (15) the actual taking of a man in execution, and discharging him upon a letter of licence, is no satisfaction as to any of the antecedent parties.

Nor (16) is it a satisfaction, that one of the parties has been charged in execution on the bill or

---

(14) Claxton v. Swift, 2 Show. 441. 494. Lutw. 882. To an action against the indorser of a bill, the defendant pleaded that the plaintiff had recovered a judgment against the drawer, and that the judgment was still in force; and upon demurrer, the court of king's bench held the plea good, but the court of exchequer chamber held otherwise, and the judgment was reversed.

(15) Hayling v. Mulhall, Blackst. 1235. A bill was indorsed by Sheridan to Boon, and by him to the plaintiff: he sued Boon, and took him in execution, but discharged him upon a letter of licence; he then sued Sheridan, for whom the defendant became bail; and upon an action against the defendant, *he* contended that the debt was satisfied by the imprisonment of Boon: but the court was clear it was not, and Mulhall was obliged to pay the money. Vide post.

(16) M'Donald v. Bovington, 4 Term Rep. 825. A bill drawn by M'Donald on Bovington, was indorsed to Thompson, who charged Bovington in execution upon it; Bovington was discharged as an insolvent, and then Thompson sued M'Donald and recovered. M'Donald paid the bill, sued Bovington, and charged him in execution; and on a rule nisi to discharge him, and cause shewn, it was urged that Bovington had satisfied the bill by being charged in execution at the suit of Thompson. Sed per Lord Kenyon, nothing can be clearer than that he has not; it was a mere formal satisfaction as to Thompson, not like actual payment; and when M'Donald was obliged to pay the bill, a new cause of action arose against the defendant by the payment, without regard to what passed in the former action; and per Buller J. the consequence would be, that because the

note and discharged as an insolvent, unless as to the party at whose suit he was so charged.

If a customer deposit with his banker bills or notes of a third person *on account*, and they are suffered to remain with the banker after they are due, it will be no satisfaction of them, that at the time they became due, and at subsequent periods, the balance between the banker and his customer was in favour of the customer. (17)

And if the balance is afterwards against the customer, the banker may sue the third person on such bills or notes. (17)

If a bill or note is mislaid, and an agent for one of the parties tenders payment, on condition that

---

drawer was obliged to pay the holder, the acceptor would be discharged without paying either. Rule discharged.

(17) Attwood v. Crowdie, 1 Stark. 483. Defendants lent their acceptances for the accommodation of Mattingley and Co., to two bills at three and four months after date, payable to Mattingley and Co., or order; Mattingley and Co. having been pressed by their bankers for security, sent them these and other bills on account: at the time these bills became due, and at several periods afterwards, the balance between Mattingley and Co. and the bankers was in favour of Mattingley and Co.; but Mattingley and Co. failed, and the balance then was the other way: the bankers sued defendants upon these acceptances; defendants insisted that as the balances were against the bankers when these bills became due, and afterwards, these bills must be considered as satisfied, or at least that plaintiffs must stand as if the bills had been indorsed to them after they became due: but Lord Ellenborough held, that as the bills were sent *on account*, which must have meant the floating account, though they were periods at which the plaintiffs had no claim upon them, and they might have been demanded back, yet as

the bill or note is delivered up, such tender is no satisfaction of the demand; and if the agent fail with the money in his hands before the bill or note is found, it will be no answer to an action upon the bill or note against the principal. (18)

But payment of interest shall cease from the time of such tender. (18)

(19) Discharging, or (20) giving time to any

---

they were suffered to remain, the plaintiffs' claim reverted when by fresh advantages the balance turned in their favour, and plaintiffs had a verdict.

(18) Dent v. Dunn, 3 Campb. 296. An executor deposited money with an agent to pay notes of the testator: plaintiff had some of the notes, but could not find them: the agent tendered him the money if he would give up the notes, but they could not be found, and the agent failed with the money in his hands: plaintiff afterwards found the notes, and brought this action. It was urged for defendant, that plaintiff ought to bear the loss, for had he not mislaid the notes, they would have been paid. Sed per Lord Ellenborough, here was only a tender, which could not extinguish the debt; plaintiff did nothing to make the stakeholder his agent; he continued defendant's agent: verdict for plaintiff, but interest to the time of the tender only.

(19) Ex parte Smith, 3 Bro. C. C. 1. Lewis and Potter indorsed certain bills and notes to Esdaile, and became bankrupt. Esdaile proved the amount of the bills and notes under their commission, and afterwards received a composition from the acceptors of the bills, and the makers of the notes, and gave them a full discharge, without the knowledge of the assignees of Lewis and Potter. On petition by the assignees to have the debt in respect of the bills and notes expunged, the chancellor held that, by discharging the acceptors and makers, without the consent of the indorser, the latter was discharged also. To the same effect is the case of ex parte Wilson, 11 Ves. 410. See also Smith v. Knox, 3 Esp. N. P. C. 46.

(20) English v. Darley, 2 Bos. and Pull. 61. The holder of

any of the parties, is a discharge of every other party, who, upon paying the bill or note, would

---

a bill sued the indorser and acceptor, and took out execution against the acceptor, but received 100*l.* from him, and took his bond and warrant of attorney for payment of the remainder by instalments, with interest and costs, excepting only a nominal sum to enable him to support actions against the other parties: he then brought on to trial this action against the indorser. Lord Eldon thought that the bargain to give indulgence to the acceptor was a bar, and nonsuited the plaintiff; and on motion for a new trial, the court was clear that the nonsuit was right; because giving time to the acceptor was a pledge that he should have time from all the other parties, and the holder had no right to give such pledge and yet hold the other parties liable.

Gould v. Robson, 8 East. Rep. 576. The holder of a bill, upon its becoming due, received part payment from the acceptor, and took a bill from him at a future short date for the remainder, and agreed to keep the original bill in his hands in the interim, as a security. He now sued the defendants as indorsers, and this was relied upon as a defence. Lord Ellenborough thought at the trial, that it did not amount to a giving time to the acceptor, and the plaintiff had a verdict; but upon motion for a new trial, he and the court were satisfied that it did, and a nonsuit was entered.

Laxton v. Peat, 2 Campb. N. P. C. 185. Indorsee of a bill against the acceptor. It appeared that the bill had been accepted for the accommodation of the drawer, which circumstance was known to the plaintiff, who gave value for the bill. When the bill became due, the plaintiff received part payment from the drawer, and gave him time to pay the remainder, without the concurrence of the defendant. Lord Ellenborough held, that this being an accommodation bill, within the knowledge of all the parties, the acceptor could only be considered as a surety for the drawer; and in the case of simple contracts, the surety is discharged by time being given, without his concurrence, to the principal. Nonsuit.

be entitled to sue the party to whom such discharge or time has been given;

Unless the right to sue in such case result from facts out of ordinary course, as from the signatures being accommodation signatures.

And if the party who would be entitled to sue assent (21) to the giving time, or if, knowing of its having been given, he (22) promise to pay the bill or

---

And see Rees v. Berrington, 2 Ves. Jun. 540. Rees became surety in a joint and several bond conditioned for the payment to the obligee, of a certain sum with interest by two instalments; the first on the 31st of December, 1789, and the second on the 31st of December, 1790. In September, 1790, the whole sum being unpaid, the obligee took promissory notes from the principal obligor, for payment of the debt by instalments at extended periods, which notes were afterwards exchanged for others payable at more distant days. This arrangement was without the knowledge of Rees. The principal obligor afterwards became bankrupt; and the executor of the obligee sued Rees, the surety. And on a bill filed for an injunction, the chancellor held, that the surety was discharged by this indulgence having been given without his consent to the principal. See also 2 Bos. and Pull. 62.

(21) Clarke v. Devlin, 3 Bos. and Pull. 363. Atkinson, the acceptor of a bill, having been arrested by the holder, offered him a warrant of attorney for the amount of the bill, payable by instalments: this offer the holder mentioned to the defendant, the drawer, proposing to accept of it; who said, "you may do as you like, for I have had no notice of the non-payment." In fact he had had notice. The court held that this amounted to an assent on the part of the defendant to the security being taken, and therefore that the defendant was not discharged by this indulgence to the acceptor.

(22) Stevens v. Lynch, 12 East Rep. 38. The defence in this action, which was by an indorsee against the drawer of a bill,

note, his liability will be continued in the former case, and revived in the latter; and it will make no difference in the latter case, though the promise were made under a misconception of the law, the party believing himself to be still liable, unless the holder is instrumental in raising that belief.

Release to payee of note, does not discharge the maker; (23)

Though the note were an accommodation note; (23)

Unless that fact were known to the releaser when he gave the release. (23)

Agreeing after a bill has become due, and been regularly protested for non-payment, and notice thereof given, not to press the acceptor, will (24) not discharge the drawer.

---

was, that the plaintiff had given time to the acceptor; in answer to which, it was proved that the defendant knew of such time having been given, but that, conceiving himself to be still liable, three months after the bill became due, he said to the plaintiff, "I know I am liable, and if Jones (the acceptor) does not pay it, I will." Upon this, Lord Ellenborough directed a verdict to be found for the plaintiff; and upon a motion for a new trial, the court held the direction right, and refused a rule.

(23) Carstairs v. Rolleston, 5 Taunt. 551. Assignees of first indorsee of note against the maker. Plea, that defendant made the note as surety for the payee, and not on his own account, and that plaintiff had released the payee from the note and from all claims and sums of money due thereon: there was no allegation that plaintiff knew that defendant was only surety, and on demurrer the plea was held bad, and plaintiff had judgment.

(24) Walwyn v. St. Quintin, 1 Bos. and Pull. 652. In an action by indorsees against the drawer of a bill, it appeared that after the bill had become due and been protested for non-payment,

Nor will (24) receiving part of the money on account from an indorser.

Giving time to the payee will not discharge the drawer, for indulgence to the payee cannot affect the drawer: he may nevertheless pay and enforce his remedies. (25)

Giving time to the acceptor will not discharge the drawer, if the acceptance was to accommodate the drawer, and the drawer, as between him and the acceptor, is the person to pay the bill. (26)

---

though no notice thereof had been given to the defendant, he having no effects in the hands of the acceptor, the plaintiffs received part of the money *on account*, from the indorser; and that to an application from the acceptor, stating that it was probable he should be able to pay at a future period, they returned for answer that they would not press him. It was urged that either of these facts discharged the drawer: but the court after argument, and time taken to consider, held that they did not, and awarded the postea to the plaintiff. Eyre C. J. said, that, had this forbearance to sue the acceptor taken place before noting and protesting for non-payment, so that the bill had not been demanded when due, it was clear that the drawer would have been discharged: it would have been giving a new credit to the acceptor. But that after protest for non-payment, and notice to the drawer, or an equivalent to notice, a right to sue the drawer had attached, and the holder was not bound to sue the acceptor: he might therefore forbear to sue him.

(25) Claridge v. Dalton, 4 Maule, 226. Indorsee against drawer. Defence, that plaintiff's agent had given time to the payee: it did not appear that plaintiff had authorized him so to do: but on rule nisi for nonsuit, and cause shewn, the court expressed a clear opinion, that if he had it would not affect the drawer or give him any ground of defence, and rule discharged.

(26) Collott v. Haigh, 3 Campb. 281. In an action against the drawer of a bill, it appeared that plaintiffs had given time for

Discharging any of the indorsers will be a discharge of all (27) subsequent, though not of prior, indorsers.

An agreement between holder, drawer, and acceptor, that the acceptor shall pay, discharges the drawer, if the acceptor is to pay to a limited extent only;

As the bill without expences. (28)

---

some weeks to the acceptor, but it appearing also that the acceptance was an accommodation acceptance, without value, Lord Ellenborough was clear that the drawer continued liable; for the reason why indulgence to the acceptor without the drawer's consent discharges the drawer is because it may affect his remedy over against the acceptor; and that reason does not apply where he is not entitled to a remedy over. Verdict for plaintiff.

(27) Smith v. Knox, 3 Esp. N. P. C. 46. Per Lord Eldon, "It is said that the holder may discharge any of the indorsers after taking them in execution, and yet have recourse to the others. I doubt of the law as stated so generally; I am disposed to be of opinion, that if the holder discharge a prior indorser, he would find it difficult to recover against a subsequent one."

So also in English v. Darley, 2 Bos. and Pull. 62. Lord Eldon, after adverting to the inaccuracy of the marginal abstract of the case of Hayling v. Mulhall, said, had the plaintiff first sued a prior indorser and discharged him from execution, it would have afforded a sufficient objection to an action against a subsequent indorser. See Hayling v. Mulhall, ante, p. 268. n. (15).

(28) De la Torre v. Barclay, 1 Stark. 7. The drawers of a bill having become bankrupts, an agreement was entered into between their assignees, the holder (plaintiff), and the acceptor, by which the acceptor agreed to pay the amount of the bill, provided he were not called upon to pay more: the agreement recited the bill, the acceptance, and the probability it would be sent back for non-payment. Plaintiff having afterwards sued

Taking the separate notes of one of several partners, at distant dates, as a collateral security, will not discharge the others, if the party insists at the time it shall not prejudice his claim upon the partnership, and he does not bind himself to wait till the notes are due; (29)

Though the partnership is dissolved before such notes are given: (29)

Otherwise, if he do bind himself to wait. (29)

Receiving dividends under a commission of bankruptcy is a satisfaction pro tanto only.

After a partial satisfaction, the holder must (30)

---

the drawers, Lord Ellenborough held this new agreement, which varied the condition of the acceptor, was a waiver of the right of action against defendants, who were represented by their assignees, and nonsuit.

(29) Bedford v. Deakin Bickley and Hickman, 2 Stark. 178. Defendants were drawers of a bill, which was dishonoured; they dissolved partnership, and Hickman became bankrupt: Bickley afterwards proposed to give his own notes at four, eight, and twelve months as a security, and one Rushbury added his name as surety: plaintiff, who held the bill, agreed to take the notes, reserving to himself the security he held from the three, and he retained the bill. Interest was calculated on the notes till they would become due. In an action afterwards upon the bill against the three, it was urged, that the taking these notes discharged Deakin and Hickman: Lord Ellenborough said, he should have acceded to the objection had plaintiff agreed to postpone his remedy upon the bill, but as he had not, and on the contrary had retained the bill, and expressly reserved to himself that security, he thought the taking the notes did not alter the original liability of the three defendants; and plaintiff had a verdict.

(30) Bacon v. Searles, 1 H. Bl. 88. Upon a bill for 95*l.* 10*s.* The drawer paid the plaintiff 60*l.* 10*s.* and on an action against the acceptor, *he*, the acceptor, paid the residue with the inte-

not in an action take a verdict for more than the sum remaining due; if he do, the court will (31) either make him correct the verdict, and pay any expence the mistake may have occasioned, or grant a new trial.

Satisfaction of a bill or note, as to one of several

---

rest into court; the plaintiff however proceeded, and after a verdict for the defendant, with liberty to the plaintiff to move to enter a verdict for him, he contended that the acceptance having made the defendant liable for the whole, and a personal contract not being divisible, he was entitled to recover, and to stand as a trustee for the drawer, but the court held otherwise, and the verdict stood.

Pierson v. Dunlop, Cowp. 571. In an action against the acceptor upon a bill for 300*l.* the plaintiff took a verdict for the whole sum; the defendant filed a bill against him in the Exchequer, and he admitted in his answer that he had previously received 180*l.* from the drawer; this (among others) was urged as a ground for a new trial, and after cause shewn, Lord Mansfield said, "The verdict is certainly taken for 180*l.* more than was due; there was no admission of this payment at the trial, which was very wrong, and has been the occasion of filing a bill in the Exchequer, therefore there ought to be a deduction of the money received, and a proportionable part of the interest, together with all the costs in the Exchequer;" and though the court discharged the rule for a new trial, they made the plaintiff remit the 180*l.* with interest upon it from the time it was paid, and pay the costs of the bill and answer in the Exchequer.

However, in Johnson v. Kennion, 2 Wils. 262., the defendant drew a bill for 1000l. in favour of Benson or order, and Benson indorsed it to the plaintiff; Benson paid the plaintiff 232*l.* notwithstanding which he took a verdict against the defendant for the whole 1000*l.* and upon a rule nisi for a new trial upon this ground, the court are represented to have held that he did right; but in Bacon v. Searles, supra, Wilson J. considered the report inaccurate, and the authority questionable.

(31) See Pierson v. Dunlop, supra.

partners, is a satisfaction as to all; and if a person is a partner in two firms, satisfaction as to one firm is (32) so as to both. What would bar one firm will bar the other, and it will make no difference though one common partner is, in fact, ignorant of the circumstances which constitute the satisfaction.

Thus if one house receive funds from the drawer to take up a bill, and misapply them, no other house to which any member of the first house belongs can sue the drawer;

Or if he stands in the place of the drawer, the acceptor. (32)

In an action upon a bill or note, the plaintiff is in general entitled to recover the money payable thereby, with (33) interest, and (34) all incidental

---

(32) Jacaud and Gordon v. French and others, 12 East's Rep. 317. Jacaud was in partnership with Blair in Ireland, and with Gordon here. Jacaud and Gordon had a bill drawn by Farrell and Co. on defendants, and Farrell and Co. had supplied Jacaud and Blair with funds to pay this bill: Blair misapplied those funds, and on an action on the bill by Jacaud and Gordon, the defence was, that the misapplication by Blair was a misapplication by Jacaud also, and that after being guilty in one house of disappointing payment by misapplying the payment-fund, he could not endeavour to enforce payment in another: and in case the court was of that opinion, and the postea was awarded to the defendants.

(33) D. Mar. 2d ed. 13. Blaney v. Bradley, Blackst. 761. By the court. "Interest is due on all bills of exchange and notes of hand payable at a day certain, or after demand, if payable on demand." See also Bunb. 129. 2 Term Rep. 58.

(34) Vide Mar. 2d ed. 13. In Simmonds v. Parminter, ante, p. 262. note (1), the plaintiff recovered interest, exchange and

expences occasioned by non-acceptance or non-payment.

The interest is, in general, to be computed from the time the bill or note would regularly have been payable, and it is, in general, to be carried down to the time when final judgment may be signed. (35)

Thus, upon a bill or note payable on presentment, interest (36) must be computed from the presentment.

But if a bill or note payable at a given time after date be for a specified sum, "bearing interest," interest shall be computed from the date. (37)

---

re-exchange; and in Auriol v. Thomas, (post, p. 284. n. 45.) 10*s.* per pagoda in lieu of interest, exchange, and all other charges.

(35) Robinson v. Bland, Burr. 1077. In an action upon a bill of exchange, and for money lent, a case was reserved, and the court was of opinion that the plaintiff could not recover upon the bill, but that he might for the money lent; but they took time to consider, with a view to settle the future practice, to what time the interest upon money lent should be computed, and afterwards determined that it should be computed to the time of giving judgment.

(36) Blaney v. Bradley, ante p. 278. note (33). Cotton v. Horsemanden, Pract. Reg. 357. The court held, that in actions upon promissory notes, payable on demand, interest should be given from the time of the demand proved; but in this case, where it appeared upon the face of the note to be for money lent, interest should be given from the date of the note. 9 Mod. 138. By the court, interest upon a bill of exchange commences from demand made.

(37) Kennerly v. Nash, 1 Stark. 452. Action on bill at four months after date for 25*l.* 4*s.* bearing interest; and per Lord Ellenborough, these words entitle plaintiff to interest from the date of the bill; without them, he would have been entitled to it from the time it became due.

It has, indeed, been held (38), that if a party, entitled to notice of the dishonour of a bill or note, offer to pay it within a reasonable time after the notice is given, he is not liable for interest from the time of the dishonour: but perhaps there might be risque in acting upon that decision.

Where all that is due is tendered, and the holder has mislaid the bill or note, so that he cannot give it up, and payment is, on that account, postponed, the interest shall be computed up to the time of such tender only. (39)

The language of 3 & 4 Ann seems to imply, that

Hopper v. Richmond, 1 Stark. 507. By the terms of a note defendant undertook to pay legal interest on demand: Lord Ellenborough held, that must mean from the date of the note.

(38) Walker v. Barnes, 5 Taunt. 240. A bill for 10*l*., due 11th June, was presented for payment on that day, and dishonoured. On the 12th notice was sent by letter to the drawer, and early on the 13th he tendered the 10*l*.; the 10*l*. was not accepted, and on an action against the drawer, it was urged for the plaintiff, that the tender was insufficient, for that defendant ought to have tendered the interest from the 11th to the 13th; but on the point being reserved, the court held it sufficient, if the drawer, within a reasonable time after the notice, tendered the principal without the interest; and judgment was given for the defendant.

Note, the interest would have been under three farthings,—one fifteenth part of ten pence. But quære, whether non-payment by the drawee was not a breach of the drawer's contract, and whether the holder was not entitled to interest for not receiving on the 11th what defendant undertook he should receive on that day. It may be observed, however, in support of this decision, that the constant form in assumpsit against a drawer or indorser, makes him promise only for the amount of the money mentioned in the bill. It is silent as to interest. It is, however, silent also as to expences.

a neglect to procure a protest upon any inland bill for the payment of 20*l.* upon which a protest might have been made (39), would preclude the holder from recovering such interest or expences from any person entitled to notice of the non-acceptance or non-payment; but the contrary is now settled. (40)

Whether it would preclude the holder of a coal-note given under 3 G. 2. c. 26. § 7. is not decided.

A jury is not bound to give interest upon a bill or note, and where the bill or note has lain dormant for many years without any claim being made upon it, they may properly refuse it. (40*)

And for any time that it has been in the hands of an alien enemy interest ought not to be allowed, because during that time payment of the principal would have been illegal. (40*)

---

(39) See 3 & 4 Anne, c. 9. § 5. ante, p. 216. note (86).

(40) See Windle v. Andrews, ante, p. 215. n. 85.

(40*) Du Belloix v. Lord Waterpark, Hilary, 1822. Payee against maker on note for 800*l.* of 27th December, 1787, payable six months after date. The cause was tried in 1821; there was no evidence of any claim upon the note from the time it was made, and for many years of the intermediate time plaintiff had been an alien enemy: the jury asked if they were bound to give interest, and Abbot C. J. told them *that* was for their consideration; and they gave none. A motion was made to increase the verdict by adding the interest, or for a new trial, but the court was clear that the question of interest was within the province of the jury; that it was in the nature of damages for the non-payment of the debt, that they were to say whether there should be any and what damages on that account, and that in this instance there was no ground for saying they had not exercised their discretion rightly. Abbot C. J. added,

The only incidental expence in the case of the person who made the presentment is the charge of the notice and protest; in the case of any antecedent party, that of the return of the bill or note must be added.

Upon a foreign bill the (41) re-exchange forms a part of the expence of the return, and let the bill be returned through ever so many hands, the (41) drawer is liable for the re-exchange upon each return.

And the (42) drawer is liable for the re-exchange

---

that during the time the plaintiff was an alien enemy, it would have been illegal to have paid him the debt, and that for that interval therefore damages could not legally have been given; the rule was refused.

(41) Mellish v. Simeon, 2 H. Blackst. 378. A bill was drawn in London upon Paris, and negotiated through Holland; before it became due the French government prohibited the payment of any bill drawn in England, in consequence of which it was dishonoured, and sent back through the different hands by which it had before been negotiated, to London; the re-exchange between Paris and Holland, raised the bill from 608*l.* 19*s.* 10*d.* to 905*l.* 13*s.* 9*d.*, and the re-exchange between Holland and London to 913*l.* 4*s.* 3*d.*, which the plaintiff (the payee) paid; and upon an action by him against the drawer, Eyre, C. J. left it to the jury, whether the defendant was liable for the re-exchange occasioned by returning the bill through Holland, and they found that he was. An application was made for a new trial upon the ground that the defendant was not liable for the re-exchange, because there was no default in him, the payment being prohibited by the government of France; but the court held it immaterial why the bill was not paid, that as it was not paid, he was liable to all the consequences, of which the re-exchange was one, and the rule was refused.

(42) See the preceding note (41). Vide Detastet v. Baring, 11 East's Rep. 265.

and every other expence arising from the non-acceptance or non-payment, notwithstanding the dishonour of the bill is expressly ordered by the country on which it is drawn.

But the acceptor is (43) not liable for re-exchange; his contract cannot be carried farther than to pay the sum specified in the bill, together with legal interest, where interest is due.

If, by the terms of a note, the holder has the option of being paid either at the place where it was made, or, "according to the course of exchange" between that place and another, he (44) may insist upon being paid according to such

---

(43) Thus in Napier v. Schneider, post., the court was clearly of opinion that the defendant, who was acceptor of a bill, was not liable for re-exchange. S. P. R. acc. in Woolsey v. Crawford, 2 Campb. 445.

(44) Pollard v. Herries, 3 Bos. and Pull. 335. The defendant gave the plaintiff a note for payment, at seven days' sight, of 1200 livres Tournois, and interest, drawn at Paris, and expressed to be "payable as above in Paris, or, at the choice of the bearer, at the Union bank in Dover, or at my usual residence in London, according to the course of exchange upon Paris." In an action on this note the defendant paid 18*l*. 16*s*. 6*d*. into court. The jury found a verdict for the plaintiff with 40*l*. 6*s*. 10*d*. damages, subject to the opinion of the court upon a case stating the making of the note, and the due presentment in London, and that, at the time when the note was made, there was a direct course of exchange between London and Paris, that that exchange had fallen, and before the note became due had altogether ceased; that, according to the last direct course, 18*l*. 16*s*. 6*d*. would be sufficient to pay the note: that when the note became due there was no direct course, but that a circuitous course of exchange through Hamburgh existed, and

course of exchange as exists between them at the time when the note becomes due.

And it makes no difference, that at the time when the note was made there was a direct course, and at the time when it becomes due, there is no direct, but only a circuitous course of exchange between them.

On the return of a bill drawn here for the payment of pagodas in the East Indies, the (45) practice is to allow for the sum payable by the bill interest and all incidental charges, after the rate of 10*s.* for each pagoda, and five per cent. thereon from the expiration of thirty days after notice of the bill's dishonour; and it has been (45) determined that this practice was lawful, even where the price

---

that, according to that circuitous course, the sum of 59*l.* 3*s.* 4*d.* would be due upon the note. The court held, that the plaintiff had a right to insist upon being paid according to such circuitous course, and the verdict therefore was entered for 40*l.* 6*s.* 10*d.*

(45) Auriol v. Thomas, 2 Term Rep. 52. Upon executing a writ of enquiry on a bill for the payment of 800 star pagodas returned protested from India, it appeared that the usage was to charge 10*s.* per pagoda for bills returned from India protested, and five per cent. after the expiration of thirty days from the notice to the defendant of the bill's dishonour, which included all incidental charges, and that the defendant had agreed to pay accordingly; upon which the jury assessed the damages at 10*s.* per pagoda, with the five per cent., though the plaintiff discounted the bill at the rate of 6*s.* 6*d.* a pagoda; that being then the current price. A rule nisi was obtained to set aside the inquisition, on the ground that this allowance was exorbitant, and the agreement for it usurious; but the court, on cause shewn, thought otherwise, and discharged the rule.

allowed for each pagoda on the discount of the bill was only six shillings and six-pence.

The action usually brought on account of a bill or note, is a special action of assumpsit thereon, but perhaps a special action (46) of debt, debt on an indebitatus, or an (47) indebitatus assumpsit, might be maintained thereon.

And assumpsit will lie upon a bill or note against a corporation, where such corporation is empow-

---

(46) In Anon. Hardr. 485. It was held that the payee of a bill could not maintain debt against the acceptor, because there was no privity between them, and because the acceptance was a collateral undertaking only. In Welch v. Craig, Str. 680. 8 Mod. 373. it was held that debt will not lie upon a note; but it does not appear by or against what particular party that action was brought. In 1 Mod. Ent. 812. pl. 13., it is said that debt will lie against the maker of a note, not against the indorser. And in Morgan's Precedents, 458, is an entry of a declaration in debt by the administratrix of the payee of a note against the maker; and in Rumball v. Ball, 10 Mod. 38, an action of debt was brought upon a note.

(47) In Brown v. London, 1 Freeman, 14. 1 Mod. 285. 1 Vent. 152. It was held, that an indebitatus assumpsit would not lie upon the acceptance of a bill, Twisden J. dubitante. And there is a dictum to the like effect in Comb. 204. But in another report of Brown v. London, Lev. 298, the court is stated to have resolved in favour of the defendant, because the custom was not set out in the count. In Skinn. 346, it is said it will only lie against the drawer upon a bill importing to have been given for value received. In Salk. 125. 12 Mod. 37, it is laid down generally, that an indebitatus assumpsit will not lie upon a bill; and in 12 Mod. 345, it is held that the payee of a bill importing to have been given for value received, may maintain an indebitatus assumpsit against the drawer. And it may be observed, that the demand of an indorsee upon a bill or note against indorser, drawer, maker or acceptor, is continually allowed as an item of set-off under the statutes of set-off.

ered by statute to issue, indorse or accept bills or notes. (48).

Debt (49) may be maintained by the payee against the maker of a note expressed to be for value received.

But instead of suing upon the bill or note, the holder may use it merely as evidence in another action.

A bill is primâ facie evidence of money lent by the payee to the drawer, and a note of money (50) lent by the payee to the maker, and each conse-

---

(48) Murray v. East India Company, 5 Barnew. and Ald. 204. Assumpsit against the East India Company as acceptors of certain bills of Exchange: it was urged, that assumpsit could not lie against a corporation; but the court, without intimating how that would be in general, held, that as the East India Company was, by 53 G. 3. c. 155. § 57., and other acts, expressly authorized to accept bills, those statutes were to be considered as virtually making them liable to the ordinary remedies upon bills, and consequently to the action of assumpsit.

(49) Bishop v. Young, 2 Bos. and Pull. 78. This was an action of debt by the payee, against the maker of a promissory note, expressed to be for value received. The first count of the declaration was upon the note; and upon general demurrer to this count, the court, after time taken to consider, held, that in this particular case, the action of debt was maintainable. But Lord Eldon, who delivered the opinion of the court, said, "We do not say how the case would stand if the action were brought by any other person than he to whom the note was originally given, or against any other person than him by whom it was signed and made, or if the note itself did not express a consideration upon the face of it." Judgment for the plaintiff.

(50) Clarke v. Martin, Lord Raym. 758. Holt C. J. expressed his disapprobation of declaring upon promissory notes

quently of money (51) had and received by the drawer or maker to the use of the holder, and of money paid by the holder to the use of the drawer or maker.

An acceptance is (52) also primâ facie evidence

(before the statute) as if they were within the custom of merchants; and assigned as a reason, " because there was so easy a method, as to declare upon a general indebitatus assumpsit for money lent." The same was laid down in 12 Mod. 380. and in Burr. 1525. Lord Mansfield says, " I do not find it any where disputed, that an action upon an indebitatus assumpsit generally, for money lent, might be brought on a note payable to one or order." And see Smith v. Kendall, ante p. 29. n. 62.

(51) Grant v. Vaughan, Burr. 1516. The bearer of a note payable to " Ship Fortune, or bearer," brought an action upon it, and inserted a count for money had and received. Lord Mansfield left it to the jury whether such a note was negotiable, and whether the plaintiff took it fairly, and they found for the defendant; but upon a rule nisi for a new trial, the court was clear the first point should not have been left to the jury; and per Lord Mansfield, " Upon the count for money had and received, the case is clear beyond dispute; for undoubtedly an action for money had and received to the plaintiff's use, may be brought by the bonâ fide bearer of a note payable to bearer. It was certainly money received for the use of the original advancer of it, and if so, it is for the use of the person who has the note as bearer;" and Wilmot and Yates Js. expressed themselves to the same effect. A new trial was granted, and the plaintiff recovered.

(52) Tatlock v. Harris, 3 Term Rep. 174. In an action at the suit of the indorsee of a bill payable to a fictitious payee against the acceptor, who was also one of the drawers, the declaration contained counts for money paid and for money had and received; it appeared upon the evidence, that the defendant was indebted to one of the indorsers, and sent him this bill, for which he was credited in account, and that the plaintiff paid

of money had and received by the acceptor to the use of the holder, and of money paid by the holder to the use of the acceptor, and (53) an indorsement of money lent by the indorsee to the indorser.

But if it appear that at the time of accepting the drawee says he has nothing in his hands except a bill of the drawer's for a larger amount, but that he expects the drawer will remit, and will therefore take all risques upon himself, the acceptance will not be evidence of money had and re-

---

that indorser the value of the bill: and upon a demurrer to the evidence, the court held that the plaintiff was entitled to recover under the counts for money paid and money had and received, and he had judgment accordingly.

Vere v. Lewis, 3 Term Rep. 182. This was a similar action to that of Tatlock v. Harris, except that the defendant was not one of the drawers, and there was no evidence that he received any value for the bill; upon which it was urged the plaintiff could not recover upon the money counts; but the court said the acceptance was evidence that he had received value from the drawers, and the plaintiff had judgment.

Thompson v. Morgan, 3 Campb. 101. Plaintiff drew on defendant, payable to plaintiff or order, defendant accepted it; plaintiff sued on the acceptance, but there being a variance between the bill as stated, and the real bill, plaintiff resorted to the money counts. Lord Ellenborough at first doubted, because indebitatus assumpsit would not lie on the bill against the acceptor; but it being pointed out to him that plaintiff was drawer and payee, so that there was no intermediate party between plaintiff and defendant, he admitted the bill as evidence under the count for money had and received; but he would not allow interest. Verdict for plaintiff.

(53) Kessebower v. Tims, B.R.E. 22 G. 3. Lord Mansfield held, that the indorsee of a note might maintain indebitatus assumpsit for money lent, against the person who indorsed it to him.

ceived by the acceptor to the use of the holder, unless there is proof that the larger bill is paid; (54)

Or other money remitted;

With that proof it will. (54)

Proof that the drawee has received a remittance from the drawer specifically for payment of the bill, will also make the drawee, though he has not accepted the bill, answerable to the holder for money had and received, if he has done any thing which can be deemed a pledge to the holder for so applying it.

And proof that the acceptor's banker has received the money from the acceptor specifically for

---

(54) Whitwell v. Bennett, 3 Bos. and Pull. 559. This was an action by the indorsee against the acceptor of a bill. The bill was incorrectly stated, and the plaintiff was therefore obliged to resort to the money counts. The evidence was, that when the defendant accepted the bill (which was for 30*l.*), he said, that though the drawer had not remitted to him, he expected that he would, and that, as he had a bill of his for 80*l.* which would be paid, he would take all risks upon himself. Lord Alvanley directed a verdict for the plaintiff, with liberty to the defendant to move for a nonsuit. Rule nisi accordingly; and on shewing cause against this rule, it was urged, that if the bill for 80*l.* was paid, the defendant was liable as for money had and received; and that, as the defendant had not at the trial produced that bill, the presumption was, that it was paid. The court said, that if that bill was paid, the action for money had and received would be maintainable, on the ground of the defendant's specific appropriation of that money to the payment of the plaintiff's demand: but that the declaration being upon the bill for 30*l.* it was a surprise upon the defendant to call for proof of the non-payment of the other bill; and that therefore it would be too much to presume payment of that bill. Rule absolute.

the bill, will make the banker liable to the holder for money had and received, if he does any thing which can be deemed a pledge to the holder. (55)

Taking the bill as agent to the holder to receive payment thereon, if payment is offered, is such a pledge, and will make him answerable for money had and received, if the money is paid to him whilst the bill is so in his possession;

At least if it be owing to such possession that he receives the payment. (55)

But a specific remittance will not make the drawee, if he do not accept, answerable to the holder as for money had and received, unless there is something which can be deemed a pledge to the holder; without such pledge there is no privity between the holder and the drawee, and the drawer

---

(55) De Bernales v. Fuller, 2 Campb. 426. 14 East. 590. Plaintiff held a bill accepted by Puller, payable at defendant's, Puller's bankers: plaintiff sent the bill to his own bankers, and they, according to the course amongst bankers, sent it to defendant's. Puller found the bill was at defendant's, and sent the money there to pay it: defendant's clerk took the money, but refused to give up the bill, and defendant insisted on keeping the money for a debt Puller owed them. Plaintiff thereupon brought an action for money had and received. Lord Ellenborough thought it not maintainable, and the defendants had a verdict; but, on an application for a new trial, and cause shewn, the court held, that as defendants made themselves agents for plaintiff by taking the bill from his bankers, and as they would not have had the money paid them had they not had possession of the bill, they were not at liberty to say they did not receive the money for plaintiff's use: a new trial was accordingly granted, and plaintiff afterwards had a verdict.

is the only person who can call the drawee to account for the misapplication. (56)

An acknowledgment of the debt by the defendant will enable the holder to recover upon a count for the account stated. (57)

---

(56) Yates v. Bell, 3 Barnew. and Ald. 643. Ingram remitted 800*l.* to defendant to take up, amongst others, a bill for 743*l.*, but that bill being returned dishonoured, defendant wrote to Ingram that he should carry the money to his credit: the bill coming back, the holder brought an action against the defendant for money had and received, on the ground that defendant was bound to apply the money to his bill. Abbot C. J. thought he was not, and nonsuited; and on a rule to shew cause why the verdict should not be entered for plaintiff, and cause shewn, the court held the nonsuit right, for there was no privity between plaintiff and defendant, unless defendant assented to apply the money as Ingram directed; if he did not follow Ingram's directions, he might be accountable to Ingram, but not to the plaintiff, and the rule was discharged.

Stewart v. Fry, 7 Taunt. 339. A bill made payable at defendant's was dishonoured for want of advice; the same day defendant received the money from Aspinall, the to pay it, and he sent to plaintiff, who had presented it, but the bill was returned to Ireland. Aspinall called back the money, and defendant paid him: the bill came back to plaintiff, and he sued defendant for the money; the jury found for defendant, and on rule nisi for a new trial, the court held the verdict right, and discharged the rule.

S. P. upon a remittance to pay a common debt, Williams v. Everitt, 14 East. 582.

(57) Highmore v. Primrose, 5 Maule, 65. In an action against the acceptor of a bill, plaintiff was precluded from recovering on the special count because of a variance, but he proved that defendant had acknowledged the acceptance, and pleaded inability to pay; and upon the point reserved, the court held, this entitled plaintiff to a verdict on the count for the account stated, and he had judgment accordingly.

Against the very person also from whom he received the bill or note, the holder may sue for the consideration upon which the bill or note was given.

For, in general, a bill or note is (58) no satisfaction of any debt or demand for which it has been given; it is only primâ facie evidence of payment, rendering it necessary that the party receiving it, should (59) account for it, before he will be entitled to recover the consideration.

---

(58) Puckford v. Maxwell, 6 Term Rep. 52. The defendant having been arrested by the Plaintiff for 80*l.*, gave a draft for 45*l.*, and promised in a few days to settle the remainder, on which the plaintiff consented to his being discharged out of custody. The draft was dishonoured, and the defendant was again arrested on the same affidavit. On rule to shew cause why he should not be discharged out of custody, and cause shewn, it was urged, that the draft, having been accepted as part payment, could not be treated as a nullity. But per Lord Kenyon: In cases of this kind, if the bill which is given in payment, do not turn out to be productive, it is not that which it purports to be and which the party receiving it expects it to be, and therefore he may consider it as a nullity and act as if no such bill had been given. These questions have frequently arisen at nisi prius, where they have always been determined the same way. Rule discharged.

Owenson v. Morse, 7 Term Rep. 64. The plaintiff bought some plate of the defendant, and gave him some country bank-notes in payment; the notes were dishonoured, on which the defendant refused to deliver the plate. The plaintiff brought trover, and insisted that the notes were payment; but on a case reserved, the court held that they were no payment unless the defendant had agreed to take them as payment, and to run the risk of their being paid. Nonsuit entered. See also Tapley v. Martens, 8 Term Rep. 451.

(59) Kearslake v. Morgan, 5 Term Rep. 513. Assumpsit for goods sold and delivered, and for money lent. The defendant pleaded the general issue; and that as to 4*l.* 14*s.* 6*d.* one W. P.

But the holder will be precluded from recovering for the consideration, if it appear that the bill or note has been, by (60) laches, made to operate as a satisfaction of the debt or demand for which it was given; or if he originally received the bill or note (61) as cash, and took upon himself the risk

---

made his note for 10*l.* payable to the defendant or order, at a time which elapsed before the commencement of the suit: and that the defendant, before the note became due, indorsed it to the plaintiff "for and on account of the said sum of 4*l.* 14*s.* 6*d.*, and the sum of 5*l.* 5*s.* 6*d.*," paid by the plaintiff to the defendant, and that the plaintiff accepted the note "for and on account" of those sums. To this plea there was a general demurrer, and it was urged, that the plea ought to have alleged that the note was received in *satisfaction* of the debt. But the court, on argument, held the plea good, and advised the plaintiff to withdraw his demurrer, and reply; which he did.

Dangerfield v. Wilby, 4 Esp. N. P. C. 159. The declaration contained a count upon a note made by the defendant, payable to the plaintiff and the money counts. At the trial the note was stated to have been lost, but no evidence of that fact was offered. It was proved, however, that on the money being demanded, the defendant had apologized for not having paid the money *on account of the note.* This was the whole of the plaintiff's case; and he contended that the note was only evidence of the consideration (which was stated to have been money lent), and that he might abandon the note, and go for the consideration. But Lord Ellenborough said, that as the note for any thing that appeared in evidence was in existence, it might still be in circulation, so that the defendant might be subjected twice to the payment of the same demand; without therefore proving the note lost, the plaintiff was not entitled to recover. Nonsuit.

(60) Vide ante, cap. vii. p. 171, 2.

(61) In Owenson v. Morse, 7 Term Rep. 66. ante, p. 291. n.(58) Lord Kenyon said, "If the defendant had agreed to take the notes as payment, and to run the risk of their being paid, that would have been considered as payment whether the notes had

of its being paid; or if it was transferred to him by way of (62) sale; unless indeed, in the two latter cases, it be proved that the person transferring the bill or note (63) knew at the time, that it was of no value.

---

or had not been afterwards paid." See also Clark v. Mundal, 1 Salk. 124.

(62) Fydell v. Clarke and another, 1 Esp. N. P. C. 447. The plaintiff had been in partnership with his brother R. Fydell; and the latter, on his own account, but in the partnership name, drew certain notes to the amount of 8000*l.* which he discounted with Hurlock and Co. bankers. The plaintiff, after his brother's death, voluntarily paid the 8000*l.* to the bankers, supposing that his brother had received the amount of these notes in *money:* he afterwards discovered that they had only given other bills and notes, which they had not indorsed, in lieu of his brother's notes, some of which bills and notes to the amount of 4300*l.* proved unproductive; and to recover that sum the present action was brought against the defendants, who were trustees of the insolvent estate of the bankers, and who had reserved funds to answer the event of the action. Lord Kenyon said, that the bankers by not indorsing the bills and notes, had refused to pledge their credit to their validity, and that R. Fydell must be taken to have received them on their own credit only; and that therefore the action could not be supported. Nonsuit.

Ex parte Shuttleworth, 3 Ves. 368. Newton gave the bankrupt before his bankruptcy, cash for a bill, but refused to allow the bankrupt to indorse it, thinking the bill better without his name. He now proved the amount under the commission, and on petition to have the debt expunged, the chancellor granted the petition, observing that this was a sale of the bill.

(63) In Fenn v. Harrison, 3 Term Rep. 759. Lord Kenyon said, "It is extremely clear that if the holder of a bill send it to market without indorsing his name upon it, neither morality or the laws of this country will compel him to refund the money for which he sold it, if he did not know at the time that it was not a good bill. If he knew the bill to be bad, it would be like

A bill or note will satisfy a preceding debt, if the holder makes it his own by laches. (64)

As by not presenting it for payment when due; (65)

Though it were taken from a third person; (65)

And in such case plaintiff must prove the bill was duly presented; (65)

But he need not prove notice to such third person of the bill's dishonour. (65)

---

sending out a counter into circulation to impose upon the world, instead of the current coin. In this case, if the defendants had known the bill to be bad, there is no doubt but that they would have been obliged to refund the money.

(64) Bridges v. Berry, 3 Taunt. 130. Defendant accepted a bill for 119*l*. due 20th October, but did not pay it: plaintiff was the holder: defendant afterwards lodged in plaintiff's hands as a security, a bill drawn by defendant upon one Ivory, for 117*l*. 11*s*. 2*d*. and paid plaintiff the difference: this bill was dishonoured, but no notice thereof was given to defendant: action by plaintiff on both bills. It was admitted at the trial that defendant was discharged from the second bill, but it was urged that he continued liable on the first: but Mansfield C. J. and the court held he did not, and nonsuit; and rule to set it aside refused.

See Swinyard v. Bowes, ante, p. 233. note (114).

(65) Bishop v. Rowe, 3 Maule, 362. Plaintiff sued the drawer and acceptor of a bill, and proved the necessary facts: defendant gave in evidence that after the bill was due, and part paid, one Tucker, who had been connected with the bill, but had not indorsed it, drew for the balance on Lewis at two months, and gave plaintiff the draught: plaintiff could not prove that the draught was presented for payment, but he nevertheless had a verdict: the court however thought that proof essential, and granted a new trial. On the second trial plaintiff gave this proof, but he could not prove that he had given notice to Tucker of the dishonour: the point was saved, whether he was bound to give this proof? and on rule nisi for nonsuit, and

If the holder of a bill or note employ a particular agent to get it discounted, but refuse to indorse it, and the agent guarantee its payment, the principal will (66) not be bound by such guarantee; and not being bound, a subsequent promise by him to pay the amount of the bill or note, will be (66) nudum pactum.

But if no restraint be imposed on such agent, the principal (66) may be bound by his guarantee; at least such guarantee will be a (66) sufficient consideration to support a subsequent promise by the principal to pay the bill or note.

---

cause shewn, the court held it sufficient for him to prove presentment and non-payment, for that shewed there had been no payment in fact; and if the defendant insisted there had been such neglect as amounted to payment in law, he should have shewn it. The rule was discharged.

(66) Fenn v. Harrison, 3 Term Rep. 757. and 4 Term Rep. 177. The defendants employed F. Huet to get a bill discounted, but said that they would not indorse it; F. H. employed his brother James H. and said he would indemnify him if he would indorse it; James indorsed it, and the plaintiffs discounted it; the bill being dishonoured the plaintiffs applied to the defendants who promised to take it up, but did not; and this action for money had and received and money paid, was brought against them. Lord Kenyon told the jury, that if they thought that James H. had made himself answerable as agent for the defendants, that was a sufficient consideration for their promise. A verdict was found for the plaintiffs; and on a rule nisi for a new trial, and cause shewn, Lord Kenyon inclined to think the verdict right; because though the agent had exceeded his authority, he thought the principal bound by what he did: the other judges differed, because F. H. was a *particular* agent only: and the rule was made absolute. On the next trial it did not appear that the defendants had told F. H. that

In case of a transfer by delivery, no action can be brought against the deliverer, except on account of the consideration.

If a bill or note be destroyed by fire or other accident, an action may perhaps be brought thereon as if it were in esse. (67)

But if a bill or note be lost, there can be no remedy upon it at law, unless it was in such a state when lost that no person but plaintiff could have acquired a right to sue thereon. (68)

As if it were specially indorsed to plaintiff, and had no indorsement from him upon it. (69)

---

they would not indorse the bill. A verdict was found for the plaintiff, and on a rule nisi for a new trial, and cause shewn, the whole court thought the verdict right, because as F. H. was not restrained as to the mode of getting the bill discounted, the defendants were bound by his act. But Buller and Grose Js. said, that if the facts had been the same, they should have continued of their former opinion. Rule discharged.

(67) See Pierson v. Hutchinson, infra. Mayor v. Johnson, post. p. 300.

(68) Pierson v. Hutchinson, 2 Campb. N. P. C. 211. In an action by an indorsee against the acceptor of a bill, it appeared that the bill had been lost after indorsement, and the plaintiff had offered the defendant an indemnity. But Lord Ellenborough nonsuited the plaintiff, saying, that if the bill had been proved to have been destroyed, he should have had no difficulty in receiving evidence of its contents, and in directing the jury to find for the plaintiff; but that having been lost, after indorsement by the payee, it might still be in the hands of a bonâ fide indorsee for value, who might sue the defendant upon it. And as to the indemnity, he said a court of law could not enquire into its sufficiency. — S. P. ruled by Lord Eldon. See ex parte Greenway, 6 Ves. 812.

(69) Long and another v. Bailie, 2 Campb. N. P. C. 214. This was an action against the acceptor of a bill of exchange,

Where it is so specially indorsed, an action may perhaps be brought thereon. (69)

Where the person paying is entitled to require an indemnity, the only remedy on a lost bill is in equity: a court of equity can enquire into the sufficiency of an indemnity; a court of law cannot.

The acceptor is not liable to be sued upon a *lost* bill, if the loss was before the bill was due, though he promises to pay it after knowing of the loss, unless there is some new consideration for such promise. (70)

The holder's only remedy is to enforce the giving a new bill under the statute. (70)

If a bill is lost after action brought thereon, and defendant suffer judgment by default, the court

---

payable to the order of the drawer, and by him specially indorsed to the plaintiffs. It was proved that a person took the bill to have it compared with the affidavit to hold to bail, that a copy was then taken, and that the bill was afterwards stolen from such person. The correctness of this copy and the special indorsement were proved, and upon this the plaintiffs had a verdict.

(70) Davis v. Dodd, 4 Taunt. 602. Action on bill payable to Allen or order, accepted by defendant, and indorsed generally to plaintiff: plaintiff lost it before it was due, but defendant after knowing of the loss, promised repeatedly to pay it. Lord Ellenborough however held the action not maintainable, and nonsuit; and on motion for a new trial, the court agreed with him: they thought defendant under no moral obligation to pay plaintiff, who by his negligence had exposed defendant to the danger of being compelled to pay another holder, and that his subsequent promise, there being no new consideration, was nudum pactum: they said, enforcing the giving a new bill under the statute, seemed to be plaintiff's only course.

will, on a copy verified by affidavit, refer it to the master to see what is due thereon; (71)

Especially if the bill has been shewn to defendant, and he has admitted his signature, and promised payment. (71)

But if the bill is lost after action brought, and defendant resists the action, and puts the plaintiff to prove the bill, the loss will be no excuse for the non-production of the bill, and plaintiff will not be able to recover. (72).

And it will make no difference though the bill is of so old a date that the statute of limitations has attached upon it.

If a bill or note transferable by delivery is cut in halves, and half lost, the holder cannot sue at law upon the other half. Payment at law cannot be enforced unless the entire instrument is produced, or unless there is proof that the entire in-

---

(71) Brown v. Messiter, 3 Maule. 281. The acceptor of a bill desired to see the bill, and then he admitted the acceptance, and promised payment; he suffered judgment by default; and the bill having been stolen from plaintiff's attorney's pocket, rule nisi to refer on production of copy verified by plaintiff's attorney, and no cause being shewn, rule absolute.

(72) Poole v. Smith, Holt. 144. In action by indorsee against acceptor, it appeared that a few days before the trial the bill was picked out of the pocket of plaintiff's attorney's clerk; and that defendant had admitted the acceptance, but said it had been satisfied between him and the drawer: the bill had been due above six years. Gibbs C. J. thought the non-production of the bill called upon him to nonsuit plaintiff, and that the statute of limitations made no difference: he said the rule was salutary, and ought not to be relaxed.

strument, or whatever part of it is wanting, has been destroyed. (73)

A special count upon a bill or note states in their order all the facts necessary to maintain the action.

To give a full idea of this count, and open the way to the observations necessary to be made upon it, I shall insert a comprehensive one in assumpsit upon a foreign bill, which will sufficiently elucidate those on inland bills or notes, and those in debt.

Count in assumpsit upon a Foreign Bill.

London } John Mills v. Thomas Roper and Ste-
to wit. } phen Howe. For that whereas on (1) the 1st day of January, 1789, at (2) London aforesaid, in the parish of St. Mary le Bow, in the ward of Cheap, certain persons (2^2) using the style and firm of Gaunt and Co. according (3) to the usage and custom of merchants, from time immemorial used and approved of, made (4) their certain bill

---

(73) Mayor v. Johnson, 3 Campb. 324. Plaintiff's traveller took a *5l.* country bank-note, payable at Stamford or London, and cut it in halves, and sent the two halves to plaintiff; one half only arrived, the mail containing the other was stolen: plaintiff sued on the half which arrived; but as plaintiff could not shew that the other half was destroyed, Lord Ellenborough held the action could not be supported, and nonsuit.

N. He assigned as a reason, that the stolen half might immediately have got into the hands of a bonâ fide holder for value, and that such holder would have had as good a right as plaintiff: but, quære—If a man who takes half a note does not take it at his peril.

of exchange in writing, their (5) copartnership, stile, and firm aforesaid, being thereunto subscribed, bearing (6) date the day and year aforesaid, and (7) directed to one Henry Hunt, at Venice, in Italy, in parts beyond the seas, and (8) thereby requested the said Henry, at double usance, to pay in Venice (8[2]) that their first of exchange (second (9) and third of the same tenor not paid) to the said (9[2]) Thomas and Stephen, or (10) their order, a certain sum of foreign money, (10[2]) called in the said bill seven hundred ducats, value (10[3]) received, and then and there (10[4]) delivered the said bill to the said Thomas and Stephen, which (11) said bill the said Henry Hunt, afterwards, to wit, on (12) the day and year aforesaid, at Venice, to wit, at London aforesaid, in the parish and ward aforesaid, on sight thereof, duly according to the usage and custom of merchants accepted, payable at A. B. and Co.'s, Venice (12[2]); and the said Thomas and Stephen (12[3]) afterwards and before the payment of the said sum of money in the said bill mentioned, or of any part thereof, to wit, on the day and year aforesaid, at London aforesaid, in the parish and ward aforesaid, by their certain indorsement in writing then and there made upon the said bill, (12[4]) their proper hands being thereunto subscribed, according to the usage and custom of merchants, appointed the (13) contents of the said bill to be paid to one Peter White, or (14) his order, and then and there delivered the said bill so indorsed to the said Peter; and (15) the said Peter afterwards and before the payment of the said sum of money in the said bill mentioned, or of any part thereof, to wit, on the day and year aforesaid, at London aforesaid, in the parish and ward aforesaid, by his certain indorsement in writing then and there made upon the said bill, his proper hand being thereunto subscribed, appointed the contents of the said bill to be paid to the said John, and then and there delivered the said bill so indorsed to the said John, of (16) which said indorsements the said Henry afterwards, to wit, on the day and year aforesaid, at London aforesaid, in the parish and ward aforesaid, had notice; and the said John in fact says, that (17) an usance mentioned in any bill of exchange drawn in London and payable in Venice, is, and at the several times aforesaid was, three calendar months from the date of the said bill, and no other time whatever; and (18) that afterwards, and when the said bill had according to the tenor and effect thereof become payable, to wit, on (19) the 4th day of July, in the year aforesaid, at Venice aforesaid, to wit, at London aforesaid, in the parish and ward aforesaid, the said bill was duly, according to the usage and custom of merchants, and according to the tenor of the said acceptance thereof, shewn and presented to the said Henry at A. B. and Co.'s aforesaid, at Venice aforesaid for payment; and the said Henry was then and there requested to pay the said sum of money in the said bill mentioned, but the said Henry did not then (19[2]) or there pay the said sum of money in the said bill mentioned, or any part thereof, but wholly neglected and refused so to do; neither (20) did he pay the said second or third of exchange in the said bill mentioned, or either of them; nor (21) did the said persons so using the stile and firm of Gaunt and Co. pay the said sum of money in the said bill mentioned, or any part thereof, or the said second or third of exchange; and thereupon the said John, afterwards, to wit on the day and year last aforesaid, at Venice aforesaid, to wit at London aforesaid, in the parish and ward aforesaid, according to the usage and custom of merchants, caused the said bill to be protested (22) for non-payment, of all which premises the said Thomas and Stephen afterwards, to wit on the day and year last aforesaid, at London aforesaid, in the parish and ward aforesaid, had (23) notice; and by reason thereof, and by force of the usage and custom of merchants, became liable to pay to (24) the said John the said sum of money in the said bill mentioned, or the value thereof, when (25) they the said Thomas and Stephen should be thereunto afterwards requested: and (26) being so liable, they the said Thomas and Stephen, in consideration thereof, afterwards to wit on the day and year last aforesaid, at London aforesaid, in the parish and ward aforesaid, undertook, and to the said John then and there faithfully promised, to pay to him the said sum of money in the said bill mentioned, or the value thereof, when they the said Thomas and Stephen should be thereunto afterwards requested: and (27) the said John avers, that the said 700 ducats in the said bill mentioned, on the day and year last aforesaid were, and from thenceforth hitherto have been, and still are of great value, to wit of the value of *l.* of lawful money of Great Britain, that is to say at London aforesaid, in the parish and ward aforesaid; yet the said Thomas and Stephen (although often requested) have not nor hath either of them paid to the said John the said sum of money in the said bill mentioned, or any part thereof, or the value thereof, or of any part thereof, but hath wholly neglected and refused, and still neglects and refuses so to do; wherefore the said John says he is injured, and hath sustained damage to the value of *l.* and therefore he brings suit, &c.

1. "On, &c." Upon a bill or note importing to be payable within a limited time after the date, and dated on a particular day, this (74) must be that day: on a bill or note importing to be payable within a limited time after the date, and not dated, the day (75) it issued, if it can be ascertained, otherwise (76) the first day the plaintiff knew and can prove that it existed.

---

(74) Stafford v. Forcer, 10 Mod. 511. cited Str. 22. In an action on a note dated in 1704, defendant pleaded that the cause of action did not accrue within six years; the plaintiff replied a bill filed in 1714, and that the cause of action accrued within six years of that time; and after verdict for the plaintiff the court arrested the judgment, because it was stated that the note was made and dated in 1704, and then the cause of action must have accrued above six years before 1714.

(75) Vide ante, p. 201. n. (60).

(76) Vide Beawes, § 190. p. 439.

2. "At, &c." On a foreign bill this must be the place at which it bears date; but where the drawing of the bill must be proved upon a trial, some place in England or Wales should be subjoined under a videlicet, thus, "at Venice in Italy, to wit, at London," &c.

In an action against the drawer, the want of subjoining such place may be taken advantage of by special demurrer to the count, but by special demurrer (77) only.

In an action on a foreign note, it may be stated to have been made at any place in England, without naming the foreign place. (78)

Inland bills and notes, though they may bear date at a particular place, may be alleged to have been made any where in England or Wales.

2[2]. "Certain persons." A bill or note may be stated according to its legal operation.

Thus a joint or several note, or a note importing in the body of it to be made by several persons, but signed by one only (79), may be stated as a several note.

---

(77) Vide 16 and 17 Car. 2. c. 8. § 1., 4 Ann. c. 16. § 1.

(78) Houriet v. Morris, 3 Campb. 303. In an action on a note dated at Paris, the statement was, that defendant at London &c. made his note, &c.; it was urged that it should have been stated to have been made at Paris, to wit, at London, &c. but Lord Ellenborough said the contract was transitory, and the statement sufficient.

(79) Roberts v. Peake, Burr. 322. A note signed by the defendant alone, but importing in the body of it to have been made by the defendant and another person, was declared upon

Nay, where the plaintiff in an action against one of two makers of a joint or several note, stated that the defendant and another made their certain note, &c. and thereby jointly or severally promised to pay, the court held it (80) well after judgment by default; notwithstanding, as the truth of either member verifies a disjunctive proposition, the note might have been joint.

And in an (81) action against one of the several

---

as the several note of the defendant, and it was agreed that it might be declared upon according to its legal operation; but judgment was given for the defendant upon another ground. See Siffkin v. Walker, 2 Campb. N. P. C. 308.

(80) Butler v. Malissy, Str. 76. In an action on a note, the declaration stated that the defendant and another did jointly or severally promise to pay; and upon demurrer, the court held it bad, and the plaintiff obtained leave to discontinue. And in Ovington v. Neale, Str. 819., Lord Raym. 1544., the plaintiff declared upon a note by which the defendant and another jointly or severally promised to pay; and upon error, the court of kings bench held it bad, because the plaintiff had not shewn a title to bring a separate action against the defendant, for he only says he has this or some other cause of action; and judgment for the plaintiff was reversed. However, in Rees v. Abbott, Cowp. 832., the declaration upon a note stated that the defendant and another made their note, by which they jointly or severally promised to pay; and upon error after judgment by default, Butler v. Malissy, and Ovington v. Neale, were cited as in point. Sed per Lord Mansfield, "If *or* is to be considered in this case as a disjunctive, the plaintiff is to elect, and by the action he has made his election to consider the note as several; but in this case it is synonymous to *and*, and both and each promise to pay." Judgment affirmed.

(81) Per Buller J., Rees v. Abbot, supra; and see Rice v. Shute, Burr. 2611., and Abbot v. Smith, Blackst. 947.

makers of a joint note, or one (82) of several drawers of a joint bill, if it be stated as a several one made by one alone, the objection can only be taken by plea in abatement.

A bill or note made by a servant for his master may be stated to have been made by the master, because that (83) is its legal operation.

3. "According, &c." It is (84) not requisite to set out any part of the custom, and even a reference to it is (85) unnecessary.

In actions upon notes, instead of referring to the custom of merchants, the count refers to the statute, but this reference is unnecessary.

4. "Made." Where a man signs his name upon a blank paper, stamped with a bill stamp, and delivers it to another to draw above the signature what bill he pleases thereon, and he draws one

---

(82) Evans v. Lewis, E. 1794. cit. 1 Barnew. and Ald. 226. In an action against defendant as drawer of a bill, the declaration stated that he made his certain bill of exchange &c.; it appeared in evidence that the bill was drawn by defendant and another person jointly: the point was saved whether this was a variance, and the court on motion were of opinion it was not, and that the only mode by which the defendant could have made the objection was by plea in abatement.

(83) See ante, p. 305.

(84) Soper v. Dible, Lord Raym. 175. In an action upon a bill the defendant demurred, because the declaration did not set out the custom, the court held it unnecessary, and said the better way was to omit it.

(85) This was determined in Ereskine v. Murray, Lord Raym. 1542., on error after judgment by default; and see Lord Raym. 88., Carth. 83. 269, 270., Lutw. 279.

accordingly, the (86) bill may be stated to have been made by the person whose signature it bears.

5. "Their, &c." A signature, when essential, is (87) implied by the preceding word "made;" this allegation, therefore, is not strictly necessary, and had better be omitted, lest there should be a (88) variance between the signature stated and that proved.

6. "Bearing, &c." This allegation (89) also

---

(86) Collis v. Emett, 1 H. Blackst. 313. Emett signed a piece of blank paper stamped with a bill stamp, and delivered to Livesay and Co. that they might write above his signature such bill as they should please: they wrote one accordingly; and an action being brought thereon against Emett, in which it was stated that he drew the bill, the court thought the statement proper; and upon a special verdict stating these facts, the court gave judgment for the plaintiff upon a count which alleged that the bill was drawn by the defendant.

(87) This was ruled upon demurrer in Elliot v. Cooper, Lord Raym. 1376., Str. 609., and Smith v. Jarvis, Lord Raym. 1484.; and on error after judgment by default, in Ereskine v. Murray, Lord Raym. 1542. Vide ante, p. 31. n. 67.

(88) Jones and another v. Mars and another, 2 Campb. N. P. C. 305. The declaration in an action against the drawers of a bill, stated it to have been made by the defendants, "their own proper *hands* being thereunto subscribed." The bill was in fact signed by only one of them "Mars and Co." Lord Ellenborough doubted whether the variance was material; but refused to nonsuit the plaintiffs. He said had it been "their own proper *hand*," he should have held it clearly sufficient.

See also Levy v. Wilson, 5 Esp. N. P. C. 180., post, 319. and Helmsley v. Loader, 2 Campb. N. P. C. 450., and Heys v. Heseltine, 2 Campb. 604.

(89) De la Courtier v. Bellamy, 2 Show. 422. In an action upon a foreign bill payable at double usance from the date

may be dispensed with; for it shall be intended, when the date is material, that a bill or note was dated when drawn.

Where the date is immaterial, and this allegation is omitted in the declaration, this intendment shall (90) not operate so as to render a variance between the date of the bill and the day on which it is stated to have been drawn fatal.

7. "Directed, &c." In an action against the acceptor upon a bill directed to him, or, in his absence, to I. S., the (91) conditional direction to I. S. need not be stated.

So in an action against the acceptor of a bill, though the bill were directed to him and another

---

thereof, the declaration stated that the drawer on such a day drew the bill, but the date was not set forth. An exception was taken on this ground; but, by the whole court, "It is well enough; we will intend it was dated when it was drawn:" judgment for the plaintiff. S. P. R. acc. Hague v. French, 3 Bos. and Pull. 173.

(90) Coxon v. Lyon, 2 Campb. N. P. C. 307. n. The declaration stated that the defendant, on the 3d of Feb. 1810, made his bill, requesting the drawee to pay on a particular day. The bill was in fact dated the 6th of Feb. 1810, but no date was stated in the declaration. Thompson B. held that the variance was immaterial

(91) Anon. 12 Mod. 447. A bill directed "to A., or, in his absence, to B.," began thus: "Gentlemen, pray pay, &c." A. accepted it; and in an action against him on his acceptance, the declaration described the bill as directed to A., without any notice of B.; and Holt C. J. held it well.

person, it may be described as directed to him, without naming the other person. (92)

In an action against an acceptor, if the bill were not directed to him, it has been held to be a fatal variance to state that it was. (93)

If a bill is directed to Messrs. A., B. and Co., it is no variance in setting out the bill according to its tenor to put *Mess*[s.] A., B. and Co., without the r instead of Mess[rs.] with it. (94)

8. "In Venice." If a bill or note in what is strictly part of it, fixes a specific place for pay-

---

(92) Mountstephen v. Brooks, 1 Barnew. and Ald. 224. In an action against three as acceptors of a bill, the declaration stated that J. S. made his bill directed to defendants, and thereby requested them to pay, &c.; it appeared in evidence, that it was in fact directed to them and one Richard Smith, with whom they were in partnership, and that it was accepted by him and them. Lord Ellenborough thought this a variance, and nonsulted the plaintiff; but on an application for a new trial, he changed his opinion; and the rest of the court concurring with him, a new trial was granted.

(93) Gray v. Milner, 2 Stark. 336. In an action against the acceptor of a bill, the declaration stated that the bill was directed to the defendant; it appeared to have no direction: Lord Ellenborough held this a fatal misdescription, and nonsuited the plaintiff.

(94) Rex v. Oldfield, Mich. 1815. An indictment for forging an indorsement upon a bill imported to set out the bill according to its tenor; the bill was directed to "Mess[rs.] Masterman and Co;" but upon the indictment the r in Messrs. was omitted, and it stood Mess[s.]; the point was saved for the consideration of the twelve judges, and they were unanimous that as it appeared by the context that Mess[s.] must mean Mess[rs.], the variance was immaterial, and the conviction unobjectionable.

ment, it is a fatal variance to omit stating it in setting out the bill or note. (95)

On the other hand, if it be stated as the import of the bill or note that the money should be paid at a specific place, when the provision for that purpose is not strictly part of the bill or note, it is a fatal variance. (96)

In such case, however, stating that the party made the bill or note, and that he *then and there* made it payable at the specified place, without

---

(95) Roche v. Campbell, 3 Campb. 247. A note was in this form, "31 days after date I promise to pay J. S. or order, at the house of N., No. 6. Grafton-street, Dublin, 40*l*. &c." In an action by indorsee against indorser, the bill was described generally to pay J. S. or order, without naming the place; and it was urged that this was a misdescription, for it implied that the note was payable generally, while it was only payable at one given house. Lord Ellenborough thought it a fatal misdescription, and nonsuited plaintiff.

Hodge v. Fillis, 3 Campb. 463. A bill was addressed to Messrs. Fillis and Co., Plymouth "payable in London;" they accepted it, payable at Sir John Perring and Co.'s, London. In an action against them the first count, in stating the bill, omitted to allege that the address made it payable in London. Lord Ellenborough thought the omission fatal on that count; but on proof of a promise by defendants to pay after the bill was due, he thought the plaintiff entitled to recover on other counts; and verdict accordingly.

(96) Exon v. Russell, 4 Maule and Selw. 505. At the bottom of a note was written, "at Messrs. Brown and Co.'s, bankers, London:" in stating the note, the declaration alleged that defendant made the note, and thereby promised to pay, &c. and made the same payable, and to be paid according to the tenor and effect, at the house of persons described as Messrs. Brown and Co., bankers, London. On rule nisi for a nonsuit

X 4

stating that he *thereby* made it so payable, is not fatal. (97)

9. "Second, &c." In an action upon a bill consisting of several parts, if the plaintiff has each part, it may be doubted whether he need take notice of this condition, because all the parts collectively make an unconditional bill; and where he has not each part, it should seem more correct to state that the drawer made his certain bill of exchange in writing in three parts, his proper hand being subscribed to each of the said parts, bearing date, &c. and directed, &c. and by each of the said parts requested, &c.; but the form I have adopted is the usual one.

9[2]. "To the said Thomas and Stephen." A bill or note importing to be payable to a fictitious person, and to be indorsed by him, may be stated to be payable to the person in whose favour the indorsement is made, or if it import to be indorsed

---

upon another ground, the court thought it a misdescription of the note to state as its import that it was made payable at a particular place; for as the place was mentioned by way of memorandum only, and not as part of the contract, that was not its import; and on that ground the rule for a nonsuit was made absolute.

(97) Hardy v. Woodroffe, 2 Stark. 319. In an action against the maker of a note, it was alleged in the declaration that defendant made the note, &c. and that he then and there made it payable at No. 32, Castle-street, Holborn; the defendant had written upon the note "payable at No. 32, Castle-street, Holborn," and Abbott J. held that memorandum supported the statement in the declaration; and plaintiff had a verdict.

in blank, it may be stated to be payable to (98) bearer.

A bill or note intended to have been made payable to A. that he might guarantee the payment to B., but through ignorance or mistake made payable to B. and by him indorsed to A., and then indorsed back by A. to B., may perhaps (99) be stated to have been made payable to A.

The payee of a bill or note payable "to his order," may (100) state it to have been made payable to himself.

---

(98) Vide ante, p. 26. n. (61). In Vere v. Lewis, ante, p. 27. note (61). Lord Kenyon, Ashhurst and Buller Js., thought that the plaintiff might recover on the count which stated that the bill was drawn payable to bearer; and in Collis v. Emett, ante, p. 28. n. (61.) it was so decided.

(99) Bishop v. Hayward, 4 Term Rep. 470. A note payable to the plaintiff or order was indorsed by him to the defendant, and indorsed back again by the defendant to him; these facts being stated on the declaration, the court arrested the judgment. It was suggested in the argument that the plaintiff had refused to take the note, unless the defendant put his name upon it, and that as he was made payee, his indorsement was mere form; and per Lord Kenyon, "Had it been understood by all parties that the note, though nominally payable to the plaintiff, was substantially to be paid to the defendant, it should have been declared on according to its legal import, as was held in Minet v. Gibson; a name may be omitted in the declaration, if the legal operation of the instrument requires it."

(100) Frederick v. Cotton, 2 Show. 8. In an action against the acceptor of a bill, it was objected, in arrest of judgment, that the bill was stated to be payable to the order of the plaintiff, and no order was alleged; but the court resolved without any difficulty, that money to be paid to a man's order was due to himself; and judgment was given for the plaintiff.

If the intended payee's name is miswritten, so as to give it a different sound and make it a different name, it may be stated to have been made payable to the person intended, and evidence may be given to shew who was intended. (101)

10. "Or order, &c." In an action by the assignee of a bill or note, it is necessary to shew that the bill or note authorizes a transfer; in an action by the payee (102), not.

10². "Money." If a bill or note is for money of the same appellation as ours, but of different value, it must not be stated as if it were for our money; (103)

As if it be for so many pounds, and is drawn and payable in Ireland, it must not be stated to be for so many pounds generally, without something to shew that pounds Irish were meant. (103)

---

(101) Willis v. Barrett, 2 Stark. 29. E. Willis sued as payee of a note: the note, when produced, imported to be payable to E. Willison, but Lord Ellenborough allowed evidence to prove that plaintiff was the person meant; and he had a verdict.

(102) See ante, p. 29. note (62.) Moore v. Paine, Ann. 288. In error upon a judgment by default in an action upon a note, it was objected that it was only stated to be payable to the plaintiff, and not *to his order*; but by Lord Hardwicke, that has been overruled often: the judgment was affirmed.

(103) Kearney v. King, 2 Barnew. and Ald. 301. In an action against the acceptor the declaration stated that A. B. at Dublin, to wit, at London, drew a bill on defendant requiring him to pay the sum of 542*l*. 1*s*. 8*d*. The bill, when produced, appeared to be drawn in Ireland, and to be payable in Ireland, and though it was for 542*l*. 1*s*. 8*d*. sterling, that sum Irish was only equal to

10[3]. "Value received," It is not necessary to state that a bill or note was for value received.

And if it be so stated, and the statement give a wrong meaning to those words, it will be a fatal misdescription. (104)

Upon a bill payable to the drawer's order, if the bill is for value received generally, without saying by whom, it is giving them a wrong meaning to state it as for value received by the drawer. (104)

If the bill is payable to a third person, it is not. (105)

500*l.* 7*s.* 9*d.* English; and on rule nisi for a nonsuit, and cause shewn, the court were clear that the bill, as stated, must be taken to have been for English money; and the bill produced being for Irish, there was a clear variance; and the rule was made absolute.

(104) Highmore v. Primrose, 5 Maule and Selw. 65. A bill payable to the drawer's order was for value received generally; the declaration stated that it was for value received by the drawer. The court thought that value received by the drawer could be no foundation for his drawing to his own order, and considered this a variance; but there being an acknowledgment of the debt by the defendant, the plaintiff recovered on the account stated.

(105) Grant v. Da Costa, 3 Maule and Selw. 351. In an action against the acceptor on a bill payable to J. S. or order, it was stated to be for value received by the drawer; on production, it appeared to be for value received generally: and on a rule nisi for a nonsuit, the court held that the meaning of value received on such a bill, payable to a third person, was, that the value had been received by the drawer of the payee; that it was natural the drawer should give the drawee that information; but why should he tell him that he, the drawee,

10[4]. "Delivered, &c." It is (106) not necessary to state that the drawer of a bill "delivered" it to the payee; it is implied in the allegation that he "made" the bill.

If it be stated that the bill was delivered to the drawee, and that he accepted it, it is (107) not necessary to allege that he delivered it back.

11. "Which, &c." Except in actions against acceptors, or on bills payable within a limited time after sight, the acceptance need not be stated.

---

had had value from the drawer? and yet that could be the only other object of the words. Rule discharged.

(106) Churchill v. Gardner, 7 Term Rep. 596. In an action by the payee of a bill against the acceptor, the declaration stated that the drawer made his certain bill of exchange, but there was no allegation that he delivered it to the plaintiff, and the defendant demurred specially for that cause. But the court was clearly of opinion that there was no foundation for the objection, the delivery of the bill to the plaintiff being sufficiently implied in the allegation that the drawer "made" the bill.

(107) Smith v. M'Clure, 5 East. Rep. 476. The plaintiff declared on a bill payable to his own order, and averred that he delivered it to the defendant, to whom it was addressed, and that he accepted it according to the custom of merchants, by reason of which premises, &c. the defendant became liable to pay. The defendant demurred specially, because it was not alleged that the defendant delivered back the bill: sed per Lord Ellenborough, the acceptance must be considered as perfect; and if so, it gave the plaintiff a right to sue upon it: if, after the acceptance, the defendant improperly detained the bill, the plaintiff might nevertheless sue him upon it. Judgment for the plaintiff.

If stated, though unnecessarily, it has been held at nisi prius that it (108) must be proved.

12. "On, &c." Where the time of payment depends on the presentment, and the action is against the drawer of a bill, or the indorser of a bill or note, this should be the very day of the presentment; in other cases, exactness as to the day is not requisite.

If, however, the plaintiff allege in terms that the acceptance was made before the time limited by a bill for its payment, it has been laid down that he will (109) be precluded from giving in evidence an acceptance afterwards; but this may perhaps be doubted. (110)

Though the time of payment depend upon the presentment, as in bills payable a given time after sight; yet, if the action is against the acceptor,

---

(108) Jones v. Morgan and another, 2 Campb. 474. In an action on a bill, drawn on Burt by the defendants, payable to their own order, and indorsed by them to the plaintiff, the declaration unnecessarily stated an acceptance by Burt. And Lord Ellenborough was of opinion, that the plaintiff having stated an acceptance, was bound to prove it.

(109) Jackson v. Pigott, Lord Raym. 364., 12 Mod. 212. In an action against the acceptor of a bill, per Holt C.J. "If the plaintiff declares that the acceptance was before the day appointed for the payment, and that the defendant accepted to pay according to the tenor and effect of the bill, and it appears upon the evidence that the acceptance in fact was after the day of payment, this would be against the plaintiff."

(110) See Young v. Wright, post. p. 318. note (114.)

exactness as to stating the day of presentment is not essential. (111)

12². "At A. B. and Co.'s." If an acceptance import to make the bill payable at a banker's, or any other particular place, this need not be stated in an action against the acceptor, nor, perhaps, in an action against the drawer or an indorser, unless the acceptance is prior to the 1st of August, 1821, or unless it expresses that the party accepts the bill payable there, and not otherwise or elsewhere. (112)

If this be expressed in the acceptance (112), or if the acceptance be prior to 31st August, 1821, the acceptance must be stated as a special acceptance, to pay at such place. (113)

12³. "Afterwards, &c." It is (114) not a ma-

---

(111) Forman v. Jacob, 1 Stark. 46. Indorsee against acceptor on bill dated Constantinople, and payable fifty days after sight. The declaration averred an acceptance on the day the bill bore date, whereas the acceptance was not till five weeks afterwards: it was objected that this was a fatal variance; but Lord Ellenborough held otherwise, and plaintiff had a verdict.

N. The date was 11th August, the acceptance 19th September.

(112) See 1 & 2 G. 4. c. 78. § 1. ante, p. 157.

(113) See Rowe v. Young, ante, p. 178.

(114) Young and another v. Wright, 1 Campb. N. P. C. 139. This was an action by indorsees against the drawer of a bill. The declaration stated all the indorsements to have been made before the bill became due; but it appeared that the immediate indorsement to the plaintiffs had been made after the bill had become due. Lord Ellenborough, on the authority of Russell v. Langstaffe, Dougl. 514. (ante), held that the variance was

terial variance, that an indorsement is stated to have been made before, and is proved to have been made after, the bill became due.

12. "Their proper hands." This is an unnecessary allegation, being implied in the preceding words; it is better to omit it, because there are cases in which it may occasion risque. For instance, if a bill be indorsed by procuration, and it be thus stated to have been made by the hand of the party himself, the variance (115) will be fatal.

13. "The contents." On an indorsement for less than the full sum mentioned in the bill or note, the plaintiff must (116) shew that the residue was paid.

14. "Or his order." These (117) words are unnecessary.

---

immaterial; he said that this was the converse of that case, but was to be governed by the same principle.

(115) Levy v. Wilson, 5 Esp. N. P. C. 180. In an action by an indorsee of a bill, the declaration stated the indorsement to have been made by the payee "his own hand-writing being thereunto subscribed." The bill appeared to have been indorsed by procuration. Lord Ellenborough held this variance fatal, and nonsuited the plaintiff. See also Jones v. Mars, ante p. 308.

(116) Hawkins v. Gardner, 12 Mod. 213. The declaration stated that the defendant drew a bill for 46*l*. 19*s*. payable to Blackman or order, and that Blackman indorsed 43*l*. 4*s*. thereof to the plaintiff; the court held, that an indorsement for part only of what was due upon the bill was bad, and said, if Blackman had brought an action for part, he must have acknowledged satisfaction for the residue.

(117) Vide ante, p. 104.

A full and blank indorsement are stated in the same manner.

15. " And the said Peter, &c." Every indorsement essential to a transfer must be stated; unnecessary ones may (118) be omitted.

Where the plaintiff would omit an indorsement, he should represent that which precedes the indorsement to be omitted to have been made in favour of the person who is indorsee upon that which follows.

Thus if a bill payable to A.'s order be indorsed by him in blank, and delivered to B. and indorsed by B. to C., if C. would omit stating B.'s indorsement, he should state that A. indorsed it immediately to him, C.

16. " Of which, &c." This (119) allegation is unnecessary.

---

(118) In Peacock v. Rhodes, ante, p. 100. note (11.) the bill was payable to Ingham, and indorsed by him and by John Daltry; the plaintiff declared as indorsee of Ingham, and recovered.

Chaters v. Bell and others, 4 Esp. N. P. C. 120. The declaration stated, that a bill was drawn payable to Curry, by him indorsed to the defendant, and by the defendant to the plaintiff. There were in fact, several intermediate indorsements between Curry and the defendant, which were omitted in the declaration; and it was contended that the plaintiff should have either declared, as the immediate indorsee of the payee, or have stated all the indorsements. But Lord Ellenborough overruled the objection. Vide Waynam v. Bend, and Critchlow v. Parry, post.

(119) Anon. Pract. Reg. 358. In an action by an indorsee of a note against the maker, the defendant demurred, and shewed for cause, that it was not alleged that he had notice of

17. "That an usance, &c." A neglect to shew the duration of an usance is (120) fatal upon demurrer, (unless perhaps where it is alleged that the bill was presented on the day it was payable) but upon demurrer only. (121)

---

the indorsement; but by the court, there is no need of notice. Judgment for the plaintiff.

Reynolds v. Davies, in error, 1 Bos. and Pull. 625. In an action by an indorsee against the maker of a note, the declaration stated the indorsement and delivery by the payee, and then averred (in the usual form) the defendant's liability and promise to pay to the plaintiff. There was no averment of notice of such indorsement. The defendant demurred specially, but did not assign such want of notice as a cause of demurrer. After judgment in the king's bench for the plaintiff Davies, a writ of error was brought in the exchequer chamber, and such want of notice assigned as error. But Eyre C. J. said the promise to pay contained in this note is to the payee or his order; immediately then on the order being made to the indorsee, the promise attaches: nor can we add the qualification of notice to a promise which was not originally qualified with that circumstance. Judgment affirmed.

(120) Buckley v. Campbell, Salk. 131. The plaintiff declared upon a bill drawn at Amsterdam and payable in London, at two usances, and did not shew what the two usances were: and the court gave judgment for the defendant, because they could not take notice of foreign usances, which are longer in one place than another.

(121) Smart v. Dean, 3 Keb. 645. In an action on a bill from Paris, payable here at double usance, the defendant pleaded payment; and on issue taken thereon, demurred, and objected that it was not alleged that double usance was two months: sed non allocatur, "It being a known term among merchants, that usance is a month, double two months; and being averred he had not paid in two months, it is well enough, the defendant having waived advantage hereof by pleading payment:" but by Twysden J., had it been on demurrer to the

18. "And that, &c." In an action against the maker of a note or the acceptor of a bill, the presentment is never stated, unless the bill or note is made payable either by the original frame of it, or by the form of the acceptance at a particular place only. (122)

In an action against the drawer of a bill, or the indorser of a bill or note, it is essential to state either that (123) the bill or note was presented,

---

declaration, the plaintiff should have averred a particular custom that usance signifieth a month. Judgment for the plaintiff.

(122) Vide Fenton v. Goundry and Callaghan v. Aylett, ante, p. 178. 9. note (19). See also Sanderson v. Bowes, ante, p. 175. note (15), with which it is difficult to reconcile, in principle, the case of Fenton v. Goundry. The acceptance seems to be as much the original contract of the acceptor of a bill, as a note is the original contract of the maker.

(123) Mercer v. Southwell, 2 Show. 180. The declaration against the drawer of a bill stated that the drawee did not accept, but did not allege that the bill had been shewn or tendered to him; and upon demurrer on this account, the omission was held fatal, for otherwise it would be in the plaintiff's power to charge the drawer, when perhaps the drawee was ready to pay the money according to the tenor of the bill, if it had been tendered to him.

Rushton v. Aspinall, Dougl. 654.—680. In an action by indorsee against indorser upon a bill payable three months after date, the declaration stated that the bill, after the making thereof, to wit, on the same day and year aforesaid (referring to the day the bill bore date), was presented for acceptance, and accepted; yet the drawer, although afterwards, to wit, on the same day and year aforesaid requested, did not pay, of which the drawer, the payee, and first indorser, and the acceptor, had notice: by reason thereof defendant became liable to pay; and being so liable, on the same day and year promised to pay. After verdict and judgment for plaintiff, the court of king's bench, upon a

that the drawee or maker could not be found, or that the defendant, had he paid the bill, would have had no remedy against them.

If a bill be stated to have been accepted payable by certain persons at a particular place, so as to make presentment at that place essential, an averment in an action against the drawer of a presentment to those persons generally, without saying at that place, is insufficient.

But an allegation that it was presented to them "according to the tenor and effect of the bill, and the acceptance thereof," will (124) be sufficient.

---

writ of error brought, held the declaration bad; because it did not shew that payment was demanded of the acceptor when the bill became due, or that notice was given to the defendant of his refusal to pay; and that though it was stated that he had promised to pay, that promise was stated as an inference of law, and the declaration did not contain premises from which that inference could be drawn; and the judgment was reversed. See also Parker v. Gordon, ante, p. 180. note (22.), and Ambrose v. Hopwood, infra.

(124) Huffam v. Ellis. M. 51 G. 3. In an action against the drawers of a bill, the bill was stated in the declaration to have been accepted by Robertson, payable at the house of Kensington, Styan, and Adams, and a presentment to them was averred to have been made "according to the tenor and effect of the said bill, and the said acceptance thereof," without saying *at the house:* to this the defendant pleaded a judgment recovered, and judgment was given by the court of King's Bench for the plaintiff, the defendants having failed to produce the record of the judgment pleaded. On error to the House of Lords, the want of an averment of a presentment at the *place* where it was made payable, was assigned for error: and Ambrose v. Hopwood was cited. But the House of Lords affirmed the judgment of the Court of King's Bench. 10th of April, 1811.

If the drawee or maker cannot be found, it is (125) sufficient to aver generally that he was not found, without stating that any inquiry was made after him.

On an allegation that the bill or note was presented, and acceptance or payment refused, the plaintiff cannot (126) give in evidence that the drawee or maker could not be found.

But if a note be made payable at a particular town, and the maker has no residence there, a presentment at the banking-houses there will justify and support an allegation that it was presented there to the maker. (127)

If the allegation be that the bill was presented

---

(125) Starke v. Cheeseman, Carth. 509. In an action upon a bill drawn by the defendant on C. C. of Radcliffe, London, the declaration merely stated that the said C. C. at Radcliffe aforesaid, or elsewhere within the kingdom of England, was not found; and, after judgment by default, it was objected in arrest of final judgment, that it was not shewn that any inquiry had been made after him; but it was answered, that it was according to the custom among merchants, and the common form in the like cases, and judgment was given for the plaintiff.

(126) R. Leeson v. Pigott, sittings after Trinity, 1788; and see Smith v. Bellamy, 2 Stark. 223.

(127) Hardy v. Woodroffe, 2 Stark. 319. Action against the maker of a note made payable at Guilford, and allegation that plaintiff shewed and presented the note to defendant at Guilford for payment thereof: plaintiff proved that he presented the note at two banks at Guilford, and that defendant lived in London: it was objected that this proof did not support the allegation; but Abbot J. thought otherwise, and that a presentment at Guilford, defendant not being there, was a presentment to defendant; and verdict for plaintiff.

by one J.S., that part of the allegation which states that the presentment was by J. S. is immaterial. (128)

In an action against the acceptor of a bill or maker of a note payable on demand, a (129) presentment on demand need not be stated.

19. "On, &c." Unless there is an express averment that the presentment was made on the day when the bill or note became payable, this (130) must be that very day; where there is such averment, exactness as to the day is, probably, immaterial.

In an action against the acceptor of a bill payable a limited time after sight, if the declaration allege a presentment for payment, mistaking the day on which such presentment was made is immaterial. (131)

Especially if it is alleged that it was presented when it became due and payable, and it was in fact presented on the day it became due. (131)

---

(128) Boehm v. Campbell, Gow. 55. In an action by drawer against guarantee of acceptor, averment that the bill was presented for payment by one J. S. at the place where the acceptance made it payable: plaintiff proved a presentment there, but not by J. S.; and Dallas, C. J. held the substantive part of the allegation proved, and plaintiff had a verdict.

(129) Rumball v. Ball, 10 Mod. 38. Debt upon a note, by which the defendant acknowledged himself indebted, and promised to pay on demand: it was urged in arrest of judgment, that it was not alleged that there had been a demand; but the court held the allegation unnecessary.

(130) See Rushton v. Aspinall, ante p. 322. note (123).

(131) Forman v. Jacob, 1 Stark. 46. In an action by indorsee

19.[2] "Did not, &c." In an action against the maker upon a note payable at the house of a third person, if a presentment there is stated, it is not necessary to state a special refusal there: the general allegation at the end of the declaration, that defendant did not pay, will be sufficient; for payment at that house would have been payment by him, and it would not be true that he had not paid, had there been a payment there. (132)

20. "Neither, &c." Where the plaintiff states that the sum of money mentioned in the bill was not paid, this allegation is not (133) necessary.

---

against acceptor on a bill payable fifty days after sight, the declaration alleged an acceptance 11th August, and that when the bill became due and payable, viz. on 3d of October, it was presented for payment. It appeared in evidence that the acceptance was not till the 19th of September, nor the presentment for payment till the 11th of November; and it was urged that these mistakes were fatal: Lord Ellenborough thought not, and the plaintiff had a verdict.

(132) Butterworth v. Lord Le Despencer, 3 Maule & Sel. 150. Payee against maker on note payable at the house of Wright and Co.'s. A presentment at Wright and Co.'s was stated, and it was alleged at the end of the declaration that the defendant, although often requested, had not paid, &c.; but there was no special allegation of non-payment upon the presentment at Wright and Co.'s. Defendant demurred on this ground; but on argument, the court was clear that the general allegation of non-payment sufficiently negatived any payment at Wright and Co.'s, and judgment was given for the plaintiff.

(133) Starke v. Cheeseman, Carth. 509. The declaration stated that the defendant made three bills of exchange, all of the same date and contents, and by the second required the drawee (the first and third of the said bills not being paid) to pay, &c.; that the drawee was not to be found, and the said sum of money in

21. "Nor, &c." This (134) allegation is unnecessary.

22. "Protested, &c." The protest (135) need not be stated in an action on an inland bill; in an action on a foreign one the plaintiff (136) must

---

the said bill mentioned was not paid: after judgment by default, it was objected in arrest of judgment, that there was no averment, that the first and third bills were not paid; but it was answered, that the allegation *that the money in the said bill mentioned* was not paid supplied the want of the averment, because the sum was the same in all the bills; and the plaintiff had judgment.

East v. Essington, Lord Raym. 810. Salk. 130. Assumpsit against the acceptor of the following bill, "Pray, pay this my first bill of exchange, the second and third not being paid." After verdict for the plaintiff, it was moved in arrest of judgment, because there was no averment, that the second and third were not paid: sed non allocatur; for per curiam, though it had been ill upon demurrer, yet it is aided by the verdict; for if the second or third had been paid, the jury would have found non-assumpsit.

Wegersloffe v. Keene, Str. 214. In assumpsit against the acceptor upon a bill by which the drawer requested him to pay "that his first bill (his second not being paid)" the declaration stated that the defendant promised to pay the money, but had not; the defendant pleaded an insufficient plea, and upon demurrer to the replication, objected that there was no averment that the second bill was not paid; but the objection was overruled, and judgment given for the plaintiff.

(134) Vide post, c. 11.

(135) See Brough v. Parkins, ante, p. 214. note (85).

(136) Salomons v. Stavely, cited Dougl. 2d ed. 684. n. 144. The court held, on the authority of the precedent in Dunstar v. Pierce, Lill. Ent. 55. that the neglect to allege a protest in an action on a foreign bill, was matter of form only, and could not be taken advantage of on a general demurrer.

either state it, or (137) shew that it was not necessary; but the omission can (138) only be taken advantage of by a special demurrer.

In stating the protest, if the plaintiff allege, "*that* (139) *he protested the bill or caused it to be protested,*" it will be unobjectionable, if the defendant pleads over.

23. "Notice." If the defendant is primâ facie entitled to notice, it is essentially necessary to state that he had (140) notice, or to shew that he was not entitled thereto.

Under an allegation of notice, it may be questionable whether evidence can be given of what

---

(137) In Rogers v. Stephens, supra, p. 234. note (117). Lord Kenyon, and afterwards the court, held a protest for non-acceptance not necessary to support an action against the drawer, because it appeared he had no effects in the hands of the drawee. See Legge v. Thorpe, ante, p. 238. note (119). And see the form of averring that the drawer had no effects in the hands of the drawee, in Legge v. Thorpe, 12 East. Rep. 171.

(138) Vide supra note (136).

(139) Witherby v. Sarsfield, 1 Show. 125. The declaration upon a foreign bill stated that the plaintiff "protested it, or caused it to be protested;" the defendant pleaded that he was not a merchant, and upon demurrer had judgment. A writ of error was brought; and it was then, for the first time, urged that the allegation that the plaintiff protested the bill or caused it to be protested, was uncertain; but the court thought it well enough, reversed the judgment below, and then judgment was given for the plaintiff.

(140) See Rushton v. Aspinall, ante, p. 322. n. (123). And see the form of averring that the drawer of a bill had no effects in the hands of the drawee, in Legge v. Thorpe, 12 East. Rep. 171.

would excuse notice (141), or whether to let in such evidence, the facts to excuse notice should not be pleaded specially. (141)

24. "To the said John." In an action upon a bill or note stated upon the count to be payable to the order of the plaintiff, it is sometimes (142) usual, though (143) unnecessary, to insert here an allegation that the plaintiff made no order; but the better way upon a bill or note made so pay-

(141) Corey v. Scott, B. R. Tr. 1 Geo. 4. 3 Barnew. 619. In an action by indorsee against drawer, the declaration stated presentment for payment and dishonour, whereof drawer afterwards, &c. had notice: at the trial there was no evidence of notice, but plaintiff proved that defendant had no effects in the drawer's hands: defendant rebutted this proof by shewing that he and the acceptor only lent their names to a subsequent indorser, and therefore that defendant on paying the bill would have been entitled to sue the acceptor and that subsequent indorser. Under these circumstances Abbott C. J. held notice necessary, and nonsuited, giving plaintiff to move to enter a verdict: rule nisi accordingly. On cause shewn, it was urged that under the allegation of notice plaintiff had no right to give evidence of what went only to excuse want of notice, and of that opinion were Bayley and Holroyd Js.; but on the merits, they agreed with Abbott C. J., that defendant was entitled to notice; and the rule was discharged. See 12 East. 171.

(142) It was done in Fisher v. Pomfret, Carth. 403.

(143) Vide Frederick v. Cotton, ante, p. 314. note (101).

See Lill. Ent. 90. 29, 41. 44, 55. 73. Lutw. 1589.

Sheldon v. Occarsen, Tr. T. 41 Geo. 3. 12 June, 1801. C. B. Roll. 715. Special demurrer to a declaration on a bill stated to be payable to the *order* of the plaintiff; and the cause assigned was, that it was not stated that the plaintiff had made no order: the court said, that it was too clear for argument, and gave judgment for the plaintiff. Best Serj. was to have argued for the defendant. S. P. Smith v. M'Clure, 5 East. Rep. 476.

able, is to state according to the legal operation, that it was made payable to the plaintiff, and then this allegation would be impertinent.

25. "When, &c." In an action against the acceptor of a bill or maker of a note not payable immediately upon presentment, instead of alleging that the defendant became liable, and promised to pay *when he should be thereunto afterwards requested*, he is stated to have become liable, and promised to pay *according to the tenor and effect of the bill and acceptance* in the one case, and *of the note* in the other.

26. "And, &c." This clause is unnecessary in an action against either the (144) acceptor of a bill or the maker of a note; and it may be doubted whether (145) it is essential in any other.

27. "And the said, &c." This averment is not, it is apprehended, ever necessary; the want (146) of it is certainly cured by verdict.

---

(144) Wegersloffe v. Keene, Str. 214. In assumpsit against the acceptor, an objection was taken to the promise as stated; sed per Fortescue J., "The plaintiff need not set out any promise. In Lowther v. Conyers, which was upon a promissory note, they left out super se assumpsit, and yet it was held well enough, for the law raises a promise."

(145) Starke v. Cheeseman, Carth. 509. Salk. 128. After judgment by default in an action against the drawer of a foreign bill, it was objected in arrest of judgment, that it was not stated in the declaration that the defendant promised to pay the money after the protest was made; but it was answered, that the law did raise the promise upon the custom of merchants, and therefore it was not necessary to lay an actual promise; and the plaintiff had judgment.

(146) Simmonds v. Parminter, 1 Wils. 185. 4 Bro. Parl. Cas.

In an action by a person who has paid a bill under protest, for the honour of drawer or an indorser, it is sufficient for him to allege that he, according to the usage and custom of merchants, paid the bill; he need not specify to whom he paid it. (147)

---

604. The declaration upon two foreign bills for the payment of 4000 and 5000 dollars did not state what their value was, and after a demurrer this was urged as a ground to arrest the judgment; but the court gave judgment for the plaintiff, and upon a writ of error that judgment was affirmed.

(147) Cox v. Earle, 3 Barnew. and Ald. 430. Declaration against acceptor on bill paid by plaintiff under protest for the honour of the second indorser stated, that plaintiff, according to the usage and custom of merchants, paid the bill under protest: special demurrer, on the ground that it was not alleged to whom plaintiff paid it, or that he paid it to the holder, or that plaintiff thereby became the legal holder thereof: sed per cur. on argument, payment to a wrong person would be no payment; this payment is alleged to have been according to the usage and custom of merchants, and plaintiff would be bound to prove payment to the person entitled to receive. Judgment for plaintiff.

CAP. X.

Remedy upon a Bill or Note by proving it under a Commission of Bankruptcy, or suing out a Commission thereon.

WHEREVER the holder of a bill or note is entitled to compel a person to pay it, he (1) may, in the

(1) In ex parte Dewdney 15 Ves. 495. Lord Eldon C. held that where recovery in an action on a bill would be barred by a plea of the statute of limitations, and all relief in equity would

event of such person's bankruptcy, prove the amount under his commission; and whatever would be a defence to a suit, (2) will be an answer to such proof.

And a bill or note (3) may be proved before it

---

be equally defeated by lapse of time, to which courts of equity, in analogy to the statute of limitations, give similar effect, the bill could not be proved under a commission of bankruptcy; and after reasoning on the inconsistency which would result from a contrary doctrine, his lordship observed, "that consideration, among others, furnishes a ground for concluding that the real meaning of the legislature in those acts (the bankruptcy statutes) requiring the Lord Chancellor to give execution to all the creditors, was, that this species of execution should be given to those creditors, who, if a commission of bankruptcy had not issued, could, by legal or equitable remedies, have compelled payment.'" See 1 Sch. and Lefr. 48. Where the holder has bought bills or notes for less than the money payable upon them, (as in ex parte Lee, 1 P. Wms. 782., where he bought notes for 10*s*. in the pound) or where he has discounted them, (as in ex parte Marlar, 1 Atk. 150.) as he might have recovered in an action, so he may prove under a commission of bankruptcy, to the full amount.

(2) As to such objections as arise from the form of the bill or note, vide ante, c. 1., also ex parte Adney, Cowp. 460., and ex parte Tootell, 4 Ves. 372. As to the sufficiency of the stamp, vide ante, c. 3. As to the transfer, vide ante, cap. 5. Acceptance, cap. 6. As to the effect of laches, vide ante, cap. 7. As to the legality of the consideration, vide post, cap. 12.

(3) By 7 Geo. 1. c. 31. § 1., after reciting that traders had been obliged to sell their goods upon trust or credit, "and to take bills, bonds, promissory notes, or other persons' securities for their monies, payable at the end of three, four or six months, or other future days of payment," and that it had become a question whether "such persons giving such credit on such securities" could be let in to prove their debts before the securities become payable, it is enacted, "That all and every person

has become due, deducting, on payment of the dividend, a rebate of legal interest for such time as it may then have to run; and it may (under certain (4) restrictions) be proved, though the bankrupt's liability commenced after his act of bankruptcy, and within two calendar months before the date of his commission.

So the money payable upon a bill or note, if of the requisite amount, though not yet due (5), will

---

and persons who have given credit, or at any time or times hereafter shall give credit on such securities as aforesaid to any person or persons, who is are or shall become bankrupts, upon a good and valuable consideration *bonâ fide* for any sum or sums of money or other matter or thing whatsoever which is or shall not be due or payable at or before the time of such person's becoming bankrupt, shall be admitted to prove his her and their several and respective bills bonds notes or other securities promise or agreements for the same, in like manner as if they were made payable presently and not at a future day; and shall be entitled unto and shall have and receive a proportionable part share and dividend of such bankrupt's estate in proportion to the other creditors of such bankrupt, deducting only thereout a rebate of interest and discounting such securities payable at future times after the rate of five pounds per centum per annum for what he shall so receive to be computed from the actual payment thereof to the time such debt duty or sum of money should or would have become due and payable in and by such securities as aforesaid."—And by § 2. the bankrupt shall be discharged by his certificate, of and "from all and every such bond, note, or other security as aforesaid."

(4) Vide post, p. 338. to 340., and 46 Geo. 3. c. 135. § 2. post, p. 339. n. (12).

(5) By 7 Geo. 1. c. 31. § 3. it was provided, "That no such creditor (i. e. upon bill, bond, promissory note, or other persons' securities not yet due,) shall be deemed or taken to be a sufficient creditor, for or in respect of such debt, to petition or

be a good petitioning creditor's debt to support a commission of bankruptcy.

And a commission may issue against the drawer of a bill before it becomes due. (6)

And the commission will stand, though the bill when due is paid by the drawee. (6)

And it is sufficient, if the money payable to the

---

join in any petition for the obtaining or suing forth of any commission of bankruptcy, until such time as such debt shall become actually due and payable." But by 5 Geo. 2. c. 30. § 22. after reciting such provision, it is enacted, "That so much of the said act as disables any such person from petitioning for, or joining in any petition for a commission against any person or persons who have before committed any act of bankruptcy, is hereby repealed: and it shall and may be lawful hereafter, for such person to petition for, or join in petitioning for any such commission of bankruptcy; any thing in the said act contained to the contrary thereof, in any wise notwithstanding."

Note, that in 7 G. 1. c. 31. § 1. the language is, "other persons' securities," (and it is so in the parliament roll) but in 5 G. 2. c. 30. § 22. (which professes to recite the substance of the former) it is, "other personal securities."

(6) Ex parte Douthat, 4 Barnew. and Ald. 67. Douthat owed Wade 148*l.*, and in order to pay him drew on Eyre and Miller, in favour of Wade or order, at four months' date: Eyre and Miller accepted the bill, and paid it when due; but in the interim Douthat committed an act of bankruptcy, and Wade sued out a commission against him, and proved the bill. Case from chancery on the question, whether under these circumstances there was at the date of the commission a good petitioning creditor's debt? the court certified that there was, and their opinion seemed to be founded not on there being a pre-existing debt to Wade, but on the ground that the statutes 7 G. 1. c. 31. and 5 Geo. 2. c. 30. § 22. extended to drawers and indorsers of bills as well as acceptors; and that if such drawer or indorser committed an act of bankruptcy before the bill was due, a commission might at once be sued out thereon.

holder, be, at the time of (7) petitioning, of the requisite amount, though, by reason of the rebate of interest, it was not of that amount at the time of the act of bankruptcy; but it must be of the requisite amount at the time of the petition.

If, therefore, the bill or note be not *then* due, it would (8) seem that he must be a creditor for

---

(7) Brett v. Levett, 13 East. Rep. 213. In an action by the assignee of a bankrupt against the sheriff, and verdict for the plaintiff, a rule nisi to set aside the verdict was granted, on a question as to the sufficiency of the petitioning creditor's debt. The debt arose on two bills of exchange, each for 50*l.*, drawn by the bankrupt, and transferred to the petitioning creditor before the act of bankruptcy; both were dishonoured by the drawee. The act of bankruptcy was on the 28th Dec. 1809, and the commission was dated 8th Feb. 1810. Each bill became due before the petition for the commission, but *after the act of bankruptcy.* At the time of the *act of bankruptcy,* therefore, there was not a debt of 100*l.* due to the petitioning creditor, but only that sum minus the rebate of interest for the time which the bills had to run; and it was contended that at *that* time there ought to have been such debt due. But the court, after referring to 7 Geo. 1. c. 31. § 3., which disabled a creditor by a bill or note, payable at a future day, from petitioning for a commission in respect of such debt, "until such time as such debt shall become actually due and payable," and to 5 Geo. 2. c. 30. §. 22., which removes such disability, held clearly, that it was sufficient if a debt of the requisite amount were due at the time of petitioning. Rule discharged. See also the judgment of Lord Kenyon in Glaister v. Hewer, infra.

(8) See 7 G. 1. c. 31. §. 1. & 3., and 5 G. 2. c. 30. § 22. & 23. The petitioning creditor must, at the time of petitioning, make an affidavit that 100*l.* is due to him from the bankrupt. But if this debt arise from a bill or note for 100*l.* not then due, the sum *then* due to him is 100*l.* minus the amount of discount; and if the bill or note be drawn payable at a very distant day,

such sum as, after deducting the rebate of interest for the time which the bill or note has to run, will leave a debt of the requisite amount.

And upon bills or notes which are due at the time of the petition, interest cannot be taken into the account, unless it is expressly made payable on the face of the bill or note. (9)

Where it is so payable it may. (9)

The holder (10) may petition for a commission of

---

the discount may greatly diminish the sum then payable, and may possibly nearly exhaust it.

(9) Cameron v. Smith, 2 Barnew and Ald. 305. A commission was founded on an acceptance for 96*l.* 17*s.* 8*d.* The bill was so long over due that near 5*l.* was due for interest, but no interest was expressly made payable by the bill. The point was reserved whether this debt would support the commission, and, after argument, the court was clear it would not; for, though interest, if expressly reserved constituted part of the debt, if it was not expressly reserved, it constituted damages only, and damages cannot be considered part of the debt.

(10) Glaister v. Hewer, 7 Term Rep. 498. The plaintiff being indebted to Hewer in a sum below 100*l.* and to Wilson on a note for 11*l.* 12*s.*, committed an act of bankruptcy; on which, Wilson, for a valuable consideration, indorsed his note to Hewer to enable him to petition for a commission: the two sums together amounting to above 100*l.* In an action of trover for goods taken by the assignees, brought to try the validity of the commission, the only question was, whether Hewer's were a sufficient debt to support the commission, it not being so when the act of bankruptcy was committed, inasmuch as the whole did not then exist in *him.* Rooke J. thought it was, and on a rule nisi to enter a verdict for the plaintiff, Lord Kenyon said the statute only required that there should be an existing debt of 100*l.* in the petitioning creditor; this petitioning creditor had such a debt at the time of petitioning, and that is sufficient to support the commission. Rule discharged.

bankruptcy, in respect of the money payable upon a bill or note, or may prove the amount under a commission when issued, notwithstanding the bill or note may not have been transferred to him until after the act of bankruptcy committed, provided the bankrupt's liability had commenced before the act of bankruptcy.

For the case of a bill or note being one in which the law admits of the assignment of a chose in action, the assignee becomes a creditor as from the time of the original creation of the debt, and not from that of the assignment.

And though the bankrupt may have committed an act of bankruptcy before he became a party to the bill or note, it will not (11) invalidate a com-

---

Bingley v. Maddison, Co. B. L. 20. A note was given by the bankrupt in January, which became due in June. The act of bankruptcy was in October following, and the indorsement in November. The indorsee was the petitioning creditor, and sued out the commission. It was contended, that at the time of the bankruptcy the petitioning creditor had no debt, and that therefore the commission could not be supported. But the court said that this was a case in which the law allowed the assignment of a chose in action: that the assignment related to the original debt: that the indorsee always came in under the commission, because the indorsement related to the original debt: that it stood thus upon principle; and that the cases were clear, explicit and positive, and of the highest nature: they therefore held the commission valid.

11 By 46 G. 3. c. 135. § 5. it is enacted, "That no commission of bankrupt that shall be hereafter issued, shall be avoided or defeated by reason of any act of bankruptcy having been committed by the person or any of the persons against whom such commission shall have issued, prior to the contracting the

mission of bankruptcy issued on the petition of the holder, (12) or prevent his proving the amount under a commission, provided, in the former case, there is a subsequent act of bankruptcy sufficient to support the commission, (13) and in the

debt of the creditor or any of the creditors upon whose petition such commission shall have issued, if such petitioning creditor had not any notice of such act of bankruptcy at the time when the debt to him was contracted; but that such commission of bankrupt, and all the proceedings under the same shall be valid and effectual to all intents and purposes, notwithstanding that such prior act or acts of bankruptcy shall have been committed by such bankrupt."

(12) By 46 G. 3. c. 135. § 2. it is enacted, " That in all cases of commmissions of bankrupt hereafter to be issued, all and every person and persons with whom the bankrupt shall have really and bona fide contracted any debt or debts before the date and suing forth of such commission, which, if contracted before any act of bankruptcy committed, might have been proved under such commission, shall, notwithstanding any prior act of bankruptcy may have been committed by the bankrupt, be admitted to prove such debt or debts, and to stand, and be a creditor under such commission, to all intents and purposes whatever, in like manner, as if no such prior act of bankruptcy had been committed by such bankrupt, provided such creditor or creditors had not, at the time of such debt or debts being contracted, any notice of any prior act of bankruptcy by such bankrupt committed."

(13) E. Moss v. Smith, 1 Campb. N. P. C. 489. To an action against the sheriff for a false return of nulla bona to a writ of fi. fa. issued against David Moss's goods, the defence was the bankruptcy of D. M. before the delivery of the writ. On the 8th of December, 1807, he committed an act of bankruptcy; on which a commission issued, founded on a debt contracted for goods sold on a credit which did not expire until the 11th of December. On the 29th his goods were taken under the fi. fa.; but the execution was withdrawn on notice of the bank-

latter that he had become such party before the (14) date of the commission; and in each, that the holder had not any (15) notice of a prior act of bankruptcy.

If an indorser of a bill or note be obliged, in consequence of the bankruptcy of an antecedent party to pay it, he (16) may prove the amount under his commission, though he did not make the payment until after the commission issued. And though the indorsement were lent merely to give credit to the bill or note (17), he may prove it independently

ruptcy. Lord Ellenborough held that the commission could not be supported, as the petitioning creditor's debt was not due when the act of bankruptcy was committed; and that it was not a case within 46 G. 3. c. 135. Verdict for the plaintiff. And on motion afterwards for a new trial the court refused a rule. And per Lord Ellenborough, the grievance which that statute meant to remedy was the practice of upsetting commissions of bankrupt, by unexpectedly proving an act of bankruptcy prior to that relied upon by the assignees.

(14) See 46 G. 3. c. 135. § 2. ante, p. 339. note (12).

(15) See 46 G. 3. c. 135. § 2 and 5. ante, p. 339. note (12) and p. 338. note (11).

(16) Joseph v. Orme, 2 New. Rep. 180. The plaintiff being holder of a bill accepted by the defendant, indorsed it for a valuable consideration to Adams. Before the maturity of the bill, a commission of bankruptcy issued against the defendant: and the plaintiff was afterwards obliged to pay the bill to Adams, and now sued the defendant as acceptor. The defendant having received his certificate, obtained a rule nisi to enter an exoneretur on the bail piece: and after cause shewn, the court held that the plaintiff might have proved the bill under the commission, and therefore made the rule absolute.

(17) Ex parte Brymer, Cooke, B. L. 165. To enable Scott and Pearson to raise money, Forsyth drew three bills on Wilkins, which the latter accepted, dated the 28th of May, 1787, for

of 49 G. 3. c. 121. § 8., unless the bankrupt were the person to whom such indorsement was lent.

If the bankrupt were the person to whom the indorsement was lent, in which case the indorser is a mere surety, he will be entitled under 49 G. 3. c. 121. § 8. on taking up the bill or note to stand

---

800*l.* each, payable three months after date; two to the order of Span, and the third to the order of the drawer, which last was indorsed in blank by the drawer. They were then sent to Scott and Pearson, and by them to Span, who indorsed them, got them discounted, and remitted the money to Scott and Pearson. Before the bills became due Scott and Wilkins became bankrupt; Span was afterwards obliged to take up the bills, and was admitted to prove under Wilkins's commission; and on a petition to have that proof expunged, the chancellor said, the debt accrued by the acceptance, and Span became a holder in a fair way. Petition dismissed. And on a second petition for a rehearing the chancellor continued of the same opinion.

Houle v. Baxter, 3 East's Rep. 177. The defendant, a retail silversmith, ordered goods of Capper, a working silversmith, and to enable him to obtain silver for the order, accepted a bill drawn on him by Capper; and to encrease the credit of the bill, Capper prevailed on the plaintiff to lend his indorsement. Capper then passed the bill to Abud, who supplied the silver of which the goods were made and delivered to the defendant. On the 7th of November, 1796, the defendant became bankrupt, and afterwards obtained his certificate. On the 24th of December 1796, the day before the bill became due, the plaintiff took it up from Abud, and now sued the defendant as acceptor. A verdict was found for the plaintiff subject to the opinion of the court. And Grose, J. who delivered the opinion of the court, said, that here the plaintiff never became surety to the *defendant*; his demand arises solely on the bill, and there was nothing to prevent his proving it under the commission. The bankruptcy and certificate is therefore a bar. Nonsuit entered.

in the place of the holder, if he had proved under the commission, and to prove himself, if the holder had not, provided in such case he had not notice, when he lent his indorsement, that the person to whom he lent it had committed any act of bankruptcy or become insolvent, or stopped payment.

And a surety has this right, though he did not become surety until after the principal had committed an act of bankruptcy.

The issuing of a commission, though such commission may afterwards be superseded (18) will be deemed such notice.

---

(18) By 49 Geo. 3. c. 121. § 8. it is enacted. That in all cases of commissions of bankrupt already issued, under which no dividend has yet been made, or under which the creditors, who have not proved, can receive a dividend equally in proportion to their respective debts without disturbing any dividend already made, and in all cases of commissions of bankrupts hereafter to be issued, where at the time of issuing the commission any person shall be surety for or be liable for any debt of the bankrupt, it shall be lawful for such surety or person liable, if he shall have paid the debt, or any part thereof in discharge of the whole debt, although he may have paid the same after the commission shall have issued, and the creditor shall have proved his debt under the commission, to stand in the place of the creditor as to the dividends upon such proof; and when the creditor shall not have proved under the commission, it shall be lawful for such surety, or person liable to prove his demand in respect of such payment as a debt under the commission, not disturbing the former dividends, and to receive a dividend or dividends proportionably with the other creditors taking the benefit of such commission, notwithstanding such person may have become surety or liable for the debt of the bankrupt after an act of bankruptcy had been committed by such bankrupt,

If an acceptance for the accommodation of the drawer of a bill be given before, and renewed after, he has committed an act of bankruptcy, such renewal is a continuation of the same suretyship; and therefore if a commission of bankruptcy be issued against the drawer, and the acceptor afterwards pay the bill, he (19) will be entitled to prove

---

provided that such person had not at the time when he became such surety, or when he so became liable for the debt of such bankrupt, notice of any act of bankruptcy by such bankrupt committed, or that he was insolvent, or had stopped payment; provided always, that the issuing a commission of bankrupt, although such commission shall afterwards be superseded, shall be deemed such notice; and every person against whom any such commission of bankrupt has been or shall be awarded, and who has obtained or shall obtain his certificate, shall be discharged of all demands at the suit of every such person having so paid, or being hereby enabled to prove as aforesaid, or to stand in the place of such creditor as aforesaid, with regard to his debt in respect of such suretyship or liability, in like manner to all intents and purposes as if such person had been a creditor before the bankruptcy of the bankrupt for the whole of the debt in respect of which he was surety or was so liable as aforesaid. Vide Stedman v. Martinnant, next note. For the law before this act, vide Snaith v. Gale, 7 Term Rep. 364.

(19) Stedman v. Martinnant, 13 East's Rep. 127., and vide S. C. 12 East's Rep. 664. On 5th of January, 1807, the plaintiff accepted a bill for the accomodation of the defendant, the drawer, which became due on the 19th of March, when it was dishonoured. On the 18th of March, 1807, a docket was struck against the defendant, and on the 21st a commission of bankrupt was issued, which was superseded on the 15th of April. A meeting of the defendant's creditors was then held, when time was given him to pay his debts by instalments. On the 9th of June, 1807, the plaintiff accepted a second bill for the defendant, in order to take up the former one, for the same sum

the amount under such commission; though, before the renewal of the acceptance, he had notice of such act of bankruptcy having been committed.

Nor will the case be varied in principle, by the circumstance of the holder of the first bill, having, before the renewal (20) given time to the drawer; or by that, of (21) an additional name, as that of an indorser, having been lent upon the second bill.

Counter acceptances are good mutual considerations for such acceptances.

---

with the addition of interest and stamp: and the indorsement of a third person was lent as an additional security, which was required by the holders of the former bill. On the 6th of August, 1807, a valid commission was issued against the defendant, founded on an act of bankruptcy committed in the preceding March. The second bill became due on the 12th of September, 1807, when the plaintiff paid it. The first dividend under the commission was declared and made on the 6th of August, 1808. On the 4th of September, 1809, the defendant obtained his certificate. In an action for money paid, and the bankruptcy and certificate pleaded, a verdict was found for the plaintiff subject to the opinion of the court, as to whether the certificate were a discharge. The court (Le Blanc J. absente) held that the second acceptance was a continuation of the same suretyship, which was created by the first; and that as such suretyship commenced before any act of bankruptcy committed, and consequently before the plaintiff could have any notice of such act, the plaintiff might, by 49 G. 3. c. 121. § 8., have proved his demand under the commission, and therefore the certificate was a bar. Postea to the defendant.

(20) Vide Stedman v. Martinnant, ante, p. 343. n. (19.) It must be presumed that the holder was ignorant of the bills having been accepted for the *accommodation* of the drawer. Vide Laxton v. Peat, ante p. 271. note (20).

(21) Vide Stedman v. Martinnant, ante p. 343. note (19).

Therefore if two traders exchange acceptances and afterwards become bankrupt, each (22) may prove the other's acceptances under his commission.

Though the acceptances of neither be due at the time of such bankruptcy.

Especially where each has (23) engaged to pay his own acceptances.

---

(22) Rolfe v. Caslon, 2 H. Blackst. *570.* Rolfe and Caslon drew two bills of the same tenor and date on each other, and each accepted the other's bill, neither having effects of the other in his hands. Twenty days before the bills were due Caslon became bankrupt. He had indorsed the bill which Rolfe had accepted in part satisfaction of a larger debt, and the creditor proved his whole debt; Rolfe paid the difference of the bill he accepted, allowing for the dividend, and now sued Caslon on his acceptance and for money paid; Caslon pleaded his bankruptcy. Verdict for the plaintiff, with liberty to the defendant to move to set it aside. On motion accordingly and rule nisi, it was urged for the plaintiff that this acceptance could not have been proved under the commission, because it created no debt to Rolfe, unless he paid the bill which Caslon drew; and at the time of the bankruptcy it was uncertain and contingent whether he would pay such bill; but the court was clear that the mutual acceptances constituted a debt on each side; and that the defendant's acceptance might have been proved under the commission, and that therefore the certificate was a bar. Rule absolute. Vide also Buckler v. Buttevant, post, p. 346. note (25).

(23) Cowley v. Dunlop, 7 Term Rep. *565.* The Peters and Dunlops exchanged acceptances to the amount of 3000*l.* and upwards, under an agreement that each should provide for their own acceptances. Both houses became bankrupt, and obtained their certificates. The Peters paid part of their acceptances, and their assignees paid dividends upon the rest, and also upon Dunlop's acceptances. Dunlop's acceptances

And if one be obliged to pay the acceptances of both, and the other afterwards obtain his certificate, the party paying (24) cannot recover any of the money so paid from the other; for as to his own acceptances the party paying was bound by his engagement to provide for them; and as to the other's, they were proveable under his commission, and therefore his certificate is a discharge.

And it is immaterial whether the acceptances exchanged be the acceptances of the parties themselves, or of (25) other persons.

---

were also proved under Dunlop's commission, and a dividend paid thereon. The Peters' assignees having paid considerably more than the Peters' proportion upon the bills, brought an action for money paid against the Dunlops; the question was, whether their bankruptcy was a bar? After two arguments, the court was divided; Lawrence and Grose Js. thought it was, because the assignees had no claim in respect of the Peters' acceptances, inasmuch as by the agreement they were to provide for them; and the claim on the acceptances of the Dunlops was barred by the certificate, because at the time of the bankruptcy, they were debita solvenda in futuro; Rolfe v. Caslon: and the assignees had no better claim than if the Peters had been holders at the time of the bankruptcy. Ashhurst J. thought it no bar, because the Peters were to be considered as sureties. Lord Kenyon thought the Peters could not be remitted to their original right as drawers, because the bills had been already proved and a dividend paid under the Dunlops' commission.

(24) Vide Cowley v. Dunlop in the last note.

(25) Buckler v. Buttevant, 3 East's Rep. 72. The defendants gave the plaintiffs their bills, accepted by third persons, in exchange for the plaintiff's acceptances of bills drawn by the defendants on him. Each bill tallied in amount with that for which it was exchanged, excepting that in one instance two

Nor is it (26) essential that the bills exchanged should agree precisely in amount, or in the times at which they respectively become due; any difference, however, in these respects is evidence of the bills not having been given in exchange for each other.

But the money payable upon such counter acceptances, will (27) not be a good petitioning

---

bills were given in exchange for one of the aggregate amount of both; and in another instance there was a difference (between the bills last exchanged) of a few shillings which were paid at the time, in order (as it was expressed) "to finish the transaction." They also agreed in dates, excepting that in two instances bills were made payable two days earlier than those for which they were respectively exchanged. And the defendants' letters in which they enclosed their remittances, always spoke of "valuing" on the plaintiff "for the same amount:" and the whole correspondence pointed at nothing else than an exchange of paper. The defendants became bankrupt; when the commission was issued the plaintiff had paid the whole amount of his acceptances to the holders, excepting 49*l.* and he proved the money so paid, under the commission. He afterwards paid the balance of 49*l.* and brought this action for money paid, to recover that sum. All the bills received by the plaintiff from the defendants were dishonoured. A verdict was found for the plaintiff, subject to the opinion of the court. The court held that this was an absolute exchange of acceptances; that each party's remedy against the other was upon the other's bills only; and that therefore this action, which was founded on an implied promise, and not on the bills, could not be supported. Postea to the defendant. Vide Toussaint v. Martinnant, 2 Term Rep. 100.

(26) Vide Buckler v. Buttevant, in the last note.

(27) Sarratt and another v. Austin, 4 Taunt. 200. In trover by the assignees of a bankrupt against the sheriff for goods taken in execution, the only question was as to the sufficiency of the

creditor's debt to support a commission; unless it appear that the petitioning creditor has taken up his own acceptances.

---

petitioning creditor's debt. He and the bankrupt had drawn two bills on each other of precisely the same tenor and dates, and each had accepted the other's bills. Before any of the bills became due, the bankrupt committed an act of bankruptcy, upon which a commission was issued founded upon the acceptances so given by the bankrupt. None of the bills was due or paid when this action was brought. A verdict was found for the plaintiffs, with liberty to the defendant to move to set it aside and enter a nonsuit. On rule nisi accordingly and cause shewn, three manuscript cases were cited to shew that where there are cross acceptances neither party can prove under a commission of bankruptcy, until he has taken up his own acceptance. Mansfield C. J. said, "If those cases had not been mentioned, I should have had no doubt that either party might prove; that the debt is barred by the certificate has been decided; why is it barred? because it might have been proved under the commission: it is strange to say then that it cannot be proved; either the one or the other must be wrong." And after time taken to consider, his Lordship, in delivering the opinion of the court, said, this question depends on the construction of 7 Geo. 1. c. 31. and 5 Geo. 2. c. 30. taken together: the preamble of the former act only contemplates the case of bills and other securities being taken for *goods sold*, and has not the least mention of their being taken where a debt is not clearly due. The act does not apply to debts in their nature contingent. This debt, though not contingent on the face of the instrument, is thus far in its nature contingent that, until the party taking the bankrupt's acceptance have paid his counter bill, the court of chancery will restrain him from receiving any dividend: and it would be a singular construction of the statutes that a man, who will not be entitled to receive a shilling out of the bankrupt's estate, unless he take up his own acceptance, should be able to petition for a commission. And no case being cited to shew that he can, the court upon prin-

And though such counter acceptances may be proved, yet the party who has given the bankrupt his own acceptances in exchange, will not be allowed to (28) receive a dividend upon such proof, until he take up his own acceptances.

So where a banker from time to time advances money and accepts and discounts bills for a customer, and in return, the latter remits bills drawn by him and accepted by others, and afterwards

---

ciple think the debt not sufficient to support the commission. Rule absolute.

The enacting part of 7 Geo. 1. c. 31. § 1. only requires that the security be taken upon good and valuable consideration. And according to Rolfe v. Caslon, (ante, p. 345.) a counter acceptance is a good consideration to enable the holder of the bankrupt's acceptance to *prove;* though from this case it appears that it is not so, to enable him to petition.

(28) Whether the not having taken up the counter acceptance will prevent the proof of the bankrupt's acceptance, or whether it will only occasion a suspension of the dividend, is a point upon which there have been contradictory decisions; and the text writers have adopted different opinions. In Cooke, B. L. p. 162. it is considered as settled that the proof cannot be permitted until the counter bill be taken up. Mr. Cooke cites ex parte Brown, 23d of December, 1797. That was a petition to prove upon an indemnity bond forfeited before the bankruptcy, but the surety the petitioner had not paid his own bond at the time of the petition being heard. The chancellor said, " The debt cannot be twice proved, there is no equity, but by taking up the original bond;" and he dismissed the petition. It mnst however be observed that here the payment of the money upon the original bond must have been the very condition upon which the bond of indemnity was to be paid. This was the case of principal and surety, which that of cross acceptances has been decided not to be. In Cullen, p. 134. and in Montagu, vol. i.

becomes bankrupt, the banker, though his own acceptances may not then be due, (29) may prove the bills so remitted, under a commission issued against the customer.

But it seems that mere reciprocal accommodations without any specific exchange of bills or notes, will (30) not create a debt on either side;

---

p. 139. it is said that the proof is allowed, but the dividend witholden. And see the judgment of Mansfield C. J. in Sarratt v. Austin, ante, p. 348. n. (27) to the same effect. See also ex parte Bloxham in the next note.

(29) Ex parte Bloxham, 8 Ves. 531. The bankrupt kept an account with the Bloxhams as his bankers; in the course of which they advanced money, and accepted and discounted bills for him; and he, from time to time, remitted bills to them drawn by him and accepted by others; these remittances were made previously to the bankruptcy, some before and some after the acceptances of the bankers. At the date of the commission the bankers were under acceptances, and they held bills so remitted; neither the acceptances or bills being then due. On petition, the chancellor, after referring to ex parte Maydwell, Cooke, B. L. 159. in which Lord Thurlow held that the liability by the acceptance was a good consideration for a promissory note, ordered that the bankers should be permitted to prove the bills upon which the bankrupt's name appeared, to cover their acceptances. See also Bosanquet v. Dudman, post, p. 399.

(30) Ex parte Walker, 4 Ves. 373. Various accommodation transactions had for many years taken place between Caldwell and Co. and the Brownes. The former were the bankers of the latter. A commission of bankruptcy issued against Caldwell and Co. in March, 1793, and in the same month the Brownes became bankrupt. An account was then taken of the mutual debts and credits. That account consisted, first, of a cash account, which included good bills as well as payments in cash; and secondly, of a bill account which related exclusively to bills

each party, in such case, becomes surety for the other, and until obliged to pay bills or notes ne-

---

which had been passed by one house to the other, and which were all ultimately dishonoured. The result was, that on the cash account the Brownes were indebted to Caldwell and Co. in the sum of 40,716*l.* and that on the bill account Caldwell and Co. had received from the Brownes bad bills to the amount of 305,149*l.* 19*s.* 10*d.* and the Brownes had received from Caldwell and Co. bad bills to the amount of 204,910*l.* 5*s.* Of the bad bills received from Caldwell and Co. the Brownes had negotiated bills to the amount of 196,589*l.* 6*s.* 4*d*, and of those received from the Brownes, Caldwell and Co. had negotiated bills to the amount of 126,855*l.* 11*s.* 10*d.* having retained the residue (viz. 178,294*l.* 8*s.*) at the request of the Brownes. All the bills received by the Brownes were discountable, and upon most of them they had received the full value; and Caldwell and Co. had no consideration for them but the bad bills received from the Brownes. All the bills (or nearly so) which the Brownes had negotiated were proved against the estate of Caldwell and Co. and by far the greater part against the estate of the Brownes also; but to a large amount, viz. 80,000*l.* the Brownes had deposited bills as a security for the payment of a much smaller sum, so that the proof against them in respect of those bills was only for the sum really due, whereas against Caldwell and Co the proof was for the whole sum payable on the bills: and the consequence of this and of the unequal negotiation of each other's bills, was, that a much larger sum was proved against Caldwell and Co. in respect of bills negotiated by the Brownes, than against the latter in respect of bills negotiated by the former. And Caldwell and Co. on petition claimed the right to prove the bills which still remained in their hands in order to be reimbursed the difference. But the chancellor said, "Till Caldwell and Co. pay all the creditors of Browne, who are likewise creditors of theirs, 20*s.* in the pound, they would be, by proving, sharing with the creditors of Browne, who are likewise creditors of theirs. If I allow this petition I must do two things that are quite impossible. I

gotiated by the other, acquires no right to sue the other, or in the event of his bankruptcy, to prove under his commission.

And even after he has been so obliged to pay bills or notes negotiated by the other, his right of action, or of proof, does not arise on the other's bills or notes, but in respect of the money paid to the use of the other.

And if both become bankrupt, and the holders of the bills or notes negotiated by each, prove, and receive the dividends upon them, under both commissions, though the one party may have negotiated hills or notes to a greater amount than the other, the assigness of neither will be permitted to (31) prove or claim, under the commission of

---

must hold that the bankruptcy creates a debt which did not exist antecedently; and I must hold that the same debt may be proved twicc." The proof was confined to the balance on the cash account only. This abstract is taken not only from Mr. Vesey's but also Mr. Cooke's report of this case. Cooke, B. L. 162. See also ex parte Earle, 5 Ves. 833.

(31) See ex parte Walker, ante, p. 350. n. (30). The assignees of Caldwell and Co. were not permitted to prove, either on the bills which remained in their hands, because no consideration had been given for them; or for money paid, because it had been paid after the Brownes' bankruptcy, and because after full proof by the holders of the negotiated bills, there would have been a double proof as to part. The decision would have been the same had the case arisen subsequently to the 49 Geo. 3. c. 121. That statute only applies where the surety pays the whole debt, or a part in discharge of the whole; it does not embrace the case of a surety, or (if a bankrupt) his assignees, paying part of the debt, after the creditor has proved

the other, any dividends which they may have paid on the bills or notes negotiated by the other; because it would be permitting the same debt (to the extent of such dividends) to be twice charged on the same estate.

If a creditor receive bills from his debtor, and negotiate them, and both become bankrupt, the creditor (33) will not be allowed to receive dividends upon his debt until he take up the bills

---

and received dividends under the principal's commission; such surety, or his assignees, can derive no advantage from the creditor's proof; nor can he or they make any distinct proof in respect of the part so paid, because the creditor has already proved, and to the extent of such part there would be a double proof against the principal's estate. In ex parte Walker the Caldwells had clearly sustained an injury; but the decision only related to the right of proof, and nothing was said as to the right of action, which, it would seem, the assignees of each party had against the other for the dividends paid by them on the bills which the other ought to have taken up: nor does the right of action, in such case, appear to have been affected by the 49 G. 3. c. 121. § 8.

(33) Ex parte Metcalfe, 11 Ves. 404. Palmer had received from Williamson in cash and bills 6424*l.* 9*s.* 3*d.*, and Williamson had received from Palmer in cash 5824*l.* 19*s.* 7*d.* Both became bankrupt. Palmer had negotiated the bills; some of which to the amount of 1098*l.* were dishonoured by the drawee, and Palmer's assignees contended that the amount of these bills should be deducted from the 6424*l.* 9*s.* 3*d.* which would reduce the sum received by him to 5326*l.* 9*s.* 3*d.*, making a balance of 498*l.* 10*s.* 4*d.* in his favour, which balance they contended they were entitled to prove against Williamson's estate. On petition to prevent such proof, Lord Eldon C. ordered that the proof of the 498*l.* 10*s.* 4*d.* should be allowed; but that Williamson's assignees should retain the dividends upon such

which he has so negotiated; for otherwise the debtor's estate would be charged with both the debt and bills.

Though the drawee of a bill may have no effects of the drawer's in hand, yet if it be drawn *on account* of a person who has, and the drawee accept it on his account, he renders himself responsible to the same extent as that person would have been had he been the drawee and acceptor; and therefore if he refuse payment, and the drawer be obliged to take up the bill, the latter (34) may prove it under a commission of bankruptcy issued against such acceptor.

---

proof in order to exonerate that estate from any demand which might be made in respect of the bills, which should have been taken up by Palmer.

(34) Ex parte Marshall and others, 1 Atk. 131. Watkin having dealings with Garway, and Garway with Hatton, it was agreed between the two latter that Hatton should answer such bills as Watkin should draw on him on Garway's account. Watkin drew accordingly on Hatton for 4000*l.* having effects in Garway's hands beyond that amount. Hatton accepted the bill, though he had no effects either of Garway or Watkin in hand; he afterwards refused payment, and Watkin was obliged to pay the bill, and proved it under a commission of bankruptcy issued against Hatton. Hatton's assignees petitioned to have the debt expunged, but the Chancellor held that Watkin was entitled to prove, because of his having had effects in Garway's hands beyond the amount of the bill. Petition dismissed.

Ex parte Matthews, 6 Ves. 285. Matthews being indebted to Garland and Co. directed Caldwell and Co., his bankers, to give an order to Burton Forbes and Gregory (on whom they drew) to accept a bill to be drawn by Garland and Co. for the amount of their debt. The bill was drawn and accepted ac-

If more than one of the persons liable on account of the non-acceptance or non-payment of a bill or note become bankrupts, the holder may prove, under the separate commission of each, the full (35) amount of the money due to him upon

---

cordingly. Before it became due Caldwell and Co., and Burton Forbes and Gregory became bankrupt. Garland and Co. proved the bill under the acceptor's commission, but afterwards received the whole amount of the bill from Matthews; on which the proof was expunged; and on petition that it might be restored for Matthews' benefit, it appearing that Matthews had effects in the hands of Caldwell and Co. beyond the amount of the bill, and that he had given them credit for that amount, proof was ordered to be reinstated.

(35) Ex parte Wildman, 1 Atk. 109. 2 Vez. 113. Wildman held bills drawn by Buckle and accepted by Vanhylik: Vanhylik failed, and made a composition with his creditors, and Buckle became bankrupt. Wildman having received nothing under Vanhylik's composition, proved his whole debt under Buckle's commission, but before any dividend was made he received 2*s*. 6*d*. in the pound out of Vanhylik's estate: Buckle's assignees then contended that he ought to deduct the 2*s*. 6*d*. in the pound out of his proof, and take a dividend upon the balance only: but Lord Hardwicke held, that as the whole sum was due when he proved his debt, and the dividend and composition would not amount to 20*s*. in the pound upon his debt, he was entitled to a dividend upon his whole debt; and per Lord Hardwicke, "In cases of bills or notes, where there is a drawer, and perhaps several indorsers, suppose two of these persons become bankrupts, the holder may prove his *whole debt* under each commission, and is entitled to receive satisfaction out of both estates, according to the dividends to be made, until he has received satisfaction for his whole debt; for he has a double security, and it is neither law nor equity to take it from him: but if before the bankruptcy of one he had received payment of part from the other, he could only have proved the residue

the bill or note at the time he makes his proof, and receive dividends under each upon the sums proved, until he shall in the whole have received such amount.

But after the (36) receipt, (or even the (37) declaration,) of a dividend under one commission, he

---

under the latter bankruptcy, as the form of proving his debt shews, because no more would remain due to him." To the same effect are the cases of ex parte Royd and ex parte Bennett, cited 2 Ves. 114.

And see Cooke's Bankrupt Laws, 170.

(36) See ex parte Wildman, ante, p. 355, note (35).

Cooper v. Pepys, 1 Atk. 106. The holders of notes drawn by Reeves, and payable to Andree, accepted 6*s*. in the pound from Andree; and Reeves having become bankrupt, the question was, whether they might prove the whole debt under his commission? and Lord Hardwicke held they could not, but that the 6*s*. in the pound must go in discharge of so much of the debt, and they could only prove the remaining 14*s*. The same point was ruled in ex parte Ryswick, 2 P. Williams, 89, ex parte Lefebvre, 2 P. Williams, 409.

See Cooke's Bankrupt Laws, 170.

(37) Ex parte Leers, 6 Ves. 644. Leers was holder of a bill which had been drawn upon, and accepted by persons at Hambro', indorsed by the payees to Pierre de Ruesnas at Hambro', and by him to Leers. It was protested for non-payment. A commission under the great seal issued against the payees, and the acceptors and last indorser were also made bankrupts. Leers had the amount of the bill claimed against the estates of each of the last mentioned parties, according to the due course at Hambro', and a dividend was declared of each estate. He had not received any part of either of these dividends; and the question now was, whether he might prove the whole bill against the estate of the payees? Lord Eldon, after hearing that the practice (the principle of which he doubted) was against such proof, ordered that these dividends should be deducted.

cannot prove under any of the rest more than the sum remaining due after deducting such dividend.

If a bill or note be pledged with a person as a collateral security for the payment of a smaller sum than that for which it is drawn, the pawnee (38) may prove the full amount of the bill or note against all parties who are liable to the full amount,

---

(38) Ex parte King, Cooke's B. L. 156. Davies gave his note for 500*l.* to Turner and Toye, expressed to be for value received but in fact for their accommodation, and they being indebted to King in 300*l.* indorsed this note to him, to enable him to raise that sum. Turner and Toye, and Davies afterwards became bankrupt; and on petition, King was allowed to prove the whole amount against Davies's estate, and to receive dividends not exceeding 300*l.*

Ex parte Crossley, Cooke's B. L. 157. 3 Bro. Ch. Cas. 237. Hartley being indebted to Crossley in 147*l.* 10*s.* gave him a bill for 200*l.* which had been drawn on Livesay and Co. by a partner in that house, payable to Hartley's order. The bill was accepted, but afterwards dishonoured. Livesay and Co. became bankrupts; but before a commission issued, Hartley paid Crossley 101*l.* 10*s.* in part of his debt. It appearing that Livesay and Co. had lent this bill to Hartley, the commissioners refused to allow Crossley to prove under Livesay's commission more than the balance of 46*l.* remaining due to him from Hartley. But on petition, the Chancellor ordered the proof to be admitted for the whole 200*l.* and dividends to be received until the petitioner should be satisfied the 46*l.* Ex parte King was relied on.

See also ex parte Bloxham, 6 Ves. 449. In which Lord Eldon, C. said, "I looked upon it as settled that you cannot hold the paper of the bankrupt, and prove beyond your actual debt upon it; but that you may have the paper of third persons, those persons being indebted to your debtor in more, and you may prove to the whole amount; not exceeding 20*s.* in the pound upon the original debt."

excepting against him from whom he received it; so as he do not by that means receive more than the sum which it was pledged to secure.

Nor will such proof be prevented by the circumstance of the bill or note having been drawn (39) by way of accommodation.

But against the party from whom he received it, he can only prove the (40) actual debt.

Under a commission of bankruptcy, the holder of a bill or note is not (41) entitled, (unless the bankrupt's estate should produce a (42) surplus,) to any interest or charges accrued or incurred after the commission issued, nor where the act of bankruptcy to which the commission relates is as-

---

(39) Vide ex parte King, and ex parte Crossley, ante, p. 357. n. 38. See also Cooke's B. L. 5th ed. p. 156.

(40) Vide ex parte Bloxham, ante, p. 357. n. 38., and Cooke's B. L. p. 156.

(41) Anon. 1 Atk. 140. The question was, whether the costs and charges incurred by protesting bills after a commission of bankruptcy issued could be proved; and Lord Hardwicke ordered that the costs of the protests arisen before the commission should be proved, but no part of the costs arisen afterwards.

As to re-exchange see ex parte Hoffman, Cooke, B. L. 173. and Francis v. Rucker, Ambl. 672. and as to the latter see 2 Bro. Cha. Cas. 599. It is observable that, in that case, the drawer was (in effect) allowed to prove re-exchange under the acceptor's commission. It has been held indeed that the acceptor is not liable for re-exchange; vide ante, p. 283. Pothier (pl. 117.) expressly says that he is in like manner as the drawer: and it seems reasonable that he should be liable to all parties where he has effects; and to all, excepting the drawer, where he has not.

(42) Vide ex parte Mills, 2 Ves. 295. and Butcher v. Churchill, 14 Ves. 573.

certained, (43) to any accrued or incurred after that act of bankruptcy.

Mutual debts and (44) credits between a bank-

---

(43) Ex parte Moore, 2 Bro. Cha. Cas. 597. Previous to the 5th of May, 1785, Mrs. Tyler accepted several bills drawn upon her by Moore, and on that day committed an act of bankruptcy, but no commission issued until the 9th of March, 1786; the bills became due between May, 1785, and March, 1786, and Mrs. Tyler not paying them, Moore did; he also paid 298*l.* for damages and charges, and the interest amounted to 46*l.* 10*s.*; the commissioners allowed Moore to prove the sum for which the bills were drawn, but would not let him prove the interest, or the sum paid for damages and charges, upon which he petitioned the Chancellor, but the Chancellor held, that as the time when the act of bankruptcy was committed was ascertained, he could not carry the damages beyond that time; and the petition was disallowed.

(44) Ex parte Prescott, 1 Atk. 230. The petitioner was a creditor for 110*l.* and at the same time debtor to the bankrupt on a bond for 340*l.* with interest. The interest was payable annually, but the principal was not payable until March, 1756, this petition being in August, 1753. The petitioner prayed that he might be allowed to set off the 110*l.* against the principal and interest on the bond: it was objected that the bond not being yet due, these were not mutual debts. But Lord Hardwicke, C. held that the case came within the expression of "mutual credit," in 5 Geo. 2. c. 30. § 28., and that that act was to be construed with reference to 7 Gee. 1. c. 31., permitting certain debts to be proved before they became due. He therefore allowed the set-off.

Atkinson v. Elliott, 7 Term Rep. 378. In May, 1796, Hodges bought a parcel of goods from the defendants for 430*l.* and in September following another parcel for 230*l.*; each at six months' credit: on each occasion he gave his acceptance for the price. The first bill became due on the 6th of November, 1796, and the other on the 9th of March, 1797. On the 9th of November, 1796, in order to take up the first bill, he gave them

rupt and any other person (45), may be set off against each other under a commission of bankruptcy, provided they accrued or were given before any act of bankruptcy has been committed by such bankrupt.

So also they may be set off, (46) notwithstand-

---

a bill for 100*l.*, and the next day indorsed to them another for 500*l.* taking from them a written engagement to pay over to him the surplus viz. 170*l.* when those bills should be paid. Those bills, viz. for 100*l.* and 500*l.*, became due and were paid on the 11th of Dec. 1796. On the 13th of December, 1796, Hodges became bankrupt, and the plaintiffs, his assignees, immediately claimed the 170*l.* The defendants however contended that they were entitled to retain the 170*l.* in part satisfaction of Hodges' acceptance for 230*l.* though not then due; and therefore refused to pay the 170*l.* On which the plaintiffs in Feb. 1797, brought this action for money had and received. But on a case reserved the court held that this case was clearly within the authority of ex parte Prescott, which Lord Kenyon said was properly decided, and therefore postea to the defendants.

(45) By 5 G. 2. c. 30. § 28. it is enacted, "That where it shall appear to the commissioners, or the major part of them, that there hath been mutual credit given by the bankrupt and any other person, or mutual debts between the bankrupt and any other person, at any time before such person became bankrupt, the said commissioners, or the major part of them, or the assignees of such bankrupt's estate, shall state the account between them, and one debt may be set against another; and what shall appear to be due on either side on the balance of such account, and on setting such debts against one another, and no more, shall be claimed or paid on either side respectively." See Tamplin v. Diggins, 2 Campb. N. P. C. 312.

(46) By 46 Geo. 3. c. 135. § 3. it is enacted, "That in all cases in which, under commissions of bankrupt hereafter to be issued, it shall appear that there has been mutual credit given by the bankrupt and any other person, or mutual debts between

ing any prior act of bankruptcy committed by such bankrupt before the credit was given to, or debt contracted by such bankrupt, provided the credit were given to the bankrupt two calendar months before the date and suing forth of his commission, and the party claiming the benefit of such set-off had not at the time of giving the credit notice of such prior act of bankruptcy, or that the bankrupt was insolvent, or had stopped payment: but not otherwise.

Therefore the amount of a bill or note cannot be the subject of set-off under a commission of bankruptcy, if either the bankrupt or the person claiming the benefit of such set-off, became party to, or holder of the bill or note after such act, and either within such two months, or after such notice.

---

the bankrupt and any other person, one debt or demand may be set off against another notwithstanding any prior act of bankruptcy committed by such bankrupt before the credit was given to or the debt was contracted by such bankrupt, in like manner as if no such prior act of bankruptcy had been committed, provided such credit was given to the bankrupt two calendar months before the date and suing forth of such commission, and provided the person claiming the benefit of such set-off, had not at the time of giving such credit any notice of any prior act of bankruptcy by such bankrupt committed, or that he was insolvent or had stopped payment: provided always, that the issuing of a commission of bankrupt against such bankrupt, although such commission shall afterwards be superseded, shall be deemed notice of a prior act of bankruptcy for the purposes of this act, if it shall appear that an act of bankruptcy had been actually committed at the time of issuing such commission. Vide 49 G. 3. c. 121. § 1.

Unless perhaps where the credit upon the bill or note forms part of a credit previously created, as where goods are sold upon a credit with liberty, before the credit expires, to draw a bill or demand a note for the price.

If an indorser of a bill take it up after the bankruptcy of the acceptor, he (47) cannot set off any debt due from him to the bankrupt against the amount of such bill, because the right of set-off did not exist at the time of the bankruptcy.

A bill or note may however be the subject of set-off, though it do not (48) become due until after an act of bankruptcy committed.

---

(47) Ex parte Hale, 3 Ves. 304. The acceptor of a bill for 200*l.* became bankrupt, and Hale, who had indorsed it before the bankruptcy, was obliged after the bankruptcy to take it up, and being indebted to the bankrupt in 90*l.* he petitioned that he might be allowed to set it off. But the Chancellor said the petitioner must pay the 90*l.* and then prove the 200*l.* There was a debt created upon the estate and due at the time of the bankruptcy, but that was not due to the petitioner; in that respect therefore the set-off fails. The petition was dismissed so far as it sought to set off the 90*l.*

(48) Ex parte Wagstaff, 13 Ves. 65. A commission of bankruptcy issued against the Kershaws on the 29th of June, 1804. At that time Wagstaff was a creditor for 2277*l.* and he had accepted a bill drawn on him by the bankrupts for 399*l.* which became due, and was paid by Wagstaff, on the 5th of July, 1804. He was at the same time debtor to the bankrupt in 363*l.* the greatest part of which was for goods sold on a credit which did not expire until the 1st of May, 1805: the residue was for money had and received. He claimed to be allowed to prove his debt of 2277*l.* contending that he had a right to set off the 363*l.* against the 399*l.* on the acceptance, though not due until

after the bankruptcy. The commissioners however refused to allow the set-off. But Lord Erskine, C. on petition ordered the set-off to be allowed, and said that this was mutual credit to all intents and purposes. See ex parte Prescott, and Atkinson v. Elliott, ante p. 359. note (44).

CAP. XI.

Of the Evidence necessary to entitle the plaintiff to recover upon a Bill or Note.

To recover in respect of a bill or note upon a count for money lent, money paid, or money had and received, the plaintiff must prove such of those facts which are not admitted, as he ought to state upon a special count; and upon a special count, he must prove such of the facts which are not admitted as appear upon the face of that count necessary.

An acceptance admits the (1) ability of the drawer to make the bill, and, if made after sight of the bill, his (2) signature; an indorsement admits

---

(1) Porthouse v. Parker and others, 1 Camp. N. P. C. 82. This was an action by the payee against the drawers of a bill. The bill purported to have been drawn by Wood as agent of the defendants, upon John Parker one of the defendants. There was no proof of Wood's authority; but it was proved that the bill had been accepted by the agent of John Parker, the drawee: and Lord Ellenborough held that the bill having been accepted by order of one of the defendants, this was sufficient evidence of its having been regularly drawn.

(2) Wilkinson v. Lutwidge, Str. 648. In an action against the acceptor of a bill, Raymond, C. J. allowed the plaintiff to read the bill without proving the drawer's hand, because he thought the acceptance a sufficient acknowledgment on the part of the defendant, but he said it would not be conclusive; and if the defendant could shew the contrary, the reading the bill should not preclude him. See Cooper v. Le Blanc, post 379. note (26).

Jenys v. Fawler, Str. 946. In an action against the acceptor of a bill, Raymond, C. J. held it was not necessary for the plaintiff to prove the drawer's hand, and on the defendant's offering to call witnesses to swear they believed it was not the drawer's hand, the chief justice would not admit the evidence, and he inclined strongly that actual proof of forgery would not excuse the defendant.

Price v. Neale, Burr. 1354. Blackst. 390. Two forged bills were drawn upon the plaintiff, which he accepted and paid; on discovering the forgery he brought this action for money had and received to recover back the money, but on a case reserved, the court held it would not lie; and Lord Mansfield said, "It was incumbent on him to have been satisfied before he accepted

the ability, and (3) signature of every antecedent party.

---

or paid them, that the bills were the drawer's hand:" and in Smith v. Chester, 1 Term Rep. 655, Buller J. says, "When a bill is presented for acceptance, the acceptor looks to the handwriting of the drawer, which he is afterwards precluded from disputing, and it is on that account that he is liable, even though the bill is forged."

Smith v. Mercer, 6 Taunt. 76. A bill was drawn on Evans, payable to Temple, indorsed by him to Le Souef, and by Le Souef to defendants: defendants indorsed it, that their correspondents in town might get it paid: it had upon it, when defendants took it, this acceptance, "Smith, Payne and Smiths, Maurice Evans." This was a forgery; but defendants did not know it: when the bill became due, Smith, Payne and Smith paid it, but at the end of a week they discovered the forgery, and gave notice thereof to defendants, and on their refusal to refund the money, brought money had and received against them. On a special case, Chambre J. thought plaintiffs entitled to recover, because defendants, by indorsing the bill with the forged acceptance thereon, had impliedly vouched for its authenticity, and because there was no blame or negligence imputable to plaintiffs, and it was against conscience in defendants to keep their money, for which they got nothing; but the other judges thought plaintiffs not entitled; Dallas and Heath Js. because it was plaintiffs' duty to know their customer's hand before they paid the bill; and Gibbs C. J., because plaintiff's conduct had prevented notice to those parties defendants might have sued, and had therefore destroyed the remedy against them. Postea to defendants.

(3) Lambert v. Pack, Salk. 127. Lord Raym. 443. 12 Mod. 244. Holt. 117. In an action against the indorser of a bill, Holt, C. J. ruled that it was not necessary to prove the drawer's hand, for though the bill was forged, the indorser would be liable.

Williams v. Seagrove, 2 Barnard. B. R. 82. A rule was made absolute for delivering up a note to an indorsee, though it was proved to have been forged, upon the ground that he might

But an acceptance, though made after sight of an indorsement, does not admit the ability or (4) signature of the indorser.

---

notwithstanding bring actions upon it against the indorsers. See also Str. 442.

Critchlow v. Parry, 2 Campb. N. P. C. 182. Indorsee against the indorser of a bill. The plaintiff was the immediate indorsee of the defendant. The declaration stated several prior indorsements, and the question was, whether it were necessary to prove them. Lord Ellenborough held the proof unnecessary, and the plaintiff had a verdict.

(4) Smith v. Chester, 1 Term Rep. 654. In an action by the indorsee of a bill against the acceptor, the plaintiff was nonsuited because he could not prove the hand-writing of the first indorser, though the indorsement was on the bill at the time of the acceptance. A motion was made to set aside the nonsuit on the ground that as the indorsement was on the bill when it was accepted the acceptance admitted it, but the court thought it did not, because the acceptor only looks to the hand-writing of the drawer, and *that* he is afterwards precluded from disputing. Rule discharged.

Carvick v. Vickery, Dougl. 630—653. N. 144. ante p. 43. note (16). A bill payable to the order of father and son, who were not partners, was indorsed by the son only, after which it was presented, and the drawee wrote upon it a direction to his banker to pay it. In an action against the drawee the question was, Whether the indorsement by the son alone was sufficient? and Willes J. inclined to think the order to the banker was a recognition of the indorsement. But Ashhurst and Buller Js. thought not. However in Hankey v. Wilson, Say. 223. in an action by the indorsee of a bill against the acceptor, there was no actual proof of the hand-writing of one of the indorsers, but it appearing that the indorsement was upon the bill when the defendant accepted it, and that he promised to pay it; Ryder, C. J. left the case to the jury, who found for the plaintiff, and upon a rule to shew cause why there should not be a new trial, the court thought it a question for the jury, Whether the acceptance and promise did not amount to an admission that the name of every indorser was authentic? and refused the rule.

Nor does it admit the indorsement of the drawer where the bill is payable to the drawer's order. (5)

And if such bill imports to be drawn and indorsed by procuration, though the acceptance admits the procuration as to the drawing, it does not as to the indorsement. (5)

But upon a bill payable to the drawer's order, an acceptance admits the drawer's ability to indorse; for if he cannot indorse, he was not of ability to draw. (6)

It precludes the acceptor therefore from relying upon infancy in such drawer and indorser. (6)

So if a bill is drawn in the name of a firm purporting to consist of several persons, the acceptance admits that there is such a firm. (7)

And that it consists of several. (7)

And the acceptor will be precluded from proving the contrary, if it is only to let in a technical objection. (7)

---

(5) Robinson v. Yarrow, 7 Taunt. 455. Action by indorsee against acceptor on bill importing to be drawn by Henry, per procuration for Stachen and Co. payable to the order of Stachen and Co., and to be indorsed by Henry per procuration for Stachen and Co. Plaintiff proved the acceptance, but he did not prove Henry's signature to the indorsement, nor his authority to indorse, upon which Burrough J. directed a verdict for defendant; and on rule nisi for new trial, and cause shewn, the court held the acceptance admitted Henry's authority to draw, and his signature as drawer, but that it was no admission of his authority to indorse, or of his indorsement, for the drawing and indorsing would have contrary effects, the one would bring the amount to Stachen and Co., the latter would carry it from them; and rule discharged.

(6) See Taylor v. Croker, ante p. 39.

(7) Bass v. Clive, 4 Maule, 13. Indorsee against acceptor on

In an action, therefore, against the acceptor of a bill or maker of a note, the plaintiff must prove the defendant's signature, and the necessary indorsements; and in the former case, if the acceptance was made without sight of the bill, the signature of the drawer: in an action against the drawer of a bill, or the indorser of a bill or note, he must prove the defendant's signature, the necessary indorsements (8) between him and the plaintiff, the presentment, the non-acceptance or non-payment, the notice of dishonour (or the facts to shew such notice unnecessary), and, in the case of a foreign bill, the protest.

In an action indeed against the drawer (9) or

---

bill purporting to be drawn by Ellis, Needham jun., and Co., and payable "to our order." Plaintiff declared upon it as drawn by certain persons trading under the firm of Ellis, Needham jun., and Co., and payable to their own order; defendant proved at the trial that only one person constituted that firm, upon which Lord Ellenborough nonsuited, with liberty to plaintiff to move to enter a verdict. On rule nisi inde and cause shewn, he and the rest of the court were clear that by the acceptance defendant had admitted conclusively that there was such a firm as that stated on the face of the bill, and was not at liberty to prove the contrary; and rule absolute.

(8) Vide Critchlow v. Parry, ante, p. 367. n. (3).

(9) Waynam v. Bend, 1 Campb. N. P. C. 175. In an action against the maker of a promissory note payable to T. L. or bearer, the declaration averred an indorsement by T. L., and Lord Ellenborough held that the plaintiff, having stated such indorsement, though unnecessarily, was bound to prove it. See also Smith v. Chester, ante, p. 367. n. (4), and Bosanquet v. Anderson, 6 Esq. N. P. C. 43.

acceptor of a bill, or the maker of a note, all the indorsements stated, though some may have been stated unnecessarily, must be proved; but against an (10) indorser, the defendant's indorsement, and such indorsements only as are stated to have been made subsequently to his, need be proved.

If a bill, in consequence of having an acceptance upon it pointing out a particular house for payment, is presented there for payment, and not at the drawee's residence or personally to the drawee, such acceptance must in general be proved in an action against the drawer or an indorser; because otherwise the presentment at that particular house will not be a valid presentment. (11)

But if it can be shewn that such acceptance was upon the bill when the defendant passed it, proof of the acceptance will be unnecessary. (11)

Proof that it was upon the bill when the plaintiff took it, if he did not take it immediately from the defendant, will not be sufficient. (11)

---

(10) See Critchlow v. Parry, ante, p. 367. n. (3).

(11) Smith v. Bellamy, 2 Stark. 223. Second indorsee of bill against payee, on bill drawn on Stevenson, payable in London, with an acceptance thereon payable at Spooner and Atwood's. It had been presented there and there only; the acceptance was upon the bill when the plaintiff took it, but there was no evidence that it was so when defendant indorsed it and passed it away: it was urged that the jury might presume it was on the bill when plaintiff took it; Lord Ellenborough thought not, and as proof of the acceptance was necessary to make the presentment valid, he nonsuited the plaintiff.

*

Where plaintiffs have no title upon a bill or note, unless they constitute a particular firm, they must prove that they constitute that firm.

As if they sue upon a bill or note payable to that firm by its name of business, without specifying its members;

Or specially indorsed to it.

But though several persons join in suing as indorsees, yet if they claim under an indorsement in blank, they need not shew that they are partners, or that they have a joint interest. (12)

It is indeed stated to have been held, that if a bill indorsed in blank is sent to a particular house, and an action is afterwards brought thereon by some of the members of that house and additional parties, there must be some evidence that that house transferred the bill to the plaintiffs, or consented to their suing upon it. (13)

And this, though the bill was sent to the house for the benefit of the persons who sue. (13)

---

(12) Ord v. Portal, 3 Campb. 239. Three persons sued as indorsees on a bill; the indorsement to them was in blank: it was urged that it ought to be shewn that they were partners, or had a joint interest. Sed per Lord Ellenborough, It it not necessary; the indorsement in blank gives a joint right of action to as many as agree in suing. Verdict for plaintiffs.

Rordasnz v. Leach, 1 Stark. 446. Two persons sued as indorsees; the indorsement to them was in blank: and on question whether they were bound to shew a joint title, Lord Ellenborough held they were not.

(13) Machell Boucher and Birkbeck v. Kinnear, 1 Stark.

And in many cases the plaintiff is compellable to prove that either he or some preceding party took the bill or note bonâ fide, and for value.

As in case of a bill or note originally given without consideration, and whilst the person giving it was under duress. (14)

Or in case of a bill or note obtained by fraud. (15)

---

499. Plaintiffs were trustees of the estate of Holder, an insolvent; two of them were partners in the house of Langton and Co.: defendant being indebted to Holder, sent a bill indorsed in blank to Langton and Co. on account of Holder's estate: the trustees sued thereon; but on an objection that Langton and Co. did not appear to have transferred the bill to the plaintiffs or to have sanctioned their suing thereon, Lord Ellenborough held that proof essential, and nonsuited the plaintiffs.

(14) Duncan v. Scott, 1 Campb. N. P. C. 100. Indorsee against the drawer of a bill. It appeared that the defendant gave the bill while under duress abroad, and under a threat of personal violence and confiscation of his property, and that it was given without consideration. Lord Ellenborough held that the defendant not having been a free agent when he drew the bill, it was incumbent on the plaintiff to give some evidence of consideration; and no such evidence being given, the plaintiff was nonsuited.

(15) Rees v. Marquis of Headfort, 2 Campb. N. P. C. 574. In an action by an indorsee of a bill against the acceptor, it appeared that the drawer had received no consideration for the bill, and had been tricked out of it by a gross fraud; and Lord Ellenborough held that this made it incumbent on the plaintiff to shew what consideration he gave for the bill; and the plaintiff not being prepared to do so, was nonsuited.

Or in case of a transfer by delivery by a person not entitled to make it. (16)

As in the instance of bills or notes which have been stolen or lost. (16)

To compel a plaintiff, however, to give such proof, it has been held necessary he should be apprized before the trial that such proof would be required from him. (17)

---

(16) Vide Anon. Miller v. Race, Grant v. Vaughan, ante, p. 106. n. (23). Peacock v. Rhodes, ante, p. 100. n. (11).

Solomons v. the Bank of England, 13 East's Rep. 135. n. Trover for a bank note for 500*l*. It appeared that the note had been fraudulently obtained by means of a forged draught, and therefore when presented for payment it was stopped by the bank, who informed the plaintiff of the circumstances. The plaintiff had received it from his correspondents at Middleburgh, and by desire of the bank, wrote to them to learn how they came by it. In answer, they wrote that they had received it in payment for goods, from a stranger. The note was three years old, and was stated by the plaintiff to have been taken by him in reduction of a balance due to him from his correspondents; but how this was did not appear. Bank notes of this value were not usually current at Middleburgh. Lord Kenyon said that as it did not appear that the plaintiff had given a valuable consideration for the note before notice, he should consider him as agent to his correspondents, and he thought that they had not satisfactorily accounted for their possession of the note. The plaintiff consented to a nonsuit; and on a rule nisi to set it aside and cause shewn the court refused to interfere. See Lowndes v. Anderson, 13 East's Rep. 130.

(17) Paterson v. Hardacre, 4 Taunt. 114. In an action by indorsee against acceptor, the defence was, that an agent employed by defendant to get the bill discounted had appropriated it to his own use, and absconded: it was urged upon this

It is laid down in (18) some cases, that in an action against the indorser of a bill, the plaintiff must prove an application to the drawer for payment; but it (19) is now fully settled he need not.

And an offer, after the bill or note has become due, to give the holder another bill in lieu of it, is an (20) admission of the holder's title, so as to supersede the necessity of proving the indorsements or other special facts.

---

that plaintiff was bound to prove how he got the bill, and what consideration he gave for it; he was not prepared with such proof, and was allowed to take a verdict subject to the question, whether he was bound to give it? and on rule nisi for a nonsuit on this ground and time to consider, the court held that where such a defence was contemplated, it was incumbent on the defendant to give distinct notice to the plaintiff that such proof would be called for at the trial; and because no such notice had been given, the rule was discharged.

(18) Vide Burr. 671.

(19) This was decided after two arguments in the case of a foreign bill in Bromley v. Frazier, Str. 441.; and in the case either of a foreign or inland bill, but which does not appear, in Lawrence v. Jacob, Str. 515.; and in the case of an inland bill, Heylin v. Adamson, Burr. 669.

(20) Bosanquet v. Anderson, 6 Esp. N. P. C. 43. Indorsee of a bill against the acceptor. The bill was drawn in favour of the drawer, who had indorsed it; and his indorsement and several others were stated in the declaration. The plaintiff proved the first indorsement, and that when the bill became due the defendant, being unable to take it up, came to the plaintiff and offered another in lieu of it. Lord Ellenborough held that this was an admission of the plaintiff's title, and dispensed with the proof of the several indorsements.

So (21) part payment of a bill or note after it has become due, without any objection being made for want of notice, or a (22) promise to pay,

---

(21) Sidford v. Chambers, 1 Stark. 326. Plaintiffs sued as indorsees of Niblock and Co., who were indorsees of Sheckles, to whom defendant had indorsed: they could not prove the indorsement of Sheckles, but they proved a letter from defendant to plaintiffs offering to substitute another bill, saying they had not money to take up the bill in question, and expressing a hope that it was not in the hands of Niblock and Co. Lord Ellenborough thought this evidence of the channel through which the bill had passed to plaintiffs, and made proof of the indorsement by Sheckles unnecessary; and plaintiff had a verdict.

Horford v. Wilson, 1 Taunt. 12. In an action by the indorsee against the drawer of a bill, which had been dishonoured by the acceptor, it appeared that the defendant had paid part of the money due upon the bill, without making any objection for want of notice of the dishonour; and the court held, upon a motion for a new trial, that from this the jury were warranted in presuming that due notice had been given.

(22) Lundie v. Robertson, 7 East's Rep. 231. Indorsee against an indorser of a bill. No evidence was given of presentment or notice; but it was proved that on being called upon by the plaintiff's clerk some months after the bill was due, the defendant said, "he had not the cash by him, but if the clerk would call in a day or two, and bring the account (meaning of the expenses) he would pay it;" the bill was shewn him at the time. On a second application, he offered a bill on London for the debt and expenses, which was refused: he then said that "he had not had regular notice, but as the debt was justly due, he would pay it." Chambre J. thought this sufficient; and verdict for the plaintiff. On a rule nisi for a new trial, and cause shewn, Lord Ellenborough said the case admits of no doubt: it was to be presumed primâ facie from the promise to pay that the bill had been presented in time that due notice had been given that no objection could be made to payment and that every thing had been rightly done; this super-

furnish grounds from which a jury may presume that it has been properly presented, that notice

---

seded the necessity of the ordinary proof: the other conversation does not vary the case; for though the defendant said he had not had notice, he waived that objection. Rule discharged.

See Gibbon v. Coggon, 2 Campb. N. P. C. 188., where, from the drawer's promising to pay a bill, Lord Ellenborough directed the jury to presume that it had been duly protested. See also Taylor v. Jones, 2 Campb. N. P. C. 105.

Greenway v. Hindley, 4 Campb. 52. In an action by the indorsees of a foreign bill against the drawer, it was proved that long after the bill became due defendant called on the holder, and said he came to arrange the payment; and on being shewn it, added, " it was regular, it was due from him and his partner, and that he was come to arrange for paying principal and interest." The declaration having alleged presentment and protest, it was urged that evidence ought to be given upon those points; but Lord Ellenborough said the defendant's acknowledgment was a sufficient foundation from which the jury might infer those facts; and verdict for plaintiffs.

Hodge v. Fillis, 3 Campb. 463. A bill was made payable in London, and accepted payable at Sir John Perring and Co.'s; and in an action against the acceptor, plaintiff had alleged presentment at Sir John Perring's, but could not prove it; Lord Ellenborough held the proof essential, unless there were something to dispense with it: plaintiff then proved that after the bill was due defendant promised payment, and Lord Ellenborough thought that made the other proof unnecessary; and verdict for plaintiff.

Wood v. Brown, 1 Stark. 217. In an action against the drawer of a bill, plaintiff proved a letter from defendant after the bill was due, in which he said he was an accommodation drawer only, and that the bill would be paid before the following term; Lord Ellenborough held that this made proof of notice of the dishonour unnecessary, and the plaintiff had a verdict without such proof.

has been duly given, and that a protest (where necessary) has been made.

And such presumption may be made (23), though the promise were not made to the plaintiff or in his presence, but to a subsequent indorsee who then held the bill or note.

Though there has been no due presentation, yet if there has been a subsequent application from an indorser for indulgence, it is for the jury to consider whether at the time of the application the indorser knew there had not been a due presentation. (24)

A nonsuit, without leaving that point to the jury, is improper. (24)

---

(23) Potter v. Rayworth, 13 East's Rep. 417. Indorsee of a note against the payee and indorser. It appeared that the note (which had been negotiated in the country) had been indorsed by the defendant to Fulford, by him to the plaintiff, by the plaintiff to Kirton, and by him to others, before it became due. A fortnight after it had become due, Kirton, who had taken it up, called on the defendant, who until then had received no notice of its dishonour: the defendant then promised Kirton to pay him the next day; having failed in this, Kirton resorted to the plaintiff, who paid the amount; and the defence now being the want of notice, the question was whether the plaintiff could avail himself of this promise so made to Kirton. Graham B. directed a verdict for the plaintiff; and on motion to set it aside, the court (Grose and Le Blanc Js. absent.) held that this promise was an acknowledgment by the defendant, either of notice, or that without notice he was the proper person to pay the note, and refused the rule.

(24) Hopley v. Dufresne, 15 East. 275. Indorsee against indorser; the bill was accepted payable at Hammersley's, and

If there have been laches in not giving notice, an indorser who may be prejudiced thereby in his remedies over against other indorsers, will not be precluded from insisting on such laches by having desired that the bill may be sent to him or some other person he names as soon as he receives notice, unless the bill when so sent is kept an improper time. (25)

---

there was no presentment there proved till after the banking-hours; but after the declaration delivered, defendant had applied to plaintiff for further time to pay the bill: nonsuit, on the ground that no sufficient presentment was proved; but on rule nisi for new trial, and cause shewn, the court thought it should have been left to the jury to say, whether at the time of his promise defendant did not know there had been no due presentation; and on that account, rule absolute.

(25) Borradaile v. Lowe, 4 Taunt. 93. Bill due 19th January; defendant was fifth indorser, Trever and Co. the fourth; 25th January, letter to defendant that it was dishonoured, with reasons assigned for not writing sooner; defendant wrote for answer, "I cannot think of remitting till I receive the draught, therefore if you think proper you may return it to Trevor and Co., if you think me unsafe." It was accordingly sent to Trevor and Co., but they returned it in a few days, saying, they had applied to the third indorser, and received it back from him as out of time; and as the delay was with plaintiff, they thought themselves and defendant discharged. Action inde: laches in plaintiff were admitted, but defendant's letter was relied upon as an answer; the distinction between the situation of an indorser, whose remedy over may be lost by the holder's laches, and of a drawer, was strongly relied on for defendant; and on rule nisi for nonsuit, and cause shewn, Mansfield C. J. said this letter contained no express promise to pay at all events, and he thought it would be too much to fix defendant here: in most cases where a defendant had been held liable there had been an express promise to pay, or a promise under

A confession of his signature is sufficient evidence (26) against the party making it, but (27) not against any other party; and it is (28) sufficient, though made pending a treaty for a compromise.

---

full knowledge of being discharged, or where there was a debt binding in conscience due from defendant. Rule absolute.

(26) Cooper v. Le Blanc, Str. 1051. The plaintiff, on discounting a note, sent to the defendant to know whether an indorsement upon it was his, and the defendant said it was, and the note would be paid when due: he would notwithstanding have given evidence by similitude of hands that the indorsement was a forgery; but Lord Hardwicke would not allow it: he seemed inclined, however, to admit proof of actual forgery; but the defendant could not adduce it, and the plaintiff had a verdict. See Wilkinson v. Lutwidge, ante, p. 154. 365.

Leach v. Buchanan, 4 Esp. N. P. C. 226. The plaintiff, before he took a bill, sent a person with it to the defendant to enquire whether the acceptance upon it were his handwriting; the defendant said that it was, and that it would be duly paid. He now offered evidence of the actual forgery of the acceptance; but Lord Ellenborough held that that proof would not discharge the defendant; that after having so accredited the bill and induced a person to take it, he was bound to pay it. Verdict for the plaintiff.

(27) Hemmings v. Robinson, Barnes, 3d ed. 436. In an action by the indorsee of a note against the maker, it was reserved as a point whether the acknowledgment of an indorser was sufficient evidence to prove his indorsement; and the court held not. See Gray v. Palmer, p. 381. n. (33).

(28) Waldridge v. Kennison, Espinasse, 143. In an action against two as acceptors of a bill, the only evidence of the signature by one was an admission he made pending a treaty for settling the cause: it was objected that this admission ought not to be received in evidence, because it was made under the faith of a compromise; but Lord Kenyon held that the admis-

Proof of the signature by a person who has no knowledge of the handwriting, except from having seen the party once write his name, may be sufficient, if the party then wrote his name at length. (29)

Or as much thereof as the signature to be proved contains. (29)

Otherwise it is not sufficient. (29)

In an action against the drawer of a lost bill, Holt C. J. (30) held proof that the defendant owned he had made the bill sufficient.

So in an action against an indorser, proof that the defendant admitted to have received a bill corresponding with that upon which the action was brought, that after issue joined he had declared that he came to town to hasten the trial of

---

sion of a handwriting might be received in evidence, though it was made under faith of a compromise; and he admitted it accordingly.

(29) Powell v. Ford, 2 Stark. 164. To prove an acceptance in which the defendant wrote his Christian name at length, plaintiff called a witness who had no other knowledge of defendant's handwriting but from having once seen him sign his name, where he put the initial only for his Christian name, "M. Ford." Lord Ellenborough thought his evidence might have been sufficient, had he ever seen defendant write his name at length; but that as he had never seen him write his Christian name, the Christian name could not be inferred to be genuine from evidence as to the sirname, any more than proof by a person who had seen him write some only of the letters which occurred in the sirname could be competent to prove the whole sirname. Nonsuit.

(30) This was the case of Hart v. King, 12 Mod. 309.

a cause brought against him on an indorsement he had made upon a bill, and that he carried the cause down by proviso, was (31) held sufficient.

But in an action by the indorsee of a bill against the drawer, proof that one of the indorsers had confessed his signature (32) is insufficient; and in an action against several drawers, indorsers, or acceptors, an admission upon the pleadings by one of his signature will (33) not exempt the plaintiff from proving it against the others, if they contest it.

---

(31) Dale v. Lubbuck, 1 Barnard. B. R. 199. In an action against an indorser the evidence was, that he had written a letter stating that he had received a bill from A. upon B. bearing date such a day, and payable to him or order six months after date (in all which circumstances the bill stated in the letter corresponded with the bill declared upon), but not mentioning the sum; that he had said he came up to town to hasten on the trial of an action brought against him on an indorsement he had made upon a bill, and that in fact he carried down the cause by proviso; and Raymond C. J. held this sufficient evidence to prove that the defendant indorsed the bill stated; and the jury found for the plaintiff.

(32) Hemmings v. Robinson, p. 379. n. (27).

(33) Gray v. Palmer, Espinasse, 125. Action against James Palmer John Palmer and Hodgson, as makers of a note; Hodgson pleaded a judgment recovered, and each of the Palmers non-assumpsit: upon the trial on the non-assumpsits, the plaintiff proved the subscription by each of the Palmers, and there rested his case. The Palmers contended that he ought to prove Hodgson's subscription also, but the plaintiff insisted that *that* was admitted by the plea of nul-tiel record; Lord Kenyon, however, held that it was only admitted as against Hodgson, not against the Palmers, and that the plaintiff could not recover against them without proving it.

Though a person sued as acceptor of a bill prove that the acceptance was forged, yet if it appear that he and the party who committed the forgery had been connected in business, and that the defendant had paid other bills drawn by such party and accepted similarly to that on which the action is brought, it will be sufficient, because it shews that he (34) had sanctioned such acceptances, and rendered himself liable to pay them.

The signature of a partner or servant, importing to have been made on the partnership or master's account, is to be considered as the signature of the (35) partnership or master.

On a signature by a servant, the servant's authority must be proved.

An authority by parol is (36) sufficient.

---

(34) Barber v. Gingell, 3 Esp. N. P. C. 60. In an action against the defendant as acceptor of a bill, he proved that the acceptance was forged by Taylor the drawer; in answer to which it was proved that the defendant had been connected in business with Taylor, and that he had paid several bills drawn as the present by Taylor, and to which Taylor (as it was supposed) had written the acceptances in the defendant's name. And Lord Kenyon held that this was an answer to the case of forgery set up by the defendant; for though he might not have accepted the bill, he had adopted the acceptance, and thereby made himself liable to pay the bill. Verdict for the plaintiff.

See Gibson v. Hunter, 2 H. Bl. 288.

(35) Vide Pinkney v. Hall, Lord Raym. 175., Smith v. Jarvis, Lord Raym. 1484., Carvick v. Vickery, Dougl. 630. n. 134.

(36) 12 Mod. 564.

Subsequent assent is (37) evidence of precedent authority.

Usual employ is evidence (38) of a general authority; and a general authority is supposed to continue until its determination is notorious.

Therefore, after the discharge of a servant usually employed, a (39) man will be bound by his signature until his discharge is generally known.

The clerk who signs bank notes need not have authority for the purpose under the common seal of the bank. (40)

And now, by 1 G. 4. c. 92. s. 3., his signature may be impressed by machinery.

Where notice is to be sent by the post, proof of putting it into the post is (41) sufficient.

Proof of sending one of two duplicate notices by the post may be established by the duplicate notice, without giving notice to produce that which was sent. (42)

Proof of sending notice by letter may be established, without giving notice to produce that letter. (42)

---

(37) Comb. 450.

(38) 12 Mod. 346., Malynes, B. 3. c. 5. § 6. p. 264., 10 Mod. 110.

(39) Vide Beawes, § 231. p. 445. Molloy. B. 2. c. 10. § 27.

(40) Brown v. Messitor, ante, p. 299.

(41) Saunderson v. Judge. ante, p. 174. 227.

(42) Roberts v. Bradshaw, 1 Stark. 28. In an action by indorsee of a bill against drawer, plaintiff's clerk proved that on the day the bill was dishonoured his master gave him two papers to compare, purporting to be notices of the dishonour of

Proof that duplicate notices were written in order that one might be sent, and that a letter was sent to defendant at that time, will be sufficient evidence that such letter contained the notice, if defendant, on notice, does not produce such letter. (42)

But it has been held that proof that a notice was put into the post either the day it ought to have been sent *or the day following* is not (though notice to produce is given) sufficient evidence that the notice was sent in time. (43)

And that it cannot be submitted to the jury for their consideration. (43)

---

the bill, one of which he produced; it was objected that the one produced could not be read unless notice had been given to produce the other; Lord Ellenborough thought otherwise, and said a letter acquainting a party with the dishonour of a bill was in nature of a notice, and it was unnecessary to prove notice to produce such a letter; plaintiff could not then prove specifically that any notice was sent, but he proved that the same day he sent a letter to defendant, the contents of which his witness did not know, and that he had given due notice to produce that letter; Lord Ellenborough thought this sufficient evidence that the letter amounted to notice, for if it did not, defendant might produce it; and plaintiff had a verdict. Defendant moved for a new trial, but the court of king's bench refused a rule.

(43) Lawson v. Sherwood, 1 Stark. 314. In an action against an indorser, it was necessary for plaintiff to prove that notice was sent to the defendant the second day after the bill became due; a witness proved that he sent him a notice two or three days after the bill became due, but whether it was the second or third day he could not state; notice to produce was proved, and it was urged for plaintiff, that as defendant did not produce what had been sent, this was evidence to go to the jury that

Production of the instrument is (44) sufficient evidence of a protest.

On a judgment by default in an action upon a bill or note, no (45) evidence need be given.

---

the notice was sent on the second day: but Lord Ellenborough thought otherwise; he said the non-production only intitled plaintiff to give parol evidence of its contents; plaintiff was bound to give notice on the second day, and evidence that he gave it either on that or the following day could not be left to the jury as evidence that he gave it on the second. Plaintiff was therefore nonsuited.

(44) Anon. 12 Mod. 345. To prove a protest, the plaintiff produced an instrument attested by a notary public; and though it was insisted that he should prove this instrument or at least give some account how he came by it, Holt C. J. ruled that it was not necessary.

(45) Bevis v. Lindsell, Str. 1149. On executing a writ of inquiry in an action on a note, the plaintiff did not produce the subscribing witness, but offered other evidence that it was the defendant's hand, and the court held *that* sufficient; "for the note being set out in the declaration is admitted, and the only use of producing it is to see whether any payment is indorsed upon it."

Mills v. Lyne, B. R. H. 26 G. 3. On a writ of inquiry in an action upon a note, the sheriff directed the jury to give nominal damages only, because the plaintiff could not prove the note. Lawrence insisted that the plaintiff was bound to produce the note (because a receipt of part might have been indorsed thereon) and to prove the defendant's signature; but per Buller J. "If you had paid part you might have pleaded it, but you have let judgment go for the whole;" and the court set aside the inquisition.

Green v. Herne, 3 Term Rep. 301. Upon a rule nisi to set aside an inquisition against the acceptor of a bill of exchange, it was urged that the bill, though *produced* before the jury, was not *proved;* but the court held that by suffering the judgment the defendant admitted the acceptance of the bill, and that he was

The court (46) will therefore upon such judgment, even in assumpsit, if the bill or note is for the payment of British money, refer it to an officer to ascertain the sum due for principal interest and costs, and give the plaintiff final judgment without a writ of enquiry.

And if the bill or note be lost pending the action, they will refer it on a verified copy. (47)

But the (48) court will not refer it, if the bill or note is for the payment of foreign money.

Nor will they refer it, to ascertain the amount

---

liable to its amount; and Buller J. said, "the only reason of producing the bill is to see whether any part of it is paid."

(46) Shepherd v. Charter, 4 Term Rep. 275. The defendant having suffered judgment by default in an action on a bill, the plaintiff obtained a rule to shew cause why it should not be referred to the master, to compute what was due for principal and interest. The rule was opposed upon the general ground that a reference in such cases was improper; but the court thought otherwise; and Grose J. observed, that the judges in the common pleas gave the case before them great consideration before they referred the question to one of the prothonotaries; and the rule was made absolute. The same had previously been done in Rashleigh v. Salmon, 1 H. Bl. 252., Andrews v. Blake, 1 H. Bl. 529., Longman v. Fenn, 1 H. Bl. 541.; and it is now every day's practice in the king's bench and common pleas, but not in the exchequer, vide Chilton v. Harborn, 1 Anstr. 249.

(47) Brown v. Messiter, ante, p. 299.

(48) Maunsell v. Lord Massareene, 5 Term Rep. 87. The court discharged a rule nisi for referring it to the master to compute principal, interest, and costs, upon a bill of exchange, because the bill was for the payment of 200*l.* Irish money. See also Napier v. Schneider, p. 387. n. 50.

of (49) charges and expences; or to compute (50) re-exchange upon a foreign bill.

And though the action be in fact brought to recover the money due upou a bill or note, yet the court will not refer it to the officer (51), unless the bill or note be stated in the declaration.

Nor will the court make such reference, in an

---

(49) Goldsmid v. Taite, 2. Bos. and Pull. 55. On a rule to shew cause why a bill of exchange should not be referred to the prothonotary to compute principal, interest, exchange, re-exchange, charges, expences, and costs, it was objected that charges and expences were not matter of mere computation; and the counsel for the rule consenting to strike out those words, the court made the rule absolute. But as to re-exchange, see the next note.

(50) Napier v. Schneider, 12 East's Rep. 420. A bill was drawn in Scotland upon and accepted by the defendant in England, and on motion to refer it to the master to compute principal, interest, and costs on this bill, the court was prayed to direct the master to allow re-exchange; but this they refused, saying that they would not refer it to the master to try foreign customs and facts, but only to compute what was due upon the bill itself. They therefore granted the rule in the common form.

(51) Osborne v. Noad, 8 Term Rep. 648. The declaration contained only counts for goods sold, and work and labour, and the common money counts. On judgment by default, the plaintiff obtained a rule nisi to refer it to the master to compute principal and interest on two notes; and in support of the rule an affidavit was produced, stating that the action was brought to recover the amount of these notes, and that such amount was recoverable under the money counts. The court, however, said that the rule was confined to cases in which it appeared by the declaration that the action was brought on the notes or bills Rule discharged.

action of debt brought on a (52) judgment recovered on a bill or note.

Where one count in the declaration is on a bill or note, and the defendant demurs to that count, and judgment is given for the plaintiff, the court (53) will refer it to the officer to ascertain what is due for principal interest and costs, on that count, though there are other counts on which the parties are at issue.

---

(52) Nelson v. Sheridan, 8 Term Rep. 395.

(53) Duperoy v. Johnson, 7 Term Rep. 473. The declaration contained many counts, one of which was on a bill; to that there was a demurrer, on which the plaintiff had judgment; to the others there was a plea, on which issue was joined: a rule nisi was obtained to refer it to the master to compute principal interest and costs on the bill; and on shewing cause against this rule, it was urged that the plaintiff ought either to have waited for the result of the trial of the issue on the other counts, or to have entered a nolle prosequi as to those counts. In support of the rule, Fleming v. Langton, 1 Str. 532., was cited; and the court thought that case decisive of the present, and made the rule absolute.

See Tidd's Practice, 5th ed. 569., stating that a nolle prosequi must be entered on the other counts; but that such entry need not be made *before* the reference to the master; that it is sufficient if done at any time before final judgment.

CAP. XII.

Defence to an Action on a Bill or Note.

ONE species of defence sometimes attempted upon a bill or note is, that there was some bargain when they were given or transferred, for a renewal or indulgence.

But it is a settled rule that no such defence can be supported by oral evidence, where it is inconsistent with the tenor of the bill or note. (1)

Thus upon a bill or note payable at a specified

(1) Woodbridge v. Spooner, 3 Barnew. and Ald. 233. Action against executors, on note payable on demand for value received: evidence was given that the bargain was at the time the note

time, parol evidence of a bargain when it was issued, that it was not to be paid till I. S. should die, or certain estates should be sold, is inadmissible. (1)

So upon a general indorsement of a bill or note, the like evidence of a bargain at the time of the

---

was given, that it should not be payable till after the maker's death, and should then be in nature of a legacy, and on that ground nonsuit: but on rule nisi to enter verdict for plaintiff, and cause shewn, the whole court held the evidence should not have been received, because it imported a different bargain and intention from what the note expressed; and rule absolute.

Free v. Hawkins, 8 Taunt. 92. In an action upon a note by indorsee against indorser, defendant insisted upon want of notice of the dishonour: plaintiff offered parol evidence that at the time the note was given and defendant (who only lent his name) indorsed it, it was understood that payment was not to be required until certain estates of the maker were sold, nor then unless they produced sufficient, and that therefore the defendant knew the note had not been honoured. Gibbs C. J. rejected the evidence, and nonsuited the plaintiff; and on a rule nisi for a new trial, the court held the evidence rightly rejected, because it contradicted the note, and the rule was discharged.

Rawson v. Walker, 1 Stark. 361. In an action by the payee against the maker, on a note payable on demand, defendant offered parol evidence, that it was given for goods sold to a bankrupt by his assignees, and that defendant was not to be called upon, unless his allowance under the commission should not be sufficient to pay the amount: per Lord Ellenborough, I am ready to admit evidence to shew the consideration illegal, but I cannot receive parol evidence inconsistent with the terms of the note; upon a note payable on demand, parol evidence to shew it was not to be payable upon demand, but on a contingency only, is not admissble. Verdict for plaintiff.

Same Point, Campbell v. Hodgson, Gow. 74.

indorsement, that the bill should be renewed, cannot be received. (2)

But parol evidence of a bargain after a bill or note was given or transferred, will be admissible; and the bargain, if there is a sufficient consideration to support it, will be binding. (2)

Where the ground of defence is an engagement to renew, it will be incumbent on the defendant to shew that he has taken the proper steps towards such renewal. (3)

It is a defence to an action on a bill, that it was passed to plaintiff by the first indorser for the special purpose of his getting it discounted for the first indorser, and that instead of so doing he

---

(2) Hoare v. Graham, 3 Campb. 57. Indorsee against payee of a note payable two months after date. Defence, that defendant refused to indorse unless plaintiffs would agree the note should be renewed when due, and that plaintiff acceded to that condition: sed per Lord Ellenborough, I cannot admit this evidence; it is inconsistent with the written instrument: I will receive evidence that the note was indorsed to plaintiffs as a trust; there may, after a bill is drawn, be a binding promise for a valuable consideration to renew it, but if the promise be contemporaneous with the drawing, the law will not enforce it; it would be incorporating with a written contract an incongruous parol agreement. Verdict for plaintiff.

(3) Gibbon v. Scott, 2 Stark. 286. In an action by drawer against acceptor on a bill for the freight of a chartered ship, the defence was, that plaintiff had engaged to renew the bill if the charterer did not return before the bill was due; but no application appearing to have been made to plaintiff to renew, Lord Ellenborough thought the defence failed, and the plaintiff had a verdict.

claimed to hold it for a debt owing to him by the second indorser. (4)

Another species of defence to an action in respect of a bill or note, is (5) want or inadequacy of consideration for giving or transferring it.

---

(4) Delaunay v. Mitchell, 1 Stark, 439. E. Clewer held a bill payable to herself or order, and indorsed first by herself, and secondly by her son: to prevent a commission against her son she delivered the bill to plaintiff, that he might get it discounted for her; he did not get it discounted, but insisted on holding it for a debt the son owed him, and sued the acceptor; but Lord Ellenborough thought it clear he could not maintain the action, and directed a nonsuit.

(5) Jefferies v. Austen, Str. 647. In an action by the payee of a note against the maker, Eyre, C. J. of the common pleas, allowed the defendant to prove, that it was given as a reward in case the plaintiff procured the defendant to be restored to an office, and that the defendant was not restored; and on this proof the defendant had a verdict.

Jackson v. Warwick, 7 Term Rep. 121. The defendant's son was apprenticed by indenture to the plaintiff; and the defendant gave the plaintiff a note for 10*l.* as an apprentice fee; but this premium was not mentioned in the indentures, nor were they stamped pursuant to 8 Ann. c. 9. The son remained part of his time, and then absconded. In an action on the note, and the failure of consideration (the apprenticeship) relied on as a defence, it was contended that the avoiding the indentures could not collaterally affect the note, and that at all events the consideration had not wholly failed, inasmuch as the plaintiff had maintained the apprentice during his stay. Lawrence J., however, thought that the consideration was entire, and had wholly failed; but he allowed a verdict to be taken for the plaintiff, with liberty to the defendant to move to enter a nonsuit. The court concurred in opinion with Lawrence, and directed a nonsuit to be entered.

A total failure of consideration is, where it can be insisted upon, a total bar: inadequacy, or a partial failure, a bar pro-tanto only. (6)

Thus in an action against an acceptor, it is a good defence either wholly or in part, that the acceptance was either wholly or in part for the accommodation of the plaintiff; (7)

---

(6) Barber v. Backhouse, Peake, 61. In an action on a bill of exchange by the payee, the defendant paid part of the money into court, and it appeared upon the trial that there was no consideration for the other part. Law, however, urged that the payment of the money into court admitted the bill was good for part, and if it was good for part, it was good in toto; but Lord Kenyon declared himself clearly of a contrary opinion, upon which the jury found for the defendant; and this case being afterwards mentioned by Lord Kenyon in the course of argument, Law said he was perfectly satisfied with the decision.

Ledger v. Ewer, Peake, 216. In an action by the payee of a bill against the acceptor, the consideration appeared to be that the plaintiff had taken the defendant into partnership; but on the defendant's friend's advice he broke off the connexion: there was evidence of fraud on the plaintiff's part in drawing the defendant into the engagement, which Lord Kenyon left to the jury; but he told them if they were against the defendant on the evidence of fraud, they should take into consideration the damages the plaintiff had really sustained by the non-performance of the contract, and were not obliged to find the whole amount of the bill; the jury, however, found for the defendant.

(7) Darnell v. Williams, 2 Stark. 166. Payee against acceptor on bill for 19*l.* 12*s.* Defendant proved that he had value for 10*l.* only, and that he accepted for the rest to accommodate the plaintiff: and per Lord Ellenborough, "Though this, as to third persons, is a bill for 19*l.* 12*s.*, yet as between these parties, their acceptance is for 10*l.* only; and that sum having been paid before the action, he nonsuited the plaintiff.

Or of some person for whom the plaintiff is trustee. (8)

So if a bill or note is given either wholly or as to a specific part, as the consideration of a special contract, and that contract either fails in toto or is in toto rescinded, it will be an answer to an action on the bill or note either wholly or protanto, if the plaintiff stands in a situation which makes him liable to such a defence. (9)

But the partial failure of consideration will constitute no defence if the quantum to be deducted

---

(8) Jones v. Hibbert, 2 Stark. 304. Defendant accepted a bill for 415*l.* to accommodate Philips and Co.: Philips and Co. indorsed it to their bankers for value, and became bankrupts: the bankers knew it to be an accommodation acceptance, and their demand against Philips and Co. was 265*l.* only: in an action by them upon this acceptance, it was held that they could only recover the 265*l.*; and they had a verdict accordingly.

(9) Lewis v. Cosgrave, 2 Taunt. 2. This was an action on a banker's check drawn by the defendant, and given to the plaintiff for the price of a horse sold by the plaintiff to the defendant, and warranted sound. The horse was in fact unsound, and that was relied on as a defence. The defendant proved that he had sent back the horse, but the plaintiff refused to take it; he, however, sent it again, and left it in the plaintiff's stable without his knowledge. Heath J. told the jury that as the plaintiff had refused to receive back the horse, the contract for the sale was not rescinded, and that the defendant was therefore bound to pay the check, and had his remedy by action for the deceit. They found a verdict for the plaintiff; but on a rule nisi for a new trial, and cause shewn, the court, on the ground of there being clear evidence of fraud, made the rule absolute. See Weston v. Downes, Dougl. 23., Power v. Wells, Cowp. 818., and Towers v. Barrett, 1 Term Rep. 133.

on that account is matter, not of definite computation, but of unliquidated damages.

Thus if a bill or note is given for the stipulated price of goods previously delivered, it is no ground of partial defence that the price was exorbitant. (10)

Or that the goods were damaged when they ought to have been sound; (11)

---

(10) Solomon v. Turner, 1 Stark. 51. In an action by payee of a note against the maker, the defence was that that and another note, which had been paid, had been given as the price of certain pictures, and that the pictures were not worth the amount of the other note: and per Lord Ellenborough, I will not admit evidence for the purpose of reducing the damages, that the pictures were of inferior value; if by inadequacy of value, and other circumstances, you can prove fraud, so as to shew there was no contract at all, the evidence will be admissible; if it fall short of that, it will be unavailable: it did fall short, and plaintiff had a verdict.

(11) Morgan v. Richardson, 1 Campb. N. P. C. 40. n. To an action by the drawer against the acceptor of a bill, drawn payable to the drawer's order, the defence was that the bill had been accepted for the price of some hams, and that they had proved to be so bad as to be almost unmarketable. The sum for which they were actually sold was paid into court. Lord Ellenborough held, that this partial failure of consideration was no defence to this action, but that the defendant must take his remedy by action. S. P. Fleming v. Simpson, 1 Campb. N. P. C. 40. n. From 2 Campb. N. P. C. 346. it appears that the case of Morgan v. Richardson was afterwards brought before the court of king's bench, and that the court approved of the direction of the chief justice.

In Tye v. Gwynne, 2 Campb. N. P. C. 346., the same point again arose in an action by the drawer of a bill against the acceptor, and Lord Ellenborough said that he should certainly adhere to the judgment of the court given in Morgan v. Richardson.

Unless the contract was rescinded on that ground. (12)

So it is no answer to an action on a bill or note, that it was given as the condition of a lease to be executed by the plaintiff and of letting the defendant into possession of the premises, and that plaintiff had refused to execute the lease, for he is not bound to execute till the price is paid; and as the defendant was let into possession, the consideration fails in part only; and the sum to be allowed for such failure is matter, not of mere calculation, but of unliquidated damages. (13)

So it is no answer to an action on a bill or note that it was for an apprentice fee, and that the ap-

---

Vide Broom v. Davis, cit. 7 East's Rep. 480. See also Basten v. Butter, 7. East's Rep. 479., and the cases therein cited.

(12) Lewis v. Cosgrave, ante, p. 394. n. 9.

(13) Moggridge v. Jones, 14 East, 486. In an action on a bill for 200*l*. by drawer against acceptor, the defence was that the acceptance was given as part of the consideration for a lease plaintiff was to execute to defendant, and which he had refused to execute: by the agreement plaintiff agreed to let, and defendant to take, for twenty-one years, from 29th December next; and plaintiff, in consideration of 500*l*. to be paid by defendant by three bills, agreed to execute the lease: defendant was let into possession and gave the bills, of which that sued on was one. Lord Ellenborough held the refusal to execute the lease no answer to the action; and verdict for plaintiff. Motion for new trial; but the court thought the verdict right, and that defendant must resort to his remedy upon the agreement, if plaintiff persisted in refusing to execute the lease. Lord Ellenborough's reason at the trial was, that the consideration had not wholly failed, because plaintiff had been let into possession.

prenticeship had been dissolved for misconduct in the master; (14)

Unless it appears that the fee was not to be paid unless the apprenticeship continued till a given period, and the dissolution occurred before that period had arrived. (14)

The want of consideration, in toto or in part, cannot be insisted upon, if the plaintiff, or any intermediate party between him and the defendant, took the bill or note bonâ fide, and upon a valid consideration. (15)

---

(14) Grant v. Welchman, 16 East, 207. Payee against maker, on note for 6*l.* of three years' standing: defence, first, that it was in part for an apprentice fee, and that the apprenticeship was for less than seven years; secondly, that a year before the action the apprentice was discharged, because plaintiff had enticed him to commit felony: Graham B. overruled both objections; and on motion for nonsuit, the court answered to the first objection, that the apprenticeship was voidable only, not void; and on the second, they enquired how the consideration for the apprentice was reserved, and it appearing that it was all to be paid at the time of the binding, but that the note was taken as an indulgence, they thought that decisive against defendant; and rule refused. Sed vide Ledger v. Ewer, Peake, 216. contra.

(15) Morris v. Lee, B. R. H. 26 G. 3. In an action by the indorsee against the maker of a note thirteen years old, the defendant obtained a rule nisi to set aside a judgment by default on an affidavit by a third person that he believed the defendant was swindled out of the note. An affidavit was made on the other side that the plaintiff took the note bonâ fide, and gave a valuable consideration for it; and the court held, that however improperly it might have been obtained, a third person, who took it fairly and gave a consideration for it, was entitled to

Where it is so taken, it is no defence that the bill or note was originally accommodation paper, and known so to be. (16)

And to support the defence against a person who may be a bonâ fide holder for value, the plaintiff should be apprized before the trial that he will be required to shew from whom he took the bill or note, and on what consideration; otherwise that defence may be excluded. (17)

If a banker is under acceptance for a customer

---

recover, and discharged the rule. And see Com. 43. 1 Term Rep. 40. 2 Term Rep. 71. 2 Atk. 182. Bull. Nisi Prius, 274. See also De Bras v. Forbes, 1 Esp. N. P. C. 117.

(16) Smith v. Knox, 3 Esp. N. P. C. 46. In an action by the indorsee of the drawer of a bill against the acceptor, it was urged in defence that this was an accommodation acceptance. But Lord Eldon said, if a person give a bill for a particular purpose, and that is known to the party taking the bill, as for example, to answer a particular demand, then the party taking the bill cannot apply it to a different purpose; but where a bill is given under no such restriction, but given merely for the accommodation of the drawer or payee, and that is sent into the world, it is no answer to an action brought on that bill, that the defendant accepted it for the accommodation of the drawer, and that that fact was known to the holder.

Charles v. Marsden, 1 Taunt. 224. Indorsees of the drawer of a bill against the acceptor. The defendant pleaded that he had accepted the bill for the accommodation of the drawer, without any consideration, and that after the bill became due it was indorsed to the plaintiffs, they knowing that it was an accommodation one. On special demurrer to the replication, the argument turned on the validity of the plea; and the whole court held, that there being no fraud or collusion alleged, the plea was bad, and gave judgment for the plaintiffs.

(17) See Paterson v. Hardacre, ante, 373.

to an amount beyond the cash balance in his hands, every bill he holds of that customer's he is to be considered as holding for value. (18)

And it makes no difference, though he holds other collateral securities more than sufficient to cover the excess of his acceptances. (18)

Illegality in the consideration, either wholly or in part, is another ground of defence.

The (19) debt of a third person, or a debt barred by (20) the statute of limitations, by a discharge under an insolvent or fugitive act, by a (21) bankruptcy and certificate, or by a composition, is a good consideration; and so is an apprentice fee,

---

(18) Bosanquet v. Dudman, 1 Stark. 1. Plaintiffs sued as indorsees of a bill, and it was made a question whether they were holders for value: they had it from Clarkson and Co., for whom they were bankers, and they took this and many other securities to cover their advances and acceptances: they were under acceptances for Clarkson and Co. beyond the amount of the cash balance in their hands; and a question being put as to the amount of the acceptances and cash balance, and the value of the other securities, Lord Ellenborough said he should hold that, if the acceptances exceeded the cash balance, plaintiffs held all the collateral securities for value. The enquiry was dropped, and plaintiffs had a verdict.

(19) Popplewell v. Wilson, Str. 264. A. gave a note to pay so much to B. for a debt due from C. to B.; and on error it was objected that the debt of a third person was no consideration; but the court thought otherwise, and the judgment was affirmed.

(20) Vide Lord Raym. 389. 6 Mod. 309. Burr. 2630. Blackst. 703. Cowp. 290.

(21) Trueman v. Fenton, Cowp. 544. Birch v. Sharland, 1 Term Rep. 715. Cowp. 290.

though the apprenticeship is for less than seven years. (22)

But the consideration of (23) signing a bankrupt's certificate, or withdrawing a petition (24) against it, or (25) joining in the acceptance of a composition, is illegal.

And if the creditor of a banker is also an acting commissioner under his commission, and takes a bill or note for his debt whilst the commission is in progress, he cannot enforce payment of such bill or note. (26)

Especially if he afterwards signed the bankrupt's certificate as such commissioner. (26)

Though he did not prove his debt under the commission. (26)

---

(22) See Grant v. Welchman, ante p. 397.

(23) Sumner v. Brady, 1 H. Bl. 647.

(24) By 5 G. 2. c. 30. § 11. It is enacted, that every bill, note, contract, agreement or other security whatsoever, to be made or given by any bankrupt, or by any other person, unto or to the use of or in trust for any creditor or creditors, or for the security of the payment of any debt or sum of money due from such bankrupt at the time of his becoming bankrupt, or any part thereof, between the time of his becoming bankrupt and such bankrupt's discharge, as a consideration, or to the intent to persuade him, her or them, to consent to or sign any such allowance or certificate, shall be wholly void and of no effect; and the monies thereby secured or agreed to be paid shall not be recovered or recoverable. And see Smith v. Bromley, Dougl. 670.

(25) Spurrett v. Spiller, 1 Atk. 105. Cockshott v. Bennett, 2 Term Rep. 763. Jackson v. Lomas, 4 Term Rep. 166. Cooling v. Noyes, 6 Term Rep. 263.

(26) Haywood v. Chambers, 5 Barnew. and Ald. 753. 1 Dowl. and Regl. 411. In an action by payee of a note against the

Where however a creditor *has* joined in a deed of composition, it is (27) not illegal to obtain the security of a third person for such composition.

And therefore a bill given by a third person, as such security, is (27) good;

Though such creditor's composition be thereby secured to be paid at an (27) earlier period than that of the other creditors.

But to stipulate privately for such additional security before joining in the acceptance of the composition, is a (28) fraud on the other creditors.

And if there is a private stipulation for more than the composition money from a third person,

---

maker, it appeared that defendant had been a bankrupt and obtained his certificate; that the note was given to plaintiff between the second and third meetings for a debt due before the bankruptcy; that plaintiff was one of the acting commissioners under the defendant's commission; that he did not prove his debt under the commission, but that after he had received the note he signed the defendant's certificate as one of the commissioners. Abbott C. J. thought defendant not a free agent when he gave the note, and nonsuited the plaintiff; and on motion to enter a verdict for plaintiff, the court said a security to induce a commissioner to sign a bankrupt's certificate would be clearly void, and it was against public policy to allow any thing which led to that result: a commissioner has an important public duty to perform, and this would have a tendency to warp his conduct in the discharge of it; and in giving a security under such circumstances, the bankrupt could not be deemed a free agent. Rule refused.

(27) Feise v. Randall, 6 Term Rep. 146.

(28) Leicester v. Rose, 4 East's Rep. 372.

and the third person pays the money, he cannot recover upon any bill or note the debtor may give him for reimbursement (29)

Though the creditor was induced originally to trust the debtor upon a representation by such third person of his responsibility. (29)

And refused to consent to the composition without such additional security on the ground of that representation. (29)

Past (30) seduction is a good consideration; future (31) prostitution an illegal one.

A note given to parish officers for a sum certain, to defray the future expences of a bastard child, is (32) illegal; the officers being authorized by law to take an indemnity only.

---

(29) Bryant v. Christie, 1 Stark. 329. Back trusted Christie to the amount of 332*l.* on a representation by Bryant of Back's responsibility. Christie became embarrassed, and offered to compound with his creditors at 10*s.* in the pound. Back considered himself guaranteed by Bryant, and therefore refused to sign the composition deed unless Bryant would promise him the remainder of his debt. Bryant promised accordingly, and Back signed the deed which released Christie: the composition was paid, and Bryant paid the difference: Christie accepted bills to reimburse Bryant, and Bryant sued thereon. But Lord Ellenborough considered this as a circuitous mode of securing Back the full amount of his debt, and a fraud upon the creditors at large, and he nonsuited the plaintiff.

(30) Annandall v. Harris, 2 P. Wms. 432. Cray v. Rooke, Forrest 153. Turner v. Vaughan, 2 Wils. 339.

(31) Walker v. Parkins, Burr. 1568.

(32) Cole v. Gower, 6 East's Rep. 110.

Dropping (33) a criminal prosecution, or suppressing evidence thereon, is an illegal consideration: but where a person has been convicted of a misdemeanour, and the court offer that if he will pay a certain sum for the expences of the prosecution, the sentence shall be for a shorter period of imprisonment than it otherwise would, a note given by him for such sum is (34), as far as respects the consideration, unobjectionable.

And where there are both civil and criminal proceedings, an agreement to compound the civil proceedings and to take a given sum for costs, and to give a bill for the amount, will not make the bill illegal, if the criminal costs do not appear to have been included, and it is no part of the bargain that the criminal proceedings shall be abandoned. (35)

---

(33) 3 P. Wms. 279. Collins v. Blantern, 2 Wils. 349.

(34) Beely v. Wingfield, 11 East's Rep. 46.

(35) Harding v. Cooper, 1 Stark. 467. In an action against the acceptor of a bill, it appeared that plaintiffs had sued the drawer, and taken out a commission of bankruptcy against him; and, on his having obtained his discharge as an insolvent, had indicted him for fraud in obtaining it. They then came to an agreement that plaintiffs should have 2*s*. 6*d*. in the pound for their debt, 220*l*. for costs, without taxation, and that the commission should be superseded, and defendant gave his acceptance for the amount. Plaintiffs afterwards consented that the indictment should be quashed. It was urged that this was an illegal consideration; and Lord Ellenborough said, a stipulation

So the release by an excise officer of a person apprehended for penalties under the excise laws, is a (36) sufficient consideration for a note given, with the approbation of the commissioners, for the amount of such penalties.

Or if an officer who has a warrant to levy excise penalties take a note for the amount, though such a transaction is to be looked upon with extreme jealously, yet if there has been no extortion in the officer, nor other improper conduct, the consideration will be unobjectionable, and the note valid. (37)

Especially if the commissioners afterwards approve what has been done. (37)

---

to drop the prosecution would, without doubt, have been illegal, but if the civil rights only were compounded, and plaintiffs chose afterwards to forego the prosecution, the transaction was not illegal: and there being no evidence that the costs of the prosecution were mentioned during the negotiation, or included in the 220*l.*, or that there was any stipulation for dropping the prosecution, the plaintiffs had a verdict.

(36) Pilkington v. Green, 2 Bos. and Pull. 151.

(37) Sugars v. Brinkworth, 4 Camp. 46. Defendant was convicted in excise penalties to the amount of 340*l.*, and plaintiff, a supervisor, had a warrant to levy the amount. Plaintiff took defendant's note at two months for that sum, and though he had no previous authority from the commissioners to take it, they approved of it when they knew it. In an action upon the note it was urged, that there might be great abuses if the taking a note for penalties were allowed: and Lord Ellenborough said if there were any reason to think the law had been abused by plaintiff, he would not be allowed to enforce payment; that such a transaction was to be looked to with extreme jealousy;

A (38) recommendation to an office in the king's household though of a private nature, and not within the statute of the 5th and 6th Edw. 3. a (39) smuggling, an (40) usurious, a (41) stock-jobbing contract, a wager upon the future amount of any branch of the (42) public revenue, or selling spirituous liquors in small quantities, contrary to 24 G. 2. c. 40. § 12., is an illegal consideration. (43)

So money lost by gaming, (except (44) in some part of a royal palace in which the King is then actually resident, the freehold and inheritance of which part is in the crown, and which is not in lease) or betting on the sides of persons so gaming, money knowingly lent for such gaming or betting, or money lent at the time and place of such play to any person either then gaming or betting, or who shall, during the play, play or bet, is (46) an illegal consideration.

---

but that here plaintiff appeared to have acted with perfect good faith; and defendant, to whom indulgence had been extended, was not to criminate his benefactor when nothing wrong had been done. Verdict for plaintiff.

(38) Harrington v. Du Chatel, Bro. C. C. 114.

(39) Guichard v. Roberts, Blackst. 445.

(40) 12 Ann. St. 2. c. 16. post. 411. note (63).

(41) 7 G. 2. c. 8. See Faikney v. Reynous, Burr. 2069. Petrie v. Hannay, 3 Term Rep. 418. and Steers v. Lashley, 6 Term Rep. 61.

(42) Shirley v. Sankey and others, 2 Bos. and Pull. 130. and Atherfold v. Beard, 2 Term Rep. 610.

(43) See Scott. v. Gilmore, post. 406.

(44) 9 Ann. c. 14. § 9.

(46) 9 Ann. c. 14. § 1.

Betting on a game at cricket (47), a horse race, or (48) a foot race against time, is gaming within 9 Ann.: insuring (49) in the lottery not.

So also the (50) ransom, or money knowingly (51) lent to enable the owner to obtain the ransom, of the ship or vessel of any British subject, or any merchandise or goods on board the same, (unless in the case of extreme necessity, to be allowed by the court of admiralty,) is an illegal consideration.

If a bill or note is in part upon a consideration which the law has made illegal, and in part upon a good consideration, it has been held that the illegality will taint the whole bill or note; and that the holder, if barred at all by such illegality, will be barred in toto as to his claim on the bill or note. (52)

---

(47) Jeffryes v. Walter, 1 Wils. 220.

(48) Lynall v. Longbotham, 2 Wils. 36.

(49) Lewis v. Piercy, 1 H. Bl. 29.

(50) 45 Geo. 3. c. 72. § 16. 17.

(51) See Webb v. Brooke, post. p. 412. n. (65).

(52) Scott v. Gillmore, 3 Taunt. 226. Action against acceptor: the bill was given to the keeper of a coffee-house by the drawer, partly for money lent, and partly for spirits in small quantities under 20*s*. worth at each time: nonsuit on the ground of 24 G. 2. c. 40. § 12. On motion for new trial, Mansfield C. J. said the statute makes the consideration illegal, not merely void, and the security is entire, and cannot be apportioned; and since it is partly given for an illegal consideration, the whole bill is void. See Spencer v. Smith, 3 Campb. 9.

N. The case does not state whether plaintiff was indorsee:

But if there be a privity between him and the defendant as to the good part of the consideration, he may recover that part exclusively of the bill or note. (53)

If a new bill or note be substituted for one which was given upon an illegal consideration, it will be open to the same objections as the original bill or note, unless it is reformed so as to exclude what made it illegal. (54)

Though the new bill or note is given to an indorsee who took the first security innocently, and gave value for it. (54)

Especially if he was apprised of the illegality in the first bill or note, before he took the second. (54)

If the new bill or note is so reformed as to exclude what made the first illegal, it will be unobjectionable. (55)

Thus if a bill or note is substituted for one which was given upon an usurious contract, it will be open to the same objections as the original bill or note, if it is not confined to what remains due for principal and legal interest. (56)

---

if plaintiff were the coffee-house keeper, still as defendant was a stranger to the original transaction, he could not be liable otherwise than on the bill.

(53) See Robinson v. Bland, post, p. 410.

(54) See Chapman v. Black, infra.

(55) See Preston v. Jackson, p. 408. note (57).

(56) Chapman v. Black, 2 Barnew. 588. White got money from Akers upon usurious interest, and indorsed to Akers a bill

And if it were given to an indorsee of the first bill or note who took it bonâ fide and for value, he could not before 58 G. 3. have sued any of the parties whom the usury would have protected from the first bill or note. (56)

Especially if he knew of the usury when he took the substituted security. (56)

But a bill or note substituted for one given upon an usurious contract will be valid, if it is given for principal and legal interest only; (57)

Or for what remains due for principal and legal interest, after reforming all prior payments, and excluding all usurious interest. (57)

---

for 40*l.* upon the transaction: this bill came into plaintiff's hands bonâ fide and for valuable consideration, but when it became due it was not paid, and plaintiff was apprised of the usury; it was then arranged that Akers should draw for the amount upon defendant, and that defendant should accept for the accommodation of White, which was done accordingly: nonsuit; and on rule nisi to set aside the nonsuit, and cause shewn, the court thought that as defendant really stood in the place of White, whatever would be a defence for White was also a defence for defendant, and as plaintiff's recovery in this action would enable Akers to keep the usurious interest he had received, and plaintiff by taking this new security, in which White's name was studiously omitted, was lending himself to screen Akers, the usury was a bar to this action, and the nonsuit right.

(57) Preston v. Jackson, 2 Stark. 237. Wyer lent defendant two sums on usurious interest, and took defendant's bonds for the amount; the bonds were afterwards given up, the account settled, and a note given for the usurious interest: Wyer indorsed that note to the plaintiff, and Holroyd J. held,

If a bill or note is given in part upon a legal, and in part upon an illegal consideration, and several bills or notes are afterwards substituted in lieu thereof, the effect of the illegality may be confined to some only of the substituted bills or notes, and the other stand exempt. (58)

As where a bill or note is given as to half for a gaming debt, and as to the residue for money lent, and two bills or notes of equal amount are afterwards substituted for it, if the giver does any thing which may be considered an election to ascribe the gaming debt to the one, he will be liable upon the other. (58)

Promising to pay one whilst both remain unpaid, shall be deemed an election to ascribe the gaming debt to the other. (58)

---

that though a new security for principal and legal interest had been held binding, such a security for the usurious interest was not so, and he would not allow the plaintiff to recover on the note.

(58) Hubner v. Richardson, Michas. 1819. Richardson lost to Brown at gaming 90*l.* and owed him other money; and for upwards of 20*l.* of the gaming debt, and upwards of 70*l.* of the other, gave him a 100*l.* note: he paid part, and then gave Brown two notes for 43*l.* each, one of which was indorsed to plaintiff for a valuable consideration, and he knew nothing of the gaming debt; defendant promised him payment: and in an action on the note, case on question whether the gaming consideration vitiated the note in plaintiff's hands, and after argument, the court held it did not, for it was for defendant to make out that some of the gaming debt made part of the consideration of this note: it might be wholly included in the other note, which did not appear to have been paid, and defendant's pro-

But it is no objection to a bill or note that it was drawn in order to be discounted, and that the brokerage for getting it discounted was exorbitant, if the broker did not discount them himself, and the person who did knew nothing of his charge. (59)

The objection of illegality of consideration is in some cases confined to those persons who were parties or privy to such illegality, and those to whom they have passed the bill or note without value; in other cases it is extended even to holders bonâ fide, and for value.

The latter cases are, where the consideration is either (60) wholly or in part (61) signing a bankrupt's certificate, money (62) lost by gaming as afore-

---

mise to pay this, implied an election on his part that it should be so included in the other.

(59) See Acland v. Pearce, 2 Campb. 599. Young v. Wright, 1 Campb. 139. Dagnell v. Willey, 11 East. 43.

(60) Robinson v. Bland, Burr. 1077. A bill of exchange was partly for money lent at the time and place of play, and partly for money lost at play: and on a case reserved the court held that the plaintiff could recover nothing upon the bill, but that he might recover the money lent on a count for money lent.

(61) Vide 5 G. 2. c. 30. § 11. ante, p. 400. note (24).

(62) By 9 Ann. c. 14. §. 1. It is enacted that all notes, bills or other securities whatsoever, given, granted, drawn or entered into, or executed by any person or persons whatsoever, where the whole or any part of the consideration of such conveyances [illegible]rities shall be for any mon[illegible] or other valuable thing whatsoever, won by gaming, or playing at cards, dice, tables, tennis, bowls, or other game or games whatsoever, or by betting on the sid[illegible] or hands of suc[illegible] do game at any of

said, or by betting on the sides of persons so gaming, money knowingly lent for such gaming or betting, money lent at the time and place of such play to any person either then gaming or betting, or who shall, during the play, play or bet, (63) money lent

---

the games aforesaid, or for the reimbursing or re-paying any money knowingly lent, or advanced for such gaming or betting as aforesaid, or lent or advanced at the time and place of such play, to any person or persons so gaming as aforesaid, or that shall, during such play, so play or bet, shall be utterly void, frustrate, and of none effect, to all intents and purposes whatsoever.

Bowyer v. Bampton, Str. 1155. Several notes given by Bampton to Church for money lent to game with, were indorsed by Church to the plaintiff for a full and valuable consideration, and the plaintiff had no knowledge that any part of the consideration from Church to Bampton was money lent for gaming; and after two arguments upon a case reserved, the court held that the plaintiff could not maintain the action; for it would be making the notes of use to the lender, if he could pay his debts with them, and it would tend to evade the act, on account of the difficulty of proving notice on an indorsee; and the plaintiff would not be without remedy, for he might sue Church on his indorsement.

(63) By 12 Ann. St. 2. c. 16. It is enacted, that no person or persons whatsoever, upon any contract, take directly or indirectly, for loan of any monies, wares, merchandise, or other commodities whatsoever, above the value of *5l.* for the forbearance of *100l.* for a year, and so after that rate for a greater or lesser sum, or for a longer or shorter time; and that all contracts, and assurances whatsoever, made after the time aforesaid, for payment of any principal, or money to be lent or covenanted to be performed upon or for any usury, whereupon or whereby there shall be reserved or taken above the rate of *5l.* in the hundred, asaforesaid, shall be utterly void.

Lowe v. Waller, Dougl. 708—736. The defendant was acceptor of a bill, which he gave to Harris and Stratton upon an

on an usurious contract, the (64) ransom, or money knowingly (65) lent to enable the owner to ob-

usurious contract; Harris and Stratton indorsed it to the plaintiff for a valuable consideration, and the plaintiff had no notice of the usury; upon a case reserved, the question was, whether the usury between Harris and Stratton and the defendant was a defence against an indorsee who took the bill bonâ fide, and paid a valuable consideration for it; and after time taken to consider, the court held it was, and though Lord Mansfield had a wish the law should turn out in favour of the plaintiff, the court found the words of the act too strong, and could not get over the case of Bowyer v. Bampton, Str. 1155.

(64) By 45 Geo. 3. c. 72. (which repeals the former act 43 Geo 3. c. 160. relating to the same subject) sect. 16. it is enacted, "That it shall not be lawful for any of his Majesty's subjects to ransom, or to enter into any contract or agreement for ransoming any ship or vessel belonging to any of his Majesty's subjects, or any merchandise or goods on board the same, which shall be captured by the subjects of any state at war with his Majesty, or by any persons committing hostilities against his Majesty's subjects, unless in the case of extreme necessity to be allowed by the court of admiralty."

And by sect. 17. "All contracts and agreements which shall be entered into, and all bills, notes, and other securities which shall be given by any person or persons for ransom of any ship or vessel, or of any merchandise or goods on board the same contrary to this act, shall be absolutely null and void in law, and of no effect whatsoever."

(65) Webb v. Brooke, 3 Taunt. 6. The plaintiff and defendant (British subjects) were made prisoners by the French at Oporto, where the defendant's ship was at the same time taken; they jointly petitioned for the release of themselves, and for the ransom of the defendant's ship, and to enable the defendant to pay for the ransom, the plaintiff lent him 3000 dollars, and for this sum the defendant drew a bill in his own favour, which he indorsed to the plaintiff. Their liberation and the ransom were accordingly effected, and they returned (as had been agreed upon) in the ship to England. The drawee refused to accept

tain the ransom, of the ship or vessel of any British subject, or any merchandise or goods on board the same, as before mentioned.

Where usury is the defence, letters between the parties at the time the bill or note is given, to fix the usurer's terms, (66) are admissible in evidence against a subsequent holder, if the usury is as against him a valid defence.

---

the bill, and this action was brought against the defendant as indorser. The defence was the illegality of the purpose for which the money was lent according to 45 Geo. 3. c. 72. A verdict was found for the plaintiff, and the point of law reserved. And after a rule nisi to enter a nonsuit, and cause shewn, Mansfield C. J. said, there is a manifest distinction between the cases of Faikney v. Reynous, and Petrie v. Hannay, and the other cases, in which a man having a debt of honour borrows money to pay it, and those cases where the plaintiff previously advances the money for effectuating an illegal transaction, or causing it to be done. Here the plaintiff and the defendant are equally ransomers; equally solicitous to procure the ransom, for they were to return home by this ship. The ransom is as much the deed of the plaintiff as of the defendant. Rule absolute.

(66) Kent v. Lowen, 1 Campb. N. P. C. 177, 180. d. This was an action against the maker of a note, indorsed by the payees to Watson, and by him to the plaintiff. The defence was usury in the original consideration for the note; to prove which the defendant tendered letters from the payees to the defendant setting forth the consideration. Lord Ellenborough held that it was first necessary to shew, either by the post mark, or otherwise, that the letters were contemporaneous with the making of the note, after which they would be evidence of an act done by the payees through whom the plaintiff claimed. From the post mark it appeared that they had been written just before the date of the note, and they were read in evidence.

But now 58 G. 3. c. 93. removes the objection of usury from an indorsee for valuable consideration, if he was ignorant of the usury at the time he took the bill or note and gave the consideration. (67)

If the consideration upon which a bill or note was made is not illegal; an illegality in the consideration upon which it is afterwards transferred will be no (68) defence, if the plaintiff took it bonâ fide, and upon a good consideration, and is not bound in making out his title to state or prove the signature of the person making such transfer.

Where he is bound to state or prove such signatures, the authorities are contradictory upon the question whether the illegality is a defence.

If the bill or note were originally given upon an unobjectionable consideration, but indorsed over by the payee upon an illegal consideration, Lord Kenyon thought a subsequent indorsee, if he took the bill bonâ fide, and upon a valuable con-

---

The defendant had a verdict; and on a motion for a new trial, the court held that the letters had been properly received.

(67) By 58 G. 3. c. 93. no bill or note that shall be made after 10th June, 1818, shall, though it may have been given for an usurious consideration, or upon an usurious contract, be void in the hands of an indorsee for valuable consideration, unless such indorsee had, at the time of discounting or paying such consideration for the same, actual notice that such bill or note had been originally given for an usurious consideration, or upon an usurious contract.

(68) Daniel v. Cartony, Espinasse, 274.

sideration, was entitled to keep it in opposition to such payee; (69)

And to enforce payment in case of a bill, against the acceptor. (70)

In Lord Ellenborough's time, the court of king's bench thought he could not enforce such payment. (71)

---

(69) Parr v. Eliason, 1 East's Rep. 92. A bill was drawn in favour of the plaintiff, he indorsed it to Persent and Bodeker upon an usurious consideration, and they indorsed it over; it was afterwards indorsed back to the assignees of Persent and Bodeker, who had become bankrupts, for a debt due to their estate; upon which the plaintiff brought trover to recover back the bill. Lord Kenyon directed a nonsuit, and after a rule nisi for a new trial, the court held, that as the bill was originally good, and as the indorsement by Persent and Bodeker was unimpeached, their indorsee had a good right to the bill, and that right was transferred to the defendants. Rule discharged.

(70) Daniel v. Cartony, Espinasse, 274. Scott drew a bill on the defendant payable to his own order, and discounted it with Greensill, who took 18*l.* per cent. discount; it was afterwards indorsed to the plaintiff, and the defendant could not impeach *that* transaction; and per Lord Kenyon, This is no defence; had the note been originally given on an usurious transaction, or for an usurious consideration, it would have been void in the hands of even a bonâ fide holder; but usury in an intermediate transaction respecting it, can never make it void in the hands of a bonâ fide indorsee, where there was no usury in the original transaction.

(71) Lowes v. Massaredo, 1 Stark. 385. In an action by indorsees against acceptor on a bill payable to Lowes or order, it appeared that Lowes indorsed it to Bloxham upon usurious terms, that Bloxham indorsed it to Ambrose, and that Ambrose indorsed it to the plaintiffs upon questionable terms:

It is no objection in an action against an indorser that the bill or note was drawn upon a gaming, or usurious, or other illegal consideration; for though the statute against gaming, &c. makes such bill void to all intents and purposes, the proper construction upon those words is, that it makes it void as far as can be necessary to further the objects of the act, but it does not avoid it in favour of a party whom the statute meant to punish, not to protect. (72)

Lord Ellenborough thought plaintiffs precluded from recovery by the usury between Bloxam and Lowes, independent of the usury between them and Ambrose, but upon being strongly pressed by Parr v. Eliason, he suffered plaintiffs to take a verdict, subject to a motion for entering a nonsuit; a rule nisi was accordingly granted, and on cause shewn, the court thought the usury between Bloxham and Lowes a bar to the plaintiff's claim, because they could not bring themselves in connection with the defendant but through the medium of Lowes's indorsement, which was tainted with usury: they also thought the terms upon which Ambrose indorsed to the plaintiffs usurious, and the rule for a nonsuit was made absolute.

(72) Edwards v. Dick, Hil. 1 & 2 Geo. 4. 4 Barnew. 212. Action on bill drawn by defendant on Lord Rossmere, payable to defendant's order, and indorsed by him; defence, that defendant drew the bill for money won by him of Lord Rossmere at play. Bayley J. thought this no defence, because by indorsing the bill defendant affirmed it to be free from exception, with which this defence was inconsistent, and rejected the evidence. On motion for new trial, the court thought he did right, for defendant was not within the spirit of the act against gaming; it was not for a person standing as he did that the act intended

protection; compelling payment from him was not advancing any practice the statute meant to suppress, and giving him protection would assist a winner, whom the act meant to discountenance, and would enable him to set up his own misconduct to bar the honest claim of an innocent indorsee. Rule refused.

CAP. XIII.

Competence of Witnesses.

In an action against one of several makers of a note, another maker is a competent witness for the plaintiff, for he stands indifferent; if the plaintiff recovers he will be liable to pay contribution to the defendant; if plaintiff fails and forces him to pay, he will be entitled to contribution from the defendant. (1)

It was at one time held, that no person who had signed a negotiable bill or note was admissible as a witness to impeach its validity, because his conduct had sanctioned what his testimony would defeat.

But the contrary is now fully settled.

Thus the drawer of a bill dated abroad and not stamped is a competent witness to prove that it

---

(1) York v. Blott, 5 Maule, 71. Assumpsit against one of two makers of a note; plaintiff called the other maker, and Graham B. admitted him: on motion for a new trial, the court thought the witness stood indifferent, and was properly admitted, and refused the rule.

was made in England, and therefore not admissible in evidence. (2)

And the only objection which can now be made against the testimony of a party to the bill or note is, that he has a direct interest in the event of the suit: if he has such an interest he is not admissible, otherwise he is.

Therefore in an action against one of several makers of a note, any of the others is a competent witness for the plaintiff; for if the plaintiff succeeds in the suit, the witness will be liable to pay contribution; if the plaintiff fails in the suit and makes the witness pay, the witness will be entitled to receive contribution. (3)

So in an action against the acceptor of a bill, the drawer is a competent witness either for the plaintiff (4) or for the defendant (5) (6); for if the plaintiff recovers against the acceptor, the drawer

---

(2) Jordaine v. Lashbrooke, 7 Term Rep. 601. In an action against the acceptor of a bill purporting to have been drawn at Hamburg, the defence was that it was drawn in London, and therefore inadmissible in evidence without a stamp: the payee and indorser was called to prove where it was drawn; but it was objected that he was incompetent. Lord Kenyon, however, admitted him; and on his testimony the defendant had a verdict upon the counts on the bill. On a rule nisi for a new trial, and cause shewn, Ashhurst J. thought the witness inadmissible; but Lord Kenyon, Grose, and Lawrence Js., held that as he was neither interested in the event, nor rendered infamous by a conviction for any crime, he was properly admitted. Rule discharged. See also Adams v. Lingard, Peake, N. P. C. 117.

(3) See York v. Blott, supra, n. (1.)

(4) Dickinson v. Prentice, 4 Esp. N. P. C. 32. This was an

pays the bill by the hands of the acceptor; if the plaintiff fails against the acceptor, the drawer is liable to pay the bill himself. (4)

And the drawer has accordingly been admitted for the plaintiff, to prove the defendant's handwriting; and for the defendant, to prove that (5) the plaintiff discounted the bill upon an usurious consideration, or that (6) the bill had been paid.

And it is no objection to the competence of the

---

action against the defendant as acceptor of a bill; the defence intended to be set up was that the acceptance was a forgery: to prove the defendant's handwriting the plaintiff called the drawer. It was objected, that having drawn the bill, the forgery of the acceptance could only be imputable to him; and that as he might be committed for a capital offence, if the forgery were established, he had such an interest as ought to disqualify him. But Lord Kenyon said that this was matter of observation as to his credit, but was no objection to his admissibility. He was admitted, and the plaintiff had a verdict. See also Barber v. Gingell, 3 Esp. N. P. C. 62.

(5) Rich v. Topping, Peake N. P. C. 224. The drawer himself had indorsed the bill to the plaintiff for an usurious consideration; he had a release from the acceptor, which Lord Kenyon thought was necessary. The reporter, however, in a note upon the case, considers that the witness stood indifferent, and ought to have been received even without a release; and in Brard v. Ackerman, 5 Esp. N. P. C. 119., the drawer (under precisely similar circumstances) was admitted without a release; at least it is not stated that he had any.

(6) Humphrey v. Moxon, Peake N. P. C. 52. This was an action by an indorsee; and a distinction was attempted to be taken between this case, and one wherein the payee was the plaintiff; but Lord Kenyon held that there was no difference in principle, and admitted the drawer.

drawer, when called to prove the acceptor's handwriting, that he is in custody upon a charge of having forged it. (7)

But in an action against the acceptor upon an acceptance for the accommodation of the drawer, the drawer or his wife is not a competent witness for the defendant; for he has a direct interest to defeat the suit, because if plaintiff recovers against the acceptor, the drawer will be liable to the acceptor not only for the amount of the bill, but for all the costs the acceptor may sustain: whereas if plaintiff fails against the acceptor, the drawer will be liable for the amount of the bill only, not for the costs. (8)

In an action by indorsee of a note against an indorser, the maker is a competent witness for the plaintiff: for if the indorser is made to pay, the

---

(7) See Dickinson v. Prentice, ante, p. 419. n. (4.), and in Barber v. Gingell, 3 Esp. N. P. C. 62., the drawer was called to prove that he had paid the bill. Being at that time a prisoner on a charge of having forged the bill, and brought up by habeas corpus, he was objected to as incompetent; but Lord Kenyon overruled the objection.

(8) Jones v. Brooke, 4 Taunt. 464. Action against acceptor of a bill: the acceptance was without value, to accommodate the drawer; the drawer's wife was called as a witness for the defendant, to prove that the drawer indorsed away the bill upon an usurious consideration; the witness was objected to, but admitted: but on rule nisi, cause shewn, and time to consider, the court held the drawer had a direct interest to defeat the action, because otherwise he must indemnify defendant against the costs as well as pay him the amount of the bill; that the wife therefore was incompetent. Rule absolute.

maker will be liable to pay him; if the indorser is not made to pay, the maker will be liable to pay the indorsee; and his liability to the one cannot exceed in extent his liability to the other. (9)

So in an action by indorsee against drawer or acceptor, an indorser is in general a competent witness either for plaintiff or defendant: for plaintiff, because, though the plaintiff's succeeding in the action *may* prevent him from calling for payment from the indorser, it is not certain that it will; and whatever part of the bill or note the indorser is compelled to pay, he may recover again from the drawer or acceptor; and he is competent for defendant, because if plaintiff fails against drawer or acceptor, he is driven either to sue the indorser or to abandon his claim.

Thus he has been admitted upon a bill drawn for his accommodation to prove for the plaintiff that (10) the plaintiff gave him value for it, and he has been admitted for the defendant to prove that he had paid the bill (11), or to prove that an un-

---

(9) Venning v. Shuttleworth, 24th February, 1796, at Guildhall. In an action by Venning, as indorsee of a note, against Shuttleworth as payee and indorser, the plaintiff called the drawer to prove notice to the defendant; he was objected to, but per Lord Kenyon stat indifferenter, and he was accordingly admitted.

(10) Shuttleworth v. Stephens, 1 Campb. 408.

(11) Charrington v. Milner, Peake, N. P. C. 6. The note had been indorsed by Monk to the plaintiff, and the defendant was allowed by Lord Kenyon to call Monk to prove that he had paid the note to the plaintiff.

stamped bill, dated abroad, had in fact been made here. (12)

So he has been admitted for the plaintiff to prove his own indorsement. (13)

And, where the indorsement has been negatived by another witness (not being an attesting witness)

Birt v. Kershaw, 2 East's Rep. 458. The defendant drew a bill in favour of Wilby, which Wilby indorsed to Glover, whose assignees now sued the defendant on the bill. The defendant called Wilby to prove that he had paid the bill to Glover, and had been reimbursed by the defendant. It was objected that Wilby (who had no release from Kershaw) came to discharge himself, and was therefore interested; his evidence, however, was received, and a verdict found for the defendant. And on rule nisi to set it aside, and cause shewn, the court was clearly of opinion that this testimony had been properly admitted; that this case fell directly within the principle of that of Ilderton v. Atkinson, 7 Term Rep. 480.; that the witness stood indifferent. Rule discharged. Lord Ellenborough said, It is true that in an action by the defendant against Wilby for the money received by him, if the plaintiffs recover, Wilby may also be liable for the costs of this action; but that argument was urged in Ilderton v. Atkinson, without effect.

(12) See Jordaine v. Lashbrooke, ante, p. 419.

(13) Richardson v. Allen, 2 Stark. 334. In an action by indorsee against acceptor, a witness called to prove the indorsement said it was not the supposed indorser's writing; plaintiff then proposed to call other witnesses to prove it was, but Lord Ellenborough held that as plaintiff was not obliged to have called the witness he did, from his being an attesting witness, it was not competent for him to call other witnesses to contradict him; plaintiff then proposed to call the indorser himself, and Lord Ellenborough thought he might, because he could speak from knowledge, other witnesses from belief only, and he came to charge himself: he was examined accordingly, but negatived the handwriting; and plaintiff was nonsuited.

whom plaintiff had called, he, or some person who saw it written, is the only witness who can be called to prove it. (14)

In an action against the drawer of a bill, it has been held that the acceptor is not a competent witness for defendant to prove a set-off, on the ground that he is answerable to the drawer only to the amount to which plaintiff recovers against defendant. (15)

But if the drawer is protected against the holder by a cross-demand he has against the holder, quære, is not such cross-demand, when set off, equivalent to payment; and will not the drawer be intitled to call upon the acceptor for the full amount of the bill, as much as if he had paid the full amount in money?

---

(14) See Richardson v. Allen, ante, p. 423.

(15) Mainwaring v. Mytton, 1 Stark. 83. In an action against the drawer of two bills, he called the acceptor to prove that the acceptor had indorsed to defendant a bill drawn by him on the plaintiff, and accepted by plaintiff, and that defendant was therefore entitled to set off this acceptance; objection being made to his competence, it was urged that he was indifferent, for if plaintiff failed against the drawer, he might sue the witness; but Dampier J. said the witness was interested in lessening the balance, being answerable to defendant for what plaintiff should recover; and he was rejected, and plaintiff recovered his whole demand.

CAP. XIV.

Forgery of Bills or Notes.

FORGING or causing to be forged, or assisting in forging, any bill or note, or any indorsement or assignment thereof, with intention to defraud any person whatever; or uttering the same as true, knowing it to be forged, with a like intent, was made a capital offence by 2 Geo. 2. c. 25. (1)

---

(1) By 2 Geo. 2. c. 25. s. 1., made perpetual by 9 Geo. 2. c. 18., if any person after 29th June, 1729, shall falsely make, forge, or counterfeit; or cause or procure to be falsely made, forged, or counterfeited; or willingly act or assist in the false

This act did not extend to Scotland. (2)

By 7 Geo. 2. c. 22. it is applied to acceptances, and the term *alter* is used as well as forge. (3)

By 31 Geo. 2. c. 22. s. 78. (4) the second of

---

making, forging, or counterfeiting, amongst other things, any bill of exchange or promissory note for payment of money, or any indorsement or assignment of any bill of exchange or promissory note for payment of money, with intention to defraud any person whatsoever; or shall utter or publish as true any false, forged, or counterfeit bill of exchange or promissory note for payment of money, or any indorsement or assignment of any bill of exchange or promissory note for payment of money, with intention to defraud any person, knowing the same to be false, forged, or counterfeited; then every such person shall be deemed guilty of felony, without benefit of clergy.

(2) By 2 Geo. 2. c. 25. s. 4., provided always, that nothing in this act contained shall extend to that part of Great Britain called Scotland.

(3) By 7 Geo. 2. c. 22., which recites that by 2 Geo. 2. c. 25. no punishment is inflicted upon any person who shall falsely make, alter, forge, or counterfeit, or cause or procure to be falsely made, altered, forged or counterfeited, or willingly act or assist in the false making, altering, forging, or counterfeiting, any acceptance of any bill of exchange, or who shall knowingly utter or publish the same as true: it is therefore enacted, that if any person, after the 24th day of June, 1734, shall falsely make, alter, forge, or counterfeit, or cause or procure to be falsely made, altered, or counterfeited, or willingly act or assist in the false making, altering, forging, or counterfeiting any acceptance of any bill of exchange with intention to defraud any person whatsoever; or shall utter or publish as true any false, altered, forged, or counterfeited acceptance of any bill of exchange, with intention to defraud any person, knowing the same to be false, altered, forged, or counterfeited; then every such person shall be deemed guilty of felony, without benefit of clergy.

(4) By 31 Geo. 2. c. 22. § 78., which recites that doubts might

Geo. 2. is extended to cases where the intent is to defraud, not an individual, but a corporation; and by 18 Geo. 3. c. 18. (5) the seventh of Geo. 2. c. 22. is in like manner extended.

---

arise whether the punishment inflicted by 2 Geo. 2. c. 25. extends to the commission of forgeries with intention to defraud any corporation, it is enacted, that if any person from and after the 1st of July, 1758, shall falsely make, forge, or counterfeit, or cause or procure to be falsely made, forged, or counterfeited, or willingly act or assist in the false making, forging, or counterfeiting, any bill of exchange or promissory note for payment of money, or the indorsement or assignment of any bill of exchange or promissory note for payment of money, with an intention to defraud any corporation whatsoever; or shall utter or publish as true, any false, forged, or counterfeited bill of exchange or promissory note for payment of money, or the indorsement or assignment of any bill of exchange or promissory note for payment of money, with intention to defraud any corporation, knowing the same to be falsely forged or counterfeited; then every such person shall be deemed guilty of felony, without benefit of clergy.

(5) By 18 Geo. 3. c. 18., which recites that doubts had arisen whether the punishment inflicted by 7 Geo. 2. c. 22. extended to such forgeries when committed with an intention to defraud any corporation, it is enacted, that if any person after the 25th of March, 1778, shall falsely make, alter, forge, or counterfeit, or cause or procure to be falsely made, altered, forged or countterfeited, or willingly act or assist in the false making, altering, forging, or counterfeiting, any acceptance of any bill of exchange, with intention to defraud any corporation whatsoever; or shall utter or publish as true any false, altered, forged, or counterfeited acceptance of any bill of exchange with intention to defraud any corporation whatsoever, knowing the same to be false, altered, forged, or counterfeited; every such person, being thereof lawfully convicted, shall be deemed guilty of felony, and shall suffer death as a felon without benefit of clergy.

And by 45 Geo. 3. c. 89. (6) forging or altering or causing to be forged or altered, or willingly acting or assisting in the forging or altering any bill or note, or any indorsement or assignment, or acceptance thereof, with intent to defraud any person or body politic, or offering, disposing of, or putting away any such forged or altered bill, note, indorsement, assignment, or acceptance, with a like intent, knowing it to be forged or al-

---

(6) By 45 Geo. 3. c. 89. § 1., which recites 2 Geo. 2. c. 25. and certain other acts, and states that certain provisions had been made and enacted for the preventing and punishing the forgery of bank notes, and other notes, bills, and instruments, in those acts respectively mentioned; and that it was expedient that such provisions should extend and be in force in every part of Great Britain, with such alterations and amendments therein as were thereby made; it is enacted, that if any person or persons shall, from and after the passing of this act, falsely make, forge, counterfeit, or alter, or cause or procure to be falsely made, forged, counterfeited, or altered, or willingly act or assist in the false making, forging, counterfeiting, or altering (among other instruments) any bill of exchange, promissory note for payment of money, indorsement or assignment of any bill of exchange or promissory note for payment of money; or acceptance of any bill of exchange with intention to defraud any person or persons, body or bodies politic or corporate whatsoever; or shall offer, dispose of, or put away any false, forged, counterfeited, or altered bill of exchange, promissory note for payment of money, indorsement or assignment of any bill of exchange or promissory note for payment of money, or acceptance of any bill of exchange, with intention to defraud any person or persons, body or bodies politic or corporate, knowing the same to be false, forged, counterfeited, or altered, then every person or persons so offending shall be deemed guilty of felony, without benefit of clergy.

tered, is a capital offence; and this act extends to every part of Geat Britain. (7)

By 43 Geo. 3. c. 139. s. 1. forging or uttering any bill or note purporting to be the bill or note of any foreign prince, state, or country, or of any person or company of persons residing in any foreign country, or of any body corporate, or body in the nature thereof, constituted by any foreign prince or state, with intent to deceive his Majesty, or any such foreign prince, &c. or any person or body politic here or abroad, is made a felony, and punishable by transportation for a term not exceeding fourteen years.

There are other provisions as to bank notes, bank post bills, and certain other securities, as to which the different statutes which refer to them must be consulted.

Forgery may be committed either by altering or adding to what has a genuine signature, or by introducing a false signature.

And a signature will be false, though in a man's own name, if he attaches to it or adopts the description or addition of any other person of the same name.

And a signature in a false name assumed for the purpose, or in the name of a non-existing person, will be as much a forgery as a signature in the name of an existing person.

---

(7) And by 45 Geo. 3. c. 89. § 8. all and every the clauses and provisions in this act contained, shall extend to every part of Great Britain.

Altering a bill or note from a lower to a higher sum is a forgery; the instrument, as altered, is a false instrument. (8)

Discharging one indorsement and inserting another, is altering the indorsement; (9)

---

(8) Rex v. Teague, Mich. 1802. Prisoner altered a 10*l*. country bank bill to 50*l*; it was on a sixteen-penny stamp, and had been thrice paid and reissued. The indictment charged, first, that the prisoner forged the bill, and secondly, that he uttered it knowing it to be forged: two objections; first, that the charge should have been for altering; and secondly, that this being a bill, not a note, could not legally be reissued without a new stamp. Prisoner was convicted, and the judges held the conviction right.

Rex v. Elsworth, Pasch. 1781. An indictment stated that a bill was drawn for 8*l*.; that persons unknown feloniously did alter it by falsely forging and adding a cipher to the 8*l*. and a y to the eight; that the prisoner had in his possession the said false, forged, altered, and counterfeited bill, and that he feloniously did utter as a true bill, the said false, forged, altered, and counterfeited bill with intent, &c., and knowing, &c. Motion in arrest of judgment, on the ground that the forgery was stated to be by persons unknown, and that the statement should have been that they feloniously *forged*, not that they feloniously *altered;* the statute 2 Geo. 2. c. 25. s. 1. making it capital to *forge*, but saying nothing as to altering; but it was answered that the *altering* was *forging*, and the judges were unanimous that the conviction was right.

And see Rex v. Post, ante, p. 8.

(9) Rex v. Birkitt, July, 1813. After conviction generally upon a bank indictment, it appeared there was one count only upon which the conviction could be supported; that count stated that the prisoner had in his possession a bank bill of exchange with a falsely altered indorsement thereon, and that he disposed thereof. The genuine indorsement was by Grant Burbey and Co., to Ladbroke and Co.; the prisoner discharged

And forging it.

If a bill or note import to be payable at any of several places, substituting a new place for one of those named, if with intent to defraud, is a forgery. (10)

Substituting the new place by introducing over the old place a piece of paper containing the new one, is a forgery. (10)

Adding a false addition to a fictitious name to delude a party to present a second time a bill he had before presented without success, under pretence

---

the whole of that indorsement, and wrote de novo, "Grant Burbey and Co.:" the judges thought this alteration made the bill what the indictment described it, and that on this count the conviction was right.

Rex v. Bigg, 3 P. Wm. 419. By 8 & 9 W. 3. c. 20. s. 36. altering or rasing any indorsement on any bank bill or note of any sort is made felony, without clergy. Upon a bank note for 100*l.* the bank paid 90*l.* and wrote upon the face of the note in red ink, "paid ninety pounds;" this writing the prisoner discharged by some liquid, probably lemon-juice: indictment thereon. The indictment stated that quoddam scriptum, anglice an indorsement, on the said note was duly made, specifying that 90*l.* was paid, and that the prisoner feloniously erased that indorsement: special verdict, finding inter al. that at the time of the act and till the 28th Nov. 1696, the only way used for indorsing bank notes, was by writing in black ink on the back side of the notes, but from the 28th Nov. 1696, it was by writing in front in red ink; special verdict. Many objections were taken; one that this was not an indorsement: after argument, the judges differed, but the majority held the conviction right. The prisoner was transported, not executed.

(10) See Rex v. Treble, ante, p. 93.

that it was for want of that addition that the bill had been before dishonoured, is a forgery. (11)

If there are two persons of the same name, but of different descriptions or additions, and one signs his name with the description or addition of the other, it is a forgery. (12)

Thus, if a bill be addressed to A. B. of London, merchant, and A. B., not of London, or not a merchant, accept it, the acceptance will be a forgery, if there be any A. B. of London, merchant; (12)

If there be no person of that name, description, and addition, not. (12)

---

(11) Rex v. Francis, Mich. 1811. John Francis took a lodging in the name of Cooke; and in less than a month passed to his landlord's wife a draft he drew on Praeds and Co. for 15*l.*, and she gave him a bank note for it to that amount. It was returned, on the ground that no person of that name kept cash there: the prisoner said it was a mistake for want of his adding "jun." to his name; which he accordingly added, and the note was again taken to Praeds, who again refused payment; but before it was brought back the prisoner absconded. Chambre J. left it to the jury whether he did not assume the name of Cooke, or at least of Cooke, *jun.*, with intent to defraud his landlord; and the jury thought he did, and he was convicted. On case, the conviction was held right.

(12) Rex v. Webb, Mich. 1819. A bill was addressed to Thomas Bowden, baize manufacturer, Rumford, and prisoner uttered it with an acceptance thereon made by a Thomas Bowden, who did not live at Rumford, and was not a baize manufacturer; and on indictment for uttering a forged acceptance, it appeared that there was no such baize manufacturer at Rumford; and on case, the majority of the judges held that the adopting a false description and addition, where a false name

So if a man of the same name as the payee or special indorsee of a bill or note indorse the bill or note, such indorsement is a forgery, because an indorsement by any other person than the right, is a false indorsement. (13)

But if the real payee or indorser of a bill or note indorse his own name thereon, without any false description or addition, his assuming at the time he utters it to be a different person of the same name, but with a different description or addition, will not make his signature a forgery, nor his uttering a capital offence.

If the signatures to a bill or note are genuine, a false pretence by the person who utters it that he bears a character he does not, will not make him liable to a prosecution for forgery. (14)

So as to any other genuine signatures upon a bill or note, though they may be intended to be passed as and for the signatures of other persons, and

---

was not assumed, and where there was no person answering that description or addition, was not a forgery; and the prisoner was pardoned.

(13) See Mead v. Young, ante, p. 110.

(14) Rex v. Hevey, Hil. 1782. The prisoner uttered a bill purporting to be payable to Bernard M'Carthy or order, and having the indorsement "B. M'Carthy," thereon, he was indicted for forging that indorsement, and uttering it knowing it to be forged: the jury found that there was such a man as B. M'Carthy, and that the indorsement was his hand-writing, but that the prisoner passed himself off as that B. M'Carthy when he uttered the bill: and on case, the judges were unanimous that as the indorsement was not forged, the prisoner was not liable to be convicted.

are passed accordingly, yet if there be nothing upon the bill or note to apply them to those persons, they are not forgeries.

A signature in an assumed name is a forgery if the name was assumed to defraud in that particular instance. (15)

---

(15) Rex v. Marshall, R. Michaelmas, 1804. Prisoner was paying away a bill payable to Ward, or order, and indorsed by Ward, and was desired to put his name upon it, and he wrote, Luke Marsden, when his real name was Thomas Marshall: he paid the bill to Harland for a horse: Harland did not know him before, but supposed from his writing it that Luke Marsden was his name. Question for the judges whether this was forgery, and they held it was.

Rex v. Whiley, Trinity, 1805. Whiley assumed the name of Milward 27th of December, and ordered goods of Thurston in that name: on 5th January following he gave Thurston a draft in the name of Milward, on Stephenson and Co., for ten guineas more than the amount of the goods, and Thurston gave him the difference. Thurston would have trusted the prisoner equally if he had used his own name: the draft was not paid, and prisoner was indicted as for a forgery. Thomson B. left it to the jury whether the prisoner assumed the name of Milward, when he ordered the goods and gave the note, with intent to defraud the prosecutor: they found that he did, and on case, the judges held the conviction right.

Rex v. Dunn, Michaelmas, 1765. Indictment that prisoner forged a note for payment of money, the tenor of which is as follows: "London, 27th July, 1765. I promise to pay Mr. Edward Hooper the sum of three pounds thirteen shillings and sixpence, or order, seven days after date, value received by me Mary ⋈ Wallace, her mark," with intent to defraud Edward Hooper: it appeared that her real name was Dunn; that she assumed the name of Wallace to represent herself as a seaman's widow; that she got three guineas and a half of Hooper, a navy agent, under that pretence, and that he wrote the no n question as a security for it, and she put her mark

Or for a system of fraud within which that signature fell. (16)

And it makes no difference, though the bill or note would have been equally taken had the party used his own name. (17)

---

to it; that he then asked her what name he should put to her mark, and she said "Mary Wallace;" upon which he wrote "Mary Wallace, her mark." The recorder doubted whether this addition after her signature could be deemed part of the note she forged; but Perrot B. and Aston J. held it was. Case on the ground that this was the prisoner's own note, and offered as her own; and nine judges against Aston J. held it a case within 2 G. 2. c. 25., and that the prisoner was properly convicted.

Rex v. Toft, Pasch. 1777. A bill of exchange for 150*l.* indorsed in blank, was stolen at Leicester; the same night the prisoner got cash for it at the Harboro' bank; but before it was cashed he was told it was the rule of the house that the person for whom they cashed a bill should indorse it, and he wrote the name John Williams; his real name was Toft. The jury found him guilty, and the judges were of opinion it was forgery.

Rex v. Peacock, Pasch. 1814. Prisoner went to Nuneham, in Gloucestershire, with intent to defraud by getting money upon bills he should draw: he went in the name of White, and in that name he drew a bill: he was indicted for forging this bill, and it was proved that his real name was Peacock; but it was not proved by what name he had passed for six years before he went to Nuneham: the jury found that he assumed that name, and went to Nuneham under it with a view to get money on bills he should draw in that name; and on case the judges held his conviction right; and that if he had used the name of White before he went to Nuneham, it was incumbent on him to prove it.

And see Rex v. Francis, ante, p. 432.

(16) See Rex v. Whiley, p. 434. and Rex v. Peacock. *supra.*

(17) See Rex v. Marshall, Rex v. Whiley, (ante, p. 434.) and Rex v. Francis, ante, p. 432.

And though it was taken upon the credit of other names upon the bill or note, not upon the fictitious name. (18)

And though the party had passed for some time by that name. (19)

But a signature in an assumed name will not be a forgery though the name were assumed for concealment or fraud, if it were not assumed with a view to that transaction, or for a system of which that is part.

Signing a mark in an assumed name, and suffering the assumed name to be ascribed to the mark, is forging the name. (20)

And it makes no difference, though the assumed name is not ascribed to the mark till after the mark is made, if it be ascribed to it in the prisoner's presence. (20)

Procuring a man to forge a bill or note is a capital offence. (21)

Procuring to utter, a common law felony only. (21)

Rex v. Shepherd, Michaelmas, 1781. The prisoner bought some things at a silversmith's, and uttered a forged cheque in payment: the silversmith took it as *his* draught, and he knew it. On conviction a doubt was entertained, as much as the silversmith gave credit to the prisoner, not to the draught, for he supposed it to be the prisoner's cheque; but on point saved the judges were unanimous the conviction was right.

18) See Rex v. Hough, post. p. 442. 447.

(19) See Rex v. Whiley, ante, p. 434.

(20) See Rex v. Dunn, ante, p. 434.

(21) Rex v. Morris, Pasch. 1814. The prisoner was con-

But procuring to utter, if the person procured is ignorant of the forgery, and therefore free from crime, may make the procurer chargeable for the uttering, and subject him to an indictment capitally on that charge.

Shewing a man forged notes to raise a false idea in him of the party's substance, would probably not be an uttering within 2 G. 2.; it has been held not to be an uttering of the sham notes to which 13 G. 3. c. 79. applies. (22)

Nor would the leaving them with him sealed up, under colour that he may take charge of them as being too valuable to be carried about. (22)

To constitute an uttering it probably would not

---

victed of procuring his wife to utter a forged order for payment of money, and the judges held he could only be punished as for a common law felony; but they held that had he been found guilty of procuring her to forge it, the offence would have been capital.

(22) Rex v. Shuckard, Michaelmas, 1811. Prisoner had two sham notes for paying *550d.*, but the numbers were in white letters on a black ground, so that they had the appearance of bank notes for *550l.*; he shewed them to J. S. with intent to make him suppose he was a man of fortune, but they were folded up so that the numbers only were visible: he then said he did not like to carry so much property about him, sealed them up in a cover, and delivered them to J. S. that he might take charge of them for the prisoner; the prisoner was afterwards suspected; J. S. opened the cover, discovered what the notes were, and the prisoner was indicted on 13 G. 3. c. 79. for uttering and publishing them; but on case, the judges held, that what he had done did not amount to an uttering or publishing within the statute, and that the conviction was wrong.

be deemed necessary it should be uttered in payment.

Uttering under the false pretence that it had been given in change by the person to whom it is uttered, in order to obtain from him a good note in lieu thereof, would probably be deemed an uttering; it has been so held in the case of counterfeit coin. (23)

And under 45 G. 3. c. 89., offering, disposing of, or putting away, is described as the offence; uttering is not mentioned.

The offence of disposing of and putting away may be complete, though the person to whom they were disposed of was an agent to detect utterers. (24)

---

(23) Rex v. Franks, Leach, 736. The prisoner sold Redit some apricots, and Redit paid him a good shilling, the prisoner put it into his mouth, and took from thence a counterfeit, and gave it to Redit as the shilling received from him, desiring him to change it, which he did: the prisoner practised the same trick with a second and third good shilling Redit gave him, on which Redit apprehended him. Conviction. — Objection that the indictment did not state that the shilling was uttered as and for a good one; the court thought an uttering not in payment within the statute, and the indictment right.

(24) Rex v, Holden, Michaelmas, 1809. Indictment charged that prisoner disposed of and put away a forged bank note with intent to defraud the bank, he knowing it at the time to be forged. The evidence was, that Shaw and Whitehead were employed by the magistrates, with the approbation of the agents for the bank, to detect utterers: that they applied to the prisoner, who procured the notes, and sold them, not as genuine, but as forged: it did not appear by any direct evidence that prisoner had the notes in his possession when first applied to,

And though the prisoner was applied to by such agent for the bill or notes. (24)

And though he might not have them when the agent first applied. (24)

And though he disposed of them, not as genuine, but as forged. (24)

Giving a confederate a forged bank note that he may utter it, is a disposing and putting away thereof. (25)

Forging or uttering a bill or note for less than 20*s.*, or a bill or note for (26) less than 5*l.*, which does not comply with the requisites of 17 G. 3. c. 30., or any other bill or note the legislature has declared void, is not within the statutes against forgery.

---

but he produced them at a subsequent meeting. It was urged, 1st, That the indictment was insufficient as not stating in what manner and to whom the notes were disposed of; and 2dly, That the disposal was insufficient, as the prisoner was solicited to commit the act by the bank's agent: but Chambre J. overruled the objections, and, on case for the twelve judges, they were unanimous that the objections had no weight.

(25) Rex v. Palmer, Pasch. 1804. Palmer and Hudson were jointly indicted, 1st, for uttering a forged bank note; and 2dly, for disposing and putting away: Hudson tendered it in payment, but Palmer was not with her: the shop-keeper stopped it as suspicious, and Palmer came afterwards with Hudson, and claimed it as his, and said he would have either the note or change. The jury found Palmer alone guilty; and seven judges against four, held him well convicted on the second count.

(26) Rex v. Moffat, Hil. 1787. Indictment for uttering a forged acceptance on a bill for 3*l.* 3*s.* The bill did not specify the payee's place of abode, and had no subscribing witness, and was therefore void by 17 G. 3.; and on a case reserved the judges held this not a forgery within 7 G. 2.

But a bill or note for payment of so many pound, instead of pounds, is. (27)

And so is a bill or note for payment of ten, twenty, thirty, &c. omitting "Pounds," if the figures with an £. affixed are put upon it to denote the amount. (28)

And so is a bill on the commissioners of the navy, though it is not warranted by 35 G. 3. c. 94., if it has the requisites of a bill of exchange. (29)

But a bill or note is not within the statutes

---

(27) See Rex v. Port, ante, p.

(28) Rex v. Eliot, Michaelmas, 1777. The prisoner was found guilty of forging this note, "No. 17.73 I promise to pay to Mr. Jos. Crook, or bearer, on demand, the sum of fifty, London, the 20th day of June. For the governor and company of the Bank of England. Thos. Thompson. £Fifty. Entered C. Blewerse." One count called it a note for payment of money only, describing it however as for payment of fifty pounds, and setting out the tenor; on the trial, the judge left it to the jury whether it was not to be considered as for *50l.*: the prisoner was found guilty, and on case, the judges were unanimous of opinion the conviction was right.

(29) Rex v. Chisholme, Pasch. 1815. Prisoner was convicted of uttering a bill on the commissioners of the navy for *22l. 6s. 9d.* for pay due to J. S. as acting lieutenant of the Zealous. Acting lieutenants have no power under 35 G. 3. to draw, and it was admitted therefore that the indictment could not be maintained on 35 G. 3.; it was urged, that it could not be deemed a bill of exchange, because the commissioners of the navy were removeable, and the instrument, if genuine, would not have been drawn for the purpose of being accepted by the commissioners, but in order to obtain an assignment under 35 G. 3.; but the judges on case held, that it was, in form, a bill of exchange, and 35 G. 3. would not prevent its being so.

against forgery, unless it is for payment of money in specie; (30)

And at all events.

Therefore a bill or note to pay in cash or bank notes is not. (30)

And it is questionable whether a bill or note payable to , or order, leaving a blank for the payee's name, is within the statutes. (31)

Forging or uttering a note without a maker's name is not a capital offence. (31*)

Forging or uttering a bill or note importing to be payable to A. B., or order, is a complete offence, though there is no indorsement upon it in A. B.'s name. (32)

---

(30) See Rex v. Wilcox, ante, p. 8.

(31) See Rex v. Randall, ante, p. 31.

(31*) Rex v. Pateman, Pasch. 1821. Prisoner was convicted of uttering and publishing as true a forged promissory note. The note was as follows: "No. 16,209. Bedford Bank. I promise to pay the bearer forty pounds on demand, here, or at Sir Charles Price, Baronet, and Co.'s, bankers, London. Value received. Bed d, the 17th day of October, 1817. For Barnard Barnard and Green." It was objected that this was no note, because it had no maker's name, and imported to bind nobody: the point was saved for the consideration of the judges, and they held the objection good, and the conviction wrong.

(32) Rex v. Birkett, Pasch. 1805. Indictment for forging and uttering a note payable to the prisoner's order: it appeared that he deposited it for his bill at an inn unindorsed, with a promise that he would pay the bill in a few days, saying, he wished not to discount it. Conviction.—Doubts whether it should not have been left to the jury to consider, whether he did not really mean to pay his bill, and get back the note, and make no further use of it. The judges thought not, and the conviction stood.

Forging on unstamped paper a bill or note which requires a stamp is as much an offence as if it were on stamped paper. (33)

And altering a bill which has once been paid, and which has been reissued without having a new stamp thereon, where such new stamp is requisite, is as much an offence as if the bill had never been paid, or as if it had had the additional stamp. (34)

An intent to defraud the person who would have to pay the bill or note if it were genuine, is to be inferred. (35)

---

* Rex v. Hough, Michaelmas, 1806. Indictment for uttering a forged bill importing to be drawn by Hastings, payable to Higgins, or order, with intent to defraud Green; the indictment did not state any indorsement in Higgins's name; the prisoner passed it to Green, and Green, at the time, enquired who Hastings and Higgins were, and the prisoner said he did not know much about Hastings, but he spoke of Higgins as a considerable manufacturer, and Green took the bill on the prisoner's representation of Higgins. Sutton B. doubted whether prisoner could properly be convicted, as Green took the bill on the credit of Higgins, and there was nothing in the indictment about his indorsement; but all the other judges thought the conviction right.

Rex v. Wicks, Pasch. 1809. Prisoner uttered a forged bill importing to be payable to the order of the drawers, Rimmington and Co.; it had not their indorsement thereon, though it had one indorsement beside prisoner's. On conviction thereon a case was reserved, and on consideration, the judges (nine) held the conviction right; for the instrument was a bill, and though it would not be available against the drawers without their indorsement, they might be compelled to indorse it, if they passed it away for good consideration. Lawrence J. for some time doubted, but at last seemed satisfied.

(33) See Rex v. Hawkeswood ante, p. 63.

(34) See Rex v. Teague, ante, p. 430.

(35) Rex v. Mazagora, Pasch. 1815. On indictment for

And this inference ought to be drawn, though, from the manner of executing the forgery, or from that person's ordinary caution, it would not be likely to impose on him. (35)

And though, from its being negotiable, it would be likely to defraud others, before it reached him. (35)

And though the object was general, to defraud whoever might take the instrument, and the particular intention of defrauding the person who would have to pay it, if genuine, never entered into the prisoner's contemplation. (35)

An intent to defraud a body politic or corporate is equally criminal with an intent to defraud an individual. (36)

Where the forgery is by alteration, the indictment may charge that the prisoner forged the altered instrument (37); or that he altered by forging; for altering is forging. (38)

And discharging one indorsement, and inserting another, may be charged as altering the indorsement. (39)

---

disposing of forged bank notes, the intent was charged to be to defraud the bank: the jury stated that the intent was to defraud whoever might take the notes, but that the intention of defrauding the bank in particular did not enter into the prisoner's contemplation, and they found the prisoner guilty. On case, the judges thought it too clear for discussion; that the prisoner must be taken to have intended to defraud the bank, and that the conviction was right.

(36) See 45 G. 3. c. 89. ante, p. 428.

(37) See Rex v. Teague, ante, p. 430.

(38) See Rex v. Elsworth, ante, p. 430.

(39) See Rex v. Birkitt, ante, p. 430. 441.

If the bill or note omit the word pounds in the body, but has an £. with figures prefixed to the amount in the margin, it may be described as a bill or note for payment of that amount. (40)

The indictment must set out the bill or note in the very words: it is not sufficient to set out the substance. (41)

And if the bill or note contain figures, the indictment must follow it in that respect. (42)

And if the bill or note be in a foreign language, a translation of it must be set out, that it may appear upon the record in a language the courts understand that it is what the law considers a bill or note. (43)

---

(40) See Rex v. Eliot, ante, p. 440.

(41) Rex v. Mason, Pasch. 1793. Indictment stated that the prisoners having in their possession a bill of exchange purporting to be drawn by J. S. on J. N., thereby requiring J. N., two months after date, to pay A. B., or order, 91*l.*, and purporting to have been indorsed by A. B., together with a forged acceptance, written on the same bill, and purporting to have been written by the said J. N., feloniously did utter, &c. Thomson B. saved the question whether the indictment ought not to have set out the bill and acceptance in their words and figures; and the judges held it ought, and that for want thereof it was bad.

Note. It would not otherwise appear on the record whether the bill was what the law considers a bill.

(42) See Rex v. Powell, post. p. 445.

(43) Rex v. Goldstein, Michaelmas, 1821. The prisoner was convicted under 43 G. 3. c. 139. of forging a note purporting to be a note of the king of Prussia: the note was in the German language, and was set out verbatim: the indictment did not set out any English translation of it, and on that account an application was made to arrest the judgment: the point was saved

Alleging that the prisoner forged a bill or note "as follows," or that he had a bill or note "as follows," implies, that what follows is in the very words of the bill or note, and makes it necessary to prove the bill or note verbatim. (44)

On an indictment for forging a bill or note with a false name ascribed to the prisoner's mark, the words ascribing the name to the mark, if written in the prisoner's presence, may be described as part of the bill or note. (45)

If the false signature contain an initial only for

---

for the consideration of the twelve judges; they directed it to be argued, and after argument, the opinion of the majority was, that a translation ought to have been set out upon the indictment, for it might be a question whether the instrument was within the statute; a court of error ought to have the means of deciding upon that point, to give them those means they ought to have the instrument before them in a language they understand, and unless they had a translation sanctioned by the jury which tried the indictment, they had no means of getting a translation upon which they could judicially rely; and the judgment was arrested.

(44) Rex v. Powell, Michaelmas, 1771. Indictment against prisoner for forging a stock receipt with intent to defraud, 1st, Taylor Barrow, and 2dly, T. Sykes. The indictment stated that the prisoner forged a certain receipt as follows, viz. &c. The receipt, as set out, contained certain sums in figures, and it was signed T. Barrow. Three objections: 1st, That this was not equivalent to setting out the tenor; but the judges held it was, and that any variance would be fatal: 2dly, That the sums should not have been set out in figures; but the judges held the receipt must be pursued literatim, or it would be a variance; and 3dly, That it should have been averred that T. Barrow, as signed, meant Taylor Barrow; but the judges thought not, and prisoner was executed.

(45) See Rex v. Dunn, ante, p. 434.

the Christian name, it is not necessary to aver what Christian name it means. (46)

The indictment ought not to describe the bill or note *as signed* by the person whose name is supposed to have been forged; such an allegation is inconsistent with the charge of forgery, and makes the indictment bad. (47)

And an indictment must not describe a bill or note as having a purport different from what appears upon the face of the instrument. (48)

On an indictment for forging the indorsement of a payee, it is not necessary to shew by the drawer or maker who was intended as payee, if there is proof that the prisoner has himself admitted who it was. (49)

---

(46) See Rex v. Powell, ante, p. 445.

(47) Rex v. Carter, Hil. 1801. Indictment for forging and uttering a bill in Hutchinson's name, described it as signed by Hutchinson; and after conviction the judges held it bad upon the face of it, and that the prisoner might be indicted de novo.

(48) Rex v. Reading, Hil. 1794. East, 981. Upon a bill directed to John Ring, there was an acceptance in the name of John King. The indictment described the bill as purporting to be directed to John King by the name of John Ring; and after conviction for forging and uttering, the judges held this a repugnant and absurd description, for the bill could only purport to be what it appeared upon the face of it to be; and the judgment was arrested.

S. P. Rex v. Gilchrist, East, 982.; and see Rex v. Jones, Dougl. 302. East, 883.

(49) Rex v. Downs, Michaelmas, 1789. Indictments for forging the payee's indorsement on a bill payable to John Sowerby, or order; when prisoner passed the bill, he said Sowerby was a cheesemonger at Liverpool, and John Sowerby of Liverpool, cheesemonger, was called; who proved that there was no other

To support a charge of forgery by subscribing a fictitious name, there must be evidence on the part of the prosecution that that is not the party's real name. (50)

And if there is no evidence affirmatively what the real name is, there ought to be proof that it was assumed for the transaction in question; (50)

Or for a system of which that was part. (50)

But if there is proof affirmatively what the real name is, it is for the prisoner to shew a prior independent use of the assumed name. (50)

And in such case an absence of proof on the part of the prosecution by what name the prisoner has passed for several years, will not be material. (50)

On an indictment for uttering, proof that the prisoner had in his possession other bills or notes ejusdem generis is admissible, because if unexplained it tends to shew that he knew the bill or note in question was a forgery. (51)

---

cheesemonger at Liverpool of that name but himself, and that the indorsement was not his; there were letters from prisoner after his apprehension implying guilt generally in this transaction. It was urged, that the drawer should have been called to prove what John Sowerby he meant; but Wilson J. left the case as it was to the jury, who convicted; and on a case reserved the judges thought the evidence sufficient to go to the jury, and that the conviction was right.

(50) See Rex v. Peacock, ante, p. 435.

(51) Rex v. Hough, Michaelmas, 1806. Indictment for uttering a forged bill, purporting to be drawn by Hastings on Esdailes, and proof that no such person as Hastings kept cash at Esdailes': when the prisoner was apprehended, which was four months after the uttering, there were found upon him two

And bills on the same house with a bill in question, importing to be drawn by persons not known at that house, will be deemed ejusdem generis with the bill in question. (51)

And proof that the prisoner had pointed out where bills or notes ejusdem generis were hid, is admissible, because if unexplained it raises a presumption that he had hid them. (52)

So proof that he had uttered other bills or notes ejusdem generis, is also admissible. (53)

---

other bills, importing to be drawn by Walters on Esdaile, and another, importing to be drawn by Newman on Esdaile; and evidence was given that no such person as Walters or Newman kept cash at Esdailes': Sutton B. allowed these bills to be read as evidence that prisoner knew the bill he uttered to be forged: and after conviction the judges thought it right.

(52) Rex v. Rowley, Pasch. 1806. Waring, a person employed by the solicitor to the bank, applied to the prisoner, who twice procured him forged bank notes; he applied a third time, prisoner went out, and after some time returned, and told Waring they were in an old shoe, in a particular lane; they went together, and prisoner threw a stone into a bush, and said, there they are: Waring found the shoe there, and the notes in it: the prisoner was indicted on 45 G. 3. c. 89. § 6. for having these notes in his possession, and Graham B. told the jury that if prisoner had the notes in his possession on their passage to the shoe, it was sufficient, and they convicted prisoner: the judges held the conviction right.

(53) Rex v. Wylie, 1 New Rep. 92. Upon an indictment for uttering a forged bank note, knowing, &c. the uttering was proved, and its being forged, and to prove the knowledge evidence was offered that the prisoner had passed other forged notes: this was objected to on the ground that it was evidence of other felonies, and the prisoner could not be prepared to resist it, but Lord Ellenborough, Heath J., and Thompson B., held it admissible, and the prisoner was found guilty.

Rex v. Ball, Michaelmas, 1807, P. C. 1 Campb. 324. P. C.

But such bills or notes must be produced, and their being forgeries proved. (54)

Proof that the prisoner took them back and changed them with the word "forged" written thereon, is not sufficient. (54)

And evidence may be given of the prisoner's conduct on such other utterings, and that he passed by different names. (55)

On indictment for uttering a forged bank note, evidence was given that three months before prisoner had passed another note, forged in the same manner, namely, with a camel-hair pencil, by the same hand, and with the same materials, and that fifteen other notes of the same fabrication had been found filed at the bank with the prisoner's writing thereon: point saved whether the evidence was admissible: all the judges except Chambre J. thought it was, though its weight would depend on the number of notes issued, and the time, and the probability, from the prisoner's situation in life, of his taking them in business.

See Rex v. Hough, pp. 442. 447.

(54) Rex v. Millard, Pasch. 1813. The prisoner was tried for uttering a *5l.* bank note, and to prove the guilty knowledge it was proved that he had before uttered two *1l.* Leicester notes; that in about a fortnight one having been objected to as bad, he changed it, and that when under charge for the uttering in question, the other was brought to him with the word "forged" upon it, and he changed that, but neither of these bills were produced, nor had any notice been given for producing them; and on case, the judges held that this evidence should not have been admitted, without proper proof that these notes were forged, and without deciding whether bills of a different description and denomination were admissible, (which Le Blanc J. thought they were); an application for a pardon was recommended.

(55) See Rex v. Millard, supra.

But quære, whether other evidence to impeach his conduct on those occasions is admissible? because he cannot be expected to be ready to meet such evidence.

Proof that the prisoner had uttered other forged bills or notes of a different kind is questionable.

On an indictment for forgery, the person whose name is forged, or upon whose genuine name a forgery is committed, is not a competent witness to prove the forgery if he has an interest in the destruction of what is supposed to be forged. (56)

And the reason perhaps is, that the indictment may be considered in some degree as a proceeding in rem, and a conviction would warrant a judicial cancellation of the forgery.

And he is not competent to prove any fact which has a tendency to make out the forgery. (56)

When the forgery is established by other evidence, whether he is competent on the part of the prosecution to any points unconnected with the forgery, is not settled. (56)

---

(56) Rex v. Crocker, 2 New Rep. 87. Indictment for forging a note. There was an indorsement on it in the prisoner's writing that a year's interest had been paid, and Le Blanc J. permitted the party whose name was forged to prove that he had never paid interest on this or any other note; but on case on this and another point, the prisoner was pardoned, and it was understood that a majority of the judges were of opinion that he ought not to have been admitted.

Note. Lord Ellenborough, Lawrence C. B., and Le Blanc

If he has no interest in the destruction of the forgery, he is a competent witness.

Thus if the holder of a forged note release the person in whose name it is made, such person will be a competent witness to prove the name forged. (57)

And he will be competent though the note was not payable to order or to bearer, so as to be negotiable, but simply to the prisoner, if the prisoner passed it to the owner for full value. (57)

So on an indictment against the payee of a bill for forging an acceptance, a release from the indorsee will make the supposed acceptor competent to prove the forgery. (58)

J., thought him admissible, because it was sufficiently proved before that the note was not signed by him, and they thought him admissible to all points but that of the forgery: some of the other judges seemed to think that to points perfectly collateral he would have been admissible, but they considered the point to which he was called as contributing to prove the forgery. Le Blanc's MSS.

(57) Rex v. Akehurst, Leach, 136. Akehurst was indicted for forging a note payable to himself, but not payable to order; he paid it away in part discharge of a debt, but did not indorse it; the holder gave the drawer a general release, and the drawer being offered as a witness to prove the forgery, Lord Mansfield, after argument, admitted him.

(58) Rex v. Mott, Hil. 1821. Indictment against payee of a bill for uttering it with the forged acceptance of Dover thereon; prisoner had indorsed it to Hood and Co. on having value to the amount of half the bill; Hood was examined as a witness, and so, on release from Hood, was Dover: case saved on the question whether Dover was competent without release from prisoner also, for if the acceptance were genuine,

And so will an abandonment of his claim by the person who would be entitled to sue the supposed acceptor if the acceptance were genuine.

And it will have that effect though such indorsee advanced the payee only part of the amount of the bill, and would be liable to him, if the bill were genuine and paid, for the residue. (58)

And the indorsee in such case is a competent witness also. (59)

Where the forgery consists in altering a genuine instrument, and consists in what gives the bill or note a better credit, but does not vary the responsibility of the drawer or maker, the drawer or maker is a competent witness to prove the forgery.

---

prisoner would have a claim against Dover for one half the bill, but the judges thought the release from Hood and Co. sufficient, because the indorsement vested the whole legal interest in them, and if the release destroyed any claim by prisoner on Dover, it gave a claim pro tanto against Hood and Co.: it was then urged that Hood was incompetent, for he had a direct interest in the prisoner's conviction; for if he was acquitted and could prove the acceptance genuine, he might sue Hood and Co. for giving the release: but a great majority of the judges held him competent.

(59) Rex v. Usher, Leach, 44. Usher forged the acceptance of a bill, making it payable at Sir Charles Asgill's in the name of Mr. Merry. Sir C. Asgill paid the bill, and charged it to Mr. Merry's account; but on being satisfied of the forgery, they gave him credit to the amount of the charge. Usher was indicted for the forgery, and Mr. Merry produced as a witness against him; upon which his counsel objected to Mr. Merry's admissibility; but Lord Mansfield, Smythe B.,

He has been held competent where the forgery introduced a new place for payment. (60)

---

and Wilmot J., held that as Sir C. Asgill had given up his claim, it was immaterial to Mr. Merry whether Usher was convicted or acquitted, inasmuch as no demand could be made upon Mr. Merry for the money, and they therefore over-ruled the objection.

(60) Rex v. Treble, Pasch. 1810. Indictment for forgery by substituting in a country bank note the name of a solvent town banker as one of the places where it was payable, instead of an insolvent one: the signature was genuine, the maker was admitted a witness, and on point saved, the judges held it right.

APPENDIX.

Trueman v. Hurst, 1 Term Rep. 40. An action was brought on a note given for board and lodging, and for teaching the defendant hairdressing; and upon an account stated, the defendant pleaded infancy, and the plaintiff replied for necessaries. Defendant demurred, and insisted that an infant could not bind himself by a note, even for necessaries, and that no action would lie against him on an account stated. The court desired the plaintiff's counsel to confine himself to the last point, from whence it may be inferred that they thought the first was with him, but they decided against him upon the last.

March v. Ward, Peake, 130. A note signed by Bowling and Ward, began "I promise to pay," and in an action against Ward alone, it was objected that the note was *joint only*, and not several; but Lord Kenyon held it was several as well as joint, and said it had been so decided on a case from Chester. "*I* applies to each severally." Verdict for the plaintiff.

Manning v. Livie, before Lord Kenyon, sittings after Michaelmas Term 1796. In an action on a note by an indorsee, the stamp appeared to be a seven shilling deed stamp; and Lord Kenyon said the note could not be read, and the plaintiff was accordingly non-suited.

Banks v. Colwell, Launceston Spring Assizes, 1788, before Buller J. cited 3 Term Rep. 81. Indorsee of a note payable on demand, against the maker. The note was given for smuggled goods; part of it was paid; and it was not indorsed to the plaintiff till a year and a half after it was given; no privity was brought home to the plaintiff, but Buller J. was clearly of opinion he ought to be nonsuited; and he said it had been repeatedly ruled at Guildhall, that if a bill or note was indorsed over after it was due, the indorsee took it on the credit of the indorser, and stood in his situation.

Brown v. Turner, 7 Term Rep. 630. Pritchard paid some stockjobbing differences for Turner, and drew on him for the amount; Turner accepted the bill, and after it became due Pritchard indorsed it to the plaintiff for a prior debt. Lord Kenyon however thought that as Pritchard could not have recovered on the bill, the plaintiff could not, and directed a verdict for the defendant; and the court was clearly of opinion that the direction was right, and refused a rule nisi for a new trial. See also Good v. Coe, cit. 7 Term Rep. 427. 429.

Jameson v. Swinton, 2 Taunt. 224. In an action on a bill, by the plaintiff, who was the indorsee of Elsham, against an indorser, the defence was, that due notice of the dishonour, which took place on the 10th of July, had not been given. Elsham (the last indorser) who lived at Back-hill, Holborn, received notice on the 10th at four o'clock in the afternoon, and he gave notice on the 11th, between eight and nine o'clock at night, to the defendant, who lived at Islington. Lawrence J. held, that this was sufficient to entitle Elsham to recover from the defendant, and therefore sufficient to enable the plaintiff, who received the bill from Elsham, to recover. Verdict for the plaintiff; and on motion to set it aside, it was urged, that the notice should have been given within the hours of business, but the court held the notice sufficient. Rule refused.

Bishop v. Chitty, Str. 1195. Chitty, the drawee of a bill, wrote upon it, by way of acceptance, " Messrs. Caswell and Mount pay this bill when due for Thomas Chitty:" it became due 2d of January, 1741: Caswell and Mount paid till the 19th, when they stopped; and no notice was given to Chitty of its non-payment till the 21st; and Lee C. J. held that Chitty was discharged, for though the holder might have refused this acceptance, he had agreed to it, and it was in nature of a draught, which is considered as payment when a reasonable time to receive it in has elapsed. However, in Smith v. De la Fontaine, B. R. T. 25 Geo. 3. Where an action was brought against the acceptor of a bill upon an acceptance to pay at his banker's, and the plaintiff could not prove a presentment at the banker's, notwithstanding which the jury found for him; the court held the proof unnessary, and refused to grant a new trial. Bishop v. Chitty, was cited. See Fenton v. Goundry, and Callaghan v. Aylett, ante, p. 177, 178.

Buckland v. Tankard, 5 Term Rep. 578. This was an action by an indorsee against the acceptor of a bill. The bill was drawn by Gregson payable to his own order, and indorsed by him in blank. And the defendant called Gregson to prove that he had indorsed and delivered it to the plaintiff that he might get it paid, and not to give him any interest in it; and that he had no consideration for it, and was still entitled to it. The witness had a release from the acceptor. Lord Kenyon thought him interested and rejected him. And on a rule nisi for a new trial, the court held that his situation would be better or worse according to the event of the verdict, and therefore that he was properly rejected. Rule discharged.

TABLE

OF

PRINCIPAL MATTERS.

STATUTES cited.

THE END.

Spotted something that isn't quite right?

Let us know and we'll fix it for future reprints.
And as a thank you for your diligence, we'll
send you a free Sothis book of your choice.

publisher@sothis.press

This page intentionally left blank

Made in United States
Orlando, FL
04 November 2026

90207192R00289